. . . .

Criminology: Applying Theory

Criminology: Applying Theory

John E. Holman
University of North Texas

James F. Quinn
University of North Texas

WEST PUBLISHING COMPANY
ST. PAUL · NEW YORK · LOS ANGELES · SAN FRANCISCO

Composition: Graphic World Inc.
Copyediting: Maggie Jarpey
Text and Cover Design: Roslyn M. Stendahl, Dapper Design
Cover: Robert Birmelin, "The Shooting Outside the Jewelry Store" Reprinted courtesy of Claude Bernard Gallery, Ltd., New York.
Production, Prepress, Printing, and Binding by West Publishing Company

COPYRIGHT ©1992 By WEST PUBLISHING COMPANY
50 W. Kellogg Boulevard
P.O. Box 64526
St. Paul, MN 55164-0526

99 98 97 96 95 94 93 92   8 7 6 5 4 3 2 1 0
Library of Congress Cataloging-in-Publication Data

Holman, John E.
   Criminology : applying theory / John E. Holman, James F. Quinn.
     p. cm
   Includes bibliographical references.
   ISBN 0-314-92142-7
   1. Criminology. 2. Crime—United States—Case studies.
I. Quinn, James F. II. Title.
HV6025.H633 1992

364—dc20
                  ∞   91-37256
                        CIP

CONTENTS

4 Biological Perspective

5 Psychiatric Perspective

6 Psychological Perspective

7 Social-Learning Perspective

8 Societal-Reaction Perspective

Preface

Many methods have been used to introduce criminological theory to undergraduate students. Some focus on the historical development of criminological theory, while others are devoted to the presentation of a particular theoretical view. Either approach, we believe, has difficulty holding the attention of undergraduate students, who generally lack a good understanding of critical methodological issues. Our chief goal in writing this book was to overcome this problem and attempt to inculcate a fascination with theoretical explanations of crime in students. Simultaneously, we sought to demonstrate that all the major perspectives in criminology have worthy contributions to make to our understanding of the causes of crime and its distribution in society.

Our experience in college classrooms has convinced us that most undergraduate students of criminology and criminal justice prefer to approach the causes of crime from a psychological orientation. This reflects their customary perception of the causes of the specific behaviors they observe in everyday life. Although it is very natural for students to attempt to deal with issues related to crime in the same way that they deal with other situations in life, criminological theory can improve their understanding of crime-related phenomena by allowing them to view such situations from a variety of theoretical perspectives. We are thus advocating an instructional method that concentrates on the application of criminological theory to the world as it is experienced by most citizens, and especially criminal justice students, rather than on the validation of a specific theory with aggregate data. While the distribution of crime is a macro-level concern, criminal laws define crime as the acts of individuals. Therefore, macro-level perspectives must be demonstrably relevant to micro-level variables if their explanations are to avoid the appearance of being spurious.

Our use of the *case-study approach* is not intended to diminish the importance of theory validation with aggregate data, but rather to separate methodological issues from theoretical ones to facilitate the learning process. By using criminological theory to explain particular criminal cases, we introduce many basic methodological concepts and issues in a somewhat painless way. This text examines all the principal theories used by criminologists, and assesses their strengths and weaknesses in as impartial a manner as possible. The case study method uses hierarchical arrangements of criminological theory. Each theoretical hierarchy progresses from the most general level, the perspective, through a series of descending levels of specificity: approach, theory, and hypothesis. A tripartite scheme of causal factors—consisting of precipitating, attracting, and predisposing forces (Benjamin and Masters, 1964)—is also used to describe each theory's main strengths and weaknesses.

This case-study method is employed to bring criminological theories to life for undergraduate students at the microlevel where, in general, people are initially most comfortable. This sensitizing strategy for approaching new subject matter is not new to the study of criminology and has been used extensively over the past several decades by many notable criminologists—for example, Clifford R. Shaw's (1930) study of muggers, Edwin H. Sutherland's (1937) study of professional thieves, and Abadinsky's studies of organized crime (1981) and jewel thieves (1983).

The cases are used for illustrative instructional purposes, not for scientifically validating theory, and should promote the development of both deductive and inductive reasoning. As the basic ideas of each theory are mastered by the student, they should become an aid to explaining other cases, as well as patterns and trends in aggregated data. By using well-documented criminal cases, rather than merely discussing abstract theories and statistical data on crime, the authors hope to keep the student focused on the construction and use of criminological theory, rather than on the problems encountered in interpreting research data. In this way, students simultaneously gain substantive knowledge of criminological theory and its application to actual events, as well as a more complete view of the possible causes of crime. This approach avoids the confusion inherent in the "mixed" findings that are almost inevitably present in reviews of the theory-validation literature.

Very few, if any, criminal acts can be fully explained by one criminological theory. This is because the "causes" of criminal behavior occur simultaneously at all levels of analysis and constantly interact with one another as well as with other environmental, structural, and internal forces. The case-study method of explaining crimes used in this text allows the student to see how various factors are involved in crime when applying either a macro- or micro-level theory to actual cases. It is very effective in transforming theory from a mere object of study to a useful explanatory device. Deduction from our examples to other applications of the theories is encouraged. It must be remembered always that the explanations offered are only examples of how theories should be used; they are not definitive descriptions of why a specific crime occurred. The interpretations provided by students and instructors are not the "final word," nor are they intended to be. Instead, the goal is to encourage students to think in a scientific fashion by testing and challenging the application of criminological theory to fact.

Such challenges to the veracity of theory applications are also vital to the development of criminology as a science because they force scholars to constantly refine their theoretical perspectives and revalidate them in the real world. In this way, the case-study method indirectly lends itself to theoretical advancement. Were it not for such disagreements among scholars, social science would never keep pace with changing social realities, and criminology would fail to take full advantage of relevant developments in related fields. This book aims to help establish in some small way criminological theory as the basis of a scientific discipline *sui generis,* without perverting the intent or content of the contributing disciplines.

This book could not have been written without the love and support of our families. Therefore, our first thanks go to Carla Mullen-Quinn and Betty Holman, as well as Brandon, Mitchell, and Carley Holman. We would also like to thank Carla Mullen-Quinn for her valuable critiques of our early drafts.

Our mentors during our graduate student days deserve recognition, too, for their contribution to this effort. Most prominent among these are Richard Caston, now at the University of Baltimore, Bill Bankston and Michael Grimes of Louisiana State University, Shearon Lowery of Florida International University, and Melvin DeFleur, currently at Syracuse University.

The technical aspects of this endeavor were made easier by the skilled professionals of West Publishing Company. We would like to thank Tom LaMarre, West's acquisitions editor, and Bernice Carlin, his editorial assistant, for their patient guidance and advice in producing this text. We would also like to thank the following reviewers for their time and effort in producing useful and erudite critiques of our early drafts.

Roger Barnes   Incarnate Word College
Werner Einstadter   Eastern Michigan University
Paul Friday   Western Michigan University
Peter Kratcoski   Kent State University
Emily LaBeff   Midwestern State University
Frank Lee   Middle Tennessee State University
Marlene Lehtiner   University of Utah
Martha Meyers   University of Georgia
Bob Regoli   University of Colorado
Jim Thomas   Northern Illinois University
Prabha Unnithan   Colorado State University

CHAPTER **1**

Introduction

The Use of Theory

Theories serve a variety of important purposes for criminologists and practitioners in related professions such as law enforcement, corrections, and social work. Among the most common uses of theory are (1) to explain and predict events, patterns and trends occurring in the real world; (2) to broaden understanding of particular issues; and (3) to help design programs and policies to improve society. Before theory can be used for such broad and optimistic purposes, however, the theory-user must understand the methods by which theories are constructed. The logic and limitations of particular theories must be understood if they are to be truly useful in explaining the causes of crime—and thus aid an intelligent response to current and future issues by scholars, policymakers, and practitioners.

In essence, theory provides a method of limiting one's view to the information that is considered most relevant to the situation in order to develop a relatively simple explanation of a usually complex event. However, there is a price to pay for the simplification of complex events. In reducing the amount of data used, one inevitably loses information. The correct application of criminological theory seeks to minimize the amount of truth lost while maximizing the degree of simplicity in the explanation of a situation.

We have found that most people, including students of criminological theory, seem to approach the causes of crime from a more or less psychological orientation that reflects their customary perception of the causes of these specific behaviors. This we attribute to their exposure to the media's (television and movies) stereotyping of criminals as psychotic, or at least seriously psychologically disturbed, as well as to their lack of exposure to other criminological explanations. A far better understanding of criminal phenomena, however, is afforded by viewing them from a variety of perspectives. Indeed, this is true for understanding any type of **social phenomena**—that is, social events that can be scientifically described. Each perspective assigns different values to the available facts and emphasizes different causal forces. In reality, these causal forces are operating constantly and simultaneously. Theory allows us to impartially separate and analyze each causal force as a separate factor. In this way we gain the fullest possible understanding of the phenomena.

Criminological theory accomplishes this by the use of rigorous logic. Each theory is based on a set of explicit assumptions. These assumptions reflect beliefs about the nature of human behavior and society. Assumptions cannot hope to reflect all of reality but serve to make the task of interpreting the social world manageable by limiting the nature of the questions we ask and the type of data we need to answer them.

Individual theories are developed out of unique viewpoints and are at times competing explanations of the same phenomenon. More often, however, they are complementary explanations for different aspects of the same case. Each, of necessity, excludes some evidence. But one theory developed from one viewpoint may include all or some of the evidence excluded from a different theory developed from a different viewpoint. Thus, theories focused on entirely different types of facts may have to be considered together in order to provide a comprehensive view of a situation.

The view provided by each theory is only as correct as the assumptions upon which it is based. Therefore, each theory has some validity if its assumptions reflect at least part of reality. Obviously, some theories will have more validity than others and therefore offer greater explanatory power. Also, some theories are more appropriate to the specific circumstances and available facts. Using theories correctly is ultimately a matter of judgment that must be developed over time.

Consider the possible viewpoints from which one might approach the problem presented in Exhibit 1.1. There are four interrelated and overlapping facts in the situation: (1) addiction to drugs, (2) criminal acts, (3) economic frustration, and (4) the desire to use illegal drugs. These four facts give four possible bases on which an explanation might be built: (1) the presence of addiction; (2) the observation of serious, predatory criminal behavior; (3) the issue of economic status or need; and (4) the status of illegal drug laws. Depending on the base used to build the explanation of this crime, explanations targeted at the four divergent phenomena would focus on (1) the prevention and treatment of illegal drug addiction; (2) the punishment of addicts and armed robbers; (3) the training and employment of addiction-prone groups, such as the inner-city poor; or (4) the legalization of drugs to make them less expensive.

It is not possible to address all four phenomena simultaneously because some of them are mutually exclusive of others. For example, it would make no sense to punish addicts while legalizing drugs, or to train them for good jobs so that they can afford to purchase illegal drugs. This mutual exclusiveness is a direct result of the fact that there are different viewpoints from which problems can be approached. The conclusions reached as to (1) the nature of the problem, (2) its scientific explanation, and (3) the best method of improving the situation, will differ greatly depending on which fact becomes the focus of attention.

Intent and Organization of This Book

. . . .

Most people experience the world in a very personal way—that is, in a case-by-case, situation-by-situation manner. This book was written to accommodate that fact. Rather than use statistical studies to validate one theory or another, we concentrate instead on the application of theory to the world as it is experienced by most citizens and criminal justice practitioners. In doing so we do not mean to refute the importance of theory validation with **aggregated data**—that is, a set of facts about a group of cases in which individual identities are ignored in order to examine patterns and trends within the entire group and/or among its subgroups. That approach has its place, and indeed is the

---

People addicted to illegal drugs are committing **armed robberies** to **obtain money** to buy the **illegal drugs** for their own personal use, because they are unable to find other ways to obtain that money.

Exhibit 1.1

. . . .

Addicts who rob

basis of most criminological theory texts. Research based on aggregated data is used to illustrate the degree to which various theories can be applied to a specific area of criminological concern (e.g., prostitution, robbery, murder). The limitations of each theory are then usually described in the same way. Much valuable information has been provided thus. We have not, however, found research studies based on aggregated data to be very helpful in illustrating the strengths and weaknesses of theories. Instead, we believe that illustrations of this type often leave the student confused as to the relevance of the theories to everyday events. This, we feel, is due primarily to two facts: (1) criminological research studies generally report mixed findings (i.e., some studies support a theory, others do not); and (2) research studies and aggregated data are too abstract for the purpose of an introduction to theory. In essence, studies reporting mixed findings are, by nature, problematic for the student in learning theory, as is the inherent complexity of the theory-validation process.

In this text, we use theory to explain particular criminal cases that are in some ways similar to those encountered in the daily operation of the criminal justice system.[1] The **case study method** is employed throughout the text in large part to bring the theories to life. Case studies are extensive, qualitative examinations of illustrative or exemplary cases of a phenomenon.[2] This way of approaching criminological theory represents a sensitizing strategy for discussing new subject matter.[3] Cole and Weston, for example, used this method to introduce the linkages between drug abuse and criminal behavior in *Case Studies of Drug Abuse and Criminal Behavior*.[4] It should be noted that the case study method is not new to the study of criminology—it has been used extensively over the past several decades. Notable early criminologists, such as Clifford R. Shaw in his 1930 study of muggers and Edwin H. Sutherland in his 1937 study of professional thieves, used the case study method.[5] More recent criminological inquiries, such as Abadinsky's 1981 study of jewel thieves and 1983 study of organized crime, have continued to employ the method.[6]

This utilization of the case study method for theory application is justified on the grounds that the cases are used throughout the text for illustration purposes, not for scientific validation of theory.[7] That is, the cases are used to show how theories explain actual events. They are not presented as evidence that the theory is true. Concern focuses not only on the events of the crime but also on the motives of the individual(s) involved, the central issue being the processes involved in the crime.[8]

As the basic concepts of each theory are mastered by the reader, the theory should become an aid to explaining other cases, as well as patterns and trends in aggregated data. Therefore, this book encourages the use of an *inductive* approach (reasoning from the specific to the general) for the application of criminological theory to criminal cases rather than a *deductive* one (reasoning from the general to the specific).

Many ways of introducing the study of theory have been used in criminology. Some texts are primarily concerned with the historical development of criminological theory, while others are devoted to the presentation of one particular view. Texts of the latter type seem to be the more common. They tend to evaluate evidence and other views in a restricted way that supports the central viewpoint of their presentation.

In the early 1980s, Liska suggested that textbooks on criminological theory introduce the full range of theories rather than a single one, thus broadening the reader's understanding of the causes of crime.[9] We adhere to this view. Accordingly, we have attempted to examine all of the principal theories used by criminologists, and assess their strengths and weaknesses in an impartial manner. This book, like many others written in the 1980s, is organized around these major theories in a logical, rather than historical, fashion. Each theory is introduced as a separate, equally valid way of describing the causes of crime. This text is unique in that illustrations of each theory's usefulness and limitations are then provided by explaining the facts of a single criminal act through the viewpoint provided by that theory. Rather than merely discussing abstract theories and statistical data on crime, we demonstrate how particular theories help to explain the facts of well-documented criminal cases. (In doing so, we also specify those aspects of a crime with which the theory cannot deal.) The idea is to keep the reader focused on the construction and use of the theory, rather than on the problems encountered in interpreting the research data. The reader is neither required nor expected to immediately grasp the interrelationships between these theories, but should gradually note the way in which the theories complement each other in explaining particular examples of human behavior.

In short, the authors' goal is to explore the use of criminological theory in a practical way, by applying it to real cases, taking note of its inherent limits, so that it might become a useful tool in the daily lives of new criminal justice practitioners.

The book is organized into chapters and subsections. Each chapter is devoted to a single *perspective*. Subsections deal with *approaches* and the specific *theories* contained within them. Discussion of each theory begins with a discussion of how and why it was developed and then focuses on the most important *concepts* in the theory, the theory's application to actual cases, and the major limitations on the theory's use.

At this point the reader should become familiarized with the common terms of criminological theory, including those just emphasized in the preceding paragraph. Let us consider the structure of criminological theories in order to explore the meanings of these terms.

The Structure of Criminological Theories
. . . .

The basic components used in theory construction are: (1) concepts, (2) variables, (3) statements, and (4) formats. **Concepts** are, essentially, terms used to identify specific phenomena that are of interest to theory-builders and theory-users. They usually represent very thorough definitions of those phenomena. The concepts used in criminological theories tend to be abstract ideas (e.g., peer group, role, status), rather than concrete things (e.g., gang, husband, judge). They are universal, rather than specific, in their identification of phenomena. That is, they do not identify any specific particular person, place, or thing but refer to attributes that are common among a group of people, places or things.[10]

Variables are labels or names given phenomena so that they can be distinguished from other phenomena or used to describe degrees of differences among phenomena (e.g., young people, middle-aged people, old people).[11] Variables constitute measurable and concrete versions of concepts and are especially critical in the process of validating theory with aggregate data.

Theoretical statements connect the variables used in a theory or explanation to one another. They indicate the relationship between the variables, and provide an interpretation of that relationship.[12] Although there are several other approaches to developing theoretical statements (e.g., metatheoretical, analytical, modeling), the *propositional approach* is the one that is used to organize and introduce the theories presented in this book. A **proposition** is a theoretical statement that specifies the connection between two or more variables or how one affects the other.[13] For example, the statement, "Poverty causes street crime," is a theoretical statement indicating the relationship between two phenomena, and it implies that changes in poverty will affect street crime. **Theoretical formats** are simply the ways in which theoretical statements are grouped together.[14]

Criminological theory is generally viewed as consisting of three hierarchically related levels of assumptions. In essence, specific criminological theories can be thought of as part of a nested hierarchy of assumptions. That is, assumptions contained in each theory are *subsumed* (meaning incorporated and/or accounted for) by an approach, and the assumptions contained in each approach are subsumed by a perspective. **Hypotheses** are simple statements about variables, describing the relationship of a single fact to some other fact, that can be empirically tested by researchers to determine their validity. This is usually done with aggregate data that describe a fairly large number of cases or situations.

The broadest or most encompassing level is commonly referred to as a *perspective* (Exhibit 1.2), a term often used as a synonym for *paradigm* and *viewpoint* (as it is in this text), although some theoreticians and textbook authors use the term to denote broad subdivisions within paradigms. A criminological perspective can be thought of as a particular way of looking at crime, or as a particular point of view regarding criminality. It is a model of the basic causes of the phenomenon of crime. Each individual perspective is

Exhibit 1.2
. . . .

Theory structure

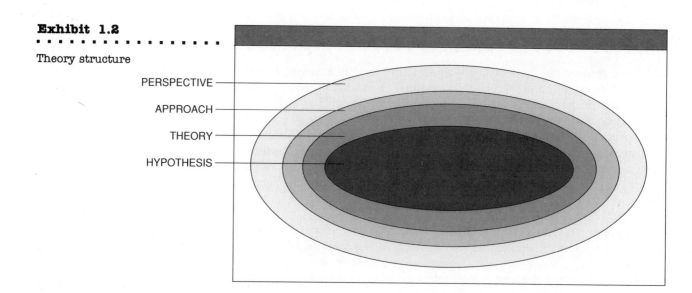

PERSPECTIVE

APPROACH

THEORY

HYPOTHESIS

built upon its own unique set of assumptions. Assumptions specified by perspectives are usually broad general statements that have universal applicability within the perspective itself.

Perspectives subsume *approaches,* the next broadest level of assumptions. Criminological approaches can also be thought of as subdivisions within a perspective. The main difference between a perspective and an approach is that the particular point of view of an approach must be consistent with that of the perspective by which it is contained. The approach, by definition, includes the assumptions of the perspective in which it is contained and then extends them in a particular direction. Approaches thus tend to be less abstract than the perspectives containing them because they link the general assumptions to specific aspects of crime or the motives for it.

Once the assumptions of the theoretical approach have been made explicit, the specific *theories* included in that approach must be addressed. Specific theories constitute the most confining level of assumptions. This is because the assumptions they contain must be consistent with both those of the perspective and the approach in which they are contained. Accordingly, theories are somewhat less abstract than the approaches that contain them. To the degree that the assumptions contained in theories are correct, they provide a brief and to-the-point outline of the processes we expect to find operating in real-life cases.

The assumptions contained in theories can be used to limit, and thus simplify, our focus at any level of analysis. They also serve to limit the theory's application, and thus restrain users from overextending the theory's usefulness. In effect, they alert us to the limits of the theory's applicability, since, as we have already shown, these assumptions are never completely accurate. Theory, in other words, is valid only when, and to the extent that, its assumptions are valid.

In addition, because theories often make general predictions that cannot be directly tested in a scientific manner (i.e., they cannot be proven false) and are usually rather subjective in nature, they require us to make judgments about situations or people that are not well-known to us. That is, judgments must be made about the nature of social situations we have not encountered or experienced, and about the innermost thoughts and emotions of people unknown or barely known to us. Speculative judgments such as these cannot be tested and verified in a scientific fashion.

If social theory went no farther than this, we would be better advised to talk of social philosophies than of the social sciences. Therefore, specific theories are only an intermediate step in the process of explanation. Holding the assumptions of the theory in mind as a rough description of how human beings and/or society "really are," the theory-user examines the predictions made by specific theories in an effort to deduce the sorts of behavior that might be expected if the theory is indeed correct.

Theories, therefore, lead to a series of predictions based on their assumptions that are commonly referred to as *hypotheses.* These are the least abstract of any theoretical device. As defined earlier, a hypothesis describes the relationship between facts within a single case and is generally stated in a single sentence. Hypotheses should resemble a "true-false" question on an examination. That is, we must be able to show them to be false, if indeed they are. Hypotheses translate the assumptions of a theory into concrete statements of what actions should be expected if (or to the degree that) the theory is correct. An example of a hypothesis would be the statement, "Substance abuse leads people into crime."

Only after the hypotheses are derived from the theoretical assumptions can they be tested and verified. If research shows that the hypotheses generated from a theory have the power to explain a significant portion of a phenomenon, we say that the theory has "empirical support." However, more than one theory is often able to account for such research results. Therefore, regardless of how much support a theory or perspective may have, we can never say with scientific certainty that a theory or perspective has been proven true.

If the hypothesis that drug use causes criminality is correct, then we would predict that very few criminals would have committed illegal acts prior to when they began using drugs. Such a statement can be tested with relative ease in the real world with aggregate data and/or case studies. (In fact, the data suggest that most criminal-addicts were criminals prior to the beginning of their drug use. Thus, a more accurate, if less appealing, hypothesis would assert that involvement in crime encourages drug use and/or addiction.)[16]

Hypotheses are traditionally associated with the methodological concerns of social science. However, hypotheses derived from theories also provide a method for matching theories to specific cases. As the theory is translated into testable hypotheses, the theory-user is forced to specify the variables involved and the relationship(s) between them. These variables function to link the theory to the facts of the case. The degree to which these same variables are present in, and relevant to, a specific case is a good indicator of the theory's fit with the facts of the case. Not only should roughly the same variables appear in both the case and the hypothesis, but their relationship to one another should be virtually identical in both the case and the hypothesis.

The Nature of Theory Application

The application of abstract theory to concrete events is, by nature, speculative and controversial. As explained, theories are usually generated from, and/or supported by, research using aggregate data. As we apply a theory to a particular case, however, we must attribute one or more motives for the criminal act to the offender's conscious intentions, and here we are attempting to act as psychotherapists. Yet, unlike a real psychotherapist, the criminological theorist has rarely met and become intimate with the offender. This is a limitation that cannot be wholly overcome.

This fact also helps to explain why more than one theory may be used to explain the same, or very similar, phenomena. Because theories seek to make the world a simpler, more manageable entity, they each tend to focus on one level or type of causal fact and neglect others. Yet all the causal forces operate simultaneously at all levels of analysis. Consequently, most theories can be applied to most crimes with some degree of validity. The problem is to determine which theory explains *more of the important facts* of a particular crime.

In any given case, a variety of facts will seem to be related to the crime in some sort of causal fashion. The more factors that can be included in an analysis, the more convincing that analysis is likely to be. Most theories are able to deal with several factors at the same or similar level of analysis. However, no fact can be meaningfully interpreted in isolation from the settings and people with which it is concerned. To fully comprehend the causes of a crime, one must carefully consider the context of the act, the social situation of the offender prior to and during the crime, and the forces operating in and around the situation. Factors that appear to cause crime in one situation may have no effect in another or may even work toward positive ends in different settings. In other words, the effects of each factor present in a particular case must be examined within the entire context of the offender's life and the situation in which the crime occurred.[17] For example, broken homes are a popular single-factor explanation of juvenile delinquency, but in some cases a divorce may prevent additional conflict in the home or help the child avoid the negative influence of a dysfunctional parent. In such cases, the "broken home" actually helps prevent crime rather than cause it.

It must also be recognized that the causes of crime are not always negative forces in themselves. Some criminogenic factors (e.g., poverty, addiction) are unfortunate whenever they occur. But consider, for example, the computer. Generally seen as a good thing, it has also made certain new types of crime possible and certain other crimes easier to commit than before. There is growing agreement among scholars that positive social developments (such as the computer) can have unforeseen results that are unfortunate—including crime.[18]

The issue of which theory explains the most is related to the broader dilemma of the proper function of criminological theory itself. Some criminologists suggest that the function of criminological theory is to develop perfect (valid and comprehensive) explanations of criminal behavior. Others propose that its function is to develop less than perfect explanations that address the most immediate needs of society. These less than perfect theories must be developed by fitting the available "criminological facts" into cohesive descriptions of particular issues. Such theories are then validated or refuted by examining the results of the policies and programs based on them. The testing of imperfect theories in real-world settings, it is further suggested, should lead to additional knowledge upon which even better theories can be developed.[19]

In accordance with this latter argument, we have matched theories with cases for illustration purposes even though the fit is less than perfect. Our method of applying theories to facts associated with particular crimes will be simultaneously guided and limited by the assumptions or propositions contained in the theories.

To a large degree, the application of particular theories to particular crimes is a judgmental issue. However, we offer three criteria that can help to guide the process:

1. the types of facts about the case that are available to us,
2. the types of facts for which the theory was designed, and
3. the assumptions made by the theory about the nature of human behavior and society.

To combine criteria, we simply weave between the facts of the case and the assumptions of the theory to build an explanation of the crime. By combining these criteria, we are able to formulate certain hypotheses that link the assumptions of the theory to the facts of the case. As explained earlier, these hypotheses should be worded so that they can be shown to be true or false in an empirical manner. Some of the possible theoretical explanations can then be eliminated. To the degree that these hypotheses accurately describe the case's pertinent features, we will assert that the theory "fits," or explains, the case. The number of significant facts that a theory can address, along with the validity of the manner in which it links them to the crime, together determine its appropriateness.

We can first narrow the range of theories that provide plausible explanations of real crimes by examining the **level of analysis,** a term that refers to a hierarchy of levels at which social factors operate. Identifying these levels is crucial to the process of fitting cases to theories. Analytical levels vary in both their main focus of attention (e.g., society, small groups, or individuals) and their reliance on abstraction. Some theories are designed to explain the distribution of crime(s) in a society, region, or administrative unit (the macro-level) while others are primarily concerned with the role of various sorts of groups in guiding behavior (the meso-level). Still others focus on the internal perceptions and motivations of the individual offender (the micro-level). This subject will be discussed in more detail in the next chapter. Generally, however, the higher the level of analysis, the more abstraction is involved in applying a theory to a particular situation. This fact is partly responsible for the preference for micro-level explanations shown by many of those without training in social science.

Further aiding this process of theory application are the assumptions of each theoretical perspective and the specific theories within that perspective. By comparing the level of analysis for which a theory is designed with the relevant facts of a criminal case, we can significantly reduce the number of possible theoretical explanations. For example, some theories assume that humans are relatively unselfish, caring creatures by nature. These theories use negative factors in society to explain criminal behavior, which is seen as the result of society's "corrupting" effect on human nature. Other theories presume just the opposite—that people are self-centered and callous by nature. These theories must take on the task of explaining how society can keep people under control at all. In reality, human nature appears to be both egocentric (self-centered) and altruistic (generous and caring), so the assumptions of both views are partially correct and the choice between them is largely one of personal ideology. This is very typical of theoretical assumptions.

It is understood that the assumptions defining each analytical level can never be completely true. They serve only to simplify the task of analysis, which would otherwise be impossible. Without the use of simplifying assumptions, we would soon find that everything was related to everything else, and the explanation of an actual event would turn into a far-ranging, never-ending discussion of the nature of society, the physical world, and human behavior. Theoretical assumptions thus serve as guides to the type(s) of data with which the theory is best equipped to deal.

Finally, we need to look at the sorts of variables involved in a case to determine which theory is best suited for application. To a large extent, the theory chosen will reflect the extent of our knowledge of various aspects of that case (the variables) as well as our personal beliefs about the nature of people and society. The less forthcoming offenders are in revealing their reasoning processes to authorities, and/or the less information provided by others familiar with the criminals and victims, the more likely it is that scientific explanations will be based at a broad, macro-social level of analysis. This is because many basic facts about the offender (e.g., age, sex, socioeconomic status) will be available to us even though we cannot be sure of what experiences, thoughts, and beliefs actually led to the crime, and these available facts will weigh heavily in our choice of explanation for the crime.

If we have strong personal beliefs about the basic nature of people, we will tend to favor theories that share our assumptions. Our understanding of behavior, and especially crime, is severely limited by such biases. The result is an incomplete view of the issue(s), often leading to erroneous explanations and conclusions, even when guided by the best of intentions. By being aware of our biases, we pave the way for a fuller and more accurate understanding of crime and its perpetrators.

All crimes consist of a multitude of various types of facts. Some are very obvious, like the choice of weapon and the victim-offender relationship. Others, like motivation, are less clear and require some degree of speculative attribution because they may not even be clearly understood by the offender. We should avoid simplistic approaches that attribute unknown psychopathologies to all criminal offenders simply because they perceive and reason in a fashion that is not immediately familiar to us. By examining each level of social analysis separately, we can begin to see their interrelationships and uses as well as their contradictions and limitations and probably arrive at more accurate conclusions.

The Process of Explaining Crimes with Theory
· ·

Unfortunately, very few, if any, acts can be fully explained by one theory. As explained earlier, this is because the "causes" of behavior occur simultaneously at all levels of analysis and constantly interact with one another as well as with all sorts of environmental, structural, and internal forces. Broadly speaking, theoretical explanations in criminology can be divided into two ideological types, *conservative* and *liberal*.

Conservative theoretical explanations are usually designed to deal with the influence of facts associated with the individual's perceptions of the immediate situation, and the opportunities and choices available to them. They are considered conservative because they focus on facts that lie within the control of the individual and can be interpreted as relieving society of responsibilty for its inequalities and other problems that may have affected the individual's logic and perceptions.

Conservative explanations tend to revolve around a set of facts associated with the particular time, setting, and people involved in the criminal act. Theories focused on this sort of data attempt to explain the peculiarities of the specific crime, devoting most of their attention to the specific people, places, and objects involved in the act. They ask questions such as, "What facts explain why this crime was committed when it was committed?" "Why were these particular people involved?" "Why did it occur where it did?" (For example, "Did it occur in a bar as a result of a spontaneous argument, or was the crime scene selected and the act planned long in advance?")

Conservative explanations typically assume humans to be creatures driven by selfish desires that must be controlled by external forces, such as the threat of punishment. Simultaneously, these types of facts are thought to operate through the structure of values with which the offender defines social reality and appropriate behavior. The theories that focus on these types of facts tend to emphasize the individual's responsibility to follow the rules of society. Such theories also tend to presume that the rules are appropriate and that the individuals who violate them are different from the rest of us in some way.

Students and criminal justice practitioners tend to be of middle-class economic backgrounds. However, policies intended to control crime are fundamentally directed at the lower economic class. Therefore, those students and practitioners who are from the middle class must take into account the way differences in environment color the perceptions and logic of individuals. Conservative theories often fail to recognize these differences due to their assumption that the legal code is the best possible set of rules to govern society and that most citizens share this view of the law.

Liberal theoretical explanations are typically designed to address mitigating circumstances, or background types of facts. They are considered liberal because they focus on factors that are clearly beyond the individual's control and thus might be used to absolve offenders from responsibility for their acts. This is due to the fact that liberal explanations tend to presume that human beings are basically malleable creatures that are too often corrupted by their environments, and only then become self-serving.

Liberal theoretical explanations tend to revolve around a different set of facts than those that conservative explanations focus on. For example, the types of criminal acts that particular people commit (e.g. a person that might commit a fraud might never commit a murder) and the particular types of people most prone to commit crimes (i.e., the lower or "under" class) are subjects of concern to liberal theoreticians. Individual perceptions of the specific situation, and the opportunities and choices people perceive to be available to them under these particular circumstances, are the crucial data here.

Offenders may be aware of the impact of some of the more immediate causal forces on their thoughts and behavior, and are likely to explain their crimes in terms of these facts. In this way their thinking parallels that of conservatives. However, the ultimate causes of any action also include the forces that have shaped the offender's perceptions and logic. Such facts generally lie in the offender's background and are often related to group memberships and environment. Most people presume that perceptions and logic reflect a fairly universal and objective sense of reality. Therefore, offenders (as well as most observers) are not likely to recognize the operation of such subtle forces in the narrative of a particular crime.

Facts related to the general social conditions influencing the offender's life are often quite distant in time and space from the crime itself. This set of facts is often viewed as mitigating the offender's responsibility for choosing crime (personal and family history, general economic conditions, etc.), such as in the case of battering parents who were themselves battered children. Group memberships (e.g., social class, race) as well as background facts (e.g., abuse by parents) are examples.

Simultaneously, however, mitigating facts often lie in the structure of society, and theories stressing such forces can easily be misinterpreted as holding the society responsible for the behavior of those who violate its laws. Just as conservative explanations fail to take into account the linkage of environment to logic, perception, and behavior, liberal explanations give little weight to the role of conscious choice in assigning responsibility for human actions. Thus, liberal and conservative explanations should be combined if we are to grasp the ultimate nature of the "causes" of crime.

It is important to reiterate that all the facts involved in explaining a crime rarely fit neatly into any one theoretical perspective or specific theory. While some theories tend to support one ideology over another, all theories make a valuable contribution to our comprehension of crime. Therefore, ideology can easily become an obstacle to developing a complete view of complex behaviors like criminal behavior. It is best that equal emphasis be given to each view of crime—the conservative and the liberal—when constructing theoretical explanations.

Most scientific approaches to crime cover at least several types of facts. However, their explanatory strength is usually at its maximum in regard to one set of facts and moderate to weak in dealing with the other(s). In this book we will use our professional judgment to rank the strength of each theory in reference to its ability to address the known facts of specific criminal cases. After the reader has gained some comprehension of the theories introduced in the early chapters of this text, she or he can have some fun by second-guessing or "Monday morning quarter backing" the authors' choices of theories for explaining cases presented in later chapters.

Readers should be aware that their moral stance and political ideology will probably color their opinions of the value of various theories. Biases are best overcome through awareness of the fact that scientific theory is concerned with the explanation of phenomena, while laws and courts are concerned with the assignment of responsibility and the maintenance of "justice." If a theory appears to neglect facts that the reader sees as crucial, the difficulty most likely lies in the ideological view of the reader rather than in the validity of the theory. It must also be remembered that the linkage of theory to ideology is far from absolute. The fact that ideas derived from conservative theories were used to define the "war on poverty" of the 1965–1975 era as a crime-control strategy illustrates this point.

The Nature of Celebrated Criminal Cases

According to Samuel Walker, "celebrated" criminal cases can be thought of as the top layer of a four-layer criminal justice wedding cake. Essentially, Walker's *wedding cake model* suggests that criminal justice officials react to different kinds of cases in different ways. Aside from the obvious difference of being highly publicized, celebrated cases usually involve the full criminal process, and generally involve controversial issues (e.g., insanity defense), celebrities (e.g., Sharon Tate), and/or rare events (e.g., appeals to the Supreme Court, jury trials). Cases that result in well-known Supreme Court rulings (e.g., Miranda) are also considered "celebrated" by Walker. In contrast, the great bulk of criminal cases do not involve the full criminal process, controversial issues, or rare events and are usually disposed of quietly through out-of-court negotiation (i.e., plea bargains).[21]

The second layer of this model is made up of crimes that criminal justice officials take very seriously, such as assaults by offenders who are "strangers" to the victim. These are serious crimes in which there are no obviously mitigating factors. Such cases are given much attention by officials but are often resolved through routine procedures. The third layer is composed of crimes defined as less serious by criminal justice officials. This layer includes crimes involving offenders and victims who had relationships with each other prior to the criminal act. An example of the difference between a second- and third-layer crime can be seen in the comparison of rape by a "stranger"—a second-level crime—versus rape by an ex-spouse or an acquaintance—a third-level crime (in most jurisdictions). The fourth and final level of the cake is made up of misdemeanor offenses and other minor, or "accidental," infractions that are seen as relatively petty by the practitioners involved with them.[22]

It is interesting to note that Walker found a high degree of consistency of criminal justice official response to crimes occurring within the same layer of the cake, including those committed in the celebrated layer.[24]

In this text, we use highly celebrated cases in which most of the relevant facts have been published in book form and there is little doubt as to the offender's identity, motive(s), and relationship to the victim. To attain such celebrity, a case must involve a well-known person as victim and/or offender or the crime must be especially gruesome or apparently senseless.

Although celebrated cases often involve economically upper-to middle-class offenders and victims, and sometimes involve complex motives and/or extensive premeditation, we found most of them to be fairly similar to cases involving those of the lower-to-middle classes. That is, most celebrated and uncelebrated cases involve similar crimes, are motivated by the same basic human emotions—anger, fear, greed, et cetera—and occur as impulsive acts.[23] The primary difference is that celebrated cases are more likely to go through the entire criminal justice process.

The reader should be aware that celebrated cases often involve crimes composed of multiple offenses, or what the justice system refers to as multiple "counts." That is, a single incident may involve the commission of the crime of robbery and the crime of homicide, or the commission of the crime of kidnapping and the crime of sexual assault. Although in today's society a crime must usually involve an act of homicide in order for it to achieve celebrated status, we have found that other crimes (e.g., robbery, theft, fraud, sexual assault) have been the motivating factors for most of the homicides. That is, many homicides occur as a method of achieving some other goal desired by the offender. Homicides resulting from robberies and disputes over illegal drugs are exemplary of these cases, which are dealt with in the chapters on cultural and structural theories in this book.

The original, driving motive for the offender's behavior in a homicide will therefore constantly remain at the center of our analysis and explanation. Thus, in a robbery-murder we would emphasize the decision to rob, the method of victim selection, and similar facts, rather than the manner in which the victim died.

In many ways homicide is a fairly typical, if extreme, type of violent crime.[25] Much of what is said of homicide can be applied to aggravated assault and similar crimes as well. For example, most violent crimes involve offenders who are demographically similar to, and known by, their victims. Alcohol and drugs are frequently involved in these crimes, which occur with the greatest frequency during warm weather, when social interaction is at its height. Likewise, the criminals involved in the cases used in this book vary from career criminals like Charles Manson to first offenders who led exemplary lives prior to their crime.

An additional factor favoring the selection of celebrated cases is simply that more information from a number of varied sources is available for these cases. This allows for a more comprehensive and less biased view of the crimes and criminals, as well as for more accuracy in describing the crimes and motives. In other words, the existing literature on these crimes, and especially on this group of offenders, is more trustworthy than usual.

Criminal Motivations

The motive for a criminal act can generally be labeled as either instrumental or expressive. **Instrumental** crimes are usually thought of as those committed for some type of objective personal gain, such as cases of robbery or insurance fraud. **Expressive** crimes, on the other hand, are usually seen as resulting from emotions, such as crimes of passion or vengeance.[26] However, concepts like instrumental and expressive motives are **ideal types,** theoretical devices that tend to be rather abstract. They help us to categorize objects and events in terms of their most essential and defining features. But they are rarely, if ever, encountered in their pure form. Rather, the phenomena encountered in the real world can best be described in terms of multiple ideal types in a unique mixture.

The majority of the cases presented in this text are instrumental crimes precipitated by practical goals. The immediate, instrumental motives of such crimes are generally the ones upon which the media concentrates its attention because they are more easily understood than expressive motives, which embody the offender's personal sense of reality, logic, and justice.

As you will see, the actual reasons for the commission of a crime are almost always much more complex than those presented by the media or scholarly typologies. The media provides only the more lurid details of the crimes and their aftermath, whereas the real stories lie hidden in the thought processes of the offenders.[27] The public consequently has a distorted image of the nature and distribution of both crime in general and the typical motivations for it. The middle-class worldview (or construction of reality) sees the typical criminal as a product of a lower-class, urban environment who has had little positive contact with the middle-class normative system. In reality, however, crime is routinely perpetrated by people at all levels of society.

Keep in mind throughout this text that there are usually numerous, as opposed to singular or isolated, facts that must be dealt with by scientific explanations. Many facts are not likely to be directly addressed by the immediate motive that is provided to us by the criminal and embellished by the media. Thus, as you will see in the cases presented in this text, the criminological explanation for the crime is not necessarily what led to the celebrity status of the case.

Finally, the reader should be cognizant of the fact that crimes of violence in general, and homicides in particular, are much less common than those involving offenses against property and the public order.[28] In 1986

The main shortcomings of learning about crime from the media is that often the media provides only the lurid, sensational details of the crimes. One example is the widespread publicity surrounding Jefferey Daumer in July 1991, after police found the dismembered bodies of 11 men in his Milwaukee apartment.

violent crimes accounted for only 11.3 percent of the total crime index.[29] It should also be noted that the great majority of police effort, and the largest number of arrests, involve crimes against the public order that are usually of a non-serious nature (e.g., public drunkenness).[30] In the cases covered by this text, property crime is often the initial motive for the offender's involvement in illegal activity, with violence playing an instrumental, and secondary, role.

Glossary ·

Aggregated Data   A set of facts about a group of cases in which individual identities are ignored in order to examine patterns and trends within the entire group and/or among its subgroups.

Case Study Method   A detailed analysis of one individual's experience and behavior or that of a single event. Such an analysis is an extensive, qualitative examination of an illustrative or exemplary case of a phenomenon.

Concepts   Terms used to identify specific ideas that are crucial to a theory, approach, or perspective.

Expressive Crimes   Offenses that occur as a result of emotional motivations, such as crimes of passion or vengeance.

Hypotheses   Describe the relationship of a single fact to some other fact and are generally stated in a single sentence that can be proven false with some form of data (i.e., either aggregate data or case studies).

Ideal Type   A hypothetical construct in which the essential features that define a phenomena are all present. It is used to open the world to analysis but is rarely encountered in concrete form.

Instrumental Crimes   Crimes committed for some type of objective personal gain, such as a case of robbery or insurance fraud.

Levels of Analysis   Particular levels of social interaction and causality within society. They vary in the types of facts upon which they focus our attention.

Propositions   Theoretical statements that specify the connection between two or more variables or how one affects the other.

Social Phenomena   Any events or occurrences in human society that can be scientifically described.

Theoretical Formats   The ways in which theoretical statements are grouped together.

Theoretical Statements   Connect variables used in a theory, indicate the relationship between the variables, and provide an interpretation of their relationship.

Variables   Labels or names given phenomena so that they can be distinguished from other phenomena, and they may also note degrees of differences among phenomena. They are capable of being measured in a scientific manner.

■ Notes

1. For a discussion of the usefulness of theory, see Arthur L. Stinchcombe, *Constructing Social Theories* (Chicago, IL: The University of Chicago Press, 1968), p. 4.
2. Howard S. Becker, "The Relevance of Life Histories" in *Sociological Methods: A Sourcebook,* ed. Norman K. Denzin (New York, NY: McGraw-Hill, 1978), pp. 289–295; Frank E. Hagan, *Research Methods in Criminal Justice and Criminology,* 2d ed. (New York, NY: Macmillan, 1989).
3. For a discussion on case studies as a sensitizing strategy to new subject matter, see Frank E. Hagan, *Research Methods in Criminal Justice and Criminology,* 2d ed. (New York: Macmillan, 1989).
4. Paul B. Weston and Robert W. Cole, *Case Studies of Drug Abuse and Criminal Behavior* (Pacific Palisades, CA: Goodyear Publishing Company, 1973).
5. Clifford R. Shaw, *The Jack-Roller* (Chicago, IL: University of Chicago Press, 1930); Edwin H. Sutherland, *The Professional Thief* (Chicago, IL: University of Chicago Press, 1937).
6. Howard Abadinsky, *The Mafia in America: An Oral History* (New York, NY: Praeger, 1981); Howard Abadinsky, *The Criminal Elite: Professional and Organized Crime* (Westport, CT: Greenwood Press, 1983).
7. R. D. Laing and A. Esterson, *Sanity, Madness and the Family* (New York, NY: Penguin Books, 1964), p. 12.
8. Norman K. Denzin, *The Research Act: A Theoretical Introduction to Sociological Methods,* 3d ed. (Englewood Cliffs, NJ: Prentice-Hall, 1989).
9. Allen E. Liska, *Perspectives on Deviance* (Englewood, NJ: Prentice-Hall, 1981), pp. ix–x.

10. Jonathan H. Turner, *The Structure of Sociological Theory*, 4th ed. (Belmont, CA: Wadworth Publishing Company, 1986), pp. 4–7.
11. Ibid., p. 7.
12. Ibid., pp. 7–8.
13. Ibid., pp. 7–21.
14. Ibid.
15. William N. Stephens, *Hypotheses and Evidence* (New York, NY: Thomas Y. Crowell Company, 1968), p. 1.
16. James Inciardi, The War on Drugs (Mountain View, CA: Mayfield Publishing, 1986), pp. 123–126.
17. Albert K. Cohen, "Multiple Factors Approaches" in *The Sociology of Crime and Delinquency,* eds. M. Wolfgang, L. Savitz, and N. Johnson (New York, NY: John Wiley and Sons, 1962), pp. 77–80.
18. Ibid.
19. Leonard Savitz, *Dilemmas in Criminology* (New York, NY: McGraw-Hill Book Company, 1967).
21. Samuel Walker, *Sense and Nonsense About Crime: A Policy Guide,* - 2d ed. (Pacific Grove, CA: Brooks/Cole, 1989), pp. 22–34.
22. Ibid.
23. Ibid.
24. Gresham M. Sykes, *Criminology* (New York, NY: Harcourt, Brace Jovanovich Inc., 1978), pp. 134.
25. Sykes, *Criminology*, p. 136.
26. James J. Collins, "Alcohol Use and Expressive Interpersonal Violence" in *Alcohol, Drug Abuse, and Aggression,* eds. E. Gottheil, K.A. Druley, T.E. Skoloda, and H.M. Waxman (Springfield, IL: Charles C. Thomas, 1983), pp. 5–25.
27. Richard M. Levine, Bad Blood: *A Family Murder in Marin County* (New York, NY: Random House, Inc., 1982), p. xi.
28. Sykes, *Criminology*, p. 86.
29. Timothy J. Flanagan and Katherine M. Johnson (eds.), *Sourcebook of Criminal Justice Statistics 1987* (Washington, D.C.: U.S. Department of Justice, Bureau of Justice Statistics, 1988).
30. Ibid.

CHAPTER **2**

A Strategy for the Application
of Theory

This chapter describes the case-history method used to apply criminological theories to the details of specific, real crimes. It also serves as a blueprint for applying such theories to other crimes. Also, terms and classification schemes that are employed throughout this book are explained here, with illustrations of their use in the theory-application process. While all definitions and classification systems are somewhat arbitrary, they must be used if confusion is to be avoided in the process of theory-application[1]. Every effort has been made to make the definitions and classifications consistent with those currently used by most social science practitioners.

Hierarchy of Conceptual Devices
. . . .

Historically, theoreticians have attached multiple meanings to certain terms. This is especially true in the social sciences. For example, according to Masterman, Kuhn used the term *paradigm* in more than twenty-one different ways in his book, *The Structure of Scientific Revolutions*.[2] In many instances, textbook writers have provided only vague definitions of critically important terms. Additionally, many theoreticians who subsequently use a term coined by another writer will attach new meanings or slightly different interpretations to them. As a specific example, consider the term *reference group*, which is used by social science theoreticians in at least three different ways: (1) to mean a group that serves as a point of reference for making comparisons; (2) to mean a group that one desires to join or maintain membership in; and (3) to mean a group that serves as a frame of reference for value judgments.[3]

As another case in point, many discussions of theory use the terms *perspective* and *approach* interchangeably (e.g., psychological perspective, psychological approach). In this text, however, each term will have its specific meaning, as defined in this chapter. The term **perspective** will be used to differentiate scientific disciplines (e.g., biology, sociology), as well as their subcommunities (e.g., biosocial, structuralism).[4] **Scientific subcommunities** consist of major subgroups within a particular scientific community or general discipline. The assumptions that these subgroups use are consistent with the disciplines they are contained in, but sufficiently different from each other to warrant being identified as a unique theoretical perspective in criminology. We use the term *perspective* to denote both the largest unit of agreement within a scientific community (e.g., sociological community/sociological perspective) as well as the smaller scientific subcommunities (e.g., social-conflict community/social-conflict perspective)[5] in an effort to maintain consistency with other criminological works. This usage also reflects the interdisciplinary nature of criminology and criminal justice.

The term **approach,** on the other hand, will be used to distinguish between the different focuses and emphases that one or more theorists have taken within a particular perspective. For example, in this text, theories within the psychological perspective that focus on and emphasize observable behavior are placed in the *behaviorist* approach, while those psychological theories that focus on and emphasize the thought processes of individuals are contained in the *cognitive* approach. Both share some assumptions derived from psychology (the perspective), but the differences between them are sufficient to distinguish them as approaches to crime and criminality.

The conceptual framework of a perspective has four important uses: (1) identifying the subject matter, or the issues to be examined and the sorts of questions to be raised about them; (2) proposing answers (theories) for these questions; (3) guiding the empirical testing of these answers to determine the degree to which they help to explain reality; and (4) providing policy/program suggestions.[6]

The scientific subcommunities of a perspective investigate phenomena from within that discipline but are often concerned with different aspects of the same phenomenon. These differences are especially important to an interdisciplinary area of concern such as criminology. For example, both the *social-learning* perspective and *labeling* perspective are contained in, and consistent with, the general goals of the discipline of sociology. But social-learning theorists view the learning processes that occur within small groups as the central cause of criminal behavior, whereas the labeling theorists see the labeling processes of society as the main issue in explaining criminality. Thus, although both of these sociological subcommunities see social processes as the crucial factor in explaining criminal behavior, they differ greatly on the question of which social processes are most important.

Individual *theories* can be grouped together into perspectives and approaches according to several different criteria.[7] We have elected to use the "schools of thought" method.[8] Under this classification system, theories are grouped together according to the sorts of assumptions upon which they are based. Throughout this text the assumptions held by each perspective will be referred to as **common assumptions,** and those held by each approach will be referred to as **restrictive assumptions.** Common assumptions tend to be rather abstract descriptions of humankind, society, and/or their relationship to one another. They cannot generally be tested or applied at the case level without being further elaborated. Usually, several theoreticians will have developed complementary or overlapping explanations of criminal behavior that are based on the same, or very similar, assumptions about the nature of individuals and society. These theories are then logically placed in the same perspective.

Restrictive assumptions—those held by an approach—restrict the use of the perspective or narrow its meaning and thus serve to focus it on a particular aspect of crime. Restrictive assumptions are the first step in the process of elaboration that makes theoretical ideas testable and applicable at the case level.

The critical divisions within a perspective lie in the factors each approach defines as most important to explaining the problem at hand. Thus, we may claim that approaches are less abstract than perspectives and more directly relevant to crime or criminality. In some cases approaches can be directly applied to the real world without further elaboration. Yet approaches are less concrete than the theories contained within them.

As it is used in the rest of this text, the term *theory* refers to a more specific and less abstract set of beliefs than those that form an approach. And **hypotheses** are even more specific and less abstract in their description of the relevant facts than theories. As very specific "if-then" statements that directly link two or more facts in a causal relationship, hypotheses make statements such as, "if A is present then B will occur" or "X causes Y." Such statements can be demonstrated to be false, but empirical testing cannot prove them true. For example, the theoretical proposition that "drug use causes crime" can be converted into this hypothesis: "If drug use causes crime, then drug use will precede criminal activity in most cases." This hypothesis has been shown to be false by the aggregate research cited in Chapter 1. Hypotheses are said to be supported by research data whenever they cannot be proven false.

Theories provide the most succinct explanation of crime possible without referring to specific variables or facts that are unique to the case. They take their focus and worldview from the assumptions of the perspective and approach in which they are based. They specify the concepts that will be developed into the variables used to test the theory, and link these ideas to the broader assumptions made in the more abstract conceptualizations of the problem under study. Throughout this text, the assumptions made by a theory will be referred to as **specific assumptions** because they act to specifically define the theory.

The reader should also be aware of the fact that criminological theories tend not to be abandoned or discarded. Rather, they are like the saying about old soldiers—they never die, they just fade away. This is partially due to the way the social sciences view hypotheses and hypothesis testing, which in turn is due to the complexity of human behavior itself. Generally speaking, hypotheses in the social sciences are couched in terms such as "more than," "most," and "lead to," rather than in absolutes, such as "all" and "always." Social science hypotheses contain statements such as, "The number of broken homes in a community will predict that community's crime rate," with the implicit understanding that not all persons from broken homes will become criminals. These types of statements are very unlike statements of fact—such as, "The world is flat," or, "The world is round"—which are either completely true or completely false.

Levels of Analysis

The terms *micro, meso,* and *macro* are used by theorists in essentially two ways: (1) to denote levels of social organization and analysis, such as the individual or family (micro) as one level, neighborhoods or organizations (meso) as another level, and institutions or societies (macro) as the third level; and (2) to denote levels of social facts, such as a specific person's marriage (micro-level fact), the denomination of the church that a specific person was married in (meso-level fact), and marriage itself as a social institution (macro-level fact). These levels form a continuum, and there is not universal agreement as to their precise boundaries.

In order to avoid confusion over the meaning of these terms, they will be used only to describe the level of social organization at which the theoretical analysis or explanation is being conducted. (It should be noted that many sociologists would argue that forms of social organization *are* facts.) The term **micro-level** will be used to refer to explanations of crime(s) focused on the individual or on interpersonal behavior in very small groups. The **meso-level** will refer to explanations that focus on the members and/or actions of large groups or organizations. The **macro-level** will refer to explanations that focus on the role of a society, culture, or institution.

Unfortunately, very few, if any, acts can be fully explained at one level of analysis. This is due to the fact that the "causes" of behavior occur simultaneously at all levels of analysis and constantly interact with one another, as well as with other environmental, structural, and internal forces. For example, how a person is affected by his or her position in the society's economic structure (a macro-level fact) is partially dependent on the sort of community in which the person lives (a meso-level fact), as well as on that individual's relationship with his or her parents (a micro-level fact). For most people, macro-level facts are more abstract than micro-level ones. This, in part, explains why the micro-level is the most popular level of explanation for those un-schooled in the social sciences. However, macro- and meso-level forces are critical to understanding behavior because they provide the setting and context in which actions (including crimes) are conceived and performed.

Types of Causal Factors

We have borrowed the terms *precipitating, attracting,* and *predisposing* from Benjamin and Master's discussion of prostitution to denote the roles played by a fact in a specific explanation of a case.[9] Although they are related to levels of analysis, these roles function independently of those levels in the process of theory application.

Precipitating factors are event(s) and/or circumstance(s) immediately pre-ceding a criminal act(s) and are thought to determine the unique facts of the crime. Precipitating factors are crucial to explanations of why a particular person committed a particular crime at a given point in time and space. Peer influence, financial pressure, emotional distress, and opportunity are commonly cited as factors precipitating the onset of criminal activity in general, as well as the commission of a particular crime. Such factors are usually linked to the crime in a very direct, concrete way.

As we move away from factors that are unique to the individual offense, we encounter **attracting factors.** These are the set of choices that the individual

Unemployment, financial problems, and depression can be factors pre-cipitating the onset of criminal ac-tivity. Other commonly cited pre-cipitating factors include peer influ-ence, financial pressure, emotional distress, and opportunity.

perceives to be available—that is, the individual's perceptions of alternatives to crime, and also the alternative methods of committing a crime (e.g., fraud versus robbery, stabbing versus bombing). If noncriminal alternatives are perceived as unappealing, or as less rewarding than crime, then the person is likely to choose illegal behavior. But it is the perceptions of the individual, not the reality of her or his situation (as it might be defined by an outsider), that constitute the crucial "facts" here.

Attracting factors are the social and psychological forces determining whether a certain type of criminal act will be committed by a particular individual. Less overt than precipitating factors, attracting factors are defined by the offender's perception of social reality. Group memberships often have great influence over how such alternatives are viewed. For example, some groups encourage their members to resolve conflicts in a confronting, or even violent, manner while others support more subtle ways. The value one places on being "respected" by others in a peer group, for example, could constitute an attracting factor—accounting, therefore, for some crimes of violence. How one's group defines "respect" is often the critical issue. However, the individual is not likely to be aware that his or her ideas about "respect" are the product of membership in a particular group. Therefore, these factors tend to be taken for granted and are likely to go unquestioned by the offender.

Attracting factors usually precede precipitating factors in time. They are often fairly obvious to observers, but may be given insufficient attention as the observer (and theory-user) searches for more directly relevant motives for the commission of a particular crime.

Attracting factors are especially relevant to the type of crime committed. If a particular crime (or type thereof) appears to offer more advantages than legal alternatives for obtaining the same goal(s), then criminality is likely to result.[10] Less arduous labor, excitement, sensual gratification, maintenance of a "macho" self-image, and the desire for increased income or status are often mentioned as attracting factors in the criminological literature. Perspectives and theories that attempt to explain why some people have extensive "criminal careers" are primarily concerned with attracting and/or predisposing factors (our next subject).

Predisposing factors are environmental influences, statuses, or other traits that define a person's living situation. Broken homes, lower socioeconomic class, urban residence, mental disorders, racism, and low IQ are seen as prominent predisposing factors by most criminologists. However, being poor, black, and from a conflict-ridden home in the inner city does not, in and of itself, "cause" a person to commit crime. Such predisposing factors simply make it much more likely that such an individual will be attracted to crime or other problematic behavior than would a person from more fortunate circumstances. These factors contribute to the person's sense of identity. Therefore, while not causal in a direct sense, they help to explain the distribution of crime across major status categories and other social groupings. Predisposing factors also help to explain the effect of major social institutions like the family and the economy on the level of crime in an area or group.

Predisposing factors are the basis upon which other, more immediate and apparent causes usually stand. They are also the most likely to be taken for granted by both offender and observer. This is especially true because they tend to constitute part of the social reality of the offender's (and perhaps the observer's) daily life. Along with attracting factors, predisposing factors tend to predict both the depth of commitment to crime and the frequency of criminal behavior in individuals.

A causal fact may be identified and used as a precipitating, attracting, or predisposing factor at *any* level of analysis—micro, meso, or macro. In order to correctly assign a particular fact to one of these categories, we must be attentive to the context in which it was relevant to the crime we are explaining. That is, the same fact (e.g., an extramarital affair) may be labeled and used as a precipitating fact in the explanation of one crime, but as an attracting or predisposing fact in the explanation of other crimes. However, it can only be used as one of the three types of factors (precipitating, attracting, predisposing) in the explanation of any single crime.

The following vignettes show, simplisticly, how a single fact may be identified and used as a precipitating, attracting, and predisposing factor.

PRECIPITATING FACT

Mrs. Smith has grown up in a family and neighborhood environment where violence is unusual and extramarital affairs are viewed as unfortunate occurrences that generally result in divorce. Upon learning that her husband is having an extramarital affair, Mrs. Smith is overcome by uncontrollable anger and rage. She immediately buys a gun and uses it to kill her husband. In this example Mr. Smith's *extramarital affair* would be identified, labeled, and used as a *precipitating fact*.

ATTRACTING FACT

Mrs. Smith has grown up in a family and neighborhood environment where violence is unusual and extramarital affairs are viewed as unfortunate occurrences that generally result in divorce. Learning that her husband is having an extramarital affair does not upset Mrs. Smith in the least. She is a compulsive gambler and owes a substantial amount of money. She knows that the money she would obtain from Mr. Smith's life insurance policy in the event of his death would more than cover her gambling losses (and, in fact, this particular life insurance policy will pay off even if she kills him). A month after learning of her husband's extramarital affair, Mrs. Smith buys a gun and uses it to kill her husband. She then calls the police and tells them that she has just shot and killed her husband while in a state of anger and rage over the discovery of his affair. In this example Mr. Smith's *extramarital affair* would be identified, labeled and used as an *attracting fact*.

PREDISPOSING FACT

Mrs. Smith has grown up in a family and neighborhood environment where violence is unusual and extramarital affairs are viewed as unfortunate occurrences that generally result in divorce. Upon learning that her husband is having an extramarital affair, Mrs. Smith is extremely upset but takes no immediate action. She has come to believe, because of her work with AIDS victims, that an extramarital affair is akin to an attempt to murder one's spouse, in that extramarital affairs can lead to exposure to AIDS. A month after learning of her husband's affair, Mrs. Smith buys a gun and uses it to kill her husband. She then calls the police and tells them that she has just shot and killed her husband. In this example Mr. Smith's *extramarital affair* would be identified, labeled and used as a *predisposing fact*.

It must be explicitly noted that predisposing, attracting, and precipitating factors rarely fit neatly into any one theoretical perspective or specific theory. Scientific approaches to crime usually cover one or two of these types of factors to some degree. However, their explanatory strength is usually at its maximum in regard to one set of factors and moderate to weak in dealing with the other(s). In this book we will use our professional judgement to rate the strength of each theory in addressing predisposing, attracting and precipitating factors.

Integration of Factors and Levels of Analysis

This book has been organized to accomplish two basic goals. First, we seek to present the essential elements of the various theories, such as the assumptions upon which they are based, the propositions they contain, and their central concepts. Then we attempt to rank these elements in terms of their relevance to a specific criminal act's causes. This is accomplished by integrating the three types of causal factors, and the levels of social organization with which they are associated, with the assumptions of the perspective, approach, and theory. In this process we employ hypotheses to cross conceptual boundaries and suggest concrete explanations.

Inherent in this process of theory application is the idea that the factors involved in each crime must be identified and prioritized in terms of their importance to the theoretical explanation being offered. They must also be tied to the criminal motive and the act itself. That is, known factors need to be viewed relative to one another and not as independent causal forces. The theory, and the approach in which it is contained, provide a method of ordering these facts and linking them to one another and to the crime.

The factors involved in each crime must then be analyzed in terms of which factors are the most important. We identify three such levels of causal relevance:

1. Factors of *primary* importance have the most relevance to the case, and without them no explanation or theory application is possible.
2. Factors of *secondary* importance must be understood in order to place the primary factors in the appropriate context and/or to link them together in a logical narrative.
3. Factors of *tertiary* importance are of only indirect relevance to the case at hand even though they may be interesting or insight-provoking.

Thus, a precipitating factor may be the most important factor in an explanation offered for one crime, and of little or no importance in the explanation of another.

Once the factors involved in a crime are prioritized, they can be used to identify the theoretical explanation with the most explanatory power. The process of deciding which theory is most applicable to a particular crime consists of three steps: (1) select the perspective most suited to the primary fact(s) of the case; (2) choose the approach within that perspective that best fits the primary and secondary facts of the case; and (3) select the specific theory that best explains the primary, secondary, and tertiary facts.

It should be noted that, in some cases, some types of factors (e.g., predisposing factors) cannot be identified because of insufficient information about the particular case. For example, in a murder case where the offender refuses to tell anyone what events led to the killing and no witnesses were present, we may not be able to determine the precipitating factor. We will, however, be able to examine the factors that predisposed the offender to crime and attracted her or him to violent methods of resolving conflicts.

Theory Advancement versus Theory Application

The linking of precipitating, attracting, and predisposing factors to levels of social analysis is at the heart of our method of applying theories to case histories. This approach is quite different than those used in most other criminology texts, which are aimed at **theoretical advancement**—the attempt to compare a plausible explanation of phenomena with a set of (aggregate or case-specific) facts through the use of hypotheses. The writers of such texts have either (1) proposed new theories; (2) modified or synthesized existing theories, or (3) provided logical or research-based critiques that demonstrate the limits of theories. Very often there are no expectations that the results (theory) will ever be practically applied beyond aggregate data focusing on a particular level of analysis. Therefore, such use of a theory violates its original intent to some degree, since it is being applied to a level of analysis for which it was not intended by its creator. To apply a theory to a particular case we must ultimately deal with the micro-level of analysis even though the theory may have been designed to address the macro (or meso) level.

Unlike other texts, we do not use aggregate data to demonstrate a theory's validity, nor do we attempt to logically improve the scope or quality of any theory. Instead, we apply existing theories to actual situations that are generally accepted as fundamental to criminology—which is pretty much what a practitioner or applied researcher does. In other words, established theories are used to solve a problem, even if no new knowledge is derived from the solution to the problem.[11]

Although the linking together of precipitating, attracting, and predisposing factors in this text was not developed for the purpose of theoretical advancement, it is consistent with the more recent methods for advancement in the sociological perspective. This is of some importance because many criminological theories have their origin in the sociological community.

In the beginning of the 1980s, the relationship between macro- and micro-level theories became a major issue within sociology.[12] Some of the most important and criminologically relevant reasons for the need to study the relationship between macro-level and micro-level theories are based on the observations that (1) there is no need to prioritize one level over the other; (2) there is an absence of conflict (i.e., contradiction) between these levels; and (3) the integration of the levels is useful and feasible, whereas strict differentiation between them is not.[13]

Ritzer points out that although there may be a consensus within sociology that this is a major issue, there is little agreement regarding the best solution to the issue.[14] This lack of consensus is partially due to the lack of agreement within the sociological community as to the value of existing theories designed to bridge the gap between the macro- and micro-levels of analysis. This is because some of these theories have a strong micro-level orientation that minimizes the importance and significance of macro-level events, such as Homans's exchange theory. Likewise, some of these theories have a decidedly macro-level orientation, such as Blau's structural theory, that neglects the importance and significance of micro-level events. In both cases, an emphasis on a particular level of causality tends to ignore the importance of the other levels, and thereby presents an obstacle to consensus on this issue.[15] Perhaps more important, when these types of theories are used to explain crime, insufficient attention is given to the entire context in which the crime occurs; it is only by giving equal treatment to all criminological theories that we can place an act in its full context.

In its linking of precipitating, attracting and predisposing factors, this book is consistent with this broader issue of the linkages between the micro- and macro-levels within the sociological perspective. Although causal factors, as they are defined in this text, are clearly distinct and separate from conceptual devices and levels of analysis, an important relationship exists between them. All the major criminological perspectives based on social interaction make assumptions concerning this link between the individual and society.[16] What this relationship is, however, and how it can be employed by theoreticians, is far beyond the scope and intent of this text. The integration of social facts with theoretical concepts in this text is designed to enhance the reader's appreciation of the need for further study of the relationship between macro-level and micro-level theories within the social sciences.

Theory as Problem Solving

The application of criminological theory is essentially a form of problem solving based on the rigorous use of scientific logic. In applying theories to crime, we must organize and link (1) a series of facts (from the case) to (2) beliefs about the phenomena (theories) and (3) the context in which they occurred (perspectives and approaches). The logic by which this is done receives the main emphasis of this text. Once acquired, this logic will aid readers in applying theories previously unknown to them, as well as in making the transition to the utilization of aggregate data and the problems associated with it. This same logic is used to develop policies and programs from causal theories.

Problem Identification

Before we can develop a theoretical explanation of a crime, we must be very sure of the question we are addressing. In effect, defining what is to be explained becomes the initial task. Unlike the police detective who is faced with solving the problem of "who done it," theoretical application seeks an answer to the question of "why" it was done. Most theories are formulated on the basis of information that already contains the answer to "who done it." By focusing on "why" at the micro-level, we hope to make macro-level theory, as well as micro-level theory, more useful to future practitioners of criminology and criminal justice.

At first glance, the problem of what is to be explained seems fairly simple and straightforward (e.g., why did this person rob that store). However, it is very easy to get sidetracked into explaining issues other than the causes of the crime when attempting to explain individual crimes or patterns of criminal behavior. This is due to the complex ways in which criminal behavior is related to other social and personal problems. Explanations of these other phenomena are usually related in an incidental way to what is being explained, but are not adequately focused on why the crime occurred.

An example of this would be a crime that was believed to have been caused by the effect of an organic brain tumor. In explaining the cause(s) of this crime, the criminologist must deal with the causal relationship between the brain tumor and the crime (i.e., how was the criminal act caused by the effect of the brain tumor?), and not the causes of the brain tumor itself (e.g., was the brain tumor a result of environmental pollution or genetics?). Explanations of the latter sort (i.e., the causes of organic brain tumors, etc.) must be left to scientific communities other than criminology (e.g., biology).

In the field of criminology, and particularly in the application of criminological theory, this need to identify and maintain our concentration on what is to be explained is extremely important. This is true largely because most of the causes of crime raise, but leave unanswered, many questions that are very interesting in their own right but lie beyond the scope of criminology and its theories.

To illustrate the importance of concentrating on what is to be explained, let us examine the relationship between crime and substance abuse. Exhibit 2.1 poses four possible problems to be explained in this regard. Each might lead to a different solution. Former drug czar William Bennett recently identified a number of such problems and solutions,[17] noting that very different solutions were proposed, depending on exactly how the drug-abuse problem was defined. He pointed out that many prominent people believe that the war against drugs should be ended, due to their use of problem statements that differ from Bennett's.[18]

The inference upon which some of the proposed solutions to the drug problem are based is that the relationship between drugs and crime lies in the addicts' need to commit crimes in order to obtain the money to buy the drugs to which they are addicted. Inherent in these types of solutions is the assumption that addicts are sick people and should be treated as such, not punished as criminals. Other solutions are based on the belief that addicts are poor people

---

1. Criminal Behavior under the Influence of Drugs
2. Criminal Behavior to Obtain Drugs
3. Drug Addiction
4. Laws Regarding Drugs

Exhibit 2.1

. . . .

Possible problems to be explained

who cannot afford drugs because of the inflated price structure of the black market. These solutions lead to an entirely different set of questions than those solutions that view addiction as a disease.

If we identify the disease-like nature of addiction as the problem, we are likely to use theoretical explanations based on the psychiatric-psychoanalytical approach. This employs a micro-level of analysis focusing on the disease of addiction and its effects on behavior. If we feel that the assumption that addicts are poor people who cannot afford their drugs is more important (primary), this would lead to theoretical explanations of why people use crime rather than legitimate means (e.g., employment) to obtain money for drugs. Such a discussion of labor markets and the economy would be set at the macro-level of analysis, as is the evidence that drug-using criminals tend to be poor.

Bennett also stated that a small minority of people who are pro-legalization think that enforcing drug laws is costlier to society than is drug use itself. Bennett's anti-legalization argument assumes that criminals would undercut legitimate drug sale prices if legalization were to occur. He also believes that substance abuse is essentially a moral issue from which government should not retreat.[19] Both of these possible solutions—legalizing drugs because it is cheaper, or not legalizing them because their use is morally wrong—imply that users are bad, not sick, and that political types of solutions are therefore in order.

Bennett further suggests that substance abuse follows criminal behavior in a causal sequence.[20] According to this viewpoint, most substance abusers are criminals prior to their initial use of drugs. Their substance abuse simply makes them more frequent and/or more violent criminals.[21] The opposite viewpoint would be that drug addiction causes criminal behavior. Exhibit 2.2 shows these two types of causal ordering. The implication of the second view-point (Bennett's) is that predatory criminal behavior, rather than substance abuse itself, is the main problem. The logic used here would result in the use of criminal involvement as the primary causal factor in explaining substance abuse, rather than substance abuse as a cause of involvement in crime. Now the observation that needs to be explained is why drug use makes many criminals more active and/or violent.

As you can see in this illustration, given the nature and complexity of most criminological problems, theory-users can be easily sidetracked into explanations of many different phenomena (e.g., substance abuse, violence, poverty). Thus, it is vital to remain focused on the primary relationship(s) identified as the problem to which theoretical attention will be applied. The theory-user must constantly remain aware of the fact that problems of crime and criminality, like most other social problems, are embedded in large phenomena and/or tangentially related to other phenomena of a noncriminological nature.

Exhibit 2.2
. . . .
Causal ordering

1. Do drugs cause criminal behavior?

    or

2. Does criminal behavior cause drug abuse?

Types of Crime

Some criminological theories were originally designed to explain all types of crime, while others were developed to explain only a particular type of crime or subgroup of criminals. For example, Merton's notion of "strain" was created to explain why most criminals are of low socioeconomic status, while Sutherland's formulation of learning theory was originally intended to explain crimes by respectable businessmen. Additionally, many theories that were originally proposed as an explanation for a particular type of crime or criminal subpopulation have since been applied to other types of crimes or populations. For example, Sutherland's explanation of crime by respectable citizens is now a popular method of explaining substance abuse among adolescents because of its emphasis on the power of the peer group.

Thus, the type of crime to be explained presents another issue in the theory-application process. Perspectives, approaches, and theories designed for specific types of crime or criminal subpopulations should offer better explanations than those that are more generic. The problem, then, involves identifying the type(s) of crimes to be explained in addition to selecting the appropriate perspective, approach, or theory.

Although many names have been coined for various categories of crimes, the following names will be used throughout this text: (1) street crime, (2) white-collar crime, (3) victimless crime, (4) organized crime, and (5) political crime.[22] **Street crimes** are also referred to as "lower-class" or "predatory" crimes. They are crimes that involve physical assaults on persons or the (homicide, assault, robbery, rape) or the stealing or damaging of property (theft, arson, vandalism).[23]

White-collar crime, sometimes called "respectable crime," is a somewhat ambiguous term. It may be used to refer to any crime committed by a person of the middle or upper economic classes.[24] However, its application is generally restricted to crimes directed against businesses or corporations (embezzlement, fraud) or those occurring as part of the offender's vocational position. This type of crime is also sometimes referred to as "middle-class or upper-class crime." The offenders are usually employed in some responsible position within the business or corporation that they embezzle or otherwise offend. This type of crime includes activities such as "Insider stock trading."

Corporate crime is a subtype of white-collar offenses that is viewed as the action of an otherwise legitimate business, as opposed to an individual person. Although individuals within the corporations are the actual perpetrators of the crimes, the corporations that employ them are viewed as legally responsible rather than individuals. Such offenses usually involve a conspiracy of several people with considerable power within the business. Corporate crimes generally include such crimes as defrauding stockholders or the public, or endangering the welfare of employees or the public.[25] Since it is often difficult to determine whether a crime was the act of a corporation or of one (or a few) employees, the boundary between corporate and white-collar crime is very blurred. And since American law is oriented to the actions of individuals, it is often very difficult to prove corporate guilt in such conspiracies.

Victimless crimes are also referred to as "vice crimes" or as "crimes against the public order." They include violations of laws that are designed to protect people from themselves.[26] As the term implies, these are crimes with no clear victim, such as prostitution, illegal gambling, and the sale of illegal drugs. The

Red-light district at Eighth Avenue and 42nd Street, New York City. Vice crimes, or "crimes against the public order," include prostitution, illegal gambling, and the sale of illegal drugs.

people involved voluntarily participate. Both the sellers and the buyers of illicit sex and drugs, for example, can be prosecuted and it is usually difficult to specify which is the "victim" of the act. Such crimes, however, are felt to offend the morality of many citizens and threaten the stability or welfare of society as a whole.

Organized crime is committed by established groups of people who define some type(s) of crime as their livelihood. Criminal organizations like the "Five families of the New York Mafia," certain motorcycle gangs, and the "Columbian Drug Cartels" are typical of such groups. Organized crime is defined as a conspiratorial enterprise created for economic gain, which depends upon violence, intimidation, and/or corruption to obtain its goals.[27] Typically, these groups are regional, national or international in scope. They resemble legitimate businesses in many ways but regularly engage in acts that would be defined as street, victimless, or white-collar crimes if performed by isolated individuals.

To a large degree these organizations are responsible for the development of widespread criminal networks or systems. For example, some criminals have developed networks that link the growers of the raw materials used in illegal drugs with the manufacturers (processors) of them, and the manufacturers with their distributors (sellers). Other illegal activities that are commonly associated with organized crime include gambling, loan-sharking and prostitution.

Political crime involves political officials or a government as either the perpetrator or the victim. Such crimes include acts committed by individuals against a government, such as treason, as well as governmental abuses of power such as the My Lai massacre during the Vietnam War. Other political crimes would be the embezzlement of public funds by politicians and the misuse of political authority for personal or party gain, as in the case of President Nixon in the Watergate scandal.

Theory Testing versus Theoretical Explanation

Please remember that this text does not aim to empirically test the power of particular theories to explain particular crimes (or crime in general). That is the job of basic or applied social science research. **Basic research** requires that one test a theory's validity with the facts represented in a set of aggregate data or case studies, using the cases that do not fit as evidence of the deficiencies of the theory being tested. **Applied research** uses similar types of data to determine if a policy or program is having the effect that was predicted by the theory on which it was based. Since neither the readers nor the authors of this text are attempting a scientific study, any conclusions they might draw as the "cause" of crime are merely speculative at best. Such speculative conclusions must be recognized as being based on a single case or sample of the population and thus cannot be generalized beyond that situation. Whereas such generalization is the goal of most empirical scientific research, this text intends instead to illustrate the use of various theories as explanatory devices.

The reader will quickly realize that most theories have flaws that prevent them from providing comprehensive and totally valid explanations of the cases examined in this text. The idea, however, is for the reader to gain an understanding of, and appreciation for, established theories, with insight into their most prominent strengths and weaknesses. To accomplish this end, each of the following chapters is devoted to one perspective, first examining the assumptions underlying the work of all the approaches and theories within that perspective, and then examining each of those specific approaches and theories in turn. For each approach or major theory, we present the known facts of a celebrated criminal case. We begin with the presentation of the facts of the case along with precipitating factors. Next, we present any extenuating circumstances surrounding the crime committed—that is, the attracting factors. Then we present family histories and/or other environmental background material that constitute predisposing factors. Finally, we present the final disposition of the case by the justice system. This order of presentation will be violated only when (1) no facts are available at a particular point in the sequence or (2) the theory being applied does not address a specific type of causal fact. Such violations will be explicitly noted and justified in the text.

Most of the case-specific facts are directly relevant to the theoretical explanation of the crime, but some (e.g., information on the case disposition or outcome) can be used to put the case into a broader context. This allows readers to further elaborate on the role of theory in explaining events that appear to be unjust or capricious at first glance. Each chapter concludes with a discussion of which aspects of the case the perspective can explain and which defy explanation by that perspective. It will be noted by the reader, however, that other perspectives may be quite adept at explaining these latter aspects of the case.

The authors have had to provide a linkage between the precipitating, attracting, and predisposing factors in order to apply some theories to concrete behaviors. The linkages that the authors have provided are their own. They should not be interpreted as parts of the original theories or of the works from which information about specific cases was drawn. Readers may see different linkages as more appropriate. If so, the authors have succeeded in their goal to provide a basis for discussion, re-conceptualization, and the raising of issues that are beyond the scope of a single book. Such exercises are encouraged as an exciting way of increasing the readers' knowledge of, and ability to use, criminological theories. In other words, these linkages should serve as a starting point for those who are serious about the study of criminology and seek to understand the interlocking web of "causes" that result in crime. Readers' criticism of the linkages should deepen their understanding of the intention of the original theorists whose work the authors have interpreted and applied.

We have found that most discussions of criminological theories leave students with a "so what" attitude about theory (especially those intended for the meso- and macro-levels) because such bridges to actual crimes and their relationship to the larger society are absent. In essence, our three-factor methodology for explaining crimes allows the reader to see how various factors are involved in crime when applying either a macro- or micro-level theory to actual cases. Our goal is to foster an awareness of the forces operating at all analytical levels, and their consequences, as they pertain to specific acts.

It must be remembered at all times that the explanations offered are *examples* of how theories should be used, not definitive descriptions of why the crime occurred. The application of specific theories to specific crimes in this text is a "post-factum" form of analysis. It is based on what was discovered as the case was solved, rather than on what was known to the participants at the time the crime occurred. It is understood that in some cases this could result in inaccurate explanations of the causes of the offender's behavior.

Other social scientists will not always agree with our choice of theoretical perspectives in explaining a given case. Such challenges to the veracity of theory applications are vital to the development of criminology as a science because they force us to constantly refine our theoretical perspectives and revalidate them in the real world. In this way, our method indirectly lends itself to theoretical advancement. Were it not for such disagreements among scholars, social science would become too complacent to keep pace with changing social realities, and criminology would fail to take full advantage of relevant developments in related fields. As you read this text, you will find that we, like most criminologists, draw on many disciplines and theories in our attempt to explain actual crimes, and we think you will see that criminal behavior is too complex to be defined by a singular cause-and-effect relationship.

Theory Construction versus Theory Testing

Observations concerning crime, criminal behaviors, and laws are made upon the basis of particular theoretical explanations and are then tested. Criminological theory thus has at least two distinct aspects: (1) the development, or

A STRATEGY FOR THE APPLICATION OF THEORY ■ **35**

construction, of theories and (2) their empirical testing or validation. This text will not deal with the developmental aspects of theory. As has been explained, theory testing through the case-history method will be used to familiarize the reader with criminological theory in a functional way. As a cumulative knowledge of perspectives, approaches, and theories is built, the reader will have a basis for comparison in learning subsequent perspectives, approaches, and theories, and will be encouraged to experiment with applying any of them to the actual criminal cases described.

Glossary ·

Applied Research   Uses aggregate or case-study data to determine whether a policy or program is having the effect predicted by the theory on which it was based. Its goal is to determine the best way of using knowledge to improve society.

Approach   Differentiates among the different focuses and emphases taken by individual writers, or groups or theorists, within a particular perspective. Approaches are more concrete than the perspectives that contain them but are more abstract than the theories they contain. They implicitly include the assumptions of the perspective in which they originated and supply theories with a set of assumptions that help to focus on some particular concern of the perspective.

Attracting Factors   Options perceived to be available by a person, including criminal versus noncriminal actions and alternative methods of committing a crime. These factors are the most influential in determining the type(s) of crime an individual becomes involved in—for example, violent or nonviolent.

Basic Research   Tests a theory's validity by use of the facts represented in a case study or set of aggregate data. Its goal is the acquisition of knowledge, rather than determining the best way to use that knowledge.

Common Assumptions   Those beliefs or suppositions that form the basis of a theoretical perspective. They are usually fairly abstract and broad in nature.

Corporate Crime   Crime committed under the guise of a business or corporation and viewed as the act of a business or corporation rather than that of an individual.

Hypotheses   Very specific "if-then" statements that directly link two or more specific facts in a causal relationship. They can be demonstrated to be false by empirical testing.

Macro-Level   Denotes theoretical analyses or explanations of behavior that are based on membership in a society and/or the actions of large institutions.

Meso-Level   Denotes theoretical analyses or explanations of behavior based on membership in moderately large groups and/or the routines and activities of small agencies/organizations.

Micro-Level   Denotes theoretical analyses or explanations of behavior at the level of the individual or very small group.

Organized Crime   Any conspiratorial enterprise for economic gain that relies on violence, intimidation, or corruption to obtain at least some of its goals. Members of such enterprises generally see crime of some type as their vocation.

Perspective   A conceptual framework that identifies the subject matter to be studied, proposes the form of the questions to be asked and identifies the empirical tests used to find "truth." It is the largest unit of agreement within both a science and its subcommunities and serves to differentiate scientific communities, as well as their subcommunities, from one another.

Political Crime   Refers to criminal acts involving political officials or a government as either the perpetrator or the victim. It is often motivated by ideological beliefs.

Precipitating Factors   Social events and/or circumstances that immediately precede, and act to shape, a criminal act. They help primarily in explaining why the crime occurred at a specific time and place, as well as why particular individuals were involved as victims and perpetrators.

Predisposing Factors   Environmental influences, statuses, or other background traits that help to define a person's living situation as it relates to the likelihood that they will engage in crime. These are usually more abstract than, and distant from, the criminal act than other types of factors.

Restrictive Assumptions   Those beliefs or suppositions that form the basis of a theoretical approach. They are based on the assumptions of a specific perspective and serve to focus that perspective on some particular aspect of crime.

Scientific Subcommunities   Major subgroups within a particular scientific community or general discipline that share a common view of a subject.

Specific Assumptions   Those beliefs that form the basis of individual theories. They are based on the suppositions of the perspective and approach in which the theory is contained and serve to extend and focus the approach in some specific way.

Street Crime   Crimes involving physical assaults on persons or the stealing or damaging of property. This is the most well-known type of crime and may also be referred to as "predatory" crime because the victim can be clearly identified and is aware of having been victimized at the time of the act.

Theoretical Advancement   The attempt to compare a plausible explanation of phenomena with a set of (aggregate or case-specific) facts.

Victimless Crime   Offenses committed against laws designed to protect people from themselves. Some argue that these laws function to guard public morality and/or public order. It is generally difficult to identify a specific person as the prey or victim of another because these offenses involve consensual acts such as gambling, drug sales, and prostitution.

White-Collar Crime   A somewhat ambiguous term sometimes used to refer to any crime committed by a person of the middle or upper economic classes, but generally restricted to crimes directed against businesses or corporations. These crimes usually are committed as part of the perpetrator's occupational role.

■ Notes

1. C. I. Lewis, *An Analysis of Knowledge and Valuation* (La Salle, IL: Open Court, 1945).

2. M. Masterman, "The Nature of a Paradigm" In Imre Lakatos and Alan Musgrove (eds.), *Criticism and the Growth of Knowledge* (Cambridge, MA: Cambridge University Press, 1970), pp. 59–89.

3. T. Shibutani, "Reference Groups as Perspectives," *American Journal of Sociology* 60 (1955): pp. 562–569.

4. G. Ritzer, *Sociological Theory,* 2d ed. (New York: Alfred A. Knopf, 1988).

5. Ibid.

6. Allen E. Liska, *Perspective on Deviance* (Englewood, NJ: Prentice-Hall, Inc., 1981).

7. G. Ritzer, *Sociology: A Multiple Paradigm Science* (Boston, MA: Allyn and Bacon, 1975); M. Albrow, "Dialectical and Categorical Paradigms of a Science of Society," *Sociological Review* 22 (1974): pp. 183–202; T. Kuhn, *The Structure of Scientific Revolutions* (Chicago: University of Chicago Press, 1962).

8. D. Martindale, *The Nature and Types of Sociological Theory* (Boston, MA: Houghton Mifflin, 1960); P. Sorokin, *Contemporary Sociological Theories* (New York: Harper & Row, 1928).

9. Harry Benjamin and R.E.L. Masters, *Prostitution and Morality* (New York: Julian, 1964), pp. 90–91.

10. James Q. Wilson and Richard Herrnstein, *Crime and Human Nature* (New York: Simon & Schuster, 1985).

11. J. H. Vetter and I. J. Silverman, *Criminology and Crime: An Introduction* (New York: Harper & Row, 1986), pp. 67.

12. G. Ritzer *Sociological Theory*, R. Collins, "Is 1980s Sociology in the Doldrums? *American Journal of Sociology* 91 (1986): pp. 1336–1355; S. N. Eisenstadt and H. J. Helle, "General Introduction to Perspectives on Sociological Theory," in S. N. Eisenstadt and H. J. Helle (eds.), *Macro-Sociological Theory* (London: Sage, 1985).

13. A. Giddens, *The Constitution of Society: Outline of the Theory of Structuration* (Berkeley, CA: University of California Press, 1984).

14. Ritzer, *Sociological Theory.*

15. G. C. Homans, *The Nature of Social Science* (New York: Harcourt, Brace and World, 1967); G. C. Homans, "The Sociological Relevance of Behaviorism," in Robert Burgess and Don Bushell (eds.), *Behavioral Sociology* (New York: Columbia University Press, 1969), pp. 1–24; G. C. Homans, *Social Behavior: Its Elementary Forms,* rev. ed. (New York: Harcourt Brace Jovanovich, 1974); P. Blau, *Inequality and Heterogeneity: A Primitive Theory of Social Structure* (New York: Free Press, 1977a); P. Blau, "A Macrosociological Theory of Social Structure" *American Sociological Review* 83 (1977b): pp. 26–54.

16. Liska, *Perspective on Deviance.*

17. William Bennett, "Should Drugs Be Legalized?" *Reader's Digest (March 1990): pp. 90–94.*

18. Ibid.

19. Ibid.

20. Ibid.
21. James Inciardi, *The War on Drugs* (Mountain View, CA: Mayfield Publishing, 1986), pp. 123–126.
22. D. Stanley Eitzen and Doug A. Timmer, *Criminology: Crime and Criminal Justice* (New York: John Wiley & Sons, 1985).
23. Joseph F. Sheley, *Exploring Crime: Readings in Criminology and Criminal Justice* (Belmont, CA: Wadsworth Publishing Company, 1987).
24. Ibid.
25. Ibid.
26. Ibid.
27. Ibid.

CHAPTER **3**

Criminological Schools of Thought

Overview of Major Criminological Schools of Thought

. . . .

Criminological "schools of thought" are broader and more encompassing viewpoints than criminological perspectives. Schools of thought are essentially devices for organizing fundamentally differing views of human nature and relating them to issues surrounding crime and its control. They provide a basis from which criminological perspectives are framed and interpreted.[1] By understanding the contributions of the main schools of thought, we can better understand the development and practices of the justice system and gain insight into the causes of crime.

Historically there have been three major criminological schools of thought: spiritual, classical, and positivist.[2] Each is centered on a different view of the role played by the human will in determining behavior. The classical school assumes that humans operate on the basis of **free will,** meaning they are free to choose one behavior over another, while both the spiritual and positivist subscribe to **determinism**—the idea that the causes of human action lie beyond individual control. The spiritual and positivist schools differ primarily as to the source of the presumed determinism and the appropriate methods of studying these influences. All three schools are discussed in more detail later in this chapter.

The assumptions contained in criminological perspectives, approaches, and theories are, to some degree, based on one or more of these three schools of thought, so it is obviously important to understand them. In the course of our endeavor, however, let us remember that we each have our own view of human nature and therefore tend to be biased toward the school of thought that agrees most closely with our own view. To some extent we are unable to be free of bias in this regard. Our own sense of involvement in social behavior and policy binds us to a one or the other criminological school of thought and thus subtly discourages us from being impartial towards perspectives, approaches, and theories.

The role of the will in human behavior has long been debated in criminological circles. Since the doctrine of free will holds that human beings are in control of their own behaviors, those who believe in it are in effect saying that people who commit criminal acts have freely chosen to do so; it is they, not their social or physical environments, who are morally responsible for their criminality. Determinism, in contrast, asserts that behavior is the inevitable result of forces beyond the direct control of individuals, which makes these forces responsible for the crime, not the individual. Consequently, the free-will-versus-determinism issue is relevant not only to the objective causes of crime but also to the assignment of moral responsibility for criminal acts— and therefore to the proper roles of the judicial and correctional systems.

For some criminologists, the concept of will is metaphysical in nature and thus beyond scientific examination. For others, it has material properties as well. But certainly it is agreed that the question of whether or not human beings have free will, and if they do, to what extent it is limited or modified by the supernatural (e.g., God, demons), the natural (e.g., genes, body chemistry), or the environment (e.g., wealth, culture), is essentially unanswerable. It cannot be conclusively tested in a scientific manner, and thus remains in the realm of philosophy, even though it strongly affects the activities and conclusions of social scientists.

Because science is ultimately concerned with the prediction of future events, it is very convenient for scientists to presume that there are observable forces external to individuals that control their behavior. Therefore science, and especially social science, tends to have a deterministic bias. Scientists often speak of behavior as "caused" by things such as environmental factors or genetic influences, but many such references to causality actually refer to the idea of prediction rather than cause. This is especially true of theories based on perspectives that presume free will to be the central cause of human actions.

The debate over the existence of free will and the issues surrounding it is reflected in the exceptions made in criminal codes for mitigating or extenuating circumstances and the way the legislatures and courts define such arguments.[3] Since the concept of free will or the lack thereof is integral to the study of criminology, we will examine this subject in further detail in the next section.

Principles Governing Perceptions of the Will

As explained, our own personal view of the role of the will exerts much influence over how we evaluate particular criminological theories. It is therefore helpful to understand what influences this personal view of ours. In his classic work, *War and Peace,* Tolstoy suggested some principles that might apply. He proposed that only through the examination of people's lives (e.g., case histories), in which the union of the individual will and external factors had already taken place, could the incompatibility of the two doctrines of free will and determinism be resolved.[4] Every human action, he pointed out, appears to be a combination of some degree of free will and some degree of necessity. Tolstoy posited that free will and external pressures are opposite ends of the same continuum, and our perception of the degree of free will involved in an act varies with our position on this continuum.[5]

Tolstoy saw an inverse relationship between the degree of freedom and the amount of external environmental pressure in the production of any human act.[6] That is, the more freedom a person perceives in an act, the less external social and environmental pressure perceived, and vice versa. The following passage illustrates Tolstoy's view of the relationship between external factors and free will:

> A drowning man who clutches at another man and drags him under; or a hungry mother exhausted by nursing her baby who steals food; or a man trained to discipline who kills a defenseless man at a word of command— seems less guilty, that is, less free and more subject to the law of necessity, to someone who knows the circumstances in which these people were placed and more free to one who does not know that the man himself was drowning, that the mother was hungry, that the soldier was in the front line, and so on. Similarly a man who committed a murder twenty years ago and has since then lived peaceably and blamelessly in society seems less guilty, and his act seems more subject to the law of necessity, to someone who considers the act after twenty years have elapsed than to one who examines it the day after it was committed. And in the same way every action of a madman, a drunkard, or a violently overwrought man appears less free and more inevitable to one

who knows the mental condition of him who performed the action, and more free and less inevitable to one who does not know it.[7]

Three propositions describing our perceptions of the degree to which human acts are caused by free will or by external environmental factors can be deduced from Tolstoy's work. The first proposition is that *the more we perceive individuals to be involved, connected, or bound to others, the less likely we are to attribute to their actions to free will.*[8] For example, we would attribute more free will to a single person than we would to a married person without children, and still less free will to a married person with children. Thus a single man who robs a gas station for money to buy groceries is likely to be viewed as more responsible for the crime and probably more deserving of punishment than a married man with children who commits the same crime. The latter is likely to be viewed as being motivated to rob not only for himself but also for his children. Thus, the single man is perceived to have more free will than the married man with children.

The second proposition asserts that *the more distant we are in time from an individual's actions, the more likely we are to attribute his or her actions to external social and environmental factors.*[9] That is, our awareness of the role played by free will decreases with the passage of time. Acts committed today will most likely be attributed to free will but ten years from now primarily to external factors.

We tend to judge a married person with children less harshly for committing a crime, on the assumption that she was motivated to rob not only for herself but also for her children.

An example of this can be seen in the case of friendships. If we meet someone today, we are likely to perceive ourselves as having a great deal of free will (i.e., choice) in deciding whether or not to become a friend. On the other hand, if we look at old friendships, we are more likely to attribute them to external factors, such as attending the same elementary school together, or living in the same neighborhood. The external environment in which our friendships occur is seen as having more influence than free will after much time has passed.

The third and final proposition maintains that *the more we know about the motives of individuals' actions, the more likely we are to attribute their actions to external social and environmental factors.*[10] For example, the more mitigating circumstances (e.g., substance abuse, negligent parents, poverty, etc.) we associate with an offender, the more likely we are to attribute the cause of his or her crimes to the mitigating circumstances than to free will. Where no mitigating circumstances are known, we tend to attribute the cause of the criminal behavior primarily to the individual's will.

Psychological studies have shown that we are most likely to attribute our own deviant acts to external situational factors, but that the deviance of others is usually attributed to their free will.[11] Our knowledge of our own motives and background is always greater than our knowledge of others, so this research fully supports Tolstoy's insights.

The influence of these three predictors on our view of the causes of a crime is, of course guided by the our ideological position on the free-will issue. The point to remember is that all of these influences operate within our frame of reference. They do not wholly overcome it.

Spiritual School of Criminological Thought

The spiritual school of criminological thought focuses on the relationship between criminal behavior and supernatural or otherworldly powers. Inherent in this school of thought is the belief that human beings are drawn to commit criminal acts by outside forces of a mystical nature—spirits or demons.[12] That is, criminal behavior is best explained by reference to the activities of supernatural powers.

Essentially, this doctrine argues that free will (the ability to choose to commit or to avoid crime) is compromised by the existence of supernatural powers, which are at the root of most criminal behavior. Theoretical explanations of this type are based on faith and theology. They are not subject to scientific examination and cannot be empirically disproved, because the supernatural cannot be observed with scientific procedures.[13] (Of course, neither can the other doctrines be conclusively proved or disproved by scientific means.)

Although spiritually based explanations of crime can be traced back to ancient times, one example of the spiritual frame of reference can be found in the history of the penitentiary system in the United States. The term *penitentiary* is derived from the word *penitent*, which means to repent or regret wrongdoing and be willing to atone for it.[14] In the early history of the United States' penitentiary system, criminals were placed in solitary confinement on the assumption that they would repent more quickly under such conditions.[15] Social isolation, it was hoped, would force them to reflect on their crimes and spiritually develop to a point where they could resist demonic temptation or seek the protection of a benevolent spiritual force (God).[16] In essence, this school of thought uses supernatural determinism to explain behavior, allowing for a modicum of free will in deciding to seek spiritual help.

The spiritual school of thought is not used by any modern scientific community, and therefore is not included among the common assumptions of the major criminological theoretical perspectives. The absence of spiritual explanations today can be seen in the way some of the recent notorious crimes associated with the occult (e.g., the grisly 1989 murders outside Matamoros, Mexico) have been handled.[17] Despite these crimes being committed by people associated with the occult, psychological rather than spiritual explanations have been offered. The individuals committing these crimes tend to be viewed as psychologically disturbed, or influenced by bizarre subcultures, drugs, or violent movies, rather than being possessed by demons or evil spirits.

Although no longer accepted by most people today, the spiritual school of thought dominated society up until the late fifteenth century. During the Enlightenment, concepts like free will and the value of the individual began to guide society's assumptions about the nature of human behavior. The result was a rejection of supernatural determinism in favor of the doctrine of free will. The value placed on individual rights today is largely based on the presumption of the dominance of free will in the determination of behavior.

Classical School of Criminological Thought
. . . .

The classical school of criminological thought focuses on the relationship between criminal behavior and law. It makes the assumption that behavior results from personal choices for which only the individual is responsible, and that society's laws can influence the choices made. In other words, free will operates on a sort of "cost-benefit ratio" within each individual wherein the possible costs of an act (punishment by the law) are compared against the possible rewards.[18] Such a view presumes that human decisions are governed by self-serving rationality. It argues that society must give people strong reasons to avoid criminal behavior.

This school of thought is a product of Enlightenment thought, and stresses the independence, dignity, and value of the individual. If actions are solely the responsibility of the individual, then we may take full credit for our accomplishments and full blame for our wrongs.

This **greatest-happiness principle** (also known as the "pleasure-pain principle"), which proposes that human beings act on the basis of minimizing pain while maximizing pleasure, is inherent in the classical school of thought. It suggests that four criteria guide a person's decision on whether or not to commit a criminal act: (1) the *intensity* of the expected pleasure or pain, (2) the *duration* of the expected pleasure or pain, (3) the *certainty* of the expected pleasure or pain, and (4) the *proximity* of the expected pleasure or pain.[19] Thus, if the intensity of the anticipated punishment outweighs the intensity of the anticipated pleasure from a crime, it is unlikely that the crime will occur. The longer the duration expected for the punishment for a crime, the less likely it is that the crime will be committed. The greater the certainty of being punished for a crime, the less likely it is that the crime will be committed. And the less time that is expected to pass between the commission of the crime and the enactment of its punishment, the less likely it is that the crime will be committed. It is on the basis of these beliefs that many criminologists believe that crime can best be deterred by swift, certain, and severe punishment.[20]

According to this school of thought, law must take the egocentric nature of humankind into account if it is to be an effective means of controlling behavior. Thus, punishments must slightly exceed the potential rewards of a particular crime. Of course, this view presumes that people employ similar definitions of what is rewarding or punishing. It also presumes that people are aware of the penalties for various crimes and that they consider those risks before they decide to commit a crime. The classical school implies that the value of rewards and punishments can be measured on a well-calibrated scale that is applicable to all members of society. All of these classical beliefs have been challenged, along with the assumption that human decisions are based on rational judgments. However, most agree that the classical school is well suited for explaining premeditated crimes motivated by instrumental goals.

The classical school maintains that it is important for the people who are to be controlled by society to understand the law and the penalties it assigns for various acts. This idea reflects a belief in the intrinsic value of the individual and the right of every person to be treated with dignity. It also is a reference to the belief that people weigh the risks and possible benefits of an act before performing it. Classical thinkers thus assert that the better understood and respected law is in a society, the less crime there will be. Many of their ideas about the role of law in society, and, the need for fairness and impartiality in the practice of law are embedded in the U.S. Constitution.[21]

Free will remains metaphysical under this doctrine. That is, in this frame of reference free will is akin to Freud's "id," in that it exists only in a non-physical sense. Whereas Freud proposed that the "ego" regulates the id's impulses, the classical school proposes that internalized, self-serving interests guide the exercise of free will. Accordingly, the threat of punishment for breaking criminal laws must be accepted and internalized by the individual in order for the law to play a role similar to that of Freud's superego.[22]

The classical school has made two major contributions to criminology. First, it introduced the idea of free will and individual responsibility for actions. Second, it defined the role of law and government in a free society. This school of thought is the basis for the widely held belief that the punishment should fit the crime.[23] With these and related principles, the classicists helped western civilization make the transition from monarchial rule to democracy. The ideals of equality under law and due process for all offenders originated here.[24]

Positivist School of Criminological Thought

The positivist school of criminological thought denies that free will exists because the causes of behavior are felt to lie in factors that are beyond the control of the individual.[25] That is, human behavior is believed governed by external environmental circumstances and/or internal biological conditions. Free will is therefore an illusion. An example would be a starving person, living in abject poverty without hope of obtaining money or employment, who steals food. Although some would claim that this person still has the freedom to

When intoxicated persons assault close friends, the effects of alcohol are often used to explain the assault.

choose not to steal, a positivist would argue that she or he does not—that such a person is forced into crime by external circumstances.

This doctrine's effects can be seen in various state laws that deal with juveniles, the competence of a suspect to stand trial, and in the existence of the insanity defense.[26] Such laws clearly infer an absence of free will and moral responsibility among the mentally incompetent and diseased. Juveniles are thought to be less capable of moral reasoning than adults and thus are treated less harshly in most cases.

The notion that deterministic forces are responsible for the criminal actions of individuals can also be seen in other situations, such as when intoxicated persons assault close friends. In these cases, the effects of alcohol, rather than the choices of the intoxicated person, are often used to explain the assault. While voluntary intoxication is not a legal defense, the person's behavior under the effects of alcohol is often socially excused because of the presumed absence of free will.

Positivism appeared in the late nineteenth century as science came to dominate civilized society and its view of the world. Like the spiritual school, positivists believe that human behavior has causes that are beyond the control of individuals—but unlike that school, they also believe that these causes can be observed and explained in a scientific manner. Indeed, they expect to find some set of laws governing human behavior that will be nearly as observable and predictable as Newton's law of gravity.

Cesare Lombroso, credited as the founder of the positivist school of thought in criminology.

Cesare Lombroso is generally credited with having founded the positivist school of thought in criminology. He argued that some people were less evolved than others. He referred to this condition of subnormal evolution as an **atavism,** and maintained that such individuals could not prevent themselves from committing crimes. Their criminality was a result of a biological condition. Criminals were seen as "throwbacks" to an earlier form of human that was less capable of rational self-control.[27] More recently, some writers have held that the poor cannot avoid criminality in a capitalist society because they lack power and are often excluded from the benefits of our society. This, too, is a form of determinism but unlike Lombroso's theory, it selects social forces as the likely cause rather than biological ones.

Positivism has many subtypes, and its influence on criminology is found in virtually all forms of scientific determinism. This school of thought seeks the causes of (and thus the responsibility for) crime in forces beyond individual control. It is a scientific view in that it seeks to apply the same methods of inquiry that are used to predict events in the physical world to human behavior. Positivists see human actions as merely natural material events that are governed by forces that science can identify, study, and describe.

The positivists have made two major contributions to criminology. First, they added the idea of natural determinism to our view of criminal behavior. Thus, the continuum from free will to determinism was established. Second, they put the study of crime on a scientific rather than a philosophical or theological basis. This allowed crime, and our responses to it, to be analyzed at both the case-specific and aggregate levels.

Models of Criminal Justice

This chapter has dealt with some very basic assumptions about the nature of behavior and its causes. Determinism and free will are polar opposites that define a continuum of frames of reference in modern criminology. Most people see reality as somewhere between these two extremes. Exactly where they place reality on this continuum from total free will to complete determinism has much to do with their preferences for particular solutions to the crime problem. Different positions on the continuum have led to various different models of criminal justice—among them the justice model and the medical model.

Classicists see humans as requiring the control of social norms and laws to guide their natural egocentricity in directions that will benefit society. All humans are seen as equal in the amount of choice they can exercise over their behavior. Therefore, all humans are believed to have an equal chance to choose criminal or law-abiding behaviors in any given situation. In the classicist view, society is responsible for using law in the best possible ways and for making law understandable to all citizens. This school of thought also maintains that the control function of law is inextricably tied to its fairness and impartiality.

Advocates of the classical school usually prefer to apply the **justice model** of criminal justice to lawbreakers, in which the law and courts are expected to judge the act, not the person by whom it was committed.[28] This model asserts that persons who commit the same or similar crimes should receive virtually identical punishments, regardless of their backgrounds or the circumstances of the crime. Proponents of this model prefer flat, or **determinant, sentences** to open-ended, or **indeterminate,** ones because their concern is with the equality and fairness of punishment, rather than with rehabilitation.

Since positivists, on the other hand, see biological and/or environmental forces as controlling human behaviors, they hold society responsible for helping individuals cope with the determining forces in their lives. People do not have equal abilities to control their behaviors according to this school of thought. Therefore some are less responsible for their actions than are others. In this view, some offenders cannot be held liable for their crimes. Consequently, to protect society, crime prevention through early identification and treatment of actual and potential criminals is necessary and is a major focus of this school of thought.

By putting the study of crime on a scientific footing, the positivists began the search for factors that would distinguish criminals from others. Unlike the classicist, the positivist assumes that there is a difference between criminals and ordinary citizens. Science is to be used to identify these differences, and eventually to help rehabilitate criminals and/or reduce the influence of the factors that create them.

Advocates of the positivist school usually prefer to apply the **medical model** of criminal justice to lawbreakers, in which the law and courts are expected to judge each offender as a unique individual.[29] This view is based on the positivist assumption that some people are less able to avoid crime than others.

Exhibit 3.1
. . . .
Models of criminal justice.

Criteria	Justice Model	Medical Model
Origin	Classical frame	Positivist frame
Subject	Role of law in society	Causes of crime
Goal	Fair punishment	Prevent future crime
Focus	Criminal act	Criminal person
Method	Determinant sentences	Indeterminate sentences

The medical model is more concerned with rehabilitation, or the prevention of future crime, than it is with "just" punishment. This model of the role of the judiciary asserts that people should be punished on the basis of their backgrounds and the circumstances of the crime.

Advocates of this model prefer open-ended, or indeterminate, sentences, since the time required to rehabilitate an offender varies with the individual. This preference is justified by the belief that persons who have committed very similar crimes may have had very different degrees of control over, and thus responsibility for, their behavior. Supporters of the medical model are also quick to point out that the rehabilitative needs of offenders vary with the individual, not the act for which they were convicted.

Exhibit 3.1 summarizes and compares these two models of the intent of our justice system in terms of their origin, subject matter, goals, focus, and methods. Readers should examine these criteria closely to convince themselves that the solution proposed by each model is a logical and inevitable outcome of the school of thought used. Such linkages between the presumptions of a viewpoint and the policies it advocates constitute a critical issue in both the study and practice of criminology.

To better illustrate how our conceptions of free will are embedded in the models of criminal justice through the spiritual, classical or positivist schools of criminological thought, we present the following case of Hans Huebner.

The Case of Hans Huebner · · · · · · · · · · · · · · · · ·   APPLICATION   · · · · · · · · ·

Hans Huebner, an eighteen-year-old German, was an accomplished computer programmer. By 1986 he had become a computer "hacker," a person addicted to computers. When Huebner needed money for the computer company he owned, he met with Karl Koch and Markus Hess, two other computer hackers, to discuss how they could make money with their hacking skills. Huebner suggested, and the others agreed, that they might earn money by breaking into U.S. government computer systems to steal military information for sale to Soviet bloc agents.[31]

Markus Hess was employed by a computer software company in downtown Hannover. Karl Koch, age twenty-three, was a computer programmer who needed money to support his cocaine habit as well as to pay for his overseas telephone bills, which were the result of his computer hacking hobby, breaking into others' computer systems for fun. After his meeting with Hess

Espionage
the act of covertly obtaining a military secret for a foreign government in either time of war or peace.[30]

and Koch, Huebner recruited Dirk Bresinsky, another computer programmer, and Peter Carl, a former gambling casino croupier, to assist them in their espionage plan. Huebner, along with these four other men, used intercontinental telephone and satellite communication systems to break into the U.S. Department of Defense's Defense Data Network.[32]

Beginning in the mid 1950s, the Department of Defense began developing a network to link military computers. By 1969 the Defense Advanced Research Projects Agency (DARPA) had developed an electronic network that connected more than 100,000 computers throughout the world. Today this network has come to be known as Internet. It has two separate components: (1) Arpanet, which is primarily for research activities linking university and laboratory computers, and (2) Defense Data Network, which is used primarily for military purposes. Although these two components are separate, access to one can be used to gain entry into the other. Because the Defense Data Network, which used to be known as Milnet, is prohibited from containing classified military information, little attention was paid to its security even though computers storing top-secret military information could be accessed through it.[33]

Access codes, also known as "passwords," or account names, are the only protection for the information in any computer in any network. It used to be that professional thieves (e.g., safecrackers) tried to crack combination locks on vaults. Today they try to crack access codes to computers to extort money from a corporation by holding their computers hostage or by selling stolen information. In essence, what Huebner and the others did was to subscribe to the Arpanet network, which allowed them to enter the Defense Data Network. This, in turn, allowed them to enter top-secret military computers once they had cracked these computers' access codes.[34]

Electronic and satellite communication transmission systems have made it possible to send information from computer systems in the United States to Germany in two or three minutes. Thus, the computer systems and networks, along with the communication systems (e.g., Tymenet, a communications company that connects computers around the world), allowed these five Germans to steal military information stored in computers in the United States some four to five thousand miles away in only a few minutes.[35]

Soon after they stole the military information, they began selling printouts of it to Soviet KGB agents in East Berlin (on at least a dozen occasions), as well as access codes to the American computers and information on how to break into them.[36] They were arrested in March of 1989 by the German authorities and charged with espionage. Huebner and Koch avoided prosecution by cooperating with the authorities. Hess, Bresinsky, and Carl each received sentences of one to two years and were released on probation in February 1990.[37]

Case Interpretation

The crimes of Hans Huebner and his associates can be interpreted in three basic ways, depending on the school of thought used as the foundation for analysis. Each interpretation suggests a different set of causal forces and thus a different way of assessing the offender's moral responsibility. Each has a distinct set of implications for how such crimes might best be prevented in the future.

A spiritual frame of reference might argue that demons bent on the destruction of the free world invaded Huebner's mind, and those of the other hackers, and caused them to commit repeated acts of espionage. Such an explanation would presume a belief that the Western world has a superior form of organization to that of the Communist bloc nations. On the other hand, if communism were presumed to be morally (i.e., spiritually) superior to democracy, then a spiritual explanation would assert that the crime occurred as a result of spirits bent on guarding the Soviet Union from capitalist domination. Even within the spiritual school of thought, the assignment of labels like "good" and "bad" to an act is a matter of one's larger worldview.

None of the offenders in this case claimed to have been influenced by supernatural forces, but this is not directly relevant to the question at hand. When the spiritual school of thought dominated criminology, knowledge that one was "possessed" was not required as proof of such possession; the act of committing a crime itself was usually taken as sufficient proof that spirits were present. Today, if an offender claims to have been possessed, we are more likely to conclude that he or she is mentally ill.

The important point, however, is that a spiritual point of view would force us to conclude that neither Hans Huebner, nor his society, could have prevented the crime. In addition to Huebner and associates, the U.S. Defense Department would be viewed as a victim of spiritual or demonic activity.

If the classical school's presumption of free will is used, an entirely different view of this series of crimes is taken. According to the classical school, humans seek to maximize pleasure while avoiding pain. Thus, Huebner and the other hackers might be presumed to have committed these crimes in order to obtain money with which to make life more enjoyable. Simultaneously, it must also be presumed that they believed that there was little likelihood of their being caught and punished. From the classical view, the hackers made a very rational choice, since their crime had the potential of great profit with little chance of severe punishment.

In using computers to steal money and information, offenders tend to feel (correctly) that apprehension is unlikely because there is no direct contact with the victim, and the routing of commands can be disguised to some extent. Additionally, large computer networks handle huge amounts of legitimate traffic, so detection of illicit users is very difficult.[38] In classical terms, this is a lack of proximity, swiftness, and certainty of punishment.

A truly positivist explanation, on the other hand, might assert that the value placed on monetary success by capitalist ideology compelled Huebner to seek out funds for his company in the most efficient way. Alternatively, Huebner's cocaine-using friend, Karl Koch, could be portrayed as a primary factor in this crime. Driven to theft by his addiction, Koch could be cast in the role of a tempter who pressured Heubner and the others to assist him in the illegal scheme. According to such a view, the cocaine-using hacker's behavior was *determined* by a psychobiological condition—drug addiction. This fact compelled him to crime in order to finance his habit, which required large sums of money on a constant basis. In turn, he would be seen as having applied pressure on Huebner to get help in raising money. Thus, Huebner could have been convinced to cooperate in the scheme through peer pressure.

A positivistic argument could also be made that some or all of these hackers had been born with (or otherwise acquired) a tendency to ignore social rules and do whatever they felt was most likely to benefit them. If indeed this was a group of well-educated sociopaths (see Chapter 5 for a detailed discussion of sociopathy), then their psychological condition made it virtually impossible for them to see that their actions were wrong. Rather, they would have felt that they deserved the money, that society had in some way deprived them of their rightful rewards, and that their acts were wholly justified. People with such a condition would be expected to commit whatever crime they felt would produce the most rewards.

According to this argument, the hackers would probably have been criminals regardless of their backgrounds. Had they been born into impoverished families and never received any real education, they might have become street criminals. Because they were relatively well-educated, middle-class men, they saw their greatest opportunities for profit in the area of white-collar political crime. The positivist argument in this scenario is based on the idea that some people have less ability to control their desires than do others. People with such diminished self-control are unable to avoid crime because they cannot see beyond the immediate rewards of the act(s) being contemplated.

In this particular case, the authors suggest that the classical school has the most convincing argument for the causes of this crime. This can best be explained by reference to Tolstoy's three propositions about the perception of the will. These men appear to have had few significant connections to others beyond their group. This crime was committed fairly recently (and we are still somewhat fearful of similar security leaks in our defense networks). Also, there is not enough background information on the offenders to provide mitigating factors. In other cases, as you will see, we will favor certain forms of positivism because mitigating factors are clearly present. In many of these cases, the offender's ties to others are very clear and directly relevant to the crime. These crimes also occurred longer ago than those of Huebner.

It should also be pointed out that each explanation leads to a different recommendation for controlling computer crime. From a spiritual view, society needs to discover a way of detecting individuals who are possessed or controlled by forces unfriendly to the society or its members. This was the original intent of the "witch hunts" that occurred in Europe and America between 1400 and 1700 A.D. Most scientists would be appalled at the suggestion that we return to such a mode of thought.

From a classical view, the problem can best be corrected by stiffening the penalties for illegal computer use so that such risk-taking is no longer a rational option for hackers. The deterrent threat of such legislation might have been effective with Huebner and his associates, especially because of their middle-class status. The threat of prison and/or heavy fines is usually more effective on middle-class people than on slum-dwellers whose status and material well-being could not be greatly lessened by legal punishment.

Better monitoring of who uses sensitive computer networks would also be suggested by this school of thought. The goal of such monitoring would be to increase the certainty of punishment for security violators. While such monitoring probably would help deter hackers, it would be extremely expensive and very likely would pose a great inconvenience for legitimate users. Positivists might advocate the development of methods by which sociopaths could be detected before they harmed society. Drug-testing of computer users might also be suggested to prevent addicts from gaining access to sensitive computer networks. However, such measures would be very expensive and could result in the unfair stigmatization of many people.

Conclusion

Both the classical and positivist schools of thought have made major contributions to criminology. The classicists alerted us to the fact that law is not to be taken for granted, but rather should be used to guide the choices of individuals in socially beneficial directions. They also promoted the dignity of the individual and stressed the need for fair government that is respected and understood by its citizens. The positivists applied scientific principles to the study of crime and its perpetrators. They put criminology on a scientific footing that sought to avoid the armchair speculation of classical philosophy. Elements of both these frames of reference—the free will of the classicist and the determinism of the positivist—can be found in most of the perspectives, approaches, and theories dealt with in subsequent chapters of this book.

Glossary

Atavism   A condition of being less evolved than the great majority of the species. Though posited as a cause of criminality by early positivists, its existence has never been scientifically demonstrated.

Determinant Sentences   Those in which a set period is served without regard for progress in rehabilitation or other factors. Such sentences are based solely on the specific crime for which the offender was convicted.

Determinism   The belief that individual behavior results from the operation of forces beyond the control of the individual. As such, it is the opposite of free will.

Free Will   The idea that human beings are free to choose one behavior or action over another and thus are in control of their own behavior. It is sometimes also referred to as *voluntarism*.

Greatest-Happiness Principle   Proposes that the actions of human beings are governed by the desire to obtain pleasure and avoid pain. It is sometimes referred to as the *pleasure-pain principle* or as *hedonistic calculus*.

Indeterminate Sentences   Open-ended periods of time to be served that may be adjusted on the basis of progress in rehabilitation or other factors. In theory, such sentences are more or less "personalized" to the needs of the particular offender.

Justice Model   Based on the philosophy of government advocated by the classical school. It stresses the need for fair punishments based on the nature of the act(s) for which a person has been found guilty, rather than on the attributes or circumstances of the person.

Medical Model Based on the philosophy of the positivist school of thought. It stresses the need to judge each offender as an individual in terms of the threat posed to society and/or the potential for rehabilitation.

■ Notes

1. George B. Vold and Thomas J. Bernard, *Theoretical Criminology,* 3d ed. (New York: Oxford University Press, 1986), pp. 15–17.

2. J. Robert Lilly, Francis T. Cullen, and Richard A. Ball, *Criminological Theory: Context and Consequences* (Newbury Park, CA: SAGE Publications, 1989), pp. 17–29; Vold and Bernard, *Theoretical Criminology,* 3d ed., pp. 6–10.

3. From *War and Peace* by Leo Tolstoy, translated by Ann Dunnigan, Translation copyright © 1968 by Ann Dunnigan. Introduction copyright © 1968 by New American Library. Used by permission of New American Library, a division of Penguin Books USA Inc.

4. Ibid., p. 1442.

5. Ibid., pp. 1438–1455.

6. Ibid.

7. Ibid., p. 1443.

8. Ibid., pp. 1443–1444.

9. Ibid., pp. 1444–1445.

10. Ibid., pp. 1445–1446.

11. E. E. Jones & R. E. Nisbett, *The Actor and the Observer* (Morristown, NJ.: General Learning Press, 1971).

12. Vold and Bernard, *Theoretical Criminology,* pp. 6–7.

13. Ibid., p. 8.

14. Jean L. McKechnie, *Webster's Deluxe Unabridged Dictionary,* 2d ed. (New York: Simon & Schuster, 1979), p. 1326.

15. American Correctional Association, *The American Prison: From the Beginning* (Laurel, MD: American Correctional Association, 1983), p. 31; Dennis Curtis, Andrew Graham, Lou Kelly, and Anthony Patterson, *Kingston Penitentiary: The First Hundred and Fifty Years* (Ottawa, Canada: Correctional Service of Canada, 1985), p. 16.

16. American Correctional Association, *The American Prison: From the Beginning,* p. 31.

17. Katherine Kerr, "He Had 12 Hours to Pray," *Houston Post,* April 12, 1989, pp. A–1, A–15.

18. Jeremy Bentham, "An Introduction to the Principle of Morals and Legislation" in Joseph E. Jacoby (ed.), *Classics of Criminology* (Prospect Heights, IL: Waveland Press, 1979), pp. 61–64. Cesare Beccaria, "On Crimes and Punishments" in Joseph E. Jacoby (ed.), *Classics of Criminology* (Prospect Heights, IL: Waveland Press, 1979), pp. 206–207.

19. Bentham, "An Introduction to the Principle of Morals and Legislation," pp. 61–62.

20. James Q. Wilson, *Thinking About Crime* (New York: Basic Books, 1975); Ernest van der Haag, *Punishing Criminals: Concerning a Very Old and Painful Question* (New York: Basic Books, 1975).

21. Eliott Monochese, "Cesare Beccaria" in Herman Mannheim (ed.) *Pioneers in Criminology* (Montclair, NJ: Patterson Smith, 1973) p. 48.

22. Sigmund Freud, *The Ego and the Id* (1927), trans. by Joan Riviere (London: Hogarth, 1949).

23. Sue Titus Reid, *Crime and Criminology,* 3d ed., (New York: Holt, Rinehart, and Winston, 1981), p. 86.

24. Monochese, "Cesare Beccaria."

25. Vold and Bernard, *Theoretical Criminology,* pp. 10–12.

26. Lincoln Caplan, *The Insanity Defense* (New York: Dell Publishing Co., 1987), pp. 9–14; Texas Criminal Procedure—Code and Rules, (St. Paul, MN: West Publishing Co., 1990), pp. 237–249.

27. Gina Lombroso-Ferrero, "Criminal Man" in Joseph E. Jacoby (ed.), *Classics of Criminology* (Prospect Heights, IL: Waveland Press, 1979), pp. 75–84.

28. David Fogel, "We Are the Living Proof. . ." *The Justice Model for Corrections* (Cincinnati, OH: Anderson, 1975); Sue Titus Reid, *Crime and Criminology,* 3d ed. (New York: Holt, Rinehart, and Winston, 1981), pp. 464–465; David Duffee, *Corrections: Practice and Policy* (New York: Random House, 1989), p. 121.

29. Leon Radzinowicz, *Ideology and Crime* (New York: Columbia University Press, 1971); Michael Hakeem, "A Critique of the Psychiatric Approach to Crime and Correction" *Law and Contemporary Problems* 23 (1958): pp. 650–682; Duffee, *Corrections: Practice and Policy,* p. 333.

30. George E. Rush, *The Dictionary of Criminal Justice,* 2d ed. (Guilford, CT: Dushkin Publishing Group, 1986), p. 90.

31. Cliff Stoll, *The Cuckoo's Egg* (New York: Pocket Books, 1990).

32. Ibid.

33. Ibid.

34. Ibid.

35. Ibid.

36. Ibid.

37. Ibid.

38. Ibid.

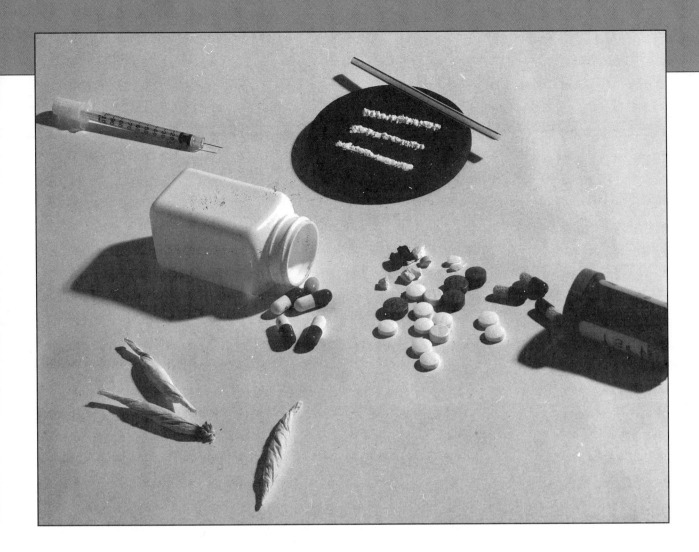

CHAPTER **4**

Biological Perspective

Overview of Biological Perspective

∙ ∙

The biological perspective (called *biocriminology*) proposes that antisocial behavior is motivated by biophysical properties unique to criminals.[1] Exhibit 4.1 details the common assumptions underlying this perspective. Its origins lie firmly within the positivist school of thought. Although the early positivists sought physiological explanations for crime as a singular phenomenon, modern biocriminology has become more specialized, with attention now directed toward the genetic, physiological, and psychophysiological aspects of the organism. Among the major biological variables that are currently viewed as most relevant to criminal behavior are brain tumors, biochemistry, hormonal imbalances, and hypoglycemia.[2] Recent research on the relationship between variables such as these and criminal behavior has focused primarily on crimes of violence that have little or no apparent motive.[3]

There are four major approaches within the biological perspective: (1) morphological, (2) hereditary/genetic, (3) biochemical-neurophysiological, and (4) biosocial. The biosocial approach is unique among these in that it allows the subject matter of other perspectives to be combined with what is known about the social-psychological causes of crime. The other three approaches differ mainly in the aspect of human biology upon which they focus.

It should be noted that only the essence of each of the various biological approaches to criminality is provided in this chapter. Many volumes have been written on every perspective, approach, and theory mentioned here. We seek only to expose the reader to the basic components of each. Because of the technical complexity of many biological theories of behavior, we will couch most of our discussion at the approach level in this chapter.

Morphological Approach

∙ ∙

The morphological approach (see Exhibit 4.2) is the oldest in biocriminology and can be traced back to Cesare Lombroso, father of positivism. This is an approach that seeks clues to the causes of criminality in the structures of the human organism. It is based on the belief that there is a meaningful relationship between certain types of physical features and personality (temperament).[4] Essentially, this approach proposes that some personalities are more prone to criminality than others—in other words, criminals are born, not made.

Exhibit 4.1

∙ ∙ ∙ ∙ ∙ ∙ ∙ ∙ ∙ ∙ ∙ ∙ ∙ ∙ ∙ ∙

Biological perspective

Common Assumptions

1. Individual human beings are biologically unique.
2. Differences in human biology account for many differences in human behavior.
3. Criminals differ from others in physical ways that can be identified through the use of scientific knowledge and procedures.

Source: George B. Vold and Thomas J. Bernard, *Theoretical Criminology*, 3d ed. (New York: Oxford University Press, 1986).

Exhibit 4.2
. . . .
Morphological approach

Restrictive Assumptions

1. Criminal behavior is inborn.
2. Behavior is associated with physical body features.
3. Criminals have physical body features that differ from those of noncriminals.

Source: Gina Lombroso-Ferrero, "Criminal Man" in Joseph E. Jacoby (ed). *Classics of Criminology* (Prospect Heights, IL: Waveland Press, 1979), pp. 75–76; Vold and Bernard, *Theoretical Criminology*, p. 58–61.

Exhibit 4.3
. . . .
Lombroso's atavism theory

Specific Assumptions

1. Criminal behavior is atavistic in origin.
2. Criminals have carnivore-like body features.
3. These external body features are associated with abnormalities of the brain that give rise to criminal behavior.

Source: Gina Lombroso-Ferrero, "Criminal Man," pp. 75–76.

Lombroso's Atavism Theory

Cesare Lombroso's atavistic theory of criminality (see Exhibit 4.3) is anthropological in orientation. First proposed in 1876 in his book, *The Criminal Man*, Lombroso's theory was heavily influenced by Darwin's theory of evolution.[5] The term **atavism** means to revert to a primitive type, and/or to resemble a remote ancestor in some characteristic.[6] Serious criminality was thought to result from the joint effects of multiple atavistic anomalies.[7] (Injuries, addictions, and diseases also were thought to result in criminal tendencies.[8]) Lombroso's reasoning was that genetic "accidents" had resulted in less than fully evolved humans who then had to live among their more modern brethren. Criminal behavior was therefore beyond individual control.

Lombroso believed that people born with abnormal features similar to those of the carnivores, such as large jaws or canine teeth, or skulls noticeably larger or smaller than normal, were in effect **born criminals**.[9] This theory was inspired by his observation of structural abnormalities in the brain of an Italian serial killer whom he autopsied.[10] Such atavism, he claimed, resulted in a form of "moral insanity" that could not be cured or controlled by any method known to society.[11]

According to Lombroso, born criminals made up about one-third of the criminal population. They were thought to be responsible for the most serious criminal offenses committed in modern societies. They were also the most frequent recidivists. The remaining criminal population, those with abnormalities less pronounced than the abnormalities of the born criminal, were thought to commit primarily minor offenses and were labeled **criminaloids**.[12]

Lombroso acknowledged that social factors like formal education, economic status, immigration, and informal learning could also produce criminal behavior. This was especially true, he felt, among criminaloids, but could occur as well in normal humans. Lombroso pointed out that serious crime is a predominantly male phenomenon, but that women were often prone to commit minor offenses like prostitution. He predicted that females would become criminal more frequently as the level of civilization increased in a society.[13]

Research conducted by Lombroso supported his atavism theory. The research methods he used, however, had serious flaws. One major flaw was that he did not include noncriminals in his research. His examination of the physical characteristics of criminals led him to the faulty conclusion that their similarities distinguished them from noncriminals. Had he compared criminals with noncriminals, as modern scientific procedures demand, he would have found that noncriminals are as likely to have the same physical characteristics as the criminals he examined. Lombroso's work, however, was crucial in establishing the positivist frame of reference in criminology, and inspired several generations of biocriminologists.[14]

Sheldon's Somatotype Theory

W. H. Sheldon focused his attention on the person's general physique or body build as a predictor of criminality. He maintained that there are three basic types of body builds, or **somatotypes**: endomorphic, mesomorphic, and ectomorphic (see Exhibit 4.4). Endomorphic body structures are those that are soft and round (i.e., fat). Mesomorphic body structures are hard, firm, and strong (i.e., muscular). Ectomorphic body structures are frail and delicate (i.e., thin).[15] According to Sheldon, endomorphs have extroverted personalities and seek comfort. Mesomorphs have assertive, aggressive personalities. Ectomorphs have introverted personalities, are sensitive and shy, and possess a strong capacity for self-control.[16]

Sheldon's morphological typology was based on a composite measurement of variations in endomorphy, mesomorphy, and ectomorphy in human physiques. He used a seven-point scale to describe the degree to which each type was present in an individual. Each person's body build, "somatotype," was described in numerical terms. For example, the somatotype 7-1-1 (endomorphy = 7, mesomorphy = 1, and ectomorphy = 1) represents the most extreme endomorph. The somatotype 1-7-1 represents the most extreme mesomorph, and the somatotype 1-1-7 represents the most extreme ectomorph. In essence, a somatotype rating indicates which body type is predominant, while simultaneously identifying the relative prominence of the other somatypes.[17]

Sheldon concluded that criminals were decidedly of the mesomorphic type, with deficiencies in ectomorphy.[18] Certain other researchers supported Sheldon's observations in their examinations of delinquent youths. Not only were a disproportionate number of male delinquents extremely mesomorphic, but the mesomorphic qualities of a masculine build, characterized by a broad chest, low waist, prominent muscles, and large bones, were found to be significantly more common among delinquent females than among law-abiding girls.[19]

Exhibit 4.4
. . . .
Sheldon's somatotype theory

Specific Assumptions

1. Criminal behavior is inborn.
2. There is a meaningful correlation between physique and personality.
3. There are three basic kinds of physiques, or somatotypes, among humans.
4. Criminality is associated with the predominance of the mesomorphic body type.

Source: W. H. Sheldon, The Varieties of Temperament (New York: Harper and Brothers, 1942), pp. 1–11; Vold and Bernard, *Theoretical Criminology*, pp. 58–61.

Exhibit 4.5
. . . .
Inheritance/genetic approach

Restrictive Assumptions

1. Factors that determine behavior are genetically transmitted.
2. Criminal tendencies are genetically transmitted.

Source: James A. Wilson and Richard J. Hermstein, *Crime and Human Nature* (New York: Simon & Schuster, 1985).

Some researchers, on the other hand, have refuted Sheldon's theory. The Gluecks study of delinquency, for example, concluded that there is no relationship between body type and delinquent personality traits.[20] Thus, the exact relationship between body types and criminal behavior—if indeed there is any relationship—remains unknown.[21]

Inheritance/Genetic Approach
. . . .

The inheritance/genetic approach (see Exhibit 4.5) assumes that behavioral tendencies toward criminality are inherited from one's parents. Unlike Lombroso's atavism theory, however, this approach does not view the criminal as a throwback to a more primitive form of the human species. Genes are seen as the indirect cause of the abnormal behavior (criminality), in that they influence the organic structures and processes of the individual human organism, which, in turn, guide behavior.[22] The various internal mechanisms and processes directly involved in criminal behavior thus originate in genetic coding but are further influenced by external factors.

Inherited behavioral traits are usually seen as general tendencies toward, for example, aggression. An inherited tendency to aggressiveness may lead a person into criminal activity under some circumstances, but under different conditions could result in that person having a successful career in sales or politics. Various methodologies for studying the presence or absence of genetic

Genes are thought to determine individual traits, which in turn guide behavior, sometimes criminal behavior.

influences on criminal behavior have been employed, including (1) general pedigree, or family tree, studies; (2) twin studies; (3) karyotype studies; and (4) adoptive studies.[23] The results indicate that many basic traits may indeed be largely the result of one's genetic inheritance.

General Pedigree Studies

General pedigree studies examine the similarities of criminal behavior within families in search of links between these similarities and the degree to which the family members are related.[24] The goal of such studies, which have been accused of oversimplification, is to assess the inheritance patterns of criminal traits (e.g., great grandparents to grandparents to parents to offspring). A fictional illustration of this was seen in the popular serial "Godfather I, II, and III" movies, where the leadership of an organized New York City crime family passed down from one generation to the next. The focus of attention in the inheritance approach is on general behavioral tendencies, such as aggressiveness, that may lead to crime.

General pedigree studies have several serious flaws. One is that they ignore the fact that, in addition to sharing genes, family members usually share environments. Thus, genetic and environmental influences are mixed very early in life. This makes it virtually impossible to determine if criminal behavior is the result of genetic transmission or environmental factors. Another problem is that in the United States the probability of arrest among juvenile males is unusually high, around 40 percent.[25] Thus, pedigree studies reporting 40 percent or less for offspring of parents with criminal records are not demonstrating that criminal behavior is inherited or genetically transmitted, but simply that these offspring are no more prone to crime than those of noncriminal parents.

Twin Studies

Twin studies take advantage of the unique genetic relationships between twins in order to address many of the flaws in pedigree research. Fraternal (Dizygotic) twins result from two ovum (eggs) within the same mother being fertilized by two separate sperm of the father. In identical (monozygotic) twins, one fertilized ovum splits into two, allowing for the creation of two individuals with identical genetic programming. Fraternal twins have 50% of their genetic programming in common while identical (monozygotic) twins have exactly the same genes.[26]

Twin studies focus on **concordance rates**, which imply similar behavioral traits or outcomes for pairs of individuals. If the behavioral traits of a set of twins are similar, the pair is said to be "concordant," or in agreement. If the behavioral traits or outcomes are found to be different, the pairs are said to be "discordant," or not in agreement. Typically, in twin criminal behavioral studies the concordance rates found for criminal behavior among monozygotic twins (identical twins) are compared with those found for dizygotic twins (fraternal twins) and/or siblings.[27]

Overall, the research with twins has been unable to demonstrate whether or not criminal traits are genetically transmitted.[28] The research has shown that monozygotic twins are more concordant than dizygotic twins regarding criminal behavior. According to Lee Ellis, however, this does not necessarily demonstrate the genetic transmission of criminal behavior, since it has been observed that monozygotic twins are treated more or less identically by others, whereas dizygotic twins are not. Thus, any differences in criminality found between the two types of twins could be due to their differential treatment (their environment).[29] Again, separating nature from nurture is a very challenging task for scientific research.

Genetic Karyotype Studies

Genetic karyotype studies examine and compare chromosomes. Although normal humans have twenty-three pairs, or forty-six chromosomes, some have an unusual number of them. The chromosomes that have attracted the most interest in biocriminology are those that determine sex: the XY chromosomes in males; and the XX chromosomes in females. The presence of the Y chromosome is what determines maleness.[30] Males, of course, have long been known to have a disproportionately high level of involvement in crime.

The interest in exploring the effects of the extra Y chromosome in males was largely the result of the publicity surrounding Richard Speck. Speck murdered eight nurses in Chicago and was believed to have an extra Y chromosome. Thus, a link was suspected to exist between males with XYY chromosomes and violence. It was later established, however, that Speck did not in fact have an extra Y chromosome.[31]

Initially, it was also thought that there was a disproportionately higher number of males in prison with the XYY chromosomes than were in the general population. This also turned out to be false. Proportionately there are about the same number of XYY males in prison as there are in the general population.[32] Finally, although early studies reported a relationship between males with XYY chromosomes and violent behavior, more recent studies have found no such relationship.[33] Indeed, most convicts with an extra Y chromosome were found to be nonviolent property offenders.[34] The difference between the earlier karyotype studies on violence and more recent ones is largely due to the relatively small number of subjects used in the earlier ones, which made their findings much less reliable than later efforts.

Although a correlation between XYY males and violence does not appear to exist, karyotype studies have found a relationship between XYY chromosome males and low intelligence.[35] Other studies on inheritance and intelligence have estimated that as much as 70 percent of intelligence may be inherited.[36] The link between the extra Y chromosome and intelligence are of some importance, because other studies have shown that a significant proportion of offenders have IQs that are below normal, though not low enough to indicate true mental retardation.[37] As with aggression, however, the most recent studies conclude that low IQ does not "cause" criminal activity, but can lead to low academic ability and frustration with conventional social norms which, in turn, can lead to criminal behavior.[38]

Adoptive Studies

Adoptive studies focus on persons who were adopted shortly after birth so that the influence of heredity and environment can be distinguished from one another. A group of known criminals (either parents or their offspring) are compared with a group of known noncriminals in these studies. The first group is referred to as "affected probands" (the term *proband* being used to describe groups of subjects who display similar traits or behaviors), and the second group is referred to as "control probands."[39]

Adoptive studies use either a *forward-trace* or *backward trace* design. In forward-trace designs, criminals who have allowed their offspring to be adopted are identified and then their children are investigated for criminal behavior. In backward-trace designs, adoptees who are criminals are identified and then their biological parents are investigated for criminal behavior. The findings for the affected probands are then compared to those for the control probands.[40]

Adoptive studies offer some advantages over other types of inheritance studies in that they provide more experimental control since they take advantage of the absence of the biological parents as an environmental factor.[41] After adoption, the only influence that the biological parents could have on their offspring would be genetic. Thus, any criminal behavior that adopted individuals display can be attributed to genetic transmission so long as the biological parents are known offenders and the adoptive parents are not.

Overall, adoptive studies suggest the existence of a genetic link between male offenders and their biological fathers. That is, male adoptees whose biological fathers are criminals are more likely to be criminals than are male adoptees whose biological fathers are noncriminals. However, the results of these studies also suggest that environmental factors serve to reduce criminal behavior irrespective of genetic background.[42] In essence, this implies that if in fact criminal behavior is genetically transmitted, environmental factors have some power to override the genetically transmitted tendency toward criminal behavior. The idea that crime may result from a combination of environmental and biological factors is currently dominant in criminology and will be discussed further as part of the biosocial approach later in this chapter.

Biochemical-Neurophysiological Approach

The human brain is best described as an electrochemical organ. The biochemical-neurophysiological approach (see Exhibit 4.6) proposes that alterations of, or abnormalities in, the normal chemical processes of brain activity adversely affect the motivational processes that guide thoughts and perceptions. These distortions of thought and perception can, in turn, result in criminal behavior. Alterations of normal chemical processes or brain activities can result from injuries to the brain, brain diseases, cancer, environmental pollutants like lead, nutritional deficiencies, and hypoglycemia.[43]

It is estimated that over 15 million Americans have some type of brain damage. In many instances, the brain damage goes unnoticed and the person is able to behave within the normal expectations of society.[44] This ability to function in a fairly normal manner despite brain damage is primarily due to the fact that there is much functional redundancy and overlap built into the organizational structure of the brain. Thus, if one part of the brain is damaged, various other parts compensate, or take over, for the damaged area(s).

The types of brain damage that are most relevant to the explanation of criminal behavior are those that affect the **limbic system,** located in the upper brain stem and lower cerebrum portion of the brain. The limbic system is thought to be directly involved with brain processes related to motivation and the regulation of aggressive behavior.[45] Very simply, when the limbic system is damaged, the person may become possessed with uncontrollable rage and act violently unless physically restrained by others. This is perhaps most notable in individuals who have been infected with rabies, a viral infection that attacks the limbic system. This disease can make even the most nonviolent person extremely hostile and inexplicably violent.[46] Thus, tumors in, and injuries to, certain parts of the brain can be the real cause of aggression and rage that may instead be interpreted as the result of a nonorganic mental illness or personality change.

This approach is relatively unique within the biological perspective because it can explain some crimes without having to refer to social reactions to bi-

---

Restrictive Assumptions

1. Chemical deficiencies or imbalances, or brain damage, adversely affect thinking patterns.
2. Such distortions of thought patterns can lead to criminal behavior.

Exhibit 4.6

Biochemical-neurophysiological approach

Source: Donald J. Shoemaker, *Theories of Delinquency,* 2d ed. (New York: Oxford University Press, 1990), pp. 152–157.

ologically induced conditions. Irrational crimes of violence that have not been provoked by any external event are often amenable to explanation by this approach. However, most criminologists agree that it only explains a rather small proportion of crimes and is applicable mainly to acts of violence that have no apparent motive.

· · · · · · · · **APPLICATION** · · · · # The Case of Charles Joseph Whitman

> **Murder**
> The act of intentionally causing the death of a person without legal justification, or unintentionally causing the death of another person while attempting or committing another crime.[47]

The application of the biochemical-neurophysiological approach to the case of Charles Joseph Whitman is intended to illustrate the utility of this approach while sensitizing the reader to the complexities of explaining crimes from the biological perspective in general. While the neurophysiological approach is the primary source of our explanation of Whitman's criminality, we are forced to synthesize this approach with the biosocial one in order to incorporate predisposing and attracting factors into this case application.

On August 1, 1966, Charles Joseph Whitman opened fire from a 307-foot-high tower on the University of Texas campus in Austin. Using a high-powered rifle, he killed twelve people and wounded thirty others before being killed by police sharpshooters. Whitman had killed his mother and wife the night before this mass murder took place.[48] He went to his mother's apartment, stabbed her in the chest, and then shot her in the head. He then returned to his own home and stabbed his wife three times in the chest.[49] Whitman was twenty-five years of age when he committed these crimes. He had been an Eagle Scout in his adolescence and was trained as a marksman during his service in the U.S. Marine Corps.

Only precipitating and attracting factors can be confidently identified in this case, but the available data allow us to speculate on possible predisposing factors as well. The *precipitating factor* for these acts appears to have been a malignant brain tumor, called *glioblastoma multiforme*, revealed upon autopsy to be about the size of a walnut, in the amygdala region of the brain. This sort of tumor is known to affect the limbic system and cause irrational outbursts of violent behavior. A team of thirty-two medical experts and scientists determined that Whitman had had the highly malignant tumor for approximately three to four months before the mass murders occurred. They predicted that he would have died in less than a year from this tumor, and they agreed that it was the probable cause of his criminal actions, although they stopped short of claiming it to be the sole cause.[50]

In the months immediately preceding the mass murders, Whitman had spoken to psychiatrists about having violent impulses that he could not control. He told the doctors that he was going to climb the university tower—a prominent part of Austin's skyline—and shoot people.[51] In a letter to his wife and mother that was written just before he killed them, Whitman said that he had many unusual and irrational thoughts, tremendous headaches, and that he was overwhelmed by violent impulses. In addition, he asked to be autopsied after his death to determine if he had any physical disorders. He also requested that some of his life insurance money be donated for mental health research on the type of crimes he was going to commit.[52]

We suggest that the tumor was the *precipitating factor* in Whitman's case.

The tumor caused him to suffer from uncontrollable outbursts of violence toward his wife and others. The tumor, however, could not have directly been responsible for Whitman's decision to use a high-powered rifle to shoot strangers from the university tower. The *attracting factors*, which we use to explain this choice of particular actions, appear to have been his Marine Corps training as a marksman and his long-term residence in Austin, which made him aware of the university tower's prominence in the city. These attracting factors dictated the form that his rage, caused by the tumor, would take. Had Whitman been trained in handling explosives or in the martial arts, his violence might have been exhibited in a different way, though at the same point in time.

We can further speculate that Whitman's exposure to violence in his own home may have acted as a *predisposing factor* in the mass murders. According to Whitman's parents, wife, friends, and psychiatrist, he was filled with hostility towards his father. His father openly admitted to beating both Whitman's mother and the woman he married after divorcing Whitman's mother.[53]

Whitman battered his own wife repeatedly during their approximately four years of marriage. Whitman told his psychiatrist of these violent domestic disputes and expressed his fear that he had inherited his father's violent traits. Further evidence of his predisposition towards violence is found in the record of his court martial from the Marine Corps for threatening to kick out another Marine's teeth.[54]

The facts used in explaining this case, along with their level of importance and their role in the explanation are summarized in Exhibit 4.7.

Because Whitman was shot and killed by police on the day of the tower murders, it is unlikely that any additional information will ever be available concerning his case. We have proposed that the biochemical-neurophysiological approach best explains Whitman's behavior. However, it could be asserted that, although the role of biology cannot be ignored in cases like Whitman's, some aspects of his behavior are better explained by situational factors such as life experiences, and career, family, societal and cultural influences.[55]

An argument could be made that because Whitman killed on two consecutive days and had written a detailed plan for the mass killing, including his escape, his crimes are not adequately explained by his brain tumor. This view of Whitman's crimes implies that biologically induced impulses to commit violent acts apply only to those acts committed simultaneously with the biologically induced experience of irrational, unprovoked rage.[56] Such a narrow view of biological determinism is common in the social sciences, but the authors

Level of Importance	Fact	Type of Fact
Primary	Tumor of the amygdala region	Precipitating
Secondary	Marine marksmanship training	Attracting
Tertiary	Knowledge of violence between parents	Predisposing
Tertiary	Feelings toward father	Predisposing

Exhibit 4.7

Summary of facts and their role in the explanation of the Whitman case

of this text believe it misrepresents the intentions of the psychobiologists who generate these theories. Here, as throughout the remainder of the book, we do not aim to defend our explanation of the case. We merely present it, along with a brief discussion of alternative explanations in order to illustrate the utility, scope, and intent of the biological perspective.

We maintain that the theoretical explanation that explains the most is the one that most closely fits the factual evidence. Any alternative explanation that unnecessarily restricts the interpretation of the role of biological factors in producing aggression would appear to be inappropriate. For example, the social-situational factors in the Whitman case, such as his mother leaving his father four months before the crimes occurred, and his hatred of his father, are tertiary factors in this particular case and are of little use in explaining his crimes.[57] This is true because the vast majority of persons whose parents separate—or who claim to hate their fathers—do not commit acts of violence. On the other hand, aggressive violent behaviors (e.g., assault, attempted murder, etc.) are considered to be fairly common among persons suffering from injury or disease to the amygdala area of the brain.[58]

As conceived by psychobiologists, there are two major varieties of aggressive behavior—instrumental aggression and aggressive aggression. Instrumental aggression was defined in chapter one as crimes motivated by practical concerns. **Aggressive aggression** refers to hostile emotional impulses that are not specific to any person or situation. This category is a peculiar subtype of expressive criminality in which the offender has not been provoked and is unconcerned with the identity of the victim. Such acts are usually seen as irrational or motivated by bellicosity, since the victim's identity is of no concern to the offender, who wishes only to vent hostile feelings in a violent manner on whatever targets attract his or her attention.

Within the aggressive-aggression category, there are numerous types of aggressive behavior resulting from brain damage or disease. Some types of brain damage or disease also allow for extreme fluctuations of mood. That is, the damage or disease allows for behavior to vacillate back and forth between aggressive and nonaggressive. Thus, Whitman's brain tumor could easily have allowed him to have a series of destructive rages over time without necessarily keeping him in a constant stage of rage.[59] Whitman's criminal behavior is also consistent with the predictions of the biochemical-neurophysiological approach. Although the brain tumor caused his impulse to commit violent acts, it did not prevent him from functioning in a fairly normal manner much of the time. Such a mental problem is quite different from that of a person suffering a psychotic episode. A psychotic is not able to function normally during a period of delusional thinking or while experiencing hallucinations.

Disorders Resulting from Psychoactive Substance Use

Psychoactive substances are chemicals that affect the central nervous system, altering the person's moods and/or behavior.[60] Although there are many specific psychoactive substances with various degrees of power, most discussions of these drugs refer to only nine basic categories: alcohol, sympathomimetics (amphetamines), cannabis (marijuana), cocaine, hallucinogens, inhalants, opiates (heroin), arylcyclohexylamines (phencyclidine or PCP), and sedatives (or hypnotics or anxiolytics).[61] Many writers combine cocaine and amphetamines into a single "stimulant" category because their effects are remarkably similar. It is also common to group alcohol in the "depressant" class along with sedatives and hypnotics. Psychoactive substances are thought to lead to criminal behavior at the individual level in at least two different ways. A third link is introduced in the chapter on culture conflicts.

First, drugs contribute to the crime problem by reducing inhibitions or by stimulating the individual to aggressive behavior. This link between such substances and crime is known as the **psychopharmacological model** and it basically refers to actions that are directly induced by drugs.[62] Psychoactive substances, in effect, have the ability to affect the internal mental controls that normally prevent, or at least discourage, an individual from committing a crime. The painful effects of withdrawal can also motivate otherwise inexplicable violent acts.

Second, addiction to psychoactive substances requires the continual purchasing of the substances, which, for many addicted persons, means committing crimes to obtain the money for purchase. This model of the drugs-crime link, referred to as **economic compulsivity**, is primarily oriented to property crimes and other instrumental acts that are explicitly intended to raise money for addictive drugs.[63] Many crimes, of course, involve a combination of the two models—as when an addict robs for economic reasons but becomes unnecessarily violent due to the presence of withdrawal symptoms.

It is possible for almost any psychoactive substance to be involved in crime in one of two ways—the substance may reduce inhibitions toward committing a crime, or the person may commit a crime in order to obtain the substance. For the sake of simplicity, we have chosen to divide psychoactive substances

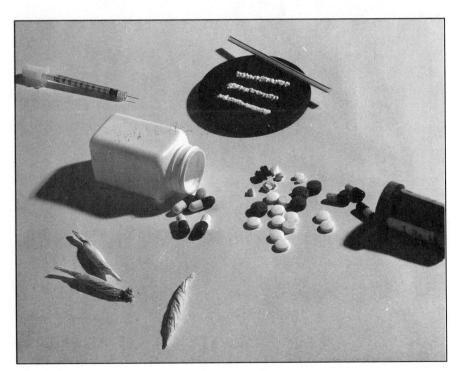

Psychoactive substances affect the central nervous system and alter moods and behavior.

into categories on the basis of their known differences in their likelihood of influencing an individual to commit a crime against persons or property.

The most important behavioral change that is brought about by marijuana, hallucinogens, and/or opiate use is impaired judgment.[64] Behavioral changes resulting from use of substances in these three categories are not generally associated with aggressiveness. In fact, there is an inverse relationship between cannabis intoxication and aggressive behavior (i.e., as intoxication increases, the likelihood of violence drops). Although property crimes to obtain money for substances contained in these classes are common, the most serious problem seems to lie with opiate addicts. Also, withdrawal from opiates is seen as having the potential to provoke violence.[65]

Alcohol, stimulants like amphetamines and cocaine, and sedatives, hypnotics, or anxiolytics impair judgment and can lead to aggressiveness. Alcohol and stimulants also lower inhibitions against sexual and aggressive impulses. Thus, one of the important links between alcohol intoxication and criminality is this drug's ability to reduce normal inhibitions. This accounts for the well-known fact that a large percentage of crimes are committed by offenders under the influence of alcohol. Like alcohol, the use of amphetamines (sympathomimetics) and cocaine can lead to crimes of violence such as assault and murder.[66] The sense of self-confidence induced by these drugs also helps account for their psycho-pharmacological linkage with crime, especially expressive forms of violence.

Inhalant and phencyclidine (PCP) intoxication can bring about changes such as belligerence, assaultiveness, and impaired judgment as well as other problematic behaviors.[67] Although somewhat rare, the use of these psychoac-

Alcohol intoxication reduces normal inhibitions and can lead to aggressiveness.

tive substances can result in brief or long-term psychotic episodes, which in some cases can be accompanied by extremely violent behavior. Psychoses associated with PCP tend to last for long periods and may even be permanent, while those associated with cocaine and inhalants tend to be fairly brief.[68]

Learning-Disabilities Approach

Learning disorders are physical handicaps that make it difficult for a person to acquire knowledge in traditional ways. The most common types of learning disabilities result from dyslexia (problems in reading), aphasia (visual and auditory problems), and hyperkinesis (hyperactivity).[69] Although the exact causes of learning disabilities are still unknown, they are thought to be organic or neurological in origin. Learning disabilities are not related to intelligence but nevertheless have a major impact upon academic achievement.

This approach proposes that there are links between learning disorders and criminal behavior (see Exhibit 4.8). The links are thought to be created by poor academic performance, inability to understand society's rules, and/or personal problems, all of which are thought to lead to criminality by lowering self-esteem and making sufferers feel rejected and misunderstood by conventional society. Also, failure to learn society's rules and behavioral expectations would result in judgmental errors that could lead to criminal behavior.[70] Like most of the approaches currently used by biocriminologists, learning disabilities cannot explain crime without referring to the interaction of biological and social factors. For this reason, many criminologists now subscribe to the biosocial approach.

Biosocial Approach

The biosocial approach (see Exhibit 4.9) is a synthesis (combination) of the inheritance, learning-disability, and biochemical approaches, with the explicit inclusion of the environment as a mediating or activating force on physiological

Exhibit 4.8

Learning-disabilities approach

Restrictive Assumptions

1. Organic or neurological disorders are thought to be the causes of learning disabilities.

2. Learning disabilities result in poor academic achievement and/or personal problems.

3. Poor academic achievement and/or personal problems can lead to criminal behavior.

Source: J. Zimmerman, W. D. Rich, I. Kelitz, and P. K. Broder, "Some Observations on the Link between Learning Disabilities and Juvenile Delinquency," *Journal of Criminal Justice,* 9 (1981): pp. 1–17; P. K. Broder, N. Dunivant, E. C. Smith, and L. P. Sutton, "Further Observations on the Link between Learning Disabilities and Juvenile Delinquency," *Journal of Educational Psychology,* 73 (1981): pp. 838–850.

Exhibit 4.9

. . . .

Biosocial approach

Restrictive Assumptions

1. Physiological tendencies toward criminality may be acquired through a number of different mechanisms.
2. Physiological tendencies toward criminality are activated by environmental factors.
3. The environment can act to encourage or discourage criminality through its interaction with innate characteristics of the individual.

Source: Sarnoff A. Mednick, "A Biosocial Theory of the Learning of Law-Abiding Behavior" in Sarnoff A. Mednick and Karl O. Christiansen (eds.), *Biosocial Bases of Criminal Behavior* (New York: Gardner Press, Inc., 1977), pp. 1–8.

factors. This approach appears to be predominant within the modern biological perspective on crime. According to this view, criminal behavior (no less than noncriminal behavior) results from the interaction of various physiological characteristics with environmental factors.[71] That is, persons with certain physiological characteristics tend to become criminal when exposed to particular environmental factors—and if those factors are not present, the physiological characteristics that are associated with criminality will not lead to criminal action.

The assumptions of this approach attempt to account for why some people are able to resist becoming criminals in the midst of criminogenic environments, while others are not.[72] These assumptions are perhaps most easily understood in relation to noncriminal types of deviant behavior, such as alcoholism. Alcoholics are presumed to have an organic or physiological makeup that is different from that of nonalcoholics and that accounts for their addiction.[73] The physiological characteristics that create the tendency toward alcholism remain dormant until alcohol is consumed.

In the same way, the restrictive assumptions on which this approach is built presume that some people have one or more physiological tendencies that can lead to criminal behavior if certain social conditions are present. Such criminal tendencies remain harmlessly dormant until triggered by environmental factors. Criminal tendencies may be activated by such things as unemployment, frustration in obtaining a desired goal, substance abuse, exposure to criminal opportunities (e.g., embezzlement), etc. Social learning and behavioral conditioning processes (see Chapter 7) may also play a significant role in the development of some biologically based tendencies like aggression.

Mednick's Biosocial Theory

Mednick's biosocial theory of crime (see Exhibit 4.10) assumes that all humans have at least occasional impulses to commit criminal acts and must learn to control these natural impulses in order to live in society. According to this theory, learning to inhibit antisocial behavior is a basic part of the socialization process in which the individual learns to avoid the punishment that is normally dispensed by family and peers when behavior warrants it. Here the influence

Exhibit 4.10
. . . .
Mednick's biosocial theory

Specific Assumptions

1. Noncriminal behavior must be learned (i.e., impulses to antisocial behavior are natural in humans).

2. Learning noncriminal behavior includes both individual abilities and environmental factors.

3. The ability to reward oneself for inhibiting antisocial impulses is critical to the formation of law-abiding social behavior.

4. Either a lack of individual ability to control antisocial impulses, environmental factors, or both, can lead to criminality.

Source: Sarnoff A. Mednick, "A Biosocial Theory of the Learning of Law-Abiding Behavior" in Sarnoff A. Mednick and Karl O. Christiansen (eds.), *Biosocial Bases of Criminal Behavior* (New York: Gardner Press, Inc., 1977).

of the classical school of thought becomes evident even within this biological perspective founded by positivists.

The state of the individual's autonomic nervous system is central to this process of learning to inhibit antisocial behavior, since the autonomic nervous system controls the physiological responses to fear, as well as other nonconscious bodily functions such as digestion and breathing. Fear of punishment is what inhibits antisocial behavior. Individuals with autonomic nervous systems that allow for a fast recovery from fear of punishment will more easily develop inhibitions toward criminal behavior. Those individuals with autonomic nervous systems that respond slowly to fear of punishment are less likely to develop such inhibitions. The reasoning is that fear causes both physiological and psychological distress in individuals. Thus, quick physiological recovery from fear-related distress provides a self-generated reward for inhibiting antisocial impulses, while slow recovery does not encourage (i.e., reward) the acquisition of self-control. Autonomic nervous systems that recover quickly from fear of punishment thus provide a lot of reinforcement for inhibiting criminal behavior, whereas those that recover slowly provide little.[74] If only for this reason, the idea of biosocial causality infers that biology alone cannot create criminality without the contributing influence of environmental factors.

Conclusion
. . . .

The idea that biological factors can cause, contribute to, or predict criminality has a long and controversial history in social science. Thousands of scholars have already addressed the "nature-nurture" issue in various ways. This perspective has been abused by racists who attempt to use it to condemn certain ethnic groups. It has also been misinterpreted by the naive who seek a single, simple explanation of criminal behavior.

The biosocial approach is felt by most to offer the most convincing set of answers to this controversy. However, the answers it provides are complex and incomplete. Much of the problem lies in our lack of knowledge of how the brain works and how thought and action are shaped by the environment.

As the leading approach within the biological perspective, the biosocial model cannot be fully employed without referring to some other social or psychological theory of the cause of crime. The positivistic biological perspective tends to remove responsibility from the criminal offender. However, the biosocial approach introduces an element of free will into the perspective by its reference to environmental and psychological factors.

The biosocial approach was developed with the intention of combining biological insights with social-psychological ones. Because such theories have yet to be introduced, we have not applied the biosocial approach to a case history. We must, however, point out that it provides a more comprehensive explanation of Charles Whitman's crimes than does the biochemical-neurophysiological approach by itself.

The biological perspective provides as reasonable a fit as possible to the facts of the Whitman case.[75] The brain tumor appears to have been the central precipitating factor. Thus, it is the primary fact of the case. This crime clearly falls within the "aggressive aggression" category of the biological perspective and is unique only because of the high toll in lives it involved. Whitman's training as a Marine sharpshooter provided the main attracting factor by familiarizing him with the use of high-powered rifles. In the overall explanation of the case, however, this is a secondary fact, since Whitman would, in all likelihood, have committed some sort of violent crime even if he had never been in the military. Had Whitman not been trained in this manner, he might have simply assaulted someone on the street and never achieved any form of notoreity. His long-time residence in Austin made the university tower a more or less "natural" place from which to commit such a crime. Thus, we can assert that his knowledge of the city was also a secondary factor in attracting him to this particular method of venting his rage.

The factors predisposing Whitman to violence are less clear, however. The available information on Whitman's relationship with his family is of tertiary importance to the explanation of this case. He may have been influenced by his father's violence toward his mother earlier in life, but we will never be able to speak of this level of causality with much certainty in the Whitman case. This, however, is the sort of social environment that the biosocial approach asserts to be a necessary mediating factor in the development of more typical forms of criminality.

This state of affairs is not unusual for any criminological perspective. The perspective is very adept at explaining one level of causality—the precipitating factors, in this case—but is of only moderate utility in addressing the next level of causality—in this case, the attracting factors. The perspective is not equipped to deal with the remaining level of causality to anyone's full satisfaction. The biosocial approach encourages us to synthesize the biological causes of the crime with the social and psychological factors that were also involved.

In other cases (e.g., low-IQ criminals), the biological perspective might be very useful in explaining the offender's predisposition to crime but would be of only moderate strength in addressing the attracting factors of the case. As a primary explanatory factor, low IQ could not, of course, deal adequately with the specific precipitators of a given crime, and analysts of such a case would have to turn to other theories to fill in these missing parts of the explanation.

Glossary ·

Adoptive Studies   Studies centering around persons who were adopted shortly after birth, usually comparing a group of known criminals (parents or their offspring) with a group of known noncriminals.

Aggressive Aggression   A subtype of expressive criminality in which the offender has not been provoked and is unconcerned with the identity of the victim. Such acts are usually seen as irrational or motivated by bellicosity, since the victim's identity is of no concern to the offender, who wishes only to vent hostile feelings in a violent manner on whatever targets attract his or her attention.

Atavism   Reverting to a primitive type and/or resembling a remote, or less evolved, ancestor in some characteristic.

Born Criminals   Identified by Lombroso as persons suffering from severely atavistic features and behavior. They were thought to be responsible for most of the serious criminality noted in modern societies. These individuals were thought to be unable to avoid criminal behavior, regardless of the sorts of environmental influences to which they were exposed.

Criminaloids   Identified by Lombroso as persons suffering from mildly atavistic features and behavior. They were associated with minor forms of criminality in Lombroso's theory, and he believed that they could be affected by environmental factors.

Economic Compulsivity   Refers to crimes, primarily against property, committed by addicted persons in order to obtain the money to purchase drugs.

General Pedigree Studies   Studies that look for similarities of criminal traits or behavior within family linages.

Genetic Karyotype Studies   Studies that examine and compare human chromosomes.

Limbic System   A set of areas in the human brain that integrate a wide variety of messages from the senses and control goal-oriented responses to environmental and internal stimuli. The limbic system is composed of the hypothalamus, hippocampus, limbic lobe, and amygdala. The amygdala is especially crucial to the aggressive responses, and disorders in this region of the system have been linked to uncontrollable and irrational rage in humans.

Psychoactive Substances   Chemicals which alter a person's moods and/or behavior.

Psychopharmacological Model   Refers to criminal actions that are directly induced by psychoactive substances. Such substances are thought to affect the internal mental controls that normally prevent or discourage an individual from committing a crime. The painful effects of withdrawal can also motivate otherwise inexplicable violent acts.

Somatotype   Numerical serial representations of the degree of endomorphy, mesomorphy, and ectomorphy in the human physique.

Twin Studies   Studies concentrated on inherited or genetically transmitted criminal behavior. Identical twins are the ideal subjects for this type of research because they share the same genes.

■ Notes

1. Larry J. Siegel, *Criminology* (St. Paul, MN: West Publishing Company, 1986), p. 146.

2. Saleem A. Shah and Loren H. Roth, "Biological and Psychophysiological Factors in Criminality" in Daniel Glaser (ed.), *Handbook of Criminology,* (Chicago: Rand McNally College Publishing Company, 1974), pp. 104–126.

3. Kenneth Moyer, "What Is the Potential for Biological Violence Control?" in C. R. Jeffery (ed.), *Biology and Crime* (Beverly Hills, CA: SAGE Publications, 1979), pp. 19–46.

4. W. H. Sheldon, *The Varieties of Temperament* (New York: Harper and Brothers, 1942), pp. 1–11.

5. George Vold and Thomas J. Bernard, *Theoretical Criminology,* 3d ed. (New York: Oxford University Press, 1986), p. 37.

6. Jean L. McKechnie, *Webster's Deluxe Unabridged Dictionary* 2d ed. (New York: Simon & Schuster, 1979), p. 117.

7. Gina Lombroso-Ferrero, "Criminal Man," in Joseph E. Jacoby (ed.) *Classics of Criminology* (Prospect Heights, IL: Waveland Press, 1979), p. 80.

8. Ibid. pp. 75–76.

9. Ibid. pp. 76–78.

10. Ibid. pp. 84–85.

11. Ibid. pp. 85.

12. Ibid. p. 76.

13. Ibid. pp. 85–88.

14. James Q. Wilson and Richard J. Herrnstein, *Crime and Human Nature* (New York: Simon & Schuster, 1985), pp. 72–75; Donald J. Shoemaker, *Theories of Delinquency* 2d ed. (New York: Oxford University Press, 1990), p. 17.

15. Sheldon, *The Varieties of Temperament,* pp. 1–11.

16. Sheldon, *The Varieties of Temperament,* p. 8; Vold and Bernard, *Theoretical Criminology,* p. 59.

17. Sheldon, *The Varieties of Temperament,* pp. 7–10.

18. Vold and Bernard, *Theoretical Criminology,* pp. 58–61.

19. P. Epps and R. W. Parnell, "Physique and Temperament of Women Delinquents Compared with Women Undergraduates," *British Journal of Medical Psychology* 25 (1952): pp. 249–255; W. H. Sheldon and Eleanor Glueck, *Physique and Delinquency* (New York: Harper & Row, 1956); James Q. Wilson and Richard Herrnstein, *Crime and Human Nature* (New York: Simon & Schuster, 1983), pp. 81–89.

20. Sheldon and Glueck, *Physique and Delinquency.*

21. Wilson and Herrnstein, *Crime and Human Nature,* pp. 88–89; Shoemaker, *Theories of Delinquency* 2d ed., pp. 18–20.

22. J. H. Vetter and I. J. Silverman, *Criminology and Crime: An Introduction* (New York: Harper & Row, 1986), p. 425.

23. Lee Ellis, "Genetic Influences and Crime" in Frank H. Marsh and Janet Katz (eds.), *Biology, Crime & Ethics: A Study of Biological Explanations for Criminal Behavior* (Cincinnati, OH: Anderson Publishing Co.), pp. 65–92.

24. Ibid.

25. Ibid.

26. Ibid.

27. Shoemaker, *Theories of Delinquency* 2d ed., pp. 21–29; Ellis, "Genetic Influences and Crime," pp. 65–92.

28. Odd Steffen Dalgard and Einar Kringlen, "Criminal Behavior in Twins" in Leonard D. Savitz and Norman Johnston (eds.), *Crime in Society* (New York: Wiley, 1978), pp. 292–307; Aaron J. Rosanoff, Leva M. Handy, and Isabel Avis Rosanoff, "Criminality and Delinquency in Twins," *Journal of Criminal Law and Criminology* 24 (1934): pp. 923–934.

29. Ellis, "Genetic Influences and Crime," pp. 65–92.

30. Ibid.

31. Larry J. Siegel, *Criminology* 2d ed. (St. Paul, MN: West, 1986), p. 158.

32. Ibid.

33. Siegel, *Criminology*, 2d ed., p. 158; Sarnoff Mednick and Jan Volavka, "Biology and Crime" in Norval Morris and Michael Tonry (eds.), *Crime and Justice* (Chicago: University of Chicago Press, 1980), p. 93.

34. H. A. Witkin, S. A. Mednick, F. Schulsinger, E. Bakkestrom, K. O. Christiansen, D. R. Goodenough, K. Hirschhorn, C. Lundsteen, D. R. Owen, J. Phillip, D. B. Rubin, and M. Stocking, "Criminality, Aggression and Intelligence among XYY and XXY Men" in S. A. Mednick and K. O. Christiansen (eds.), *Biosocial Bases of Criminal Behavior* (New York: Gardner Press, 1977), p. 187.

35. H. A. Witkin, S. A. Mednick, F. Schulsinger, E. Bakkestrom, K. O. Christiansen, D. R. Goodenough, K. Hirschhorn, C. Lundsteen, D. R. Owen, J. Phillip, D. B. Rubin, and M. Stocking, "XYY and XXY Men: Criminality and Aggression," *Science* 193 (1976): pp. 547–555.

36. Jere R. Behrman and Paul Taubman, "Is Schooling 'Mostly in the Genes'? Nature-Nurture Decomposition Using Data on Relatives," *Journal of Political Economy* 97, no. 6 (1989): pp. 1425–1446.

37. N. S. Caplan, "Intellectual Functioning" in H. C. Quay (ed.), *Juvenile Delinquency* (Princeton, NJ: VanNostrand, 1965); T. Hirschi and M. J. Hindelang, "Intelligence and Delinquency: A Revisionist View," *American Journal of Sociology* 42 (1977): pp. 571–587; W. C. Reckless and M. Smith, *Juvenile Delinquency* (New York: McGraw-Hill, 1932).

38. Hirschi and Hindelang, "Intelligence and Delinquency: A Revisionist View," pp. 571–587; Scott Menard and Barbara J. Morse, "A Structuralist Critique of the IQ-Delinquency Hypothesis: Theory and Evidence," *American Journal of Sociology* 89 (1984): pp. 1347–1378.

39. Ellis, "Genetic Influences and Crime," pp. 65–92.

40. Ibid.

41. Ibid.

42. Barry Hutchings and Sarnoff A. Mednick, "Criminality in Adoptees and Their Adoptive and Biological Parents: A Pilot Study" in Sarnoff A. Mednick and Karl O. Christiansen (eds.), *Biosocial Bases of Criminal Behavior* (New York: Gardner Press, Inc., 1977), pp. 127–141; Sarnoff A. Mednick, William F. Gabrielli, Jr., and Barry Hutchings, "Genetic Factors in the Etiology of Criminal Behavior" in Sarnoff A. Mednick, Terrie E. Moffitt, and Susan Stack (eds.), *The Causes of Crime: New Biological Approaches* (Cambridge, England: Cambridge University Press, 1987), pp. 74–91; C. R. Cloniger and I. I. Gotesman, "Genetic and Environmental Factors in Anti-Social Behavior Disorders" in Mednick,

Moffitt, and Stack (eds.), *The Causes of Crime: New Biological Approaches,* pp. 92–109.

43. Shoemaker, *Theories of Delinquency,* p. 26; Siegel, *Criminology,* pp. 152–157.

44. Roger N. Johnson, *Aggression In Man and Animals* (Philadelphia: W. B. Saunders Company, 1972), pp. 76–77.

45. Ibid., pp. 68–70.

46. Ibid., p. 77; Frank R. Ervin, Vernon H. Mark, and Janice Stevens, "Behavioral and Affective Responses to Brain Stimulation in Man" in Joseph Zubin, and Charles Shagass (eds.), *Neurobiological Aspects of Psychopathology* (New York: Grune & Stratton, 1969), pp. 58–65.

47. George E. Rush, *The Dictionary of Criminal Justice* 2d ed. (Guilford, CT: Dushkin Publishing Group, 1986), p. 158.

48. Jack Levin and James Alan Fox, *Mass Murder: America's Growing Menace* (New York: Plenum Press, 1985), pp. 16–17.

49. Ibid., p. 30.

50. Johnson, *Aggression In Man and Animals,* pp. 77–79; Lisa Hoffman, "Do the People in Texas Blame Me," *Dallas Times Herald,* July 27, 1986, p. 19A; Sott Sunde and Bob Drummond, "A Sniper's Rampage," *Dallas Times Herald* July 27, 1986), p. 18A.

51. Johnson, *Aggression In Man and Animals,* pp. 77–79; Levin and Fox, *Mass Murder: America's Growing Menace, pp. 16–17.*

52. Johnson, *Aggression In Man and Animals,* pp. 77–79.

53. Levin and Fox, *Mass Murder: America's Growing Menace,* pp. 16–17; William J. Helmer, "Madman on the Tower," *Texas Monthly,* August 1986, p. 168; Lisa Hoffman, "Do the People in Texas Blame Me," p. 19A.

54. David Nevin, "Charlie Whitman: The Eagle Scout Who Grew Up with a Tortured Mind," *Life* 61, no. 7 (August 1966): pp. 28D–30D.

55. Levin and Fox, *Mass Murder: America's Growing Menace,* p. 39.

56. Ibid., p. 32.

57. Nevin, "Charlie Whitman: The Eagle Scout Who Grew Up with a Tortured Mind," pp. 28D–30D.

58. Moyer, "What Is the Potential for Biological Violence Control?" pp. 23–24.

59. Ibid., pp. 21–41.

60. American Psychiatric Association, *Diagnostic and Statistical Manual of Mental Disorders,* 3d ed, revised (Washington, DC: American Psychiatric Association, 1987), pp. 123, 165.

61. Ibid., pp. 169–170.

62. P. J. Goldstein, "The Drugs-Violence Nexus: A Tripartite Conceptual Framework," *Journal of Drug Issues,* Fall (1985), pp. 493–506.

63. Ibid.

64. American Psychiatric Association, *Diagnostic and Statistical Manual of Mental Disorders,* 3d ed., rev. (Washington, DC: American Psychiatric Association, 1987), pp. 123, 140–152, 165.

65. James A. Inciardi, *The War on Drugs* (Palo Alto, CA: Mayfield Press, 1984) p. 135.

66. Ibid., pp. 127–159.

67. Ibid., pp. 148–149, 154–158.

68. "Cocaine Abuse," *Harvard Medical School Mental Health Letter* 2, no. 5 (1985): pp. 1–4; L. Grinspoon and J. Bakalar, "What Is Phencyclidine?" *Harvard Medical School Mental Health Letter* 6, no. 7 (1990): p. 8.

69. J. Zimmerman, W. D. Rich, I. Kelitz, and P. K. Broder, "Some Observations on the Link between Learning Disabilities and Juvenile Delinquency," *Journal of Criminal Justice* 9 (1981): pp. 1–17; P. K. Broder, N. Dunivant, E. C. Smith, and L. P. Sutton, "Further Observations on the Link between Learning Disabilities and Juvenile Delinquency," *Journal of Educational Psychology* 73 (1981): pp. 838–850.

70. Ibid.

71. Sarnoff A. Mednick, "A Biosocial Theory of the Learning of Law-Abiding Behavior" in Sarnoff A. Mednick and Karl O. Christiansen (eds.), *Biosocial Bases of Criminal Behavior* (New York: Gardner Press, Inc., 1977), pp. 1–2.

72. Mednick, "A Biosocial Theory of the Learning of Law-Abiding Behavior," pp. 1–2; Sarnoff A. Mednick, Lis Kirkegaard-Sorensen, Barry Hutchings, Joachim Knop, Raben Rosenberg, and Fini Schulsinger, "An Example of Biosocial Research: The Interplay of Socioenvironmental and Individual Factors in the Etiology of Criminal Behavior" in Sarnoff A. Mednick and Karl O. Christiansen (eds.), *Biosocial Bases of Criminal Behavior* (New York: Gardner Press, 1977), pp. 9–10.

73. W. Madsen, *The American Alcoholic: The Nature-Nurture Controversy in Alcoholic Research and Therapy* (Springfield, IL: Charles C. Thomas, 1974), p. 15; D. W. Goodwin, "Alcoholism and Heredity," *Archives of General Psychiatry* 36 (1979): pp. 57–61; H. B. Murphee, "Some Possible Origins of Alcoholism" in W. J. Filstead, J. J. Rossi, and M. Keller (eds.), *Alcohol and Alcohol Problems* (Cambridge, MA: Ballinger, 1976).

74. Mednick, "A Biosocial Theory of the Learning of Law-Abiding Behavior."

75. Harold D. Kletschka, "Violent Behavior Associated with Brain Tumor," *Minnesota Medicine* 49 (1966): pp. 1853–1855.

■ Suggested Readings

Jere R. Behrman and Paul Taubman, " Is Schooling 'Mostly in the Genes'? Nature-Nurture Decomposition Using Data on Relatives," *Journal of Political Economy* 97 no. 6 (1989): pp. 1425–1446.

Lee Ellis, "Genetic Influences and Crime" in Frank H. Marsh and Janet Katz (eds.), *Biology, Crime & Ethics: A Study of Biological Explanations for Criminal Behavior* (Cincinnati, OH: Anderson Publishing Co.), pp. 65–92.

Heinz Hafner and Wolfgang Boker, *Crimes of Violence by Mentally Abnormal Offenders: A Psychiatric and Epidemiological Study in the Federal German Republic,* translated by Helen Marshall (Cambridge, London: Cambridge University Press, 1982).

Sarnoff A. Mednick, William F. Gabrielli, Jr., and Barry Hutchings, "Genetic Factors in the Etiology of Criminal Behavior" in Sarnoff A. Mednick, Terrie E. Moffitt, and Susan Stack (eds.), *The Causes of Crime: New Biological Approaches* (Cambridge, England: Cambridge University Press, 1987), pp. 74–91.

Edward Sagarin, *Taboos in Criminology* (Beverly Hills, CA: Sage, 1980).

Saleem A. Shah and Loren H. Roth, "Biological and Psychophysiological Factors in Criminality" in Daniel Glaser (ed.), *Handbook of Criminology* (Chicago: Rand McNally College Publishing Company, 1974), pp. 104–126.

■ Suggested Books for Additional Application

Miriam Allen deFord, *Murderers Sane & Mad: Case Histories in the Motivation and Rationale of Murder* (New York: Abelard-Schuman, 1965).

Paul B. Weston and Robert W. Cole, *Case Studies of Drug Abuse and Criminal Behavior* (Pacific Palisades, CA: Goodyear Publishing Company, 1973).

David St. Clair, *Say You Love Satan* (New York: Dell, 1987).

CHAPTER **5**

Psychiatric Perspective

Overview of Psychiatric Perspective

Mental illnesses are traditionally classified into one of three major categories, each of which consists of many subcategories, or specific disorders. **Psychoses** are generally considered the most serious major category of mental disorder because their victims lose contact with reality. While some psychoses have organic causes that can be clearly identified with modern diagnostic techniques, other equally serious ones cannot be linked to any single physical abnormality. The latter type are generally referred to as "functional" psychoses in order to distinguish them from those caused by identified "organic" factors. Thus, **functional mental disorders** are those in which mental functioning is clearly impaired but no organic cause can be confidently described. The psychiatric perspective deals especially with such functional psychoses.[1] A more appropriate title for this chapter might even have been the "functional psychotic" perspective. However, psychiatry is the pivotal discipline both in organizing materials on these types of disorders and in treating their sufferers. Exhibit 5.1 gives the common assumptions of this perspective.

We will concentrate our discussion of personality disorders, the second major category of mental illnesses, in the following chapter on the psychological perspective, so as to give full attention to the Freudian approach to personality development. The third major category of mental problems, neurotic disorders, are so common among both criminals and noncriminals that their discussion is not appropriate in a criminology text.

Exhibit 5.1

Psychiatric perspective

Common Assumptions

1. The brain is a highly complex electrochemical organ, and its mechanisms are not yet fully understood by science.

2. Perceptions and behaviors are the result of electrochemical processes in the brain.

3. Early experiences help shape brain processes.

4. The processes of the brain can be affected by genetics, chemicals, and environmental factors.

5. Abnormalities in these processes are difficult to identify but cause abnormal perceptions and behaviors.

6. Only some of these abnormalities are medically identifiable by modern scientific procedures—many can be identified only by their symptoms.

7. Many of these abnormalities are common enough to have been detected and classified even though their cause is unknown.

8. Some of these abnormal processes may, at times, lead to crime.

Source: S. H. Snyder, *Madness and the Brain* (New York: McGraw-Hill, 1974); Thomas L. Bennett, *Introduction to Physiological Psychology* (Monterey, CA: Brooks/Cole, 1982), pp. 25–92, 243–287; H. Hafner and W. Boker, trans. Helen Marshall, *Crimes of Violence by Mentally Abnormal Offenders: A Psychiatric and Epidemiological Study in the Federal German Republic* (Cambridge, London: Cambridge University Press, 1982), pp. 5–46; American Psychiatric Association, *Diagnostic and Statistical Manual of Mental Disorders*, 3d ed., revised, (Washington, DC: American Psychiatric Association, 1987), pp. 97–99, 187–188.

Although the media focuses much attention on psychotic killers and rapists, they are actually quite few in number. In fact, the seriously mentally ill commit extremely few crimes when compared to the "normal" public, and one is about as likely to be killed by lightning as by a psychotic murderer. When psychotics do commit acts of violence, however, their motives and actions are often intriguingly bizarre. This accounts for the disproportionate media attention given such crimes and the consequent popular misconception that psychotics play a significant role in society's overall crime problem.

The psychiatric perspective is associated primarily with the discipline and practice of psychiatry, which was founded on the work of Sigmund Freud. The modern psychiatrist is a medical doctor with advanced training in the biology of the brain as well as various psychological theories of the causes and remedies for psychic problems. Within psychiatry, some practitioners use Freud's theory to account for the development of psychoses, while others use biological, biosocial, or psychological theories. The psychiatric perspective thus overlaps the biomedical theories at some points, as well as the psychological approaches to criminality discussed in the following chapter.

The psychiatric perspective assumes that criminality is the result of some type of mental illness or brain disorder. In this way it has much in common with the positive school of thought and the biological perspective. The biological perspective examines abnormalities in brain structure, however, whereas psychiatry is primarily concerned with disorders in brain functioning. Many psychiatrists believe that a person's early experiences help shape brain processes in a unique way and make a significant contribution to adult behavior and thought patterns. This assumption is the direct legacy of Sigmund Freud, whose ideas are dealt with in the next chapter. Freud, however, did not directly concern himself with psychosis.

Current psychiatric treatment is most closely associated with the psychotic disorders, partly because psychoses usually require drug treatment, which only a psychiatrist is trained to administer, whereas other mental disorders might be treated by psychologists. (Organic mental disorders are dealt with as part of the biological perspective.)

Although we are not primarily concerned with definitions of mental illness or explanations of why people become mentally ill in this text, some discussion of the controversies surrounding such definitions and explanations is necessary as background information. This is especially appropriate because the behavior of the disordered person is the only data from which a diagnosis of functional psychosis—the main subject of the psychiatric perspective—may be drawn. Unfortunately, definitions of functional psychoses are problematic in themselves. This is partially due to the fact that modern definitions of these disorders are interpreted differently by the different professional audiences (e.g., psychiatrists, social workers, psychologists), each of whom have their own theoretical biases. In addition, the term "mental illness" has come to refer to a large class of disorders. The defining of functional mental illnesses is a process of producing numerous definitions of the various categories and subtypes of mental illness. Thus, it requires more than the production of a single definition. It is a concept that takes in all forms, types, and degrees of mental processes that are categorized as dysfunctional. Further, these disorders can become evident through physical, social, or psychological symptoms.

Yet, the task of defining mental illnesses is critical because these definitions determine how others respond to the mentally ill through social actions.[2] For example, the definition of someone as mentally ill is often interpreted as meaning that the person is dangerous. Aggregate research shows that this belief is unfounded. Nevertheless, psychiatry, more than any other discipline, has been given the responsibility of predicting which mental patients may become dangerous in the future. Dangerousness is at least as problematic a concept as mental illness. By giving such power to psychiatry, society confirms its belief in this perspective despite the many problems that other scientists have noted in its most crucial concepts.[3]

It must be emphasized that definitions of serious functional mental disorders are medical terms or diagnoses used by psychiatrists, whereas the term *insanity* is a legal term used in the court system. These two terms are not interchangeable. A psychiatrist determines if people are mentally disordered by comparing their symptoms to those of an accepted category of mental disease. A court of law determines if they are legally insane according to whether they were able to understand the nature and quality of the criminal act at the time it was committed.[4] The legal term, *insanity,* is concerned with a person's ability to judge the appropriateness of an act from the point of view of the mainstream society. Thus, a court of law can find defendants legally insane for a number of mental conditions other than psychosis, as well as find defendants diagnosed as psychotic to be legally responsible for their act(s).[5]

Eaton identified five generic problems in defining mental health:[6]

1. Mental health is conventionally defined as a part of general health.
2. There is controversy as to the role of environmental factors in mental disorder.
3. Mental health is a matter of degree.
4. Health is not a static quality, but rather is constantly changing.
5. There is an unfounded assumption that knowledge of extreme cases of mental illness can be generalized to more typical ones.

At the basis of the problems identified by Eaton are the biological assumptions that (1) a physical brain is prerequisite to a mental functioning of any sort and (2) standards of behavior (i.e., functioning) are socially defined. Thus, some of the problems in defining mental health stem from the inseparability of the mind from the brain. Others spring from the inseparability of behavior from social beliefs and values.

One milestone that has been reached is the distinction between mental illnesses attributable to either physical (organic) or unknown (functional) conditions. This allows for distinctions to be made between mental illnesses of an organic nature (e.g., tumors), as discussed in the preceding chapter, and those of unknown origin or of a functional nature (e.g., schizophrenia).

Because mental health is ever-changing (i.e., it has a dynamic quality) and is a matter of degree, two of these generic problems in defining mental health are of particular importance to criminology. As a dynamic quality, mental illness can come and go within minutes.[7] Persons suffering from psychosis can act very normally in the absence of delusions, but the next minute, while having a delusion, behave very strangely. This accounts for why some defendants who have committed horrendous crimes while delusional are able to act in a perfectly normal manner during their trial.

The problem of mental illness being a matter of degree is enmeshed with the legal idea of **diminished capacity,** meaning a lower than average level of mental sophistication or impaired ability to deal with reality due to some temporary condition. Diminished capacity is relevant in crimes such as murder, where there are several degrees of seriousness involved in determining the precise charge to be used. These degrees of seriousness are dependent on the defendant's state of mind. Because criminal laws require that a person must have a criminal intent (**mens rea**), defendants with diminished mental capacity are viewed as having a lower degree of moral responsibility for their acts.

For example, murder in the "first degree" requires malice, premeditation, and deliberation. Murder in the "second degree" requires the absence of premeditation and deliberation, but the presence of malice. And "voluntary manslaughter" requires the absence of all three—premeditation, deliberation, and malice. Other types of homicides would be either justified, excusable, or accidental.[8]

David Berkowitz, the Son of Sam killer who terrorized New York City, said that he killed six persons and wounded seven because of some "unknown urge to kill."

Because norms for behavior are socially defined on the basis of beliefs and values, some people have reached the conclusion that mental illness cannot be defined scientifically. They claim, in effect, that science cannot establish a hierarchy of values, and therefore it cannot provide definitions of mental illness or mental health.[9] This claim sees behavior as being defined as either "good or bad" on the basis of social values through a conventional process.[10] Therefore, since values are not absolute, ultimate, eternal, or objective, and are in fact subjective, no valid scientific definitions of them can be provided.[11]

The values upon which standards of normality are based are found in the fundamental institutions of society—the family, religion, school, mythology, etc. Two variables suggested as contributing to definitions of mental illness are (1) the ordinary environmental conditions to which one is expected to adapt and (2) the tolerance limits of that social environment.[12] Thus, the social meaning of mental illness centers on the inability of some individuals to adapt to their social environment at the standard or normal tolerance level expected by others in the same social environment. Social values that either directly or indirectly relate to defining the inability to adapt to the normal social environment at a tolerable level have come to have direct relevance for defining mental illness.

The *medicalization of deviance* ("turning badness into illness") can be traced back to the European witch hunts and the asylum movement.[13] The phenomena reappeared in the United States during the mid-1850s with the founding of the American Medical Association. One of the first moral issues that the American Medical Association was involved in was that of abortion. Prior to 1850 abortion was a common practice and was not viewed as an immoral act. Members of the American Medical Association lobbied against it as an immoral act, and abortions were subsequently outlawed by legislative action.[14]

Medical ventures into the moral world of norm creation still occur today. For example, in 1973 the American Psychiatric Association voted that homosexuality was not necessarily a symptom of mental disorder. This highlights the fact that at least some of the definitions of mental disorders that have evolved through the medicalization of deviance are not founded on any scientific basis, but rather on a socio-moral process of negotiation over definitions and behavioral limits.

The medical model of mental disorder is built on the presumption that the causes of functional mental illnesses reside within the individual. Although genetic, biochemical, and psychological investigations each seek to discover different kinds of causal agents for mental illness, they all presume that the causal agent is within the individual.[15] It is often proposed that these disorders are physical in origin, but that we simply do not have a sufficient understanding of the mind/brain to identify their cause. Systematic studies of functional mental disorders that have attempted to conclusively identify the cause(s) of the illness within the individual have, however, failed. (Over 5,000 research papers on the origins of schizophrenia published over the past six decades have not adequately demonstrated the location or nature of its causes.)[16]

Because medical approaches have been inconclusive, an eclectic approach to mental illness, particularly to psychosis, seems warranted. Much current attention focuses on the processes of the brain and how they are affected by the environment. For example, our mental processes are known to be mediated by hundreds of billions of **synapses** in the brain—that is, the electrochemical junctions of two nerve endings through which pass chemical substances. The chemical substances that are involved in this process are known as **neurotransmitters.** They include noradrenaline, serotonin, dopamine, acetylcholine, certain amino acids and polypeptides. An electrical signal provides a cue for a presynaptic neuron to release particular chemicals into the synaptic cleft (i.e., the space between two neurons). The postsynaptic neuron reacts to the neurotransmitter, causing a series of biochemical events in the postsynaptic neuron. Signals are transmitted along neural pathways (sets of neurons) in this manner. Presynaptic neurons store and release neurotransmitters into synaptic clefts in response to commands via the electrical signals given off by nerve fibers. Postsynaptic neurons have receptors that react to the presence of neurotransmitters. The neuronal signal is transmitted when the receptors initiate a series of electrochemical events in the postsynaptic neuron.[17] Although we have provided only a simplified description of the process, its complexity should be clear. It is suspected that a problem with one or more aspects of this process can result in the hallucinations/delusions that characterize psychoses.

Research with antipsychotic drugs, especially the major tranquilizers, has produced strong evidence that these chemicals have the ability to alter the activity of the neurotransmitter at the synapse. For example, when chlorpromazine is given to a normal person, the drug has little effect. However, when it is given to a person exhibiting psychotic symptoms (delusions or hallucinations), the problem ceases or is at least reduced. This major tranquilizer is exclusively for use by psychotics and is known to block the uptake of dopamine, a common neurotransmitter. It is not known how this helps to prevent hallucinations.

Simple conclusions, such as the assertion that mental illness (schizophrenia) is caused by overactive dopamine synapses, are not possible, however. For one thing, too little is understood about the complexity of the mental processes. These processes involve the interaction of over 10 billion different types of neurons, a wide variety of neurotransmitters, sensory inputs from the environment and the different effects of drugs within the brain.[18] Additionally, overactive dopamine synapses may be the *result* of schizophrenia, rather than the cause. A dopamine-blocking agent may merely be controlling a symptom of the underlying disorder rather than alleviating the cause.

Nevertheless, the fact remains that certain chemicals, such as chlorpromazine, alter the behavior of persons through their pharmacological action. It is indisputable, therefore, that biochemical processes are involved in mental illness. Chemicals can alter behavior. The problem is that we do not yet understand the exact processes involved or their sequential order.

The reported genetic findings regarding mental illness and families demonstrate that the source of mental illness is not totally genetic.[19] However, these findings do indicate that genetics are involved to some extent in some mental illnesses. In Kety's study, which controlled for both in-utero and environmental factors, 13 percent of biological paternal half-siblings (same father–different mother) of adopted schizophrenics were found to be schizophrenic, in comparison with 2 percent for the control group. In this study, the only thing that the schizophrenics had in common was that 50 percent of their genetic inheritance was from their fathers. Since they had different mothers and were raised in different environments, it appears that they could only have acquired schizophrenia, or a predisposition toward it, through genetic transmission.[20] However, this percentage is too low to suggest that genetic factors are totally responsible for schizophrenia. There are also many diagnosed cases of the disease in which no family history is found.

In sum, both genetic and chemical factors play a role in the etiology of some mental illnesses, but they cannot fully account for them. Instead, an *eclectic paradigm* (i.e., integration of several different theoretical perspectives) for mental disorders is needed—one that will take these biological factors into account while linking them to a variety of environmental factors. The **diathesis-stress model** is just such a model. *Diathesis* refers to a biological predisposition or tendency toward a given disorder. Thus, this model suggests that severe stress acts to trigger an illness to which the individual was vulnerable: neither the biological predisposition nor stress alone can cause mental disorder, but mental disorder can or will result from their combined action.

No such paradigm has been accepted by all of the involved disciplines at this time, however. Theoretical explanations for several different kinds of causes of functional mental disorders (e.g., social, psychological, or physiological) have some evidence to support them; but no perspective is currently capable of accounting for all the evidence regarding mental illness.[21]

Psychotic-Disorders Approach

The central feature of psychosis is the presence of delusional and/or hallucinatory content in thoughts and emotions (see Exhibit 5.2). Among the numerous types of psychoses, those considered most relevant to the explanation of criminality are schizophrenia, delusional (paranoid) disorder, and brief reactive psychosis.

Schizophrenia is the most commonly diagnosed form of psychosis in the United States.[22] Of the several subtypes of schizophrenia (e.g., catatonic, paranoid, undifferentiated), the paranoid type is most directly connected to criminal behavior.[23]

Exhibit 5.2

. . . .

Psychotic-disorders approach

Restrictive Assumptions

1. Psychotic disorders may result from chemical, genetic, environmental or other sources.
2. These disorders render their victims unable to distinguish between reality and internally generated delusions or hallucinations.
3. Psychotics may behave in a criminal manner as a response to the content of their delusions/hallucinations.

Source: American Psychiatric Association, *Diagnostic and Statistical Manual of Mental Disorders, 3d ed.* (Washington, D.C.: American Psychiatric Association, 1987), pp. 109–111, 187–211; *The Harvard Mental Health Letter,* "Violence and Violent Patients: Part I," Vol. 7, No. 12 (1991), pp. 1–4.

Paranoid schizophrenia is characterized by unfocused anger and arbitrary violence.[24] Although schizophrenics, and especially paranoid schizophrenics, are stereotyped by the media as crazed killers, they are rarely violent criminals. While, admittedly, schizophrenia can lead to extremely violent crimes, it more frequently results in other types of criminal behavior (e.g., vagrancy, assault), which are less well publicized.

For example, in his book, *Confessions of a Criminal Lawyer,* Seymour Wishman discusses the case of Phil Lanza, who was convicted of two robberies. Lanza had been hospitalized for paranoid schizophrenia while in the Navy and was given many electroconvulsive shock therapy treatments. He claimed that he had a hallucination in which a man took over his brain, forced him to get a gun, and made him rob two stores. When Lanza was found guilty, Wishman felt that he had failed as Lanza's attorney in not proving that Lanza had been seriously mentally ill at the time he committed the crimes. Wishman felt that Lanza was convicted because his Navy medical records were not allowed as evidence during the trial.[25]

The central feature of **delusional (paranoid) disorders** that distinguishes them from schizophrenia is the less bizarre nature of the delusions/hallucinations. They tend to have a consistent theme that does not result in behavior as extreme as that of the schizophrenic individual. These delusional systems, however, do come to dominate the person's life and behavior. There are several subtypes of delusional (paranoid) disorders: erotomanic, grandiose, jealous, persecutory, and somatic.[26] The erotomania, jealous, and persecutory subtypes are more directly associated with criminal behavior than are the others.

Erotomanic delusions involve sexual fantasies that are focused on some sort of idealized notion of romantic love. Usually, the object of this idealized romantic love is someone famous or of higher status than the person suffering from the delusions. It is not uncommon for a person suffering this type of delusion to attempt to contact the object of their idealized romantic love.[27] John W. Hinckley, Jr., who shot President Reagan in 1981 and was subsequently found not guilty by reason of insanity, suffered this type of delusion. According to his psychiatrist, Hinckley suffered an erotomanic delusion that focused on Jodie Foster, a movie star.[28]

Persons suffering from a **grandiose delusional disorder** become convinced that they are actually a famous person (e.g., Caesar, Napoleon), or possess some great talent or invention. They become frustrated when the world fails to acknowledge their great importance. Persons suffering jealousy-type delusions are certain, despite a complete lack of evidence, that their spouses or lovers are unfaithful. Persons suffering this type of delusion may assault their spouses, lovers, or others in response to their delusional beliefs. An example of this type of delusion is offered by the case of Orlando Camacho, whose jealousy of his wife began early in their courtship and developed into auditory hallucinations whereby he heard his wife talk to him when he was not facing her. However, as soon as he would face her, she would stop talking. He believed that she had told him that she had sex with ten different men during their first ten days of marriage. As he did not want his wife to be with other men, he murdered her. He was found guilty in the death of his wife and sentenced to five years in prison.[29]

Persecutory delusions are, as the term implies, of a suspicious and fearful, though self-centered, nature. Persons under this type of delusional disorder generally perceive some type of plot or conspiracy against them, which, in fact, is nonexistent. Resentment, defensiveness, and anger are associated with persecutory delusions, which can result in the use of violence.[30] The common attribute of all these forms of paranoid delusions is the narcissistic belief that the psychotic is the center of much attention or activity by others.

A **brief reactive psychosis** lasts no more than a month but no less than a few hours. This type of psychosis is a reaction to an event or experience that would be considered an extraordinarily stressful event (e.g., death of a loved one, military combat) for anyone living in the same culture. Some principal features of this type of psychosis are peculiar postures, screaming, and muteness, as well as suicidal and aggressive behavior.[31]

The reader should note that although mental disorders are viewed as causal for both **psychotic criminals** and **antisocial-personality criminals**, these two types of criminals are very different. Psychotics commit crimes because of their delusions or hallucinations, whereas the antisocial personality commits crimes for instrumental (e.g., money) or emotive (e.g., revenge, pleasure) reasons.[32] The psychotic is, by definition, unable to distinguish reality from delusion, and thus may be found not guilty by reason of insanity if charged with a crime. The antisocial personality, on the other hand, is fully aware of reality and may be tried and convicted like anyone else. While Freud did not directly address psychoses or personality disorders, his conceptualization of the development of personality is a major part of the psychiatric perspective and has influenced the modern definition, explanation, and treatment of these disorders.

The Case of Joseph Kallinger · · · · · · · · · · · ·   APPLICATION · · · · · ·

In 1973 Joseph Kallinger and his thirteen-year-old son, Michael began robbing and burglarizing numerous suburban homes in Pennsylvania, New Jersey, and Maryland. About a year later, Kallinger began sexually assaulting his female robbery victims. On at least one occasion he let his son Michael rape a robbery victim.[35] In 1975 Kallinger and his son began murdering people. Their first

Burglary
The act of unlawfully entering a residence, industry, or business with the intent to commit a felony or larceny.[33]

Robbery
The act of using force or the threat of force to unlawfully take or attempt to take property that is in another person's immediate possession.[34]

victim was a ten-year-old boy. Next they killed Kallinger's older son, Joe Jr., by drowning him in the flooded basement of a vacant building. Their last homicide victim was a nurse whom they killed during one of their house robberies. Thus, before they were arrested on January 17, 1975, they had killed three people and stolen over $600,000 in cash and jewelry.[36]

The *precipitating factor* in Kallinger's case was his psychosis. He was eventually diagnosed as suffering from schizophrenia. At the age of fifteen, he began having hallucinatory experiences with a "God of the Universe." The "God of the Universe" was a large figure that would command him to do things. In 1972 the "God of the Universe" instructed Kallinger to massacre all mankind with a butcher knife. Although Kallinger knew that he had to do exactly as the "God of the Universe" commanded him, he did not believe that he had the ability or courage to kill. He therefore solicited the help of his son Michael.[37]

By the age of twelve, Michael was not afraid of anyone or anything. He was later diagnosed as suffering from an antisocial-personality disorder. Michael became a source of strength and courage to his father in carrying out commands from the "God of the Universe." When Kallinger told Michael that he needed his help to kill some people, Michael said he would be glad to help.[38]

The *attracting factors* leading to these events are related to the origins of Kallinger's psychosis. The origins of his psychosis can be traced to his psychological castration by his adoptive parents. At the age of four, he had a hernia operation. Shortly after the operation, his parents lied to him about the reasons for the surgery. They told him that the doctor had removed a demon from his penis rather than telling him the truth, which was that the doctor had repaired his hernia. They also told him at that time that he was not allowed to have penile erections, for if he did he would do wicked things; and if he did wicked things, he would go to hell when he died.[39]

These statements by Kallinger's parents left him psychologically castrated. He could not understand why he was having penile erections, since the demon that was supposed to have caused them had been cut out by the doctor. At this point in his life, he began to associate sexual arousal with knives. In Kallinger's mind the penis had now become an object of self-love and preservation. Evidence of this attraction is seen in Kallinger's cutting off the penis of his ten-year-old murder victim, then taking it home and keeping it in a plastic bag. Additional evidence of this attraction is found in the fact that Kallinger only murdered the nurse after she refused to chew off the penis of a male robbery victim.[40]

At the age of six, Kallinger had his first hallucinatory experience. He saw his penis floating toward him on a knife. These delusions about his alleged castration made him flee from big-breasted women and macho men. It also led him to stab photographs of women, macho men, breasts, and penises. By the age of twelve, he was having hallucinations about cutting open a woman's stomach or cutting off her breasts.[41]

As an adolescent, Kallinger was consumed with hostility, rage, and vindictiveness as a result of his psychological castration and other childhood abuses. At the age of thirteen, Kallinger committed his first act of aggression with a knife. He took several adolescent males into the woods and threatened to cut off their penises with a knife. However, after these threats of violence, he is not thought to have committed another serious criminal act for more than twenty years. It was as if the criminal aspects of his psychosis had gone into hiding.[42]

The factors *predisposing* Kallinger towards violence stemmed from his early family environment. Kallinger was born in Philadelphia in 1937. Kallinger's natural mother put him up for adoption when he was six days old. When he was a year old, he went to live with Stephen and Anna Kallinger. They formally adopted him two years later. Stephen Kallinger was a shoemaker who owned his own shop. He and his wife could be described as a middle-class couple. They adopted Joseph because Stephen Kallinger was unable to have any children and they wanted someone to help Stephen in his shoe repair shop, as well as to have someone to leave the business to when they died. Joseph quit school at the age of sixteen and went to work as a shoemaker in his father's shoe repair shop.[43]

Several of the behaviors of Kallinger's parents are quite common among the parents of schizophrenics whose psychoses are attributed to family environment. These families constantly place the child in **double-bind** situations— meaning the child receives contradictory information on what is appropriate behavior. For example, Kallinger's parents would tell him never to fight with other children, but when he refused to fight, they told him he was a sissy. Such families also support each other's (parent's) odd behavior, isolate the child, and show no affection.[44] Kallinger's parents also teamed up against him by supporting each other's schizoid behaviors towards him, never taking his side. They literally made him a prisoner in his own home by not allowing him to play with other children. They never kissed, caressed, or played with him, nor did they ever recognize his birthdays.[45]

Kallinger's direct exposure to violent aggressive behavior began early in his childhood. On one occasion, his mother hit him on the head four times with a steel hammer because he asked her if he could go to the zoo. This occurred despite his father having already given his approval for such a trip. On another occasion, his parents placed his fingertips in the flames of the stove as punishment for taking a roll of quarters.[46]

Kallinger was convicted of four counts of robbery, four counts of false imprisonment, and one count of burglary in Pennsylvania. He was sentenced to thirty to eighty years in the Pennsylvania State Prison for these crimes. In New Jersey he was found guilty of robbery, rape, and murder. For these robberies and rapes he was sentenced to forty-two to fifty-one years. He was also sentenced to life imprisonment for the murder of the nurse. Due to the number of years he must serve, it is doubtful that he will live long enough to be paroled.[47]

Unfortunately, Kallinger's crimes did not end with his incarceration. In 1978, at the State Correctional Institution at Huntington, Pennsylvania, he stabbed another inmate twenty times, though the inmate survived. After this attack he was transferred to the Pennsylvania State Hospital for the Criminally Insane, a maximum-security hospital for men. In 1982 doctors stated that he would probably have to remain there for the rest of his life—he was 45 years old at that time.[48] His son Michael pled guilty to two counts of armed robbery in exchange for having the "accessory to murder" charge against him dismissed.

Joseph Kallinger clutches a Bible as he enters a sheriff's car, just before his second trial for robbery and false imprisonment in 1975.

In 1975 Michael was sent to the Lancaster Detention Home. Then in 1976 he was placed on probation in the custody of foster parents until his twenty-first birthday (December 25, 1982).[49]

Joseph Kallinger

The psychiatric perspective provides an explanation of Kallinger's crimes that seems more appropriate than the possible alternatives. His psychotic delusions are clearly the precipitating factor in these acts. They are also the primary fact to be dealt with in explaining Joseph Kallinger's criminality. There is much reason to believe that abusive parental behavior distorts a child's development and creates the sort of abnormal perceptions that lead to criminality.[50] Michael Kallinger's diagnosis as an antisocial personality plays an identical role when his actions become the focus of attention.

Thus, the abuses Joseph Kallinger suffered as a child, and especially the psychological trauma he suffered as a result of the way his adoptive parents explained his hernia operation to him, can be interpreted as attracting factors in his case. This assertion is based on the way in which these experiences led him to associate pain and cutting instruments with sexuality. Assuming this to be true, there are several alternative methods of explaining how these early experiences led to Kallinger's psychosis. However, explaining how and why

Exhibit 5.3
. . . .
Summary of facts and their role
in the explanation of the Joseph
Kallinger case

Level of Importance	Fact	Type of Fact
Primary	Kallinger's psychotic delusions	Precipitating
Secondary	Kallinger's psychological castration	Attracting
Tertiary	Kallinger abused in early childhood	Predisposing

people become psychotic is of secondary importance to the explanation of this crime in this text. Therefore, these are secondary factors in our explanation of Joseph Kallinger's criminality.

When attention turns to his son Michael, we have considerably less solid information to use. However, it is reasonable to assume that Joseph's criminal orientation and psychotic behavior and teachings had a major impact on Michael. Joseph's influence on his son is thus seen as the attracting factor of secondary import in Michael's case. Of course, other explanations could compete with this one. For example, it could be argued that some sort of criminogenic factor was present in Joseph's genetic makeup and was biologically passed onto Michael at conception. Such an assertion would be based on the genetic approach within the biological perspective.

The general atmosphere of Joseph's childhood home undoubtedly added to his problems. The lack of nurturing and the double-bind situations in which he was placed as a child are thus seen as tertiary factors that predisposed Joseph to problematic behavior. Because less is known of the son's background than of Joseph's, little can be said of Michael's case at this level of explanation. The role played by each of these sets of factors in the Kallinger case is summarized in Exhibit 5.3.

The case of Joseph Kallinger is of exceptional scientific interest for two reasons. First, the origin of his psychosis can be traced to a single childhood event (the hernia operation and its explanation), within the context of an abusive home environment. Second, his psychosis can be isolated as the direct cause of the robberies and homicides he committed. In most criminal cases, however, there is no single clear cause of a functional psychosis, and the presence of psychosis is not often the singular cause of a series of violent crimes.

Conclusions

. . . .

In cases such as that of the Kallingers, the pursuit of explanations for the noncriminal aspects of the case, such as the origins of psychoses, may be productive but are beyond the scope of criminology, which is concerned with the effects of the psychosis, not its cause. Seeking the best theoretical explanation for the causes of Kallinger's psychosis would demand an exploration of both the potential physical effects of his employment environment and the psychological impact of his early childhood experiences on his psychosexual development. For example, since he was a shoe repairman, his psychosis might be attributed to his inhaling toxic fumes from glue while making or repairing shoes. This type of causal analysis would require the exploration of such questions as where he obtained such dangerous glue and why it was allowed to be sold. Genetic factors could also be included, and the biosocial approach to criminality could be employed.

Likewise, theories based on the social structure and social learning perspectives might be better suited to causal explanations of Joseph Kallinger's psychoses beyond the micro level of his family. That is, to explain why his parents were allowed to become adoptive parents by the community in which they lived, theories contained in the conflict, disorganization, or anomie perspectives would be most appropriate. Social-learning theories could be used to explain how he came to associate knives, violence, and cutting with sexual pleasure.

The psychotic-disorder approach, while fascinating, explains very little of the criminality present in modern society. This is not only true for crime in general, but for violent crime as well. For example, Holmes and De Burger have identified four types of serial murders:[51]

1. **Visionary serial murderer**—Homicides are committed in response to delusional voices or vision.

2. **Mission-oriented serial murderer**—homicides are committed because of a decision to rid the world of a certain category of people.

3. **Hedonistic serial murderer**—homicides are committed for pleasure or thrill-seeking.

4. **Power/control-oriented serial murderer**—homicides are committed for satisfaction derived out of having life-or-death control over the victim.

Among these four types, only the visionary type is linked to psychoses, while the other three are attributed to personality disorders.

At the moment, just how much crime is explicable in terms of the personality-disorder approach is not clear. Researchers estimate that over one-fourth of the felons in our prisons may suffer from antisocial-personality disorders.[52] An equal or even greater number may be free in our society. Even if we use the most conservative estimate, this type of disorder undoubtedly accounts for much crime in the United States. For this reason, along with the desire to avoid the technical complexities of psychological theories, we have chosen to further elaborate on sociopathy in the next chapter, which deals with the psychological perspective on crime.

Glossary ·

Antisocial-Personality Criminal   One who commits crimes for instrumental reasons or emotive reasons, lacks conscience, is self-aggrandizing, is intolerant of rules, and seeks immediate gratification while avoiding responsibility.

Brief Reactive Psychosis   A type of psychosis in which the psychotic episode usually lasts no more than a month though no less than a few hours.

Delusional (Paranoid) Disorders   A type of psychosis in which the delusions incurred have a theme that does not produce readily identifiable odd or bizarre behavior.

Diathesis-Stress Model   Suggests that mental illness results from the combined effects of a biological predisposition or tendency toward a given disorder and environmental stress. That is, severe stress acts to trigger an illness to which the individual was vulnerable. Neither the biological predisposition nor stress alone, however, would have caused the mental disorder.

Diminished Capacity A legal term implying a lower or lowered level of mental sophistication.

Double-Bind A situation in which a person receives contradictory imperatives or implicit commands from parental figures or significant others in authority roles. Victims of double-bind situations cannot "do right" because they have received two commands that contradict one another—to obey one imperative is to violate the other. Thus, victims of such a situation suffer immense guilt and dissatisfaction with themselves.

Erotomanic Delusions Sexual fantasies that are focused on some sort of idealized notion of romantic love.

Functional Mental Disorders Types of mental illnesses, primarily psychotic disorders and abnormal personality patterns, for which there are no clearly identifiable organic causes.

Grandiose Delusional Disorder Occurs when a person is convinced that he or she is actually a famous person, or possesses some great talent or invention that he or she in fact does not possess.

Hedonistic Serial Murderer One who commits homicides for pleasure or thrill-seeking.

Mens Rea Refers to criminal intent or "guilty mind" and is a necessary element of any crime.

Mission-Oriented Serial Murderer One who commits homicides because of a decision to rid the world of a certain category of people.

Neurotransmitters A variety of chemicals that rely messages between neurons.

Paranoid Schizophrenia A type of psychosis characterized by unfocused anger and violence.

Persecutory Delusions A type of psychosis characterized by suspicious and fearful thoughts, generally including some type of plot or conspiracy that in fact is nonexistent.

Power/Control-Oriented Murderer One who commits homicides for satisfaction derived out of having life-or-death control over the victim.

Psychosis A type of mental disorder that involves delusions and hallucinations affecting the display of emotion and the content of thought. They are generally considered the most serious major category of mental disorder because their victims lose contact with reality.

Psychotic Criminal One who commits crimes in response to delusions and/or hallucinations that result from a functional psychotic disorder.

Synapse The electrochemical junction of two nerve endings through which neurons pass chemical substances.

Visionary Serial Murderer One who commits homicides in response to delusional voices or visions.

■ Notes

1. World Health Organization, *Mental Disorders: Glossary and Guide to Their Classification in Accordance with the Ninth Revision of the International Classification of Diseases* (Geneva, Switzerland: World Health Organization, 1978); Commission on Professional and Hospital Activities, *International Classification of Diseases*, 9th rev., Clinical Modification (ICDM-9-CM) (Ann Arbor, MI: Professional and Hospital Activities, 1978); Timothy Plax, "Mental Illness," in Melvin DeFleur, *Social Problems in American Society*, (Boston, MA: Houghton-Mifflin, 1983), pp. 124–127; Donald J. Shoemaker, *Theories of Delinquency*, 2nd ed. (New York: Oxford University Press, 1990), p. 50; George Vold and Thomas J. Bernard, *Theoretical Criminology*, 3rd ed. (New York: Oxford University Press, 1990), pp. 108–111.

2. George Herbert Mead, *George Herbert Mead on Social Psychology: Selected Papers*, edited by Anselm Strauss (Chicago: University of Chicago Press, 1956), p. 167.

3. Robert J. Menzies and Christopher D. Webster, "Mental Disorder and Violent Crime" in Neil A. Weiner and Marvin E. Wolfgang *Pathways to Criminal Violence* (Newbury Park, CA: Sage Publications, 1989).

4. George Rush, *The Dictionary of Criminal Justice* (Guilford, CT: Dushkin, 1986), pp. 120.

5. Ronald Markman and Dominick Bosco, *Alone with The Devil: Famous Cases of a Courtroom Psychiatrist* (New York: Doubleday, 1989), pp. 32–33.

6. Joseph W. Eaton, "The Assessment of Mental Health," *The Journal of Psychiatry* 108 (1951): pp. 83–84.

7. Markman and Bosco, *Alone with The Devil: Famous Cases of a Courtroom Psychiatrist*, pp. 28–29.

8. Ibid, pp. 100–104.

9. Martin Hoffman, "Psychiatry, Nature and Science," *The American Journal of Psychiatry* 117 (1960): pp. 207–208.

10. R. D. Laing, *The Divided Self* (Baltimore, MD: Penguin Books, Inc., 1965), p. 36.

11. Hoffman, "Psychiatry, Nature and Science," pp. 207–208.

12. K. A. Menninger, *The Human Mind* (New York: Knopf, 1937), p. 1; F. C. Redlich, "The Concept of Normality," *American Journal of Psychotherapy* 6 (1952):p. 533; G. H. Preston, *The Substance of Mental Health* (New York: Farrar and Rinehart, 1943), p. 112.

13. David J. Rothman, *The Discovery of the Asylum* (Boston: Little, Brown and Co., 1971) pp. 122–136; Elliott P. Currie, "Crimes without Criminals: Witchcraft and Its Control in Renaissance Europe," *Law and Society Review* 3 (1968):pp. 7–32.

14. Peter Conrad and Joseph W. Schneider, *Deviance and Medicalization: From Badness to Sickness* (St. Louis, MO: C. V. Mosby Company, 1980.)

15. Thomas J. Scheff, *Being Mentally Ill* (Chicago: Aldine Publishing, 1966), pp. 7–12.

16. L. Bellak, *Dementia Praecox: The Past Decade's Work and Present Status: A Review and Evaluation* (New York: Grune and Stratton, 1948); D. D. Jackson, *The Etiology of Schizophrenia* (New York: Basic Books, 1960);

N. D. C. Lewis, "Research in Dementia Praecox," The National Committee for Mental Hygiene, New York, 1936).

17. James Fadiman and Donald Kewman, *Exploring Madness: Experience, Theory, and Research* (Monterey, CA: Brooks/Cole, 1973).

18. Ibid.

19. Ibid.

20. Ibid.

21. David F. Wrench, *Psychology: A Social Approach* (New York: McGraw-Hill, 1969), p. 198.

22. Timothy Plax, "Mental Illness" in Melvin DeFleur, *Social Problems in American Society* (Boston: Houghton-Mifflin, 1983), pp. 133.

23. American Psychiatric Association, *Diagnostic and Statistical Manual of Mental Disorders*, 3d ed, rev. (Washington, DC: American Psychiatric Association, 1987), pp. 187–198.

24. American Psychiatric Association, *Diagnostic and Statistical Manual of Mental Disorders*, pp. 187–198; J. Lanzkron, "Murder and Insanity: A Survey," *American Journal of Psychiatry* 119 (1963): pp. 754–758.

25. Seymour Wishman, *Confessions of a Criminal Lawyer* (New York: Penguin Books, 1981.)

26. American Psychiatric Association, *Diagnostic and Statistical Manual for Mental Disorders*, pp. 199–200. For delusional disorders as a special risk, see H. Hafner and W. Boker, *Crimes of Violence by Mentally Abnormal Offenders: A Psychiatric and Epidemiological Study in the Federal German Republic* (Cambridge, England: Cambridge University Press, 1982), pp. 27–28.

27. Ibid., pp. 199.

28. Lincoln Caplan, *The Insanity Defense and the Trial of John W. Hinckley, Jr.* (New York: Dell Publishing Company, 1987), pp. 18–21.

29. Markman and Bosco, *Alone with The Devil: Famous Cases of a Courtroom Psychiatrist*, pp. 19–48.

30. American Psychiatric Association, *Diagnostic and Statistical Manual of Mental Disorders*, pp. 199–200.

31. Ibid., pp. 205–207.

32. Ibid., pp. 199-200, 205-207.

33. George E. Rush, *The Dictionary of Criminal Justice*, 2 ed. (Guilford, CT: Dushkin Publishing Group, 1986), p. 27.

34. Ibid., p. 210.

35. Flora R. Schreiber, *The Shoemaker.* (New York: Simon & Schuster, 1984), p. 17

36. Ibid.

37. Ibid.

38. Ibid.

39. Ibid.

40. Ibid.

41. Ibid.

42. Ibid.

43. Ibid.

44. R. D. Laing and A. Esterson, *Sanity, Madness and the Family*, (New York: Penguin Books, 1964.)

45. Flora R. Schreiber, *The Shoemaker.*

46. Ibid.

47. Ibid.

48. Ibid.

49. Ibid.

50. M. A. Straus, J. R. Gelles, and S. K. Steinmetz, *Behind Closed Doors: Violence in the American Family* (Garden City, NY: Anchor/Doubleday, 1980); C. George and M. Main, "Social Interactions of Young Abused Children: Approach, Avoidance and Aggression," *Child Development* 50 (1979): pp. 306–318; J. Q. Wilson and R. J. Herrnstein, *Crime and Human Nature* (New York: Simon & Schuster/Touchstone, 1985), pp. 253–263.

51. Ronald M. Holmes and James De Burger, *Serial Murder* (Newbury Park, CA: SAGE Publications, 1988), pp. 55–60.

52. "The Antisocial Personality, Part I," *Harvard Medical School Mental Health Letter* 2, no. 1 (1985): p. 2.

■ Suggested Readings

Ronald M. Holmes and James De Burger, *Serial Murder* (Newbury Park, CA: SAGE Publications, 1988).

James Fadiman and Donald Kewman, *Exploring Madness: Experience, Theory, and Research* (Monterey, CA: Brooks/Cole, 1973).

John C. Goodwin, *Insanity and the Criminal* (New York: George H. Doran Company, 1924).

R. D. Laing and A. Esterson, *Sanity, Madness, and the Family* (New York: Penguin Books, 1964).

Flora R. Schreiber, *The Shoemaker* (New York: Simon & Schuster, 1984).

Terence P. Thornberry and Joseph E. Jacoby, *The Criminally Insane* (Chicago: The University of Chicago Press, 1979).

■ Suggested Books for Additional Application

Ronald Markman and Dominick Bosco, *Alone with The Devil: Famous Cases of a Courtroom Psychiatrist* (New York: Doubleday, 1989.

(L. D. Klausner, *Son of Sam* (New York: McGraw-Hill, 1981).

Lincoln Caplan, *The Insanity Defense and the Trial of John W. Hinckley, Jr.* (New York: Dell Publishing Company, 1987).

CHAPTER **6**

Psychological Perspective

Overview of Psychological Perspective

Convicted serial killer Ted Bundy erupts at the judge after receiving the death penalty for the murders of two Florida State women students in 1978.

As mentioned in earlier chapters, the psychological perspective overlaps with both the biological and psychiatric perspectives. The overlap results from the fact that all three perspectives see the causes of criminal behavior as arising from within the individual. It therefore follows, according to these perspectives, that individual criminals must somehow be different from noncriminals. But while the biological perspective focuses on physical (organic) differences and the psychiatric perspective on distinctive mental processes, the psychological perspective primarily focuses on differences in psychological functioning and personality traits as the causes of criminal behavior. Exhibit 6.1 gives the common assumptions of this perspective.

Although there are many types of psychological disturbances (e.g., mood disorders, anxiety disorders, etc.), sexual sadism and antisocial-personality disorder are of the most direct relevance to criminology. Both of these disorders are implicated in many crimes of violence such as murder and sexual assaults. The disorder of **sexual sadism** includes recurrent and extreme desires in which the psychological or physical suffering of the victim is the focus of sexual arousal. This particular disorder is associated primarily with serial killers and rapists. It must be noted, however, that fewer than 10 percent of rapists have this mental disorder.[1]

The term **personality** is usually used to describe the collective and/or most prominent psycho-behavioral trait(s) exhibited by individuals. **Personality traits** are defined as the permanent patterns developed by individuals that guide how they perceive, relate, and think about themselves and their environment.[2] For example, a person who is shy, quiet and nonengaging among strangers would usually be described as having an introverted personality. A person who

Exhibit 6.1

Psychological perspective

Common Assumptions

1. There are a series of necessary stages in the mental and sexual development of humans.

2. Abnormal mental and sexual development results in personality disorders and psychological disturbances, which usually begin in early childhood and become a characteristic feature of the individual.

3. These mental disorders and disturbances result from early experiences and may lead to criminality.

4. As these disturbances and disorders reside within the individual, it is this level of analysis that must be addressed to understand and deter criminal behavior.

Source: Sigmund Freud, "The Ego and the Id" in *The Standard Edition of the Complete Psychological Works of Sigmund Freud,* trans. James Strachey (London: The Hogarth Press and The Institute of Psycho-Analysis, 1961), pp. 12–47; Donald J. Shoemaker, *Theories of Delinquency,* (New York: Oxford University Press, 1984), pp. 41–42, 50; George B. Vold and Thomas J. Bernard, *Theoretical Criminology,* 3 ed. (New York: Oxford University Press, 1986), pp. 108–111.

is outgoing, talkative, and secure among strangers is usually described as having an extroverted personality.

Inherent in the psychological perspective is the assumption that humans develop various psychological disturbances and different types of personalities (e.g., introverted, extroverted, etc.) for various reasons. It is believed that psychological disturbances usually result from experiences in early life. Some personality traits and disorders are thought to predispose the individual to crime while others generally do not.

Much of psychology's focus is on mental development. It is believed that as children grow into adulthood they pass through a series of stages in which they acquire the ability to solve problems and make moral choices. Problems at any of these stages of development are seen by many as contributing to both adolescent and adult criminality.

Stages of Moral Development

Much of the work that has been done in the area of personality development is based on the work of Freud and involves what is usually referred to as the "moral" development of the "self." The concept of **self** can be thought of as the mental or psychic processes (the mind) underlying personality characteristics and traits, and their development. In the context of personality development, individual morality can be thought of as the values and norms (e.g., sincerity, honesty, etc.) held by the individual in relation to those held by the society in which she or he lives.

From a Freudian approach, the development of the self is viewed as a struggle between the "good" conscience (superego) and the "bad" or "evil" animal within (id).[3] The logical mind (ego) is crucial because it acts as a referee in this conflict. (These Freudian terms will be discussed more fully later in this chapter, in the section on "The Freudian Approach to Psyche and Behavior.") As the conscience becomes more and more developed, it is presumed to become more and more moral, thus becoming increasingly better equipped to control the impulses of the human animal. Erik Erikson, a student of Freud, proposed a number of stages in ego development, beginning with infancy and ending with old age, at each of which the ego faces a crisis. If the crisis is not successfully overcome, it can lead to personality disorders.[4]

The works of Jean Piaget and Charles Horton Cooley focus on the cognitive aspects of personality development. Piaget proposed that children go through a series of developmental stages through which they eventually become less and less egocentric. That is, each stage is accompanied by a greater sensitivity to the viewpoints of others.[5] **Responsible actions**—those that meet a person's needs without interfering with the needs of others—therefore increase along with cognitive development. The implication of this theory would be that the higher the degree of cognitive development there is, the less the likelihood of criminality.

Cooley developed the concept of the *looking-glass self*, meaning we learn to see ourselves on the basis of the reactions of others to us. Our concept of who and what we are in a moral, mental, physical and emotional sense is thus based on the feedback we receive from the others.[6] Cooley's work thus bridges the gap between psychological theories that focus on the individual and more sociological ideas that emphasize the relationship between the individual and the society.

Kohlberg built on Piaget's ideas, predicting six stages of moral development. The first two—the "punishment and obedience orientation" stage and the "hedonistic orientation" stage—suggest that children comply with authority initially out of fear and then out of hopes of being rewarded. In these early stages of development children respond to cultural labels of good and bad, and evaluate the morality of actions on the basis of the expected consequences or perceived power of the parent (rule-giver). The child defines "right" behavior as that which satisfies his or her own felt-needs (hedonistic), and appropriate behavior on the basis of the consequences associated with the behavior.[7]

Kohlberg's second two stages, the "interpersonal concordance" stage and the "law and order orientation" stage, usually occur during adolescence. During these stages, the maintenance of family and societal expectations are seen as valuable in and of themselves. Because the social order becomes a source of identity during these stages, conformity and loyalty to the social order is viewed as desirable. Acts that help or please others are defined as "moral" by people operating at this level of development. During these stages, an understanding of the logic and norms behind "good" and "bad" behavior develops, and "morality" consists of doing one's duty.[8]

According to Kohlberg the last two stages of development are the "social contract, legalistic orientation" stage, and the "orientation to universal ethical principles" stage. These stages of development occur around the time of early adulthood. The morality of an action is defined in more universal terms here, as well as on the basis of how well it reflects general social rules and values. **Abstract thought processes** in which symbols are used to generalize basic principles from one situation to another are required to achieve these stages. Kohlberg proposes that regression from, or fixation at, any stage of development is possible, either of which can result in personality problems.[9]

Adult-Child Issues in Personality Development

There are a number of social factors that are widely accepted as intervening in and/or inhibiting personality development. Many personality disorders are thought to be the result of growing up in a dysfunctional or unhealthy family. Therefore there has been much interest in the effects of various sorts of relationships between adults and children within households.[10] Although there is a continuum of dysfunctional families, from mildly dysfunctional to extremely dysfunctional, depending on the severity and frequency of the problems, we are going to discuss only the more extreme types here. Dysfunctions are usually parental behaviors that disrupt the family's inner processes and become the center of activity and thought for family members.

Seriously dysfunctional families generally contain one or more of the following characteristics: physical abuse/neglect, emotional abuse/neglect, sexual abuse, double binds (situations in which all choices given are negative ones), inability to have fun, demands of perfectionism, enmeshment (blurring of identities), or high threshold for inappropriate behavior/pain.[11] Generally one or both parents are alcoholic, physically abusive to the children and/or wife, or suffer from some type of serious mental disorder (e.g., schizophrenia).[12] Because there are interdependent behavior patterns within families, dysfunctional family members can act as contagions.[13] That is, the traits and behaviors of disturbed parents can spread to the children, and/or the children may develop personality disorders as a result of their attempts to deal with their disturbed parents or other family members. For example, in the case of a person exhibiting a schizotypal type personality and having been reared by schizophrenic parents, the parents' schizophrenia would be considered as a contagion. The traits and attributes of schizophrenia in this case would be viewed as a disease spreading from adult parents to their children through association. Obviously, individuals raised in dysfunctional families are at risk of developing some type of personality disorder.[14]

Substance Abuse and Co-Dependency

Numerous theories pertain directly to the influences of substance abuse on personality development. The majority of these theories focus on the intervening and/or inhibiting effects the substances have on the personality development of the abuser, but some focus on the more indirect effects, such as co-dependency. Theories that focus on the direct effects have suggested, among other things, that substance abuse causes (1) development lags resulting in immaturity, (2) personality disorganization, and/or (3) retardation of ego development.[15] Each of these problems can be expected to result in faulty reasoning processes that may lead to criminal acts.

Children and adults raised in alcoholic families have a high risk of developing a **co-dependent** personality,[16] meaning a person who permits another person's behavior to affect him or her to the extent that much time and effort is consumed with attempts to control this other person's behavior.[17] Generally speaking, a co-dependent person can be thought of as a "caretaker" for the dysfunctional person. Mild forms of co-dependency are thought to be very common in our society but severe forms render individuals incapable of functioning properly in the real world.

According to Gold's cognitive-control theory, alcohol and drug usage confirms the substance abuser's belief that she or he is unable to function on her or his own.[18] Although substance abusers can be thought of as co-dependent (either on substances or on other people), the co-dependent is generally identified as the person upon which the substance abuser relies. The co-dependent enables the abuser to continue his or her substance abuse in many ways—making excuses for the abuser, assuming responsibility for the abuser's acts and omissions, and feeling guilty each time the abuser makes a mistake. The co-dependent's "enabling" behavior is not intended to help the substance abuser continue his or her abuse, but in reality it has just this effect. Persons with co-dependent behavior patterns are likely to become spouses or "significant others" of alcoholics, drug abusers, or other types of dependent people. As such, many view them as victims of their co-dependent personality.[19] Self-help groups such as Al-Anon and Families Anonymous are specifically designed to help people with this type of personality problem.[20]

Child Abuse

It is widely suspected that some victims of child abuse are at risk of becoming child abusers.[21] That is, they develop personalities that encourage them to become child abusers themselves. Some attribute this to social learning (see Chapter 7), while others believe that it results from retarded moral development resulting in faulty thought processes and an inability to generalize learning across situations.

Freudian Approach to Psyche and Behavior

Although Freud was a physician by training, he operated as a scientist attempting to explain the irrational elements of human behavior in a rational way. Although he developed a general theory of the psyche, his work focused on the causes of abnormal behavior and was conducted largely with upper-class female patients suffering nervous disorders.[22] The term *psyche*, a synonym for the human "mind," is defined in psychology as the means by which human beings adjust their behavior and needs to the demands of their environments.[23] The Freudian approach to the psyche (see Exhibit 6.2) is based on the assumption that the human mind is composed of conscious and unconscious components. Freud's hypothetical unconscious allows for an understanding of the pathological processes in mental life.

Individual mental processes and personality traits are the unique result of interactions among three components of the psyche: the id, the ego, and the superego.[24] The **id** contains the inner world of the individual's inborn instincts and reflexes, as well as her or his passions. It is the source of animal desire and creativity. The id remains permanently in the unconscious, where it en-

Exhibit 6.2

Freudian approach to psyche and behavior

Restrictive Assumptions

1. The human psyche has two major aspects—the conscious and the unconscious.

2. The human psyche is composed of three main parts—the id, ego, and superego—which overlap the conscious and unconscious.

3. In the course of a person learning to live in society, conflicts between the individual's basic animal desires (the id) and society's rules are inevitable.

4. Many of these conflicts are so traumatic that the individual buries them in the unconscious part of the psyche.

5. Such repressed psychic material can cause an individual to become fixated at a less than fully socialized level of development.

6. Such a fixation may result in abnormal, and even criminal, patterns of perception and behavior.

Source: Sigmund Freud, "The Ego and the Id," *The Standard Edition of the Complete Psychological Works of Sigmund Freud*, trans. James Strachey (London: The Hogarth Press and the Institute of Psycho-Analysis, 1961); Calvin S. Hall, *A Primer of Freudian Psychology* (New York: The World Publishing Company, 1954).

courages the immediate release of energy or tension brought on by either internal or external stimulation. The **ego** represents the real world of the individual's conscious reason and common sense. It is oriented to practical efficiency and goal-oriented behavior. The ego is thought of as mediating between the id and the superego as the individual deals with the external world. The **superego** contains the inner world of the individual's ideal expectations and conscience. It is the moral part of the psyche, and it strives for ethical perfection. The superego contains the conceptions of what the individual considers to be morally good, as well as what others view as morally good. It is heavily influenced by inputs from society that are transmitted to the person by significant others.

In well-adjusted people, the ego is in command of the psyche, controlling the id and the superego, and interacting with the external world in the interests of the individual. The superego develops as individuals learn social norms through rewards and punishments received early in life. The ego mediates the conflicts that arise between the instinctual drives generated by the id and the controlling ideals of the superego and acts to suppress them when necessary. If the ego allows the id, superego, or external world too much power, maladjustments in the psyche will occur.[25]

Sigmund Freud (1856-1939)

Freudian Theory of Criminality

Even though Freud himself did not develop a specific theory of criminal behavior, one has been developed by others based on his view of the psyche and deviant behavior and is therefore referred to as a Freudian theory (see Exhibit 6.3). Crime is but one form of deviance. Freud proposed that much deviance resulted from an excessive sense of guilt as a result of an overdeveloped superego. Persons with overdeveloped superegos feel guilty for no reason and wish to be punished in order to relieve the guilt. Early childhood experiences and emotions that are repressed in the subconscious produce this feeling of

---

Restrictive Assumptions

1. The human psyche consists of an id, ego, and superego.

2. Perception and behavior are determined by the way in which these three components interact with one another.

3. The ego has the most direct control over behavior.

4. Excessive guilt may be generated by an overdeveloped superego but is stored in the ego.

5. Persons suffering from such an excess of guilt will desire to be punished.

6. Crimes are a method of obtaining such desired punishment and relieving guilt.

Exhibit 6.3

Freudian theory of criminality

Source: Sigmund Freud, "The Ego and the Id," *The Standard Edition of the Complete Psychological Works of Sigmund Freud,* trans. James Strachey (London: The Hogarth Press and the Institute of Psycho-Analysis, 1961).

guilt, which later rises to disturb the conscious mind. According to this theory, such people commit crimes in order to assure punishment and thus relieve guilt. In effect, by committing a crime the person provides something real to which guilt can be attached. The outcome of an excessive sense of guilt, then, is the commission of crimes.[26] According to this view, crime is not the result of a criminal personality but rather of a poorly integrated psyche.

Neo-Freudian Theory of Criminality

Because Freud's primary interest was with the neurotic personality rather than the criminal, many differing interpretations of his work have been used to apply it to the problem of crime. The fundamental distinction between Freud's original work and that of his later followers lies in the role assigned to the id, supergo, and the ego. Whereas Freud theorized that the desire for punishment was the result of an overly powerful superego, the neo-Freudians believed that crime results from a too-powerful id (see Exhibit 6.4).

August Aichorn is probably the best known of the neo-Freudians in the field of criminology. Aichorn felt that three predisposing traits had to be present before criminality would emerge as a lifestyle: (1) the desire for immediate gratification, (2) the valuation of one's personal desires over the ability to have good relationships with others, and (3) a lack of guilt over one's actions. Aichorn's view assumes that the ego is too weak to control the powerful id in criminals.[27]

Even more recent psychological theories agree, picturing the criminal as an id-dominated personality who is not able (or willing) to control impulsive, pleasure-seeking urges. This view asserts that damage to the ego early in life

Exhibit 6.4
. . . .

Neo-Freudian theory of criminality

Specific Assumptions

1. The human psyche consists of an id, ego, and superego.

2. Perception and behavior are determined by the way in which these three components interact with one another.

3. The ego has the most direct control over behavior.

4. Persons with damaged or weak egos may become so dominated by the id that they cannot conform to social rules and will commit crimes.

5. Crime may provide a method of attaining self-esteem and other needs that cannot otherwise be readily met.

6. Crime allows failure to be rationalized as being caused by the acts of the mainstream society.

Source: **August Aichorn,** *Wayward Youth* (New York: Viking Press, 1935); Fritz Redl and Hans Toch, "The Psychoanalytical Perspective" in Hans Toch (ed.), *Psychology of Crime and Criminal Justice* (New York: Holt Rinehart and Winston, 1979); David Agrahamson, *Crime and the Human Mind* (New York: Columbia University Press, 1944); Seymour Halleck, *Psychiatry and the Dilemmas of Crime* (Berkely, CA: University of California Press, 1971).

results in the id becoming overly dominant and controlling the individual's behavior. Persons with id-dominated personalities are unable to live in conventional society because they are incapable of comprehending the impact of their actions on others.[28] This view of the criminal is very close to that of the personality-disorders approach (discussed next) but is less closely bound to the specific diagnostic criteria of that approach.

Still others within this approach perceive criminality as a means of coping with the feelings of oppression and helplessness that characterize life in modern societies. Committing crimes, according to Seymour Halleck, allows people to experience autonomy in a way that is forbidden by conventional society. Crime encourages such individuals to use their abilities and creativity to achieve personal rewards, while simultaneously allowing them to excuse their failures as due to interference from the mainstream society.[29]

Personality-Disorders Approach

Personality disorders are constellations of enduring, maladaptive, and rigid personality traits that impair functioning in a variety of social contexts and are injurious to the sufferer and/or others. Persons with such disorders are sane in a legal sense but chronically exhibit problematic behaviors (see Exhibit 6.5). Some of the personality disorders most clearly associated with criminal behavior are paranoid, schizotypal, antisocial, and borderline personality disorders.[30]

Paranoid-personality disorders cause an overriding, but unfounded, tendency to interpret the actions of others as threatening to one's self. Persons suffering from this disorder are referred to as *paranoiacs*. Some of the personality traits associated with paranoid-pesonality disorders are pathological jealousy, quick anger reactions, and the bearing of grudges.[31] Unlike the psychotic, the paranoiac perceives reality correctly but assigns erroneous meanings to these perceptions. Paranoiacs constantly detect references to themselves in events that are, in fact, completely unrelated to them.[32] An example of the possible criminal effect of a paranoid-personality disorder can be seen in cases

Exhibit 6.5

Personality disorders approach

Restrictive Assumptions

1. Personality disorders are less severe than psychotic disorders— they do not interfere with an individual's ability to comprehend reality.

2. These disorders may result from genetic, environmental, or other sources.

3. Personality disorders may result in patterns of perception and behavior that are criminogenic.

Source: American Psychiatric Association, *Diagnostic and Statistical Manual of Mental Disorders* - 3d ed. (Washington, D.C.: American Psychiatric Association, 1987).

where the husband is under the paranoid belief that his wife is unfaithful to him and, as a result of this pathological jealously, assaults or kills her.[33]

Both paranoid and schizotypal personality disorders are thought to be related to schizophrenia, even though they are not psychoses. The schizotypal personality is characterized by listlessness, emotional numbness, anxiety when strangers are present, an unkempt appearance, and peculiar mannerisms. These individuals are socially isolated, have difficulty interacting with others, and may interpret some situations in a paranoid manner. This disorder is felt to be the most incapacitating of the personality disorders and blends into schizophrenia in some people.[34]

Antisocial-personality disorder is also referred to as *psychopathy* or *sociopathy*. This disorder is characterized by a marked lack of ethical or moral development. The sociopath displays a pattern of aggressive, irresponsible, and often clearly antisocial behavior. Antisocial personalities are extremely skilled manipulators of others, including mental health professionals. They usually appear to be very charming, aggressive, and carefree individuals when first encountered. Many have very high IQs. However, they are unable to tolerate constraints of any kind and do not usually plan their actions in advance. Also, antisocial personalities expect to be rewarded for meeting their most mundane obligations but will not tolerate criticism of their antisocial behavior. They firmly believe that others see the world as they do and act differently (more responsibly or morally) only because they are afraid to act on their impulses. Thus, they convince themselves that they are superior to those they victimize.

Persons with this disorder have very underdeveloped consciences and experience little or no remorse, guilt, or anxiety over their actions. Indeed, they appear incapable of experiencing any truly deep emotions. They can be very angry at a person one day and treat him or her as a dear friend the next if they can gain from such behavior. It is also suspected that antisocial personalities do not learn as rapidly from punishment as do normal people. Many serial killers, such as Theodore Bundy, are thought to have antisocial-personality disorder.[35] It is estimated that approximately 3 to 5 percent of American males and just under 1 percent of American females suffer from it. The first symptoms of the disorder usually occur prior to age fifteen. Some researchers believe that this, and similar, personality disorders may be inherited.[36]

Antisocial-personality disorder is associated with frequent and serious stealing, vandalism, and physical cruelty in childhood and adolescence. In adults, it is often characterized by a wide variety of behaviors, including violence such as spouse- or child-battering and/or confidence games ranging from investment fraud to marriage-for-swindle.[37]

It should also be noted that the effects of long-term substance abuse often bear a close resemblance to antisocial personality. However, such secondary antisocial personalities can be distinguished from primary, or true, antisocial personalities by the presence of anxiety or guilt in the secondary group. Only clinical professionals with much experience in dealing with antisocial personalities can make such a distinction, however. This is due to the highly manipulative behavior evidenced by all antisocial personalities.[38]

Personality traits associated with *borderline personality disorder* include problems with self-identity, interpersonal relationships, dramatic shifts in mood, and inappropriately intense anger that may be uncontrollable. Such people have relationships with others that tend to be very intense but unstable and shallow. They tend to see people and events as either completely good or entirely bad. Like antisocial personalities, borderline personalities are very impulsive. However, they are less skilled at manipulating others than are antisocial personalities. Borderline personalities are also more likely to engage in self-destructive behavior, such as substance abuse and suicide, than are antisocial personalities. In addition, borderline personalities, especially if they use mind-altering substances, are prone to brief episodes of psychosis. This disorder is suspected to be more common among women than among men. It is estimated that between 3 and 5 percent of the population suffers from it.[39]

The Case of Kenneth Bianchi and Angelo Buono · · · · · · · · · · · · · · · · ·

Angelo, "The Buzzard," Buono and his cousin, Kenneth Bianchi, came to be known as the "Hillside Stranglers" because most of the bodies of their fourteen victims were found on hillsides, in and around Los Angeles, California. Almost all of the nude victims had been bound or handcuffed, raped, and strangled to death. Exhibit 6.6 lists the details of these crimes.

Although they began in the Los Angeles area, when Bianchi moved to Bellingham, Washington, he continued to commit rape-murders on his own.

All of the victims were walking alone between eleven o'clock at night and two in the morning. In many of the murders, the offenders pretended to be plainclothes police officers in an unmarked car. They would ask the victim to step over to their car, request identification, and then "arrest" (in fact, kidnap) her. Other victims were picked up without the police ruse. Weckler was invited to a party, King was offered a ride home, and Hudspeth was given information about a possible job. All of these murders were premeditated. Buono and Bianchi brought cord along to strangle the victims and plastic bags to put everything in so they would not leave any incriminating evidence behind.[41]

The *precipitating factor* in this case was that Angelo Buono wanted some prostitutes to work for him and Bianchi so that he could earn some extra money for his child-support payments. In 1977 Buono and Bianchi loaned Sabra Hannan, a sixteen-year-old runaway from Phoenix, Arizona, some money, knowing that she would be unable to repay the loan. They then forced her into prostitution to repay it. When she initially tried to escape from them, they beat her and told her that they would kill her if she tried another escape. Buono and Bianchi recruited a second girl to prostitute for them by telling Hannan that she could go free if she found another girl for them. Hannan found Rebekah Gay Spears, a fifteen-year-old runaway also from Phoenix, and convinced her to live with Buono. Buono frequently and brutally sodomized Spears.[42]

In August of 1977 Buono arranged with the owner of an outcall prostitution service called Foxy Ladies to send Hannan and Spears out on calls for them. Foxy Ladies would get 15 percent of what the girls made. On one call for the Foxy Ladies, Spears was sent over to the home of an attorney. Spears told the attorney about being held prisoner in Buono's house, the beatings, the relentless sodomy, and the threats of being mutilated and/or killed if she

> **Serial Murder**
> The act(s) of killing two or more individuals in a series of homicide episodes that occur over a period of time and are usually committed in different locations.[40]

Exhibit 6.6
. . . .

Buono and Bianchi's murder
victims

1. *Yolanda Washington*: age unknown, part-time prostitute; raped and murdered by strangulation; body found in Hollywood on October 17, 1977.

2. *Judith Ann Miller*: age 15, part-time prostitute; raped and murdered by strangulation; body found in the area of Terrace and La Crescenta on October 31, 1977.

3. *Lissa Teresa Kastin*: age 21, dancer, neither a prostitute nor a drug user; raped and murdered by strangulation; body found in Glendale on November 6, 1977.

4. *Jill Barcomb*: age 18, prostitute; raped and murdered by strangulation; body found in Hollywood on November 10, 1977.

5. *Kathleen Robinson*: age 17, prostitute; raped and murdered by strangulation; body found in Hollywood on November 17, 1977.

6. *Kristina Weckler*: age 20, art student; raped and murdered by gassing to death; body found in Glendale on November 20, 1977.

7. *Sonja Johnson*: age 14, parochial-school student; raped and murdered by strangulation: body found on November 20, 1977.

8. *Dollie Cepeda*: age 12, parochial-school student; raped and murdered by strangulation; body found, along with Johnson's, on November 20, 1977.

9. *Jane King*: age 28, actress and part-time model; raped and murdered by strangulation; body found on November 23, 1977.

10. *Lauren Wagner*: age 18, business-school student; raped and murdered by strangulation; body found in November 1977.

11. *Kimberly Diane Martin*: age 17, prostitute; raped and murdered by strangulation; body found mid-December, 1977.

12. *Cindy Lee Hudspeth*: age 20, raped and murdered by strangulation; body found in Glendale on February 17, 1978.

13. *Diane Wilder*: age 27, Western Washington University student; raped and murdered by strangulation: body found in Bellingham, Washington on January 12, 1979.

14. *Karen Mandic*: age 22, Western Washington University student; raped and murdered by strangulation; body found, along with Wilder's in Bellingham, Washington on January 12, 1979.

Source: Ted Schwarz, *The Hillside Strangler: A Murderer's Mind* (Signet, New York: Signet, 1981).

ran away. The attorney put Spears on a plane to Phoenix. Because of this incident, Buono tried to threaten and blackmail the attorney. The attorney sent a 300-pound bouncer friend of his named "Tiny" over to Buono's house. That was the last the attorney heard from Buono.[45]

Shortly after the attorney sent Spears back to Phoenix, Hannan escaped from Buono and Bianchi. They then found another girl to prostitute for them by the name of Jennifer Snider. Buono bought a so-called "trick list" (list of customers for prostitutes) containing 150 names at a cost of one dollar per name from Deborah Noble, an experienced prostitute. However, Buono did not know that there are two types of trick lists. An "outcall" list contains names of clients who want the prostitute to come to their house, apartment, or motel, but the clients on an "incall" list want to come to the prostitute's house, apartment, or motel. Buono had purchased an incall list. When Snider, his new prostitute, called the clients, they wanted to come to her. Since she lived at Buono's house, the list was useless.[46]

Buono became furious, thinking Noble had deliberately cheated him on his purchase of the trick list. This incident, coupled with the incident of the attorney helping Spears escape, enraged Buono to the point that he became intent on raping and murdering a prostitute in revenge. Bianchi joined him in this plan. Bianchi initially proposed that they kill Snider because she would not let him sodomize her. Buono said they could not kill her because she was too closely linked to them. They then left Buono's house with the intention of finding, raping, and killing a prostitute.[47]

On their first attempt to rape and murder a prostitute, they picked up two teenage girls, had sex with them, but then threw them out of the car naked. On their next attempt they pretended to be plainclothes police officers, but the girl they approached was the daughter of Peter Lorre, a famous movie

> **Assault**
> The act of intentionally, knowingly, or recklessly causing physical injury to another person.[43]
>
> **Sodomy**
> Usually refers to acts of anal intercourse but may also refer to oral intercourse.[44]

Angelo Buono, one of the Hillside Stranglers, leaving the Criminal Courts Building in Los Angeles after pleading innocent to 10 counts of murder and a slate of sexual offenses.

Sexual Assault/Rape
The act of unlawful sexual intercourse with a female, using force or without legal or factual permission.[48]

Aggravated Sexual Assault
The act of causing serious physical injury, or attempting or threatening to kill a person during the commission of a sexual assault.[49]

actor, so they let her go unharmed also. Finally, they came across Yolanda Washington, a prostitute who was with Noble when she sold Buono the trick list. They were able to get Washington in their car by pretending to be plainclothes police officers. Once in the car, they handcuffed her, then Bianchi raped and strangled her. Thus Yolanda Washington became the first victim of the Hillside Stranglers.[50]

Washington's murder was reported on the back pages of a local newspaper. Disappointed, Buono and Bianchi decided that they would have to commit another murder in order to get the kind of publicity—and "respect" from prostitutes—that they wanted. They went on to kill thirteen more women before they were apprehended.[51]

The major *attracting factor* in this case was Buono's sexual sadism. By age fourteen, Buono had formed his concept of the function of women—they existed to be beaten, raped, and sodomized. He perceived his mother as something akin to a whore and regarded women in general as "stupid bitches." Buono had one son with his first wife, and four sons and one daughter with his second wife. His second wife, Mary Castillo, divorced him in 1964 for beating and sodomizing her. Buono had two more sons with Nanette Campina, a woman who lived with him for some time. By age thirty-five, he had eight children. From 1965 until he was apprehended for the Hillside Strangler Murders, Buono was routinely having sex with teenage girls as young as thirteen years old. Many of these teenage girls were friends of his sons.[52] An example of Buono's sexual sadism towards his homicide victims was the torture inflicted on one victim by administering electrical current to her hands and feet. Watching the victims suffer was sexually stimulating to Buono, which is the basis of his diagnosis as a sadist.[53]

Buono's sexual sadism did not end with the death of his victims. He and Bianchi left their first victim's body in front of the home of a woman whom Buono had dated a few times and had come to hate. This was Buono's way of letting her know that you do not drop Buono and get away with it. Buono expected that this would greatly affect this woman, but his plan failed because neither she nor the police ever made the association between the victim's body and Buono's broken relationship with the woman.[54]

Another *attracting factor* in this case was Bianchi's antisocial-personality disorder. As a chronic and habitual liar, Bianchi told his live-in girlfriend that he had cancer when he did not. He falsified another person's college diploma and used it to pass himself off as a psychologist. After his arrest for the Bellingham, Washington, murders of Wilder and Mandic, he even attempted to pass himself off as a multiple personality so that he would be found not guilty by reason of insanity. This ruse almost succeeded.[55]

Biological causes for Bianchi's criminality were ruled out when an electroencephalogram, skull series, echogram, and spinal tap by neurologists were all negative for any type of organic brain damage or tumor. An additional *attracting factor* was Bianchi's relationship with Buono, which was that of slave to master. Bianchi would do whatever Buono wanted. In many ways they had an understanding between them similar to that of an old married couple or two cell mates. In many ways Bianchi was Buono's "punk."[56]

There appear to be several minor *predisposing factors* in this case. Buono was forty-four years old in 1977 when he and Bianchi began killing women in Los Angeles. He owned and operated a small auto upholstery shop in his garage. He had had no formal religious instruction, and had quit public school at age sixteen without learning to read, write, or do arithmetic.[57] During adolescence, his hero was Carl Chessman, known as the "red light bandit," a man who had been arrested and convicted in California in 1948 for kidnapping and sexual assault. To commit his crimes, Chessman would place a red light on top of his car and pull up to couples parked in a lover's lane. This enabled him to convince the lovers that he was a policeman so that they would open their car windows or doors.[58] Another minor predisposing factor in Buono's case was his criminal record for minor offenses, which included several convictions for auto theft and a one-year suspended sentence for failure to provide child support.[59]

As with Buono, there are only minor predisposing factors for Bianchi. Bianchi was twenty-five years old when the murders began. He was born out of wedlock to a teenager who placed him in a foster home from which he was adopted before he was one year old. When he was thirteen, his adoptive father died.[60] One predisposing factor in Bianchi's case seems to be his adoptive mother's fear of the adoption authorities taking him away from her. She suffered from what might best be described as a severe anxiety complex about losing the baby that she had wanted so desperately since her marriage. By 1959 Mrs. Bianchi had become seriously disturbed for this reason. She translated her fear of losing Bianchi into a belief that he had various physical ailments. She constantly took him to doctors despite the fact that they were never able to find anything wrong with him. In 1959 the Rochester General Hospital staff felt Bianchi was completely normal for a child his age and they suggested that he and his mother see a psychiatrist. In 1962 Mrs. Bianchi was reported to the Rochester Society for the Prevention of Cruelty to Children, Inc. because of Bianchi's emotional state due to his adoptive mother's over-concern with his health. Even then she refused to see a psychiatrist for herself or Bianchi.[61]

Another predisposing factor in Bianchi's case was his teenage marriage. He had moved to Hollywood, California, from Rochester, New York, in 1975. Prior to leaving Rochester, he married a girl shortly after they graduated from high school in 1971. They were divorced after eight months of marriage. She had allegedly had affairs with other men while married to Bianchi. Bianchi felt he had been "dumped on" by his ex-wife.[62] This may have further predisposed him to violence against women.

Exhibit 6.7 summarizes the facts in the Buono and Bianchi case. Notice the roles of the precipitating, attracting, and predisposing facts.

The trial of *People v. Buono* in 1983 was the longest criminal trial in the history of the United States at that time and cost the state of California nearly $2 million. The prosecution of Buono was somewhat unusual. Because the Los Angeles district attorney's office decided it had insufficient evidence to convict Buono, it requested that the court dismiss the case against him. As a result, the California attorney general's office prosecuted the case instead. This action was highly unusual because most requests from the district attorney's office to drop charges are routinely granted by judges. When Buono's trial finally ended, he was found guilty on nine counts of homicide and received a life sentence without the possibility of parole.[63]

Exhibit 6.7
. . . .
Summary of facts and their role in the explanation of the Buono and Bianchi case

Level of Importance	Fact	Type of Fact
Primary		
(Buono)	Sexual sadist	Attracting
(Bianchi)	Antisocial-personality disorder	Attracting
(Bianchi)	Relationship with Buono	Attracting
Secondary		
(Buono)	Incidents with prostitutes	Precipitating
(Buono)	Child-support payments	Precipitating
(Bianchi)	None	
Tertiary		
(Buono)	Adolescent identification with Chessman	Predisposing
(Buono)	Criminal history	Predisposing
(Bianchi)	Adoptive mother's parenting	Predisposing
(Bianchi)	Ex-wife's treatment of him	Predisposing

Movies such as *The Three Faces of Eve* provided widespread public knowledge about "multiple personalities." While awaiting trial for the Bellingham murders, Kenneth Bianchi recalled watching this movie and faked a multiple personality disorder in an attempt to escape conviction.

In the Bellingham, Washington, murders, Bianchi initially pled not guilty by reason of insanity. He later changed his plea to guilty in exchange for a life sentence instead of the death penalty. He also agreed to testify against Buono as part of the plea bargain agreement. For the two Bellingham, Washington, murders he received two life sentences—one for each count. This assured that he would spend the rest of his life in prison. In California, Bianchi was charged with only five counts of murder but received a life sentence for each of them.[64]

Yochelson and Samenow's Criminal-Personality Approach

Yochelson and Samenow developed a view of the criminal personality that conforms to the assumptions of the psychological perspective but rejects even the hint of determinism that is present in other theories and approaches. They arrive at conclusions about the nature of criminality that are very similar to those of the personality-disorders approach and the moral-development ideas that have already been presented. However, their view of the causes of these traits is more explicitly grounded in the free will of the individual. While sympathetic to the personality-disorders approach, they feel that this view of crime fails to scrutinize the thought patterns that are the crucial determinant of crime. Their ideas are summarized in Exhibit 6.8.

The initial intention of these theorists was clinical application; their research sought to identify methods of rehabilitation that would be effective with the typical criminal. Toward this end, they studied criminals in an attempt to determine what personality traits they had in common and how these traits led to criminality. They concluded that although criminality is a matter of choice, the pattern of dysfunctional and irresponsible choices emerges so early that there may be biological factors implicated in its creation. These clinicians are not optimistic about the efficiency of rehabilitation efforts. They point out

Exhibit 6.8

Yochelson and Samenow's criminal personality

1. The roots of criminality lie in the way in which people think and make decisions.

2. Criminals think and act differently from others, even at a very early age.

3. Criminals are irresponsible, impulsive, self-centered, and are driven by fear and anger.

4. Deterministic explanations of crime result from believing the criminal who is seeking sympathy.

5. Crime occurs because the criminal wills it or chooses it, and this is the crucial fact that rehabilitation must deal with.

Source: Samuel Yochelson and Stanton E. Samenow, *The Criminal Personality Volume 1: A Profile for Change* (New York: Jason Aronson, 1976).

that if crime is a matter of choice, rehabilitation is under the offender's control. Furthermore, because their notion of the "criminal personality" is defined as a pattern of anger, fear, self-aggrandizement and impulsivity, the criminal will generally choose not to change and hence frustrate the best efforts of rehabilitators.[65]

Their work begins with a critique of biological and sociological explanations of criminality. They reject the idea of biological causes as useless rather than invalid due to inadequate knowledge of genetic influences on personality. They also reject the social-learning perspective (subject of the next chapter) on the basis that criminals (and others) consciously select their companions. Structural explanations suffer a similar fate with these theorists because they believe that institutional and peer demands encourage responsibility and the criminal is one who has chosen to act irresponsibly. Indeed, their view of the factors that create criminality is entirely centered on the individual's perceptions and choices. Thus, it stresses free will to an unprecedented extent. The exercise of willpower and choice are the dominant themes of this approach.[66]

Just as alterations of environments have not significantly affected crime rates, neither will treatment efforts, according to Yochelson and Samenow, unless the treatment is designed to destroy the old, destructive patterns of decision-making and create new, socially acceptable ones.

These theorists point that much of the literature on the causes of crime is based on the accounts of known criminals, and these accounts are self-serving methods of seeking sympathy and avoiding blame—which is typical of the sociopath as well as Yochelson and Samenow's "criminal personality". They further point out that many background variables, such as home environment and community traits have little power to predict which individuals will become criminal—a fact that helps invalidate approaches based on determinism in their eyes.

Yochelson and Samenow maintain that crime and other deviant acts result from dysfunctional thought processes, which, starting at an early age, lead a person into a series of choices that form a fairly distinct pattern of criminality. They point out that the effect of a criminalistic child on her or his parents is usually greater than the effect of the parents on child. Children who become criminal are very consistent in their thoughts and actions no matter what setting is examined. These youths do not follow the lead of their playmates. Instead, they fall into a pattern of seeking excitement and attempting to distinguish themselves from their peers, for whom they have little respect. They yearn to be older, bigger, and more important while the others are relatively content with their current situation. This means that offenders create a pattern of perception and behavior that keeps them from growing into an approved position in the social structure at a very early age.

Yochelson and Samenow believe the criminal was a child bored with, or at least rejecting of, conventional activities and thus unaffected by the presence of anti-crime programs that seek to socialize him or her into a law-abiding lifestyle. These children are exploitive at home, in school, and later, in the workplace, just as would be expected of a sociopath. It is their observation that the only treatment effective in changing this pattern is confrontation of irresponsible acts and thoughts along with control of the criminal personality's rewards.

The criminal, they believe, as a child and as an adult, seeks immediate success and will not delay rewards or invest in an activity long enough to achieve conventional success. These individuals are never content with their current position in society. They constantly seek to attain more power over other people. Like the sociopath, they feel little sense of obligation to others, and always put their own desires first. Criminal acts are stimulating to these people, and victimization of others attracts them to an ever-expanding set of criminal acts. As the child matures, the desire for excitement grows and the pattern of exploitation expands accordingly. This search for excitement and a sense of personal power are the hallmarks of the criminal personality.

Yochelson and Samenow observe that, much like the sociopath, the typical criminal presents him or herself as a victim when caught. They maintain that this pattern is established early in life and that it is not well-predicted by the quality of the home in which the child is raised. They point out that parents tend to seek the causes of such incorrigible behavior in factors beyond the child's control and their influence so as to assure their own mental comfort. Yochelson and Samenow argue that the deterministic bias of social science, which is at least implicitly supported by government programs and the media, support environmental explanations that feed the excuses made by both criminals and their parents.[67]

Yochelson and Samenow go on to paint a picture of the traits of the criminal that has great intuitive appeal. They observe that the criminal is a very energetic, spontaneous person whose thoughts pass quickly but are experienced in a very intense manner. In a sense, criminals are hyperactive both mentally and physically. However, these theorists find that fear is constant and intense in the criminal as well. They also maintain that only some of the criminal's fears can be explained by early experiences.[68] The presence of fear is a major distinction between the "criminal personality" and the sociopath.

In particular, the criminal is fearful of physical injury and death as well as of being embarrassed, rebuffed, or "put down." The criminal, even as a child, will not admit to these fears. When they escalate to the point that the individual feels completely worthless, hopeless, and a failure, a **zero state** has been reached, which has three components: (1) view of self as nothing, (2) belief that others share this view, and (3) fear that this state is permanent.[69]

These researchers present evidence that criminals are plagued by frequent and intense anger. They theorize that this chronic anger grows over time and results in a loss of perspective through which the criminal becomes increasingly illogical in her or his thought processes with advancing maturity, eventually becoming aware only of any personal threat—physical or emotional—in a situation. Such anger cannot be effectively deterred because offenders are unable to perceive the future consequences of their actions. So their anger eventually **metastasizes**, or takes over and generalizes from an isolated situation to become a hatred of the world or some category of people in it (e.g., women). The criminal's fear of being forever lost in the so-called zero state is thought to be at the root of his or her anger.[70]

Another pervasive trait among criminals found by Yochelson and Samenow is the presence of extreme pride or a sense of personal superiority. This may be a reaction to fear of the dreaded zero state. The result is a sense of entitlement to various privileges that far exceeds that of others and is inappropriate for the criminal's stage of life and actual achievements. When society rejects the criminal's unreasonable claims, the response is to conceive the self as a victim and seek sympathy. More anger rises, too, when the criminal's perceived superiority goes unrecognized.[71]

At the heart of Yochelson and Samenow's approach is the belief that criminals, regardless of their intelligence level, think differently than noncriminals do—they think in a concrete rather than an abstract manner. **Concrete thought** is associated with immaturity by most psychologists, so a link with stages of moral development is present here. Each life situation is dealt with by the criminal as an isolated case with no relation to his or her own personality or indeed to any external factors. As a result, these people do not learn from adverse experiences as do most other people; they lack the sort of symbolic thought patterns that link past experiences to present and future situations. They are therefore unequipped to live a responsible life, with an appreciation of work, interpersonal cooperation, human interdependence, justice, home, family, and consideration of others. Because of their anger, fear, grandiose self-image, and immature thinking processes, they cannot act in a reciprocal manner to others. All relationships and situations are reduced to the question of, "What's in it for me?"[72]

Still another characteristic of the criminal, referred to as **fragmentation** by these writers, is a mental state of unusually rapid fluctuations in mood (e.g., going from sentimentality to anger instantly). This results in a great deal of inconsistency in attitudes and actions over fairly short periods of time. For example, criminals are notorious for starting activities and then abandoning them without attempting to complete them.[73] This is also true of many codependent people.

The image of the criminal that Yochelson and Samenow create is much like that of the sociopath in the lack of ability or will to consider the future and examine the consequences of actions that will bring immediate pleasure.[74] Other writers have referred to this problem as an inadequate **time horizon** and have linked it to impulsivity, aggression, and low intelligence.[75] Also like the sociopath, criminal personalities are unable to consider the impact of their acts on others because they appear incapable of empathy. People are seen and dealt with as though they were merely objects placed on earth for the use or amusement of the offender.

This set of traits not only leads the offender to consistently choose to reject responsibility in favor of power and immediate gratification, but also makes them distrustful of others. They constantly seek independence on the basis of their supposed superiority to others yet take pains to avoid situations that will demand any great effort on their part. They refuse to endure adversity. Their decisions are governed by an overconcern with expediency, personal power and recognition, convenience, and momentary desire.[76]

Conclusion

The hallmark of the psychological perspective is the search for the traits that define criminality within the individual's mind rather than in biology or the relation of the person to a group or society. The Freudian conception of the psyche is pervasive in our culture's thinking about the human mind. In Freudian theories of criminology, the dominance of the id, or the weakness of the superego, renders people unable to follow the rules of society even though they are well aware of them. This approach is developmentally oriented and places emphasis on the stages of moral development. Inadequate moral development seems to be heavily implicated in criminality, especially when it results in concrete reasoning patterns.

The idea of sociopathy is well accepted and explains serial offenders quite well. The traits of the sociopath are modified by the environment, so some sociopaths become criminal offenders while others manage to live in a law-abiding way though they may make those around them miserable. Whether this disorder is inherited or acquired through some learning process is unknown at this time.

In a sense, Yochelson and Samenow's approach combines elements of the concept of moral-development stages, the neo-Freudian concept of the psyche, and the symptoms of sociopathy into a unique approach that focuses on thought patterns and choice-making processes. Their approach can be applied to virtually any crime. However, it is so adamant about crime resulting from will and choice that, if applied to certain cases, it could result in very circular reasoning.

Buono and Bianchi are clearly **serial killers**—offenders who kill repeatedly over a fairly long period of time—and many, if not most, serial murderers are sociopathic. Both of these offenders had been diagnosed as suffering from antisocial-personality disorder, a diagnosis amply confirmed by their manipulations of others and the remorseless cruelty with which they committed their crimes. The personality-disorder approach would likely maintain that this condition was determined by forces beyond their control, while the criminal-personality approach of Yochelson and Samenow would attribute this behavior pattern to choice and free will. In the final analysis, however, it is not possible to be certain of the degree to which determinism or free will guided their actions.

The motives of serial killers are fundamentally expressive in nature. Killing is the goal, and the choice of victim is often fairly random. The feeling of power that Yochelson and Samenow identify as a trait of the criminal personality, along with elements of sexual sadism, seem to be present in most serial killers. The phenomenon of the serial killer has only recently captured the attention of the media and authorities. Many criminologists believe that this is due to advances in technology that allow police departments across the nation to compare the characteristics of unsolved violent crimes so as to identify patterns that recur in different parts of the country. Others speculate that there has been an increase in the number of sadistic sociopaths in society which has, in turn, led to an increase in the number of such killings.

Although the causes of serial rape-murders such a those committed by Buono and Bianchi are complex, it is apparent that they do reside within the offenders. This is in keeping with the presumptions of the positivist school of thought. With Buono and Bianchi it is fairly evident that Buono was a sexual sadist and that both men had antisocial-personality disorders. The inheritance approach—which maintains that sociopathic traits are transmitted genetically within family lineages—would seek to examine their family trees for such evidence. Such an approach could be appealing in this case because Buono and

Bianchi were cousins, but they did not share the same genetic lineage, since Bianchi was adopted.

The biosocial approach would also be interested in evidence of a genetic predisposition to sociopathy. However, explanations using this approach would combine this belief with information on Buono and Bianchi's youth in order to explain these crimes. The idea that Buono's hatred of his mother was apparently generalized to other females whom he considered to be promiscuous could be inferred from a Freudian approach. That is, his early experiences with his mother created unconscious conflicts within his psyche that impelled him to brutalize women. Bianchi's maltreatment by his mother early in life may have distorted his psyche, especially in regards to women. His suspicions of his ex-wife's infidelity may have further reinforced this attitude.

Yochelson and Samenow would argue that these crimes resulted from Buono and Bianchi's desperate attempts to avoid the zero state. The fact that they both had had negative experiences with women indicates the possibility that their crimes were responses to perceived "put downs" from the girls they tried to force into prostitution. The murders were a method of regaining control and demonstrating their superiority to these prostitutes. These theorists would be most interested in the thought patterns of the offenders and would maintain that their crimes were the result of conscious choices.

Control theorists (see Chapter 12) would use these same facts to argue that these killers lacked adequate attachment to their parents, which resulted in inadequate bonding to society's norm system. This would have allowed them to commit these heinous acts without remorse. Social-learning theorists (see Chapter 7) would likely focus on Buono's identification with Chessman, the red-light bandit of the 1950s. By using this rapist as a role model, Buono was able to glorify his sadism and define his crimes as quasi-heroic adventures. Labeling theorists (see Chapter 8) would argue that Buono's earlier problems with the law predisposed him to define himself as a criminal, thereby facilitating this transition to more serious acts (i.e., pimping, brutalizing and killing).

All of these forces probably contributed to the Hillside Strangler killings to some degree. The personality-disorder approach, however, uses the most prominent facts of the case to construct a very viable and straightforward explanation of the crimes. This approach provides an explanation that appears more valid than the alternatives while simultaneously being less complicated than the alternatives. This quality of parsimony is a desirable trait for any scientific explanation.

Glossary ·

Abstract Thought Processes Those in which symbols are used to generalize basic principles from one situation to another.

Antisocial-Personality Disorder Characterized by patterns of irresponsibility and antisocial behavior, as well as aggressive tendencies. Sociopaths (another term for antisocial personalities) are manipulative, self-aggrandizing, and remorseless.

Co-dependency Refers to the behavior of a person who permits another person's behavior to affect him or her to the extent of being consumed with attempting to control this other person's behavior.

Concrete Thought Processes   An immature mode of cognition in which each situation is dealt with as an isolated case with its own rewards, rules, and goals. Concrete thinkers do not learn from adverse experiences as do most other people because they lack the sort of symbolic or "abstract" thought patterns that link past experiences to present and future situations.

Ego   A term used by Freud to represent the part of the psyche based on the individual's conscious reason and common sense. It acts as a mediator or "referee" between the id and the superego.

Fragmentation   A term for unusually rapid fluctuations in mental state (e.g., going from sentimentality to anger instantly), which result in extremely inconsistent attitudes and actions over fairly short periods of time.

Id   A term used by Freud to denote the part of the unconscious containing the inner world of the individual's inborn instincts, reflexes, and passions.

Metastasized Anger   The criminal personality's chronic anger generalized from an isolated situation to a hatred of the world or some category of people in it.

Paranoid-Personality Disorders   An overriding, unfounded tendency to interpret the actions of others as threatening or demeaning.

Personality   A term used to describe the collective and/or most prominent psychological trait(s) exhibited by an individual.

Personality Disorders   A set of maladaptive and rigid personality traits that impair functioning in personal and social contexts.

Personality Traits   The permanent patterns individuals develop in terms of how they perceive, relate to, and think about themselves and their environment.

Responsible Actions   Actions that meet the actor's needs without interfering with the needs of others.

Self   Refers to the mental or psychic processes (the mind) underlying personality characteristics and traits, and their development.

Serial Killer   One who kills repeatedly over a fairly long period of time. Many, if not most, of these killers are sociopaths.

Sexual Sadism   A mental disturbance in which reoccurring, extreme, sexual urges demand the psychological or physical suffering of a victim.

Superego   A term used by Freud to denote the inner world of the individual's conscience and ideal expectations.

Time Horizon   The ability to anticipate the future consequences of actions being performed or contemplated in the present.

Zero State   A mental condition dreaded by the criminal personality in which feelings that one is worthless, hopeless, and a failure are dominant. This state has three components: (1) a view of self as nothing, (2) the belief that others share this view, and (3) the fear that this state is permanent.

■ Notes

1. American Psychiatric Association, *Diagnostic and Statistical Manual of Mental Disorders*, 3d ed., rev. (Washington, DC: American Psychiatric Association, 1987), pp. 287–288.

2. Ibid., p. 335.

3. Sigmund Freud, "The Ego and the Id," *The Standard Edition of the Complete Psychological Works of Sigmund Freud*; Sigmund Freud, *Civilization and Its Discontents*, trans. Joan Riviere (Garden City, NY: Doubleday [1927] 1957).

4. Erik Erikson, *Childhood and Society* (New York: Norton, 1963).

5. Jean Piaget, *The Construction of Reality in the Child*, trans. Margaret Cook (New York: Basic Books, 1954).

6. Charles Horton Cooley, *Human Nature and the Social Order* (New York: Schocken, [1902] (1964).

7. Lawrence Kohlberg and Card Gilligan, "The Adolescent as a Philosopher: The Discovery of the Self in a Postconventional World," *Daedalus* 100 (1971): pp. 1051–1086.

8. Ibid.

9. Ibid.

10. R. D. Laing, *The Politics of the Family* (New York: Random House, 1969); R. D. Laing and A. Esterson, *Sanity, Madness and the Family* (New York: Penguin Books, 1964); R. D. Laing, *The Divided Self* (New York: Pelican Books, 1965); John Friel and Linda Friel, *Adult Children: The Secrets of Dysfunctional Families* (Deerfield Beach, FL: Health Communication, Inc., 1988), p. 17.

11. Claudia Black, *It Will Never Happen to Me* (Denver, CO: M.C.A., 1981); M. A. Fossum and M. J. Mason, *Facing Shame: Families in Recovery* (New York: Norton, 1986); A. Miller, *For Your Own Good: Hidden Cruelty in Child-Rearing and the Roots of Violence* (New York: Farrar Strauss Giroux, 1983); Friel and Friel, *Adult Children: The Secrets of Dysfunctional Families*, pp. 71–90.

12. Friel and Friel, *Adult Children: The Secrets of Dysfunctional Families*, pp. 17, 73.

13. R. D. Laing, *The Politics of the Family*; R. D. Laing and A. Esterson, *Sanity, Madness and the Family*; F. Ivan Nye and Felix F. Berado, *The Family* (New York: Macmillan, 1973), pp. 19–23; and Donald W. Calhoun, *Persons-In-Groups* (New York: Harper & Row, 1976), p. 61.

14. R. D. Laing, *The Politics of the Family*; R. D. Laing and A. Esterson, *Sanity, Madness and the Family;* R. D. Laing, *The Divided Self;* Friel and Friel, *Adult Children: The Secrets of Dysfunctional Families*, p. 17.

15. Charles R. Carroll, *Drugs in Modern Society* (Dubuque, IA: Wm. C. Brown, 1985), pp. 38–45.

16. Health communications, *Co-Dependency, an Emerging Issue* (Hollywood, FL: Health Communications, 1984); Melody Beattie, *Codependent No More* (New York: Harper & Row, 1987), pp. 28–29; Friel and Friel, *Adult Children: The Secrets of Dysfunctional Families*, p. 159.

17. Melody Beattie, *Codependent No More* (New York: Harper & Row, 1987), p. 31.

18. Carroll, *Drugs in Modern Society*, pp. 38–45.

19. Phyllis York, David York, and Ted Wachtel, *ToughLove* (New York: Bantam Books, 1983).

20. Al-Anon Family Group Headquarters, Inc., *Al-Anon Family Groups* (New York: Al-Anon Family Group Headquarters, Inc., 1986); Al-Anon Family

Group Headquarters, Inc., *Al-Anon's Twelve Steps & Twelve Traditions* (New York: Al-Anon Family Group Headquarters, Inc., 1981).

21. Friel and Friel, *Adult Children: The Secrets of Dysfunctional Families*, p. 17; Harold J. Vetter and Ira J. Silverman, *Criminology and Crime: An Introduction* (New York: Harper & Row, 1986), p. 88.

22. Calvin S. Hall, *A Primer of Freudian Psychology* (New York: The World Publishing Company, 1954), pp. 11–21.

23. Jean L. McKechnie, *Webster's Deluxe Unabridged Dictionary*, 2d ed., p. 1454.

24. Sigmund Freud, "The Ego and the Id," *The Standard Edition of the Complete Psychological Works of Sigmund Freud*, pp. 13–39; Calvin S. Hall, *A Primer of Freudian Psychology* (New York: The World Publishing Company, 1954), pp. 22–35.

25. Ibid.

26. Sigmund Freud, "The Ego and the Id," *The Standard Edition of the Complete Psychological Works of Sigmund Freud*, p. 52.

27. August Aichorn, *Wayward Youth* (New York: Viking Press, 1935).

28. Fritz Redl and Hans Toch, "The Psychoanalytical Perspective" in Hans Toch (ed.), *Psychology of Crime and Criminal Justice* (New York: Holt Rinehart and Winston, 1979), pp. 193–195; David Abrahamson, *Crime and the Human Mind* (New York: Columbia University Press, 1944) p. 137.

29. Seymour Halleck, *Psychiatry and the Dilemmas of Crime* (Berkeley, CA: University of California Press, 1971).

30. American Psychiatric Association, *Diagnostic and Statistical Manual of Mental Disorders*, 3d ed., rev., p. 335.

31. Ibid., p. 337.

32. "Paranoia and Paranoid Disorders," *Harvard Medical School Mental Health Letter*, 3., no. 2 (1986): pp. 1–4; M. Baron, R. Gruen, J. D. Rainer, J. Kane, L. Asnis, and S. Lord, "The Schizophrenic Spectrum," *Harvard Medical School Mental Health Letter* 2, no. 4 (1985): p. 7.

33. Truman Capote, *In Cold Blood* (New York: Random House, 1965), pp. 212–213.

34. "Paranoia and Paranoid Disorders," *Harvard Medical School Mental Health Letter*, pp. 1–4; M. Baron, R. Gruen, J. D. Rainer, J. Kane, L. Asnis, and S. Lord, "The Schizophrenic Spectrum," p. 7.

35. Ronald M. Holmes and James De Burger, *Serial Murder* (Newbury Park, CA: SAGE Publications, 1988).

36. "The Antisocial Personality, Part I," *Harvard Medical School Mental Health Letter* 2, no. 1 (1985): pp. 1–4; "The Antisocial Personality, part II," *Harvard Medical School Mental Health Letter* 2, no. 2 (1985): pp. 1–5; L. N. Robins, J. E. Helzer, M. M. Weissman, H. Orvaschel, E. Gruenberg, J. D. Burke and D. Regier, "Lifetime Prevalence of Specific Psychiatric Disorders in Three Sites," *Archives of General Psychiatry* 41 (1984): pp. 949-958.

37. L. N. Robins, et al., "Lifetime Prevalence of Specific Psychiatric Disorders in Three Sites," pp. 949–958; American Psychiatric Association, *Diagnostic and Statistical Manual of Mental Disorders*, 3d ed., rev. p. 342–346.

38. B. Karpman, "On the Need for Separating Psychopathy into Two Distinct Types," *Journal of Criminal Psychopathology* 3 (1941): pp. 112–137; J. Q. Wilson and R. J. Herrnstein, *Crime and Human Nature* (New York: Simon & Schuster, 1985), pp. 206–207.

39. American Psychiatric Association, *Diagnostic and Statistical Manual of Mental Disorders*, 3 ed., rev. pp. 342–346; "Borderline Personality Disorder, Part I," *Harvard Medical School Mental Health Letter* 2, no. 6 (1985): pp. 1–3; Jules R. Bemporad and Henry F. Smith, "Borderline Disorders of Childhood," *Harvard Medical School Mental Health Letter* 2, no. 1 (1985): pp. 5–6.

40. Holmes and DeBurger, *Serial Murder*, pp. 16–19; Vetter and Silverman, *Criminology and Crime*, pp. 93–94.

41. Ted Schwarz, *The Hillside Strangler: A Murderer's Mind* (Signet, New York: Signet, 1981).

42. Darcy O' Brien, *Two of a Kind: The Hillside Stranglers* (New York: New American Library, 1985).

43. **Texas Penal Code** 8th ed. (St. Paul, MN: West Publishing, 1990), pp. 31–35.

44. George Rush, *The Dictionary of Criminal Justice*, 2d ed. (Guilford, CT: Dushkin Publishing group, 1986), p. 226.

45. O'Brien, *Two of a Kind: The Hillside Stranglers*.

46. Ibid.

47. Ibid.

48. Rush, *The Dictionary of Criminal Justice*, 2d ed., p. 205; *Texas Penal Code*, 8th ed., pp. 31–35.

49. Ibid.

50. O'Brien, *Two of a Kind: The Hillside Stranglers*.

51. Ibid.

52. Ibid.

53. Ibid.

54. Ibid.

55. Schwarz, *The Hillside Strangler: A Murderer's Mind*.

56. Ibid.

57. Ibid.

58. O'Brien, *Two of a Kind: The Hillside Stranglers*.

59. Ibid.

60. Schwarz, *The Hillside Strangler: A Murderer's Mind*.

61. Ibid.

62. Ibid.

63. O'Brien, *Two of a Kind: The Hillside Stranglers*.

64. Schwarz, *The Hillside Strangler: A Murderer's Mind*.

65. Samuel Yochelson and Stanton E. Samenow, *The Criminal Personality Volume 1: A Profile for Change* (New York: Jason Aronson, 1976), pp. 104–105.

66. Ibid.

67. Ibid, pp. 246–249.

68. Ibid, pp. 255–259.

69. Ibid, pp. 259–266.

70. Ibid, pp. 268–270.

71. Ibid, pp. 270–275.

72. Ibid, pp. 302–307.

73. Ibid, pp. 308–309.

74. Ibid, pp. 369–372.

75. James Q. Wilson and Richard J. Herrnstein, *Crime and Human Nature* (New York: Simon & Schuster, 1985), pp. 53–54, 167–172, 217.

76. Yochelson and Samenow, *The Criminal Personality Volume 1: A Profile for Change*, pp. 400–440.

■ Suggested Readings

H. F. Eysenck, *Crime and Personality* (London: Routledge & Kegan Paul, 1977).

"The Antisocial Personality, Part I," *Harvard Medical School Mental Health Letter* 2, no. 1 (1985).

"The Antisocial Personality, Part II," *Harvard Medical School Mental Health Letter* 2, no. 2 (1985).

B. Karpman, "On the Need for Separating Psychopathy into Two Distinct Types," *Journal of Criminal Psychopathology* 3 (1941): pp. 112–137.

William H. Reid, *The Psychopath: A Comprehensive Study of Antisocial Disorders and Behaviors* (New York: Brunner/Mazel, 1978).

Stanton E. Samenow, *Inside the Criminal Mind* (New York: Times Books, 1984).

D. J. West, C. Roy and Florence L. Nichols, *Understanding Sexual Attacks* (London: Heinemann, 1978).

■ Suggested Books for Additional Application

David Abrahamsen, *The Murdering Mind* (New York: Harper & Row, 1973).

J. Egginton, *From Cradle to Grave* (New York: The Berkley Publishing Group, 1989).

Gerold Frank, *The Boston Strangler* (New York: The New American Library, 1966).

Edward Keyes, *The Michigan Murders* (New York: Pocket Books, 1976).

Stephen G. Michaud and Hugh Aynesworth, *The Only Living Witness* (New York: New American Library, 1983).

Jack Olsen, *Son: A Psychopath and His Victims* (New York: Dell, 1983).

Jack Olsen, *The Man with the Candy* (New York: Simon & Schuster, 1985).

Ann Rule, *Lust Killer* (New York: NAL Penguin, 1983).

Ann Rule, *Small Sacrifices* (New York: New American Library, 1988).

Carlton Smith and Tomas Guillen, *The Search for the Green River Killer* (New York: Penguin Books, 1991).

Andy Stack, *The Want-Ad Killer* (New York: New American Library, 1983).

Robert K. Tanenbaum and Peter S. Greenberg, *The Piano Teacher* (New York: NAL Penguin, 1987).

CHAPTER **7**

Social-Learning Perspective

Overview of Social-Learning Perspective

The social-learning perspective combines insights from the sociological and psychological communities. It asserts that criminal behavior originates in exactly the same way other behaviors do (Exhibit 7.1). This perspective maintains that criminals do not initially differ from others in any notable physical or psychological way. Rather, they are distinct from law-abiding citizens in the degree to which they have been exposed to definitions that portray criminal acts as appropriate. In other words, interactions with others (e.g., peer groups) who see criminal behavior as desirable or admirable lead to criminal behavior. However, close inspection of these theories reveals elements of free will in their assumptions about how people chose such reference groups and evaluate the ideas they receive from them.

Before detailing the mechanisms of behavior acquisition specified by the social-learning perspective, let us look at the macro-level context in which this theory originated. Its basis is Sutherland's and Cressey's notion of **differential social organization** wherein the various groups that compose a society are thought to have their own unique forms of organization with their own unique norms. Differential social organization attempts to explain why crime rates are unequally distributed across the subgroups of society. This concept is in direct opposition to the social-disorganization perspective, which asserts that groups with high crime rates suffer from a lack of organization. The concept of differential social organization instead claims that such groups have a form of organization that is different from that of the dominant society. This concept bridges the gap from meso- to macro-level concerns, providing a context for the development of micro-level theories about criminal behavior.

The social-learning perspective is primarily focused on the individual's relationships with various **membership groups,** that is, groups distinct from other social groupings because they are defined on the basis of active participation and face-to-face interaction. Their impact is at the micro to meso level of analysis rather than at the macro level where other types of social groups take significance. While economic classes and racial categories constitute social groups, they are not membership groups because no one is familiar with all the members of her or his race or class. The family, peer groups, and work

Exhibit 7.1

Social-learning perspective

Common Assumptions

1. Human behavior is flexible, not fixed.
2. Both criminal and noncriminal behavior stem from the same general social-psychological processes.
3. Behavior is learned through association with others.
4. Informal, intimate groups dominate the learning process.
5. Most criminal behavior is learned and committed in a group or gang context.

Source: Donald J. Shoemaker, *Theories of Delinquency* (New York: Oxford University Press, 1984).

teams are membership groups. Basically, the social-learning perspective asserts that behavior is the product of learning that occurs through direct contacts with others and from media sources.

From Sutherland's and Cressey's viewpoint, macro-level differences in social organization, and the personal associations they produce, provide an explanation of the process(es) by which individuals acquire criminal behavior patterns.[1] All individuals belong to many social groups. It is the individual's pattern of group memberships that is seen as the source of behavior. In essence, differences in group organization allow some groups to become criminally oriented while others are encouraged to be law-abiding.[2] By examining a person's group memberships, especially in small, intimate groups, one should be able to predict not only the likelihood of the person committing a crime, but also the type of crime, according to this perspective.

Case Information Sources

The Tate-LaBianca murders are among the best known and most thoroughly researched crimes in recent American history. They occurred during a time of great social change in the United States. The civil rights movement had recently established minority rights, the Vietnam War was becoming increasingly controversial, and the hippie movement was reaching its zenith. Drug use and social revolution were common topics on university campuses as well as throughout the nation. The historical context of the killings may have influenced the competing explanations of the crimes put forth at the time of Charles Manson's trial.

In our explanation of the Tate-LaBianca murders, we have synthesized several different accounts offered over the past two decades. Our analysis benefits from a couple of advantages. One is its usage of multiple sources. This was possible only because of the great notoriety given these crimes as well as the passage of time. Additionally, our analysis is more objective than that of anyone who was personally involved in the case. We have no vested interest in demonstrating the validity of any one explanation. In fact, we believe that there are elements of truth in all of the explanations offered to date.

The most well known explanation of the Tate-LaBianca murders is the one offered by Vincent Bugliosi, chief prosecutor for the Manson trial, in his book, *Helter Skelter*. Bugliosi reported that Manson was convinced a race war was imminent in the United States in which the blacks (African-Americans) would rise up against the whites and kill them all. He believed that the Beatles' song "Helter-Skelter" was a prophecy of this event. Manson and his "family" planned to wait out the "Helter Skelter" period in an underground shelter in Death Valley, then emerge to rule over all at the invitation of the blacks, who would not, according to Manson, know how to rule themselves.

Bugliosi's explanation of the murders was that Manson simply got tired of waiting for the blacks to start "Helter Skelter" and decided that he and his followers had to show them how to start the race war. The murders were Manson's attempt to inspire "Helter Skelter."[3]

Another plausible explanation for the Tate-LaBianca murders is Thomas Noguchi's music-career explanation. Noguchi was the chief medical examiner in Los Angeles at the time of the murders. While incarcerated at McNeil Island,

Manson had learned to play the guitar and drums and would sing and write songs. However, he was allegedly quite bad at all of these activities. Noguchi proposed that Manson committed the Tate-LaBianca murders because his attempts at a music career after his release from McNeil Island had failed. He suggests that Manson specifically blamed Terry Melcher, the Hollywood talent agent who owned the house where Sharon Tate lived, for his failure. Noguchi believed that Melcher was the intended victim of the attack—between the time that Manson had visited Melcher at his home and the Tate murders, Melcher had moved out of the house and Sharon Tate had moved in. Manson had also been to the house next door prior to the time of the murders.[4]

Our applications of theory to this case are based on our own synthesis of Bugliosi's, Noguchi's, and others' views. Susan Atkins, Leslie Van Houten, Patricia Krenwinkel, Linda Kasabian, and Charles "Tex" Watson were all members of the Manson "family." Although some of the same factors may have been involved for all of those participating in these crimes, we have chosen to focus on Susan Atkins, Charles "Tex" Watkins, and Manson himself in our applications.

Differential-Association Approach

Sutherland's differential-association approach to criminal behavior (see Exhibit 7.2) was developed to explain white-collar crime but has since found wider application in criminology. This theory explicitly states that criminal behaviors are acquired in the same way as conventional behaviors—they are learned. Sutherland proposed that, taken in the context of differential social organization, differential association could explain most crime. His goal was to develop an explanation of criminality that would apply equally to all social classes and groups. **Differential association** has come to be defined as a process by which individuals come to have varying levels of access to both criminal and conventional values through contacts with other people and other aspects of the larger society. Sutherland designed his approach to explain why, within the same general environment, some people become criminals or delinquents and others do not.[5]

All individuals are exposed to a number of different groups through which they come into contact with many different definitions of the same behaviors. For example, a youth who plays on a team where drug use is seen in a very negative light may also belong to a neighborhood peer group that defines the use of drugs as an appropriate form of recreation. The differential-association approach asserts that it is the frequency, duration, intensity, and priority of the definitions received that determine whether the youth will use drugs or not. (The more frequent, intense, valued, and long lasting the contact with persons who see drugs favorably, the greater likelihood there is that the youth will also use drugs.) These criteria give the theory a somewhat deterministic tone. However, concern with the priority given to various definitions adds an element of free will to this approach. Each individual is exposed to many contradictory sets of definitions of important behaviors. Thus, each person is free to assign each source a relative level of importance or credibility. While the frequency, duration, and intensity of contacts with various types of people may not be completely under the control of the individual, the priority assigned

Restrictive Assumptions

1. Criminal behavior is learned through communication with other persons.

2. Most social learning takes place within small, intimate groups.

3. This learning includes: (a) the skills required to commit the crime, (b) the motives and/or rationalizations for the crime, and (c) attitudes associated with the crime.

4. Learning consists of the accumulation of favorable and unfavorable definitions of various behaviors.

5. Criminal behavior occurs when favorable definitions of criminal behavior are given more weight than unfavorable ones.

6. The balance between favorable and unfavorable definitions of a specific behavior is determined by the frequency, duration, priority, and intensity of contacts with groups/persons supplying the definitions.

7. All of the other mechanisms and processes involved in learning criminal behavior are the same as those involved with learning noncriminal behavior.

8. Criminal expression of common needs and values does not explain criminality because noncriminal behavior is an expression of these same needs and values.

Source: Edwin H. Sutherland and Donald R. Cressey, *Criminology*, 10th ed. (Philadelphia: Lippincott, 1978).

to each source and/or definition is a matter of personal choice. Some people feel it is acceptable to use drugs, but not to rob or rape. Even among drug users there is no universal agreement as to which drugs or other crimes are acceptable. Such differences in the attitudes of criminals are best explained by the differential-association approach.

More than definitions of behaviors are acquired through this process— skills are, too. Just as we need to be taught how to drive a car safely, so also must a heroin user learn to prepare the drug and use a syringe to inject it. Likewise, certain attitudes are often associated with various definitions of behavior. For example, people who learn that stealing and drug use are appropriate behaviors are also likely to believe the police to be evil and to see law-abiding citizens as "suckers." Such attitudes are associated with criminal behavior, but need not be present for one to commit crimes. Rationalizations and justifications for various acts are also acquired in this manner.

The Case of Susan Atkins · · · · · · · · · · · · · · · · · · **APPLICATION** · · · · ·

The Tate-LaBianca murders occurred in Beverly Hills, California, on two consecutive nights in August of 1969. On August 9th, the victims at the Tate residence included Sharon Tate and her unborn child, Abigail Folger, Jay

Accomplice
A person who aids another person in committing a criminal offense.[13]

Sebring, Voytek Frykowski, and Steve Parent. On the night of August 10th, the victims at the LaBianca residence were Leno and Rosemary LaBianca.[6]

None of these victims were acquainted with their assailants. Sharon Tate was a twenty-six-year-old movie actress married to Roman Polanski, a well-known movie director. At the time of her death, she was eight months pregnant. Abigail Folger was twenty-five years old and heiress to the Folger coffee fortune. Jay Sebring was an internationally recognized men's hair stylist. He was thirty-five years old at the time of his death. Voytek Frykowski was a thirty-two-year-old friend of Tate's. Steve Parent was an eighteen-year-old who was visiting Tate's caretaker. Leno LaBianca was a forty-four-year-old businessman and Rosemary LaBianca was his thirty-eight-year-old wife.[7]

The Manson "family" was a loosely organized group of "hippies," a nomadic group whose principal base of operation was an abandoned movie set called the Spahn Ranch just north of Los Angeles, California. They lived off the profits of drug sales and theft, as well as by foraging whatever they could from garbage cans.[8] At times this group numbered more than one hundred, but the hard-core, inner circle never had more than twenty-five to thirty members. Charles Manson, an ex-convict, used illegal drugs, sex, and a self-composed, guru-like philosophy to control the members. He used the girls and women to bring motorcycle gang members into an alliance for physical protection against the outside world. In essence, Manson controlled the females, and the females helped to keep the bikers under control.[9]

In many ways Manson's leadership and control over people could be likened to that of Reverend Jim Jones. Most of the "family" members did not have any alternative groups to meet their needs. The girls and young women were primarily middle-class runaways or lower-class "throwaways." Several were college dropouts. An example of a lower-class "throwaway" was Dianne Lake. At the age of thirteen, she had been introduced to group sex and LSD

Susan Atkins, Patricia Krenwinkel, and Leslie Van Houten laugh and joke with reporters as they are escorted to the courtroom during the Sharon Tate murder trial.

trips by her parents in a commune. When she joined the Manson Family at the age of fourteen, it was with her parents' approval. She stayed with the Manson Family despite Manson's severe and repeated physical abuses. She was an emotionally disturbed adolescent who suffered from occasional LSD flashbacks. She both feared and loved Manson.[10]

The *precipitating factor* in the commission of the Tate-LaBianca murders was a misguided effort on the part of Susan Atkins, Leslie Van Houten, Mary Brunner, Lynnette Fromme, Linda Kasabian, and other Manson Family members to get another member, Robert "Bobby" Beausoleil, age twenty-two, out of jail. Beausoleil had been arrested for the murder of Gary Hinman, a music teacher who had befriended some members of the Manson family.[11]

Gary Hinman had sold some mescaline to Beausoleil, who in turn sold it to some bikers. The bikers claimed the mescaline was no good and demanded that Beausoleil return their $2,000. Charles Manson told the bikers that he and Beausoleil would return their money. Manson and Beausoleil intended to get the money back from Hinman and return it to the bikers. Beausoleil, Susan Atkins, and Mary Brunner went over to Hinman's to get the money. After two days of torture, though, Hinman still refused to give them the $2,000. At this point, they stabbed him to death. (This made Atkins an accomplice in the murder of Hinman.[12])

After Beausoleil was arrested for the murder of Hinman, Susan Atkins and others decided that if members of the Manson Family murdered several other people after the pattern of the Hinman murder while Beausoleil was in jail, the police would think that Beausoleil had nothing to do with the Hinman murder. These copycat murders involved tying up the victims, stabbing them to death, and writing "pig" in blood on doors and walls. Atkins, Watson, Kasabian, Krenwinkel, and Van Houten—all between twenty and twenty-six years of age at the time—went to the Tate and LaBianca residences to carry out this plan.[14]

As we move away from the precipitating factors toward the *attracting factors*, we find them most clearly documented in Susan Atkins's association with the Manson Family. The choice of the copycat murder strategy to free Beausoleil was rooted in the lifestyle of the Manson Family at the Spahn Ranch.

Susan Atkins had met Charles Manson in San Francisco, California, when she was eighteen years old and living in a commune. Prior to meeting Manson, she drank heavily, took drugs of all sorts, and was sexually promiscuous. She had worked as a topless dancer for a while. She had been arrested, along with her boyfriend and another man, for robbery (of several gas stations) and auto theft. As a result of her involvement in these crimes, she spent two months in jail and received two years probation.[15] Shortly after meeting Manson, she left the commune and moved to Los Angeles with five other women to join Manson's group. This was the beginning of the Manson Family. He then moved the family from Los Angeles to the Spahn Ranch.[16]

At the Spahn Ranch, the females in the Manson Family were relatively isolated from the rest of society. In addition, they were subjected to Manson's psychological and physical control techniques. For example, he told Atkins and the others that they had psychological hangups about wanting to have sex with their fathers, from which they could free themselves by having sex with him while pretending he was their father. Through this technique Manson became a father figure to the girls. This made him a symbol of authority to which they became subservient. He would also orchestrate group sex (orgies) for the family to break down their inhibitions.

Manson used manipulative techniques learned in prison. One example of this type of control was his giving Family members aliases. Susan Atkins was renamed Sadie Mae Glutz. "Glutz" is a prison inmate slang word for prison guards.[17] This helped to destroy their old identities so that Manson could assign new ones.

In his self-styled guru role, Manson would wash their feet and have them wash the feet of others, as did Jesus Christ. Manson never claimed to be Christ, but many of his guru-like behaviors indicated that he wanted others to believe this was his true identity.[18]

Manson also had Family members practice what he called "creepy-crawling," in which they secretly entered strangers' homes, and just crept and crawled around and then left. Supposedly these "creepy-crawling" expeditions were practice for committing crimes.[19]

In effect, the entire social environment in which the members of the Manson Family were living was geared toward committing criminal offenses. Since Manson Family members did not work, their very survival depended upon criminal behavior.

It can be argued that the copycat murders at the Tate and LaBianca residences were attractive to Susan Atkins and the others due to the differential association that they were exposed to at Spahn Ranch. This strategy to free Beausoleil was totally consistent with the illegal alternatives employed by the Family for obtaining goals on an ongoing, day-to-day basis. It required less labor than hiring an attorney. It offered excitement, as well as increased status within the Manson Family. It was also congruent with the worldview and morality preached by Manson.

A *predisposing factor* in Susan Atkins's case might have been dropping out of high school. She was born in 1948 to an average middle-class American family. She attended church regularly with her family. She committed minor shoplifting offenses at the age of twelve but was not involved in any serious crimes. She failed the fifth grade and repeated it. However, when she failed the eleventh grade, she decided to quit high school because she would be almost eighteen years old when she started the eleventh grade all over again. After her mother's death from cancer, her father began to drink heavily, and she left home, finally ending up in the Haight-Ashbury section of San Francisco, where she met Manson.[20] These facts *predisposed* Atkins to join the Manson Family. As a result of that decision, differential association further *attracted* her to crime, and the desire to free Beausoleil *precipitated* the homicides.

Exhibit 7.3
. . . .

Summary of facts and their role in the explanation of the Susan Atkins case

Level of Importance	Fact	Type of Fact
Primary	Free Beausoleil from jail	Precipitating
Secondary	Association with Manson family	Attracting
Tertiary	Family environment	Predisposing
Tertiary	Failure in school	Predisposing

In 1971 Susan Atkins, along with Leslie Van Houten and Patricia Krenwinkel, received the death sentence for her role in the Tate-LaBianca murders. All three of these death sentences were commuted to life imprisonment when the California State Supreme Court abolished the death penalty in 1972.[21] Atkins is currently serving her life sentence at the California Institution for Women. She has become a born-again Christian and has her own ministry within the prison.[22] Exhibit 7.3 summarizes the facts of her case.

Differential-Association-Reinforcement Theory

According to Burgess and Akers, differential-association theory is a general explanation of all human behavior, criminal and noncriminal alike, and their differential-association-reinforcement theory is essentially a modification of Sutherland's differential-association approach that includes general behavior-reinforcement theory (Exhibit 7.4). In particular, this theory specifies the pro-

Exhibit 7.4
. . . .

Differential-association-
reinforcement theory

Specific Assumptions

1. Classical conditioning produces a response without prior training.

2. Behavior acquired through the observation of others is reinforced by observing the punishment and reward consequences received by these other people.

3. Behavioral conditioning determines the likelihood of an act being repeated.

4. Criminal behavior is learned through operant conditioning.

5. Criminal behavior is learned both in social and nonsocial situations in which the behavior of other persons reinforces criminal behavior.

6. Criminal behavior is learned in groups that are major sources of reinforcements for the individual.

7. Effective and available reinforcers and other existing reinforcement contingencies are necessary components in learning criminal behavior, including specific techniques, attitudes, and avoidance procedures.

8. The specific types of criminal behaviors and their rate of occurrence result from the operation of effective and available reinforcers, and the norms by which they are applied.

9. Criminal behavior is acquired when it is more highly reinforced than noncriminal behavior.

10. The level of criminal behavior is contingent upon the amount, frequency, and probability of criminal-behavior reinforcement.

Source: Robert L. Burgess, and Ronald Akers, "A Differential Association-Reinforcement Theory of Criminal Behavior," *Social Problems* 14 (1966): pp. 128–147; Ronald L. Akers, Marvin D. Krohn, Lonn Lanza-Kaduce, and Marcia Radosevich, "Social Learning And Deviant Behavior: A Specific Test Of A General Theory," *American Sociological Review* 44 (1979): pp. 636–655.

cesses by which learning occurs. Differential association has already specified the source and content of the learning.

Burgess and Akers used the *behaviorist approach* from psychology to specify the manner in which learning occurred. They claim that learning results from four types of conditioning: positive reinforcement, negative reinforcement, positive punishment, and negative punishment. Reinforcements are rewards (punishments are self-explanatory). Negative types of conditioning involve the removal of a stimuli while positive conditioners involve the receipt of a stimuli. Thus, positive reinforcers involve the receipt of things defined as pleasing, such as obtaining money. Negative reinforcers consist of successfully avoiding or removing an unpleasant, or *aversive,* stimuli such as when someone quiets a crying infant. Positive punishments occur when a person is subjected to a stimuli that he or she defines as unpleasant, such as being put in jail. Negative punishment is associated with the loss of a pleasant stimuli as occurs when someone loses money because of a court-imposed fine. These conditioning processes are summarized in Exhibit 7.5.

Most psychologists agree that rewards are more powerful in shaping behavior than are punishments. Rewards tend to increase the likelihood and frequency of a behavior while punishers tend to reduce, and eventually extinguish, a behavior. When a behavior has been eradicated from a person's repertoire of acts through the use of punishments, scientists say that **extinction** has occurred.

Burgess and Akers also presume that there are two major types of behavioral learning. One is reflective of respondent behavior, which is governed by the stimuli with which it is associated. Such behavior is largely associated with the autonomic nervous system. This idea was critical to Mednick's biosocial theory presented in Chapter 4. The second is operant behavior, which involves the central nervous system and is a function of past and present environmental consequences. Behaviors that are quickly followed by reinforcing stimuli will increase the likelihood of the behavior being performed in the future. The six possible environmental consequences relative to behavior according to the *Law of Operant Behavior* are listed in Exhibit 7.6.

Differential-association-reinforcement theory proposes that the primary learning mechanism in social behavior is operant conditioning. That is, behavior is shaped by the stimuli that follow the act and are defined as a consequence of it. Due to its stress on conditioning processes, behaviorism is often interpreted as being deterministic. However, the fact that the individual must decide what is rewarding and what is a consequence of an act indicates that a large element of free will is presumed by this theory.

Social behavior is acquired through direct conditioning and through imitation of others' behavior. Learning through the observation of role models is known as **vicarious learning.** This concept is based on research that shows

Exhibit 7.5

Types of conditioning mechanisms

	Reinforcer	Punisher
Positive	Pleasing stimuli received	Aversive stimuli received
Negative	Aversive stimuli removed	Pleasing stimuli removed

Exhibit 7.6 . . . .

The law of operant behavior

1. Positive reinforcement results from stimuli that are defined as desirable and acts to increase the frequency of the behavior with which it is associated.

2. Negative reinforcement removes or avoids stimuli that are defined as unpleasant and acts to increase the frequency of the behavior with which it is associated.

3. Positive punishment results from stimuli that are defined as unpleasant and acts to decrease the frequency of the behavior with which it is associated.

4. Negative punishment results from the avoidance or removal of stimuli that are defined as desirable and acts to decrease a behavior's frequency.

5. Neutral reinforcement produces or removes certain stimuli that do not change a behavior's frequency.

6. Extinction reinforcement produces certain stimuli that decrease a behavior's frequency to zero.

Source: Robert L. Burgess, and Ronald Akers, "A Differential Association-Reinforcement Theory of Criminal Behavior," *Social Problems* 14 (1966): pp. 128–147; Ronald L. Akers, Marvin D. Krohn, Lonn Lanza-Kaduce, and Marcia Radosevich, "Social Learning and Deviant Behavior: A Specific Test Of A General Theory," *American Sociological Review* 44 (1979): pp. 636–655.

that people watch others perform behaviors, observe the outcome of the behavior for that person, and then model their own behavior accordingly. This concept is crucial because it means that a person need not actually perform a given behavior in order to be reinforced for it. Thus, social-learning theories can include television portrayals of crime and related behaviors as a source of learning and reinforcement. Vicarious learning is an important source of information for noncriminal as well as criminal behaviors.

Whether deviant or conforming behavior is acquired and persists depends on the nature of past and present conditioning associated with the behavior—that is, the rewards and punishments the behavior brings. Rewards and punishments administered to others, if observed, have a similar effect in vicarious situations. As they interact with the various groups to which they belong, people form valuative definitions of a behavior. These definitions are a form of verbal, cognitive behavior that can be directly reinforced. Once formed, these definitions also act as stimuli for other behavior.[23]

Reinforcers, according to this theory, can be nonsocial as well as social. The greatest behavioral effects, however, come from the influence of the groups that control individuals' major sources of reinforcements and expose them to behavioral models and normative definitions. Differential association, which refers to the acquisition of definitions through interaction with different groups, occurs first. These groups provide the social environments in which exposure to definitions, imitation of models, and social reinforcement for various behaviors takes place. The definitions are learned through the observation of others, and are socially reinforced by the individual's intimates.

Differential-reinforcement theory has been validated with regard to drug use. The research shows that individuals acquire definitions of particular drugs as good or bad. Once learned, these definitions serve as criteria for deciding between use and abstinence. After the initial use, vicarious influences become less important while the effects of definitions appear to continue. It is at this point that the actual consequences—social and nonsocial reinforcers and punishers—of the specific behavior come into play. They determine the probability that use will be continued and at what level. The consequences include the actual effects of the substance at first and subsequent use, along with the perceived reactions of others present as well as of those who find out about it later. The anticipated reactions of others important to the individual also play a role in assigning priority to these definitions.[24] Since most criminals commit many crimes before being apprehended, they have been heavily reinforced by both the profits from the crimes and by the acceptance of their peers prior to experiencing punishment at the hands of the criminal justice system. Thus, the punishment has less effect on future behavior than the earlier rewards. Also, the more isolated the group is, the less competition there will be from contradictory definitions outside the group, and the greater the frequency, duration, intensity, and priority of the group's definitions. This is apparently what led Tex Watson's involvement in the Tate-LaBianca murders.

· · · · · · · · · **APPLICATION** · · · · **The Case of Charles "Tex" Watson**

> **Drug Law Violation**
> The act of unlawfully selling, purchasing, distributing, manufacturing, cultivating, transporting, possessing, or using a controlled or prohibited drug or the attempt to commit these acts.[25]

The precipitating factor for Charles "Tex" Watson's involvement in the Tate-LaBianca murders was the same as that of Atkins, Krenwinkel, Kasabian, and Van Houten—the desire to absolve Beausoleil from guilt in the murder of Hinman. The attracting factor for Watson however, was different from those of the others. In June of 1969 Watson received $2,400 dollars from Bernard "Lotsapoppa" Crowe for some marijauna that Watson had promised to deliver to him. When Watson failed to deliver the marijuana, Crowe went to Watson's girlfriend's apartment and threatened to kill her. Watson was not at the apartment, so the girl called Charles Manson. Manson took his gun and went over to the girl's apartment with T. J. Walleman, another member of the Manson family. At Watson's girlfriend's apartment, Manson and Crowe began to argue. During the argument, Crowe attacked Manson and Manson shot him.[26]

This incident left Watson even further in debt to Manson for the assistance he provided regarding Crowe. On the night of the Tate murders, Manson reminded him of that debt, telling him it was time to do something for Beausoleil and to go with the girls and help them carry out their plan.[27] Watson agreed, eager to reduce his debt to Manson. He went with the women and helped carry out their plan at the Tate residence. The following night he again accompanied them to the LaBianca residence.

Beyond the issue of his debt to Manson, the *attracting factors* for Watson were the same as those for Susan Atkins—they lay in his association with the Manson Family. Watson, like Atkins, was literally isolated from the rest of society while being subjected to Manson's psychological and physical control, and the criminal milieu that existed with the Manson Family at Spahn Ranch. Manson controlled the conditioning stimuli and thus the definitions of what was desirable.

The *predisposing factor* in Watson's case appears to be his heavy illegal drug use. Other than dropping out of college, there appear to be no other predisposing factors in Watson's past. After the Tate-LaBianca murders, Watson fled California and returned to Texas. Although arrested in Texas on a California warrant, Watson fought his extradition back to California. In September of 1970 he was returned to California, where he was tried separately from Atkins, Krenwinkel, Van Houten, and Manson for the Tate-LaBianca murders.[28] In October of 1971 a jury found Watson guilty of seven counts of first degree murder and one count of conspiracy to commit murder.[29] He was given the death penalty, but like the others convicted of the Tate-LaBianca murders, he had his death sentence later commuted to life imprisonment. Exhibit 7.7 summarizes the facts of the Watson case.

Neutralization-Drift Theory

Sykes and Matza proposed their neutralization-drift theory (see Exhibit 7.8) to deal with what they felt to be serious defects in Sutherland's view of juvenile delinquency as a form of behavior based on competing or countervailing values and norms. Sutherland and the "subcultural" theorists (see Chapter 10) saw juvenile delinquency as a form of behavior based on the values and norms of a deviant subculture, just as law-abiding behavior is based on the values and norms of the larger society. Sykes and Matza felt that this assumption was of extremely dubious validity because the world of the delinquent is embedded in the larger world of those who conform. Criminals and delinquents only rarely escape some degree of socialization to the dominant socio-moral order.[30]

According to Sykes and Matza, many theorists imply the existence of a delinquent subculture and a system of values that represents an inversion of the values held by respectable, law-abiding society. The norms of the delinquent subcultures constitute a countervailing force directed against the conforming social order according to these views. The major difficulty with these views is that if there existed a delinquent subculture in which delinquents viewed their illegal behavior as morally correct, then feelings of guilt would be rare among delinquents and criminals. Yet there is much evidence to suggest that many delinquents and criminals do experience guilt. Thus, Sykes and Matza concluded that many delinquents do, in fact, subscribe to the dominant morality of the culture even though their behavior violates the social norms.

Another point raised by Sykes and Matza was that the juvenile delinquent frequently accords admiration and respect to law-abiding persons. Additionally, there is much evidence to indicate that juvenile delinquents often draw a sharp line between those who can be victimized and those who cannot (e.g.,

Level of Importance	Fact	Type of Fact
Primary	Debt to Manson	Attracting
Secondary	Illegal drug use	Predisposing
Tertiary	Free Beausoleil from jail	Precipitating

Exhibit 7.7

Summary of facts and their role in the explanation of the Charles "Tex" Watson case

Exhibit 7.8
. . . .
Neutralization-drift theory

Specific Assumptions

1. The normative system of a society is marked by great flexibility.

2. Criminal behavior is a matter of choice.

3. Criminals exercise their choices based on their view of the situation at a particular point in time.

4. Most criminals fluctuate between conforming and deviant standards for behavior for a long period before committing themselves to one or the other.

5. Justifications for criminal behavior that are seen as valid by the criminal are often derived from values present in the mainstream society.

6. Justifications for criminal behavior are attempts to protect the individual both from self-blame and the condemnation of others that results from committing a criminal act.

7. Justifications for criminal behavior often precede criminal behavior.

8. There are five major types of justifications for criminal behavior:
   a. denial of responsibility,
   b. denial of injury,
   c. denial of the victim,
   d. condemnation of the condemners, and
   e. the appeal to higher loyalties.

Source: Gresham M. Sykes and David Matza, "Techniques of Neutralization: A Theory of Delinquency," *American Sociological Review* 22 (1957): pp. 664–670; Shoemaker, *Theories of Delinquency.*

friends). In sum, it is doubtful that many juvenile delinquents are totally immune from the demands for conformity made by the dominant social order.[31]

According to Sykes and Matza, people belong to many groups and thus receive different and sometimes competing definitions of the same behavior. This is a condition referred to as **drift,** wherein the individual tends to fluctuate between these competing norm systems for a period of time before becoming bonded to one or the other. The idea of drift is especially applicable to young people who are experimenting with multiple group memberships and behaviors. While in this state they tend to retain some of the mainstream norms. Therefore, they feel the need to absolve themselves of guilt for criminal acts and will likely resort to techniques of neutralization to justify their actions in terms of values recognized by the mainstream society.[32]

Sykes and Matza's neutralization-drift theory suggests a modification of differential-association theory for a large proportion of juvenile delinquents. According to neutralization-drift theory, no matter how deeply enmeshed in patterns of delinquency a youth may be, and no matter how much this involvement may outweigh his or her association with the law-abiding, the delinquent cannot escape the society's condemnation of his deviance. The demands for conformity must be met and answered; they cannot be ignored

Individuals in "drift," many of whom are juveniles, fluctuate between deviant and conforming norms. At a crack house in Philadelphia, six adults and this 13-year-old boy, who is homeless, were found with assorted weapons and crack vials.

as part of an alien system of values and norms. The delinquent thus uses the reasoning of the dominant culture to excuse his actions.[33]

The specific assumptions of neutralization-drift theory are that delinquency is a matter of choice on the part of the delinquent, that juveniles exercise their choices based on the situation or circumstances at a particular point in time, and that delinquents are only somewhat alienated from society.[34] The basis for these assumptions is that the society's normative system is marked by flexibility. Flexibility, in fact, is an integral part of criminal law, which is a body of rules that are not held to be binding under certain conditions. If an individual can prove that criminal intent (mens rea) was lacking, he can avoid moral responsibility for his criminal actions and thus escape the negative social sanctions. Norms, however, are even more flexible than the criminal law.

Neutralization-drift theory is primarily based on the assumption that justifications for deviance that are seen as valid by the delinquent are not seen as valid by the legal system. They are however, part of the culture's **vocabulary of motives** commonly used to excuse or justify acts that are expected to be condemned by the greater society. These justifications are often referred to as *rationalizations*. They are viewed as preceding and facilitating deviant behavior, as well as protecting the individual both from self-blame and the condemnation of others that results from committing a deviant act.[35] Sykes and Matza called the justifications most frequently used by delinquents *techniques of neutralization*. They identified five major types:[36]

1. **Denial of responsibility:** The delinquent views the offense as resulting from forces outside of her or his control.
2. **Denial of injury:** The delinquent views the offense as not really causing any harm even though it is against the law.
3. **Denial of the victim:** The delinquent views the act as being caused by the victim.

4. **Condemnation of the condemners:** The delinquent shifts the focus of attention from his or her own deviant acts to the motives and behavior of those who disapprove of those delinquent acts.

5. **Appeal to higher loyalties:** The delinquent sacrifices the commonplace normative demands of the larger society for the primary moral demands of smaller social groups to which she or he belongs.

According to Sykes and Matza, these techniques of neutralization may not be powerful enough to shield offenders from the force of their own internalized values and the reactions of conforming others. However, they are critical in lessening the effectiveness of social controls and encouraging deviance. Thus, they are thought to underlie much delinquent behavior.[37]

These techniques are rooted in values that are held by the mainstream society but given secondary importance because they are contingent upon other, primary values. When a group elevates such *subterranean values* to primary importance, their meaning is inevitably distorted. Therefore, the behaviors they produce and justify are likely to be defined as deviant or criminal by the mainstream even though they originated in the mainstream society. For example, our culture recognizes the importance of leisure and recreation because of the emphasis it places on hard work, achievement, and self-sufficiency. When the search for leisure recreation becomes the primary value of a group of individuals, its meaning is distorted by the absence of prior hard work, achievement, and discipline. Without these primary values to modify the meaning of leisure, this normally beneficial goal becomes an impetus to delinquent behavior.[38]

· · · · · · · · · **APPLICATION** · · · · **The Case of Charles Manson**

Conspiracy
The act of agreeing to commit an unlawful act with two or more persons.[39]

The *precipitating factor* for Charles Manson's involvement in the Tate-La-Bianca murders was the same as for Atkins, Watson, Krenwinkel, Kasabian, and Van Houten—to absolve Beausoleil from guilt in the murder of Hinman. The *attracting factor* for Manson, however, was far different. Manson credited himself with the killing of a member of the Black Panthers in July of 1969. The Black Panthers were a radical group that gained notoriety during the late 1960s for their interest in weapons and their violent behavior. The day after Manson shot Bernard Crowe, he read in a Los Angeles newspaper that a member of the Black Panthers was found shot to death on the front lawn of a Los Angeles apartment building. Manson mistakenly believed that Bernard Crowe was this Black Panther. He felt certain that the Black Panthers would seek revenge.[40]

The female members of the Manson family came up with the copycat murder plan as a method to free Beausoleil from jail. However, Manson found the plan to be attractive because it would also make it appear that the Black Panthers had committed the Hinman and Tate-LaBianca killings.[41] This would not only free Beausoleil, but keep police attention away from Manson. Furthermore, the jailed Black Panthers would not be able to seek their revenge on Manson for the death of one of their members. Following the commission of the Tate-LaBianca murders, the murderers did, in fact, plant one of the victims' wallet and credit cards where they thought some Black Panthers would find them.[42]

The *predisposing factor* for Charles Manson was his early childhood environment and the fact that he had spent over half of his life (seventeen years) in juvenile and adult correctional facilities. Manson was born in 1934 to a sixteen-year-old prostitute who drank heavily. In 1939 she was sentenced to five years in a state penitentiary for armed robbery. When paroled in 1941, she reclaimed Charlie, who was then eight years old. In 1947 she tried to have him placed in a foster home, but since none were available, the court sent him to the Gibault School for Boys, a caretaker institution. After ten months at the Gibault School for Boys, he ran away and returned to his mother.[43] Although we cannot be certain of the details, the tendency toward legal trouble in Manson's youth could be partially attributable to fetal alcohol syndrome due to his mother being alcoholic at the time of his birth. This would allow for biological factors to be included in explanations of Manson's early childhood and adolescent behavior.

Charles Manson

At the age of twelve, Manson committed a burglary and was sent to Father Flanagan's Boys Town. After being there four days, he ran away and committed two robberies. For these robberies he was sent to the Indiana School for Boys, where he remained for three years. In those three years he ran away from the reformatory eighteen times.[44]

In 1951, during one of his escapes, he stole an automobile and took it across a state line, which is a federal offense. For this, he was sentenced to the National Training School for Boys in Washington, D.C. While there, he assaulted another boy by putting a razor blade to his throat and then sodomizing him. As a result he was transferred to the Federal Reformatory at Petersburg, Virginia.[45]

In 1954 Manson was paroled from the Federal Reformatory at Petersburg, Virginia. He was now nineteen years old. That same year he married Rosalie Jean Willis. He fathered one child with her while working as a busboy, service-station helper, and parking-lot attendant to support himself and his family. In 1955 he was again charged with transportation of a stolen automobile across state lines and given a five-year probated sentence.[46]

In 1956 Manson was arrested again, and his probation for the interstate transportation of stolen cars was revoked. He was sentenced to three years at Terminal Island, San Pedro, California. In 1958, while Manson was still in prison, his wife divorced him and was awarded custody of their son. By the time he was released from Terminal Island in 1958, he was what most authorities would describe as "the ideal correctional institutional inmate stereotype."[47]

In 1959 Manson was arrested for attempting to cash a United States Treasury check that he had stolen from a mailbox. He was given a ten-year probated sentence. That same year he married a nineteen-year-old girl named Leona. In 1960 he was indicted for transporting women across state lines for the purposes of prostitution (a violation of the Federal Mann Act). The court ruled he had violated his probation for the theft of the United States Treasury check and sent him to prison for ten years.[48]

In 1961 Manson began his ten-year sentence at the United States Penitentiary at McNeil Island, Washington. He was now twenty-six years old. According to correctional staff evaluation at McNeil Island, Manson felt more secure in correctional institutions than in the outside world because institutions had become his way of life. Leona divorced Manson in 1963, and there was allegedly a son from this union.[49]

Exhibit 7.9

Summary of facts and their role
in the explanation of the
Charles Manson case

Level of Importance	Fact	Type of Fact
Primary	His relationship with the Black Panthers	Attracting
Secondary	Free Beausoleil from jail	Precipitating
Tertiary	Family environment	Predisposing
Tertiary	Prisonization	Predisposing

In March of 1967 Manson was released from McNeil Island. The morning he was to be released, he literally begged the authorities to let him remain in prison. He told them that prison had become his home and that he did not think he could adjust to the outside world. After his release, Manson went to the Haight-Ashbury district of San Francisco, where the hippie movement was centered. It was in Haight-Ashbury that the Manson Family was born.[50]

Manson's involvement in the Family and the Tate-LaBianca killings is in large part explained by his socialization to crime and prison life. However, this explanation can be extended with neutralization theory. Manson's grudge against Terry Melcher (the real object of the murders, many believe, since Manson did not know that Melcher had moved out of the house) allowed him to *deny the victim*. He felt victimized by Melcher's refusal to acknowledge his musical talent, and this could have allowed him to neutralize his behavior.

Manson has repeatedly stated that he is a product of our society's welfare and correctional institutions. He is quite correct in this assertion. Because he was essentially raised by the government, he was able to *deny responsibility* for his entire personality and worldview. In addition, during the late 1960s, with extreme controversies raging about civil rights and Vietnam, it was relatively easy to dismiss the deaths of seven well-to-do citizens by *condemning the condemners*. That is, many people felt the government, and especially the "military-industrial complex," was killing thousands in an Asian war and ruining the lives of millions more through racial prejudice. Thus, Manson's condemnation of American institutions was much more in tune with the times in 1969 than it would be today.

Manson's belief in the "Helter-Skelter" prophecy also allowed him to *appeal to higher loyalties*. Also in this vein, he often implied he was a reincarnation of Jesus Christ. By twisting the syllables of his surname, he came to define himself as the "son of Man" which is a veiled reference to Christ. This belief would also have made a very convenient neutralization technique for the family members.

Exhibit 7.9 summarizes the facts of the Manson case.

Conclusion

The social-learning perspective fits the facts of this case quite well. (See Exhibit 7.10 for a summary of those facts.) Manson acted as a conduit by which prison norms were transmitted to Family members. In addition, the antiestablishment values of the hippie era provided a set of subterranean values that permitted

Level of Importance	Fact	Type of Fact
Primary	Free Beausoleil from jail	Precipitating
Secondary	Manson Family environment	Attracting
Tertiary	Manson's Black Panther relationship	Precipitating

Exhibit 7.10

· · · · · · · · · · · · · · · ·

Summary of facts and their role in the explanation of the Tate-LaBianca case

the Family to feel justified in its behavior. Manson was able to justify the control he exerted over the Family members by referring to the fact that they had already been rejected by the mainstream society. He may even have honestly believed that he was helping them since he was far more "streetwise" than they, and his presence was a guiding force in assuring the physical survival of these young people.

Drift does not, however, appear to have been a major factor in this case. At the time of the killings, the Family members seem to have had few doubts as to the necessity of their acts. However, their entry into the Family, in some cases, may be well explained by drift. The manner in which they justified their behavior can be explained by the techniques of neutralization. The social learning that went on in the Manson Family was extremely effective due to its intensity. The social isolation of the family from the rest of society, along with the severity of Manson's techniques, added to the frequency, duration, intensity, and priority of the definitions they used.

In more common circumstances, learning is more gradual and social groups are far less isolated from competing definitions of their behaviors. The social-learning perspective maintains that the crucial fact in explaining crime is that of cultural transmission. That is, (sub)cultures generate norms on the basis of their position in society, their unique environment, and their history. They then transmit these norms, along with rationalizations and techniques for them, to others. In this case, Family members learned to burglarize homes ("creepy-crawl"), sell drugs, and engage in deviant sexual acts very quickly because they were isolated from condemnation and experienced intense rewards for complying with Manson's desires. Manson taught them the norms of the prison that encouraged violence, homosexuality, racism, self-pity, and hatred of the dominant society.

A major implication of the social-learning perspective relates to the relationship between morality and crime. This perspective portrays the offender as a person caught between two worlds, or, more precisely, between two conflicting sets of definitions of right and wrong. For each act considered, the individual must choose between these sets of normative and moral guidelines. The setting in which decisions are made thus influences the choice of behaviors. The person's social contacts and observations of others are also crucial factors in such decisions. Furthermore, not all people define the same stimuli as rewarding or punishing. Going to jail would be a punishment for most people, but for Charlie Manson it was more like a long-awaited homecoming. The point is that we learn to define objects and events by experiencing them as rewards or punishments and by observing how others define them. At each point in this process, we must weigh competing definitions, and their anticipated consequences, so as to choose a behavior.

Other social-learning theorists believe that the process of acquiring definitions of behaviors is more complex than this. Daniel Glazer proposed that in addition to the processes of social learning identified by Sutherland and Akers, there is a simultaneous process of **differential anticipation** occurring in many cases. Differential-anticipation theory suggests that people are most likely to commit those acts for which they expect the greatest reward and the least punishment. The crucial idea here is that what the person anticipates in the way of rewards and punishments may differ from what the objective likelihood is.[50]

What the classical school referred to as the pleasure-pain principle is involved in differential anticipation. This concept serves to link social-learning theories with the idea of social control through bonding that is dealt with in Chapter 12. The isolation of the Manson Family may have resulted in unrealistic expectations as to the likelihood of freeing Beausoleil from jail, initiating Helter-Skelter, and similar goals that strike members of the mainstream society as somewhat fantastic.

The idea that role-models are critical in shaping behavior is accentuated in Glaser's idea of **differential identification.** This theory maintains that people establish links between themselves and particular individuals or groups, and then judge themselves and their actions by the norms of these groups. As people observe what they believe to be the typical attitudes, values, and behaviors of those they admire or desire to be like, they set up an identification with that group or individual and model their behavior on that image. They need no personal contact with the group or person they admire, however.[51] Media portrayals of crime that glorify illicit lifestyles are thought to provide a source of differential identification for many youths. In Manson's case, Charlie identified with the prison culture even though he had been free for some time. His manipulation of the identities of the Family members forced them to strengthen their identification with him while reducing their identification with other groups.

While the social-learning perspective does well in explaining the crimes of Manson and his Family, other perspectives can contribute to the explanation of these crimes. The biological perspective could speculate on the role played by Manson's mother's alcohol abuse while she was pregnant with Charlie. The Family's involvement in drugs probably played a role in lowering their inhibitions against violence and might have made them more easily influenced by Manson's guru-like self-presentation.

Some authorities would contend that Manson was a sociopath and that this personality disorder caused him to manipulate the others in a variety of bizarre ways, culminating in the Tate-LaBianca killings. Control theorists would emphasize the intense bonds that Manson developed among the family members that caused them to internalize his norms. Social-disorganization theorists would add that the turmoil of the late 1960s created a sense of normlessness throughout the nation of which the Family and its crimes were merely a symptom.

No single view can explain all the facts of these crimes adequately, but together they give a rather thorough explanation that makes these crimes more understandable.

Glossary ·

Appeal to Higher Loyalties The delinquent sacrifices the demands of the larger society for the demands of the smaller social groups to which she or he belongs.

Condemnation of the Condemners The delinquent shifts the focus of attention from his or her own deviant acts to the motives and behavior of those who disapprove of the acts.

Denial of Responsibility The delinquent views the offense as resulting from forces outside of the individual.

Denial of Injury The delinquent views the offense as not really causing any harm even though it is against the law.

Denial of the Victim The delinquent views the offense as not being wrong in light of the actions or status of the victim.

Differential-Anticipation Theory Suggests that people are most likely to commit those acts for which they expect the greatest reward and the least punishment. The crucial idea here is that what the person expects may differ from what the objective likelihood is.

Differential Association The process(es) of learning behaviors in small groups by which some individuals learn to define certain crimes as appropriate behaviors because positive definitions of these acts outweigh negative ones.

Differential Identification Theory Maintains that people establish mental links between themselves and particular individuals or groups and then judge themselves and their actions by the norms of those groups—even if they are not directly acquainted with the people in these groups. As people observe what they believe to be the typical attitudes, values, and behaviors of those they admire or desire to be like, they set up an identification with that group or individual and model their behavior on that image.

Differential Social Organization Allows for some groups within society to be criminally oriented and others not, and explains that crime rates are differentially distributed in societies because of differences between subgroups.

Drift A state in which the individual is simultaneously under the influence of both deviant and conforming norms. Persons in this situation tend to fluctuate between these competing norm systems for a period of time before becoming bonded to one or the other. The idea of drift is especially applicable to young people who are experimenting with multiple group memberships and behaviors.

Extinction Occurs when a behavior is eradicated from a person's repertoire of acts through the use of punishments.

Membership Groups Collections of individuals that participate in face-to-face interaction with one another over some period of time. There is no assumption of common traits among these groups. Rather, participation in activities with other members is their defining feature.

Vocabulary of Motives Rationalizations, excuses, and/or justifications for deviant acts that are commonly accepted by the greater society for minor norm violations.

Vicarious Learning   The acquisition of behavior and knowledge through the observation of the behavior of others and its consequences.

■ Notes

1. Edwin H. Sutherland and Donald R. Cressey, *Principles of Criminology* (Philadelphia: Lippincott, 1955).
2. Harold J. Vetter and Ira J. Silverman, *Criminology and Crime: An Introduction* (New York: Harper & Row, 1986).
3. Curt Gentry and Vincent Bugliosi, *Helter Skelter* (New York: W. W. Norton & Company, 1974).
4. Thomas T. Noguchi with Joseph DiMona, *Coroner* (New York: Simon & Schuster, 1983).
5. Edwin H. Sutherland, *Principles of Criminology*, 3d ed. (New York: Lippincott, 1939); James F. Short, Jr., "Differential Association As a Hypothesis: Problems of Empirical Testing," *Social Problems* 8 (1960): pp. 14–25.
6. Gentry and Bugliosi, *Helter Skelter.*
7. Ibid.
8. Ibid.
9. Ibid., p. 302.
10. Ibid., pp. 275–277.
11. Nuel Emmons, *Manson in His Own Words* (New York: Grove Press, 1986).
12. Ibid.
13. George E. Rush, *The Dictionary of Criminal Justice*, 2d ed. (Guilford, CT: Dushkin Publishing Group, 1986), p. 2.
14. Nuel Emmons, *Manson in His Own Words* (New York: Grove Press, 1986); Susan Atkins with Bob Slosser, *Child of Satan, Child of God* (New York: Bantam Books, 1978).
15. Atkins with Slosser, *Child of Satan, Child of God*; Lawrence Schiller, *The Killing of Sharon Tate* (New York: New American Library, 1970).
16. Ibid.
17. Atkins with Slosser, *Child of Satan, Child of God.*
18. Ibid.
19. Gentry and Bugliosi, *Helter Skelter*, p. 235.
20. Atkins with Slosser, *Child of Satan, Child of God.*
21. Gentry and Bugliosi, *Helter Skelter*, pp. 558, 661.
22. Atkins with Slosser, *Child of Satan, Child of God.*
23. Robert L. Burgess, and Ronald Akers, "A Differential Association-Reinforcement Theory of Criminal Behavior," *Social Problems* 14 (1966): pp. 128–147; Ronald L. Akers, Marvin D. Krohn, Lonn Lanza-Kaduce, and Marcia Radosevich, "Social Learning and Deviant Behavior: A Specific Test of a General Theory," *American Sociological Review* 44 (1979): pp. 636–655.
24. Ibid.
25. Rush, *The Dictionary of Criminal Justice*, pp. 83–84.
26. Gentry and Bugliosi, *Helter Skelter.*
27. Ibid.

28. Ibid., p. 483.
29. Ibid., p. 629.
30. Gresham M. Sykes and David Matza, "Techniques of Neutralization: A Theory of Delinquency," *American Sociological Review* 22 (1957): pp. 664–670; Shoemaker, *Theories of Delinquency.*
31. Ibid.
32. David Matza, *Delinquency and Drift* (New York: Wiley, 1964).
33. Ibid.
34. Shoemaker, *Theories of Delinquency.*
35. C. Wright Mills, "Situated Actions and Vocabularies of Motive," *American Sociological Review* 5 (1940): pp. 904–913.
36. Sykes and Matza, *Techniques of Neutralization: A Theory of Delinquency.*
37. Ibid.
38. Gresham Sykes and David Matza, "Juvenile Delinquency and Subterranean Values," *American Sociological Review* 26 (1961): pp. 712–719.
39. Rush, *The Dictionary of Criminal Justice,* pp. 49–50.
40. Gentry and Bugliosi, *Helter Skelter.*
41. Gentry and Bugliosi, *Helter Skelter;* Atkins with Slosser, *Child of Satan, Child of God.*
42. Atkins with Slosser, *Child of Satan, Child of God.*
43. Gentry and Bugliosi, *Helter Skelter.*
44. Ibid.
45. Ibid.
46. Ibid.
47. Ibid.
48. Ibid.
49. Ibid.
50. Daniel Glazer, *Crime in Our Changing Society* (New York: Holt Rinehart and Winston, 1965), pp. 125–126.
51. Daniel Glaser, "Criminality Theories and Behavioral Images" in D. R. Cressey and D. A. Ward (eds.), *Delinquency, Crime and Social Process* (New York: Harper & Row, 1969); Daniel Glaser, "Role Models and Differential Association" in E. Rubington and M. S. Weinberg (eds.), *Deviance: The Interactionist Perspective* (New York: Macmillan, 1973).

▪ Suggested Readings

Ronald L. Akers, Marvin D. Krohn, Lonn Lanza-Kaduce, and Marcia Radosevich, "Social Learning and Deviant Behavior: A Specific Test of a General Theory," *American Sociological Review* 44 (1979): p. 636–655.

Susan Atkins with Bob Slosser, *Child of Satan, Child of God* (New York: Bantam Books, 1978).

Robert L. Burgess and Ronald Akers, "A Differential Association-Reinforcement Theory of Criminal Behavior," *Social Problems* 14 (1966): pp. 128–147.

Nuel Emmons, *Manson in His Own Words* (New York: Grove Press, 1986).

Curt Gentry and Vincent Bugliosi, *Helter Skelter* (New York: W.W. Norton & Company, 1974).

■ Suggested Books for Additional Application

Thomas E. Gaddis and James O. Long, Killer: A Journal of Murder (New York: Macmillan, 1970).

Mike Maguire and Trevor Bennett, "Peter Hudson: From Sweets to Antiques" in *Burglary in a Dwelling* (London: England: Heinemann, 1982), pp. 90–121.

Ed Sanders, *The Family* (New York: New American Library, 1989).

Ernest Volkman and John Cummings, *The Heist: How a Gang Stole $8,000,000 at Kennedy Airport and Lived to Regret It* (New York: Franklin Watts, 1986).

John Hugner and Lindsey Gruson, *Monkey on a Stick: Murder, Madness and the Hare Krishnas* (New York: Penguin Books USA, 1990).

CHAPTER **8**

Societal-Reaction Perspective

Overview of Societal-Reaction Perspective

The societal-reaction perspective, commonly called the *labeling* perspective, was originally designed to explain the effects of apprehension for minor rule violations on future behavior. It originated as a reaction to the deterministic assumptions of psychiatry and psychology. This is a perspective most applicable to youthful offenders, but it has also been applied to the mentally ill and has been used by educators. The original proponents—Tannenbaum, Lemert, Kitsuse, Erikson, and Becker—do not suggest that it be used for explaining the initial causes of criminal acts.[1] The perspective is intended rather to broaden the area of criminological study by including the activities of *all* the people involved in acts of crime and social responses to those acts.[2] That is, the perspective includes the role of other actors such as the police and the courts as well as the criminal. These actors, in addition to psychiatrists, schoolteachers, and social workers, have the power to apply formal labels that could have a negative impact on the recipient. They are referred to as **control agents.**[3]

While some labeling theorists are primarily concerned with the activities of control agents, others are more interested in the effects of labels on behavior and its reinforcement.[4] This aspect of the perspective attempts to explain the processes by which labels are applied and the role they play in establishing and/or perpetuating patterns of criminal involvement. Subdivisions within the perspective address the offender's self-image and status or the activities of control agencies and their employees. Exhibit 8.1 gives the common assumptions of this perspective.

The process by which labels are applied to offenders by police, courts, and other control agents is the chief interest of the societal reaction perspective.

Common Assumptions

1. No human act is inherently criminal.

2. Crime is socially defined, it is a property conferred upon certain acts by societal reactions.

3. The labels assigned to people affect their self-image, material well-being and thus, their behavior.

Source: K.T. Erikson, "Notes on the Sociology of Deviance," *Social Problems* 9 (Spring 1962): pp. 307–314; T.F. Cullen and J.B. Cullen, *Toward a Paradigm of Labeling Theory* (Lincoln, NE: The University of Nebraska, 1978), p. 5.

The question of how crime is socially defined is a major concern of the societal-reaction perspective, since one of its major assumptions is that social acts become crimes only when defined as such by social audiences.[5] Societal-reaction theorists contend that crime "is not a quality of the act a person commits"[6] or "a property inherent in certain forms of behavior,"[7] but rather is external to the act and actor.[8] That is, what is defined as a criminal act is determined largely by the audience's reaction to the act and its perpetrator. Thus, criminality is not a trait possessed by individuals; it is a property conferred upon some acts by societal reactions to them.[9]

The nature of the social control system and its agents is therefore critical to this perspective. This sort of macro-level concern means that there is much overlap between the interactionist approach to labeling and the conflict perspectives dealt with in Chapters 13 and 14 of this text. In fact, this perspective can be said to represent a combination of insights from social-learning and conflict theories.

Within the societal-reaction perspective, two approaches may be identified, interactionist and consequence. Although both approaches stress interaction and are concerned with the consequences of labeling, they have different emphases. Interaction versus consequences is a basic issue of this perspective. The *interactionist approach* primarily focuses on issues involving the development and enforcement of laws, and in particular on the interaction between offenders and agents of social control. This approach is vital to understanding crime statistics and agency behavior. The *consequence approach,* on the other hand, focuses predominately on issues involved with the effects of labeling on the self-concept and behavior of the offender.[10] This approach is focused on the social psychology of the offender and those associated with him or her.

These approaches do not contradict one another. They merely focus on different actors within the criminal justice system. Because most of the key points made by the consequence approach are presumed by the interactionist approach, the consequence approach will be dealt with first.

Consequence Approach
. . . .

Frank Tannenbaum, an education historian, is generally credited with the creation of the consequence approach (see Exhibit 8.2) to labeling. Tannen-

Exhibit 8.2

· · · · · · · · · · · · · · · ·

Consequence approach

Restrictive Assumptions

1. Criminal labels can alter a person's self-image.

2. Changes in a person's self-image can encourage acceptance of a criminal identity and criminal behavior.

3. Continuation and/or intensification of criminal behavior is often the result of such changes in the person's self-image.

Source: Frank Tannenbaum, *Crime and the Community* (Boston: Ginn and Co., 1938).

baum focused attention on what he called the **dramatization of evil** in elementary and secondary schools. He noted that rule violations, even isolated ones, were given a disproportionate amount of attention by teachers. This attention led to the characterization of the child in terms of acts that were often not typical of the child's usual behavior. Focusing on such acts brought attention to the rule violation rather than the child as a person. Tannenbaum felt this was both unfair and harmful to the child's future behavior and self-image.

For societal-reaction theorists like Tannenbaum, Lemert, Becker, Goffman, and Scheff, the major concern has been with the effects of negative social reactions on individual behavior.[11] The basic idea is that criminal labels can alter the way people perceive themselves because of their direct effects on the material well-being and social status of the labeled person. It is thought that these material and social consequences are the mechanisms by which the self-image is altered.[12] This approach suggests that true and repetitive criminal behavior is often the result of accepting and conforming to the negative expectations implied by labels that have been assigned.[13]

The consequence approach to the effects of societal reaction holds that individuals pass through a transition from non-deviant to deviant status. Edwin Lemert is usually credited with developing this approach. He argued that most people who violate social rules see themselves as relatively normal until they are apprehended and labeled. At that time a **stigma** is attached to the person, meaning a negative label that has social and/or material consequences for its holder. People then react to that person differently, with the result that she or he becomes isolated from the mainstream society. Such isolation encourages increased association with others who have similar labels and the operation of social-learning processes leading to crime.

Becker extends our insight into this transformation by describing four states through which deviants pass: situational availability, the initial act, continuation of the behavior, and identification with deviant groups.[14]

Situational availability essentially refers to the opportunity to engage in illegal acts. This is a prerequisite for the act to occur. For example, illegal drugs must be available in order for them to be purchased. Customers must be available to prostitutes in order for prostitution to occur.

The *initial deviant act* is essentially that—the first time the deviant act is committed by an individual. It may be committed out of ignorance of the law, out of a desire to experiment, or as a result of peer pressure to conform, among other reasons.

Continuation of the behavior is most likely the result of being labeled deviant. That is, once the particular deviant label (e.g., "pothead," "junkie," "prostitute," "thief," etc.) has been assigned, the individual is likely to continue the type of deviance with which he or she has been identified.

Identification with deviant groups, the final stage, is simply the mental linkage of the labeled person's self-image with the label and others who share it. In essence, by joining the deviant group, the individual has accepted the deviant label and uses the other deviant group members as a reference group, rather than non-labeled members of conventional society.

Garfinkel suggests that labeling ceremonies, such as trials, are concerned with the alteration of people's identities. According to Garfinkel, there is no society whose social structure does not provide ceremonies of identity degradation. He claims that the structural conditions of status degradation are universal in all societies and that the fact of status degradation through labeling has the effect of recasting the objective character of the stigmatized person. That person comes to be seen as a different person by society and acquaintances.

In our society, the arenas of degradation where the redefined person has the widest transferability between groups are the courts, which have a near-monopoly over such ceremonies.[15] Not only are such official "ceremonies" seen as very powerful social psychological forces in themselves, but theorists like Tannenbaum would add that the ability to place negative statements about a person's behavior and/or character in an official file that is to be used by others gives much power to both official labels and the control agents who assign them.

Lemert's Labeling-Consequences Theory

Lemert's labeling theory (see Exhibit 8.3) proposes that continued criminal behavior is pathological and in need of explanation. Lemert focuses on the causes of continued criminal pathological behavior, not the causes of the initial behavior. According to this theory, criminal behavior becomes habitual as a result of stigmatizing labels being assigned to and accepted by offenders.[16]

The causes of initial criminal acts are many and varied.[17] For example, persons may commit thefts because they are insane, have no money to live on, have business debts, or just for the thrill of it. From this approach then, initial and unrecognized acts of crime are viewed as symptomatic of a tendency

---

Exhibit 8.3

Lemert's labeling-consequences theory

Specific Assumptions

1. All people commit acts that violate the society's rules, but most such infractions are of minor significance, if they are noticed at all.

2. Official criminal labels, however, alter the person's self-image and encourage conformity to the stereotype associated with the label.

3. Patterns of criminality are often the result of the self-image being altered by such stigma.

Source: E.M. Lemert, *Social Pathology* (New York: McGraw-Hill, 1951).

towards criminality, rather than a pathology. All people are believed to commit some acts that could be defined as criminal. These actions are not habitual, however. They are merely isolated incidents of little consequence for either the actor or the society. Lemert refers to such initial and unlabeled acts as **primary criminal behavior** (primary deviance). Such acts usually have few, if any, consequences for the individual's self-image or material well-being.

According to this theory, primary (initial) criminal behavior remains a minor symptom as long as it is dealt with by the offender as part of a socially acceptable **master status,** which is defined as the major social label that a person uses to define him or herself (e.g., housewife, student, business executive, truck driver, etc.).[18] This status is the central feature of the person's self-image and acts to define and modify the content of all the other roles that individual occupies. A housewife whose primary criminal behavior is part-time prostitution can retain her housewife master status, as can business executives who embezzle funds from their companies, so long as stigma and negative consequences do not occur as a result of their acts. That is, such people think of themselves as, and act like, housewives or executives except perhaps when actually committing the primary or initial criminal act(s). It is very important to note that others respond to them according to this "normal" master status. Such primary deviants do not suffer socially or materially for their criminality.

When there is a significant and/or official societal reaction to such primary criminal behavior, however, the socially acceptable master status may be replaced with a criminal one. Lemert refers to criminal behavior that occurs after a criminal label has been applied to the individual as **secondary criminal behavior** (secondary deviance) and sees it as largely the result of assigned criminal labels. As the criminal behavior becomes increasingly habitual, the actor begins to identify with the criminal role assigned by the labeling process.[19]

According to this theory, the sequence of events leading from primary criminal behavior to secondary criminal behavior is as follows:[20]

1. Primary criminal behavior is socially reacted to through the labeling process.
2. The stigmatization and penalties that occur as a result of that process lead to acceptance of and conformity to the criminal role as the new master status.
3. This new, criminal master status leads to continued and accelerated criminal behavior.

Thus, the changes in the psyches of the housewives and business executives that result from their labeling as prostitutes and embezzlers force these individuals to perceive themselves as criminals rather than as housewives and business executives, and their criminal behavior increases. Their master status has been altered by the label and society's reaction to it.

This criminal-labeling process is thought to turn occasional or isolated acts of criminal behavior into patterns of criminality—in large part due to the ostracism that occurs within the internal political and social-psychological processes of small groups.[21] Housewives who are publicly labeled as prostitutes and business executives who are publicly labeled as embezzlers (to continue our example) cannot control the ostracism of the social audiences they encounter. Thus, the social roles available to them are narrowed to those of the

criminal by the processes of differential association, reinforcement, and identification (see Chapter 7 on social-learning theory). The changes that occur
within the individual's psyche as a result of such ostracism from socially acceptable groups lead to a reconstruction of the person's identity as a criminal.
Exemplary of the changes brought about by stigmatization would be the part-
time prostitute housewife who, once labeled, takes on the life of a full-time
prostitute in self-image and lifestyle.

Stigmatized people are no longer seen and reacted to as "normal" by those
around them but are viewed instead according to their label(s). For example,
Johnny occasionally steals cars in order to go joyriding. He is committing
primary criminal acts, but sees himself as a normal kid who occasionally
"borrows" a car to go for a ride. In this state of primary criminality, the
individual commits rule violations but sees her or himself as "normal." Those
around the person share this view. Once apprehended by the police for his
crime, though, Johnny is publicly labeled a thief. Now others react to him as
a thief, rather than as a normal person who committed an act that society
defines as criminal. His law-abiding friends are no longer permitted to associate
with him, so he can get few rewards from conventional activities. However,
his label provides him access to delinquent groups that will reward him for
the label and for further criminal activity. Johnny now occupies the status of
a criminal because he possesses a stigmatizing label that has adversely affected
his social and material well-being.

The Case of Christiane F. · · · · · · · · · · · · · · · · | APPLICATION | · · · · · · · ·

Because this case involves a minor, she will be identified only as Christiane F.
When she was six, Christiane F. and her parents moved from a small rural
community in Germany to a high-rise apartment in a lower-class neighborhood
in Berlin. Her father was an alcoholic who could not support his family and
who physically abused Christiane and her younger sister. Out of fear for her
own safety, Mrs. F. would not defend her daughters from her husband's abuse.
Mr. F's alcoholism and violence seem to have been the result of his resentment
over feeling forced to marry Mrs. F. when she became pregnant out of wedlock
with Christiane. Mr. F. blamed his failures in life on getting married and having
children. He felt so strongly about this that he didn't want any of his friends
to know that he was married or that he had children. He made his wife pass
herself off as his sister and forced his children to call him "Uncle" around his
friends.[24] When Christiane was twelve years old, her parents divorced and
Christiane remained with her mother while her sister went to live with their
father. Shortly after her parents' divorce, her mother took up with a steady
boyfriend with whom Christiane did not get along.[25]

Christiane F. was of above-average intelligence. Up until the age of thirteen,
her social and mental development appeared to be quite normal. However,
she did feel rejected at school and felt lost as a result. By the age of thirteen,
she and her friends had begun abusing alcohol and hashish. Her initial reason
for getting involved with substance abusers was that she did not get along
with her mother's boyfriend. Initially she had done well in school, but her
academic performance deteriorated as her substance abuse increased.[26] Like
many youths, her illegal behavior was not immediately detected and she still

Prostitution
The act of offering or agreeing to
engage in, or engaging in, a sex
act with another person in return
for a fee.[22]

Streetwalker
Slang for a prostitute who stands
on the sidewalk or roadway to
solicit passers-by.[23]

saw herself as a relatively normal teenager who had been rejected by the school system. Because she was unhappy at home and felt that the school had rejected her, there seemed to be little to lose by deepening her drug involvement.

While she was still thirteen, Christiane left her alcohol- and hashish-abusing peer group to join a group of more serious drug abusers who were school dropouts. While with this new group, she began using more dangerous drugs, such as LSD and ephedrine (uppers). As a result of these involvements, she began doing even worse in school than before and attended school even less.[27] Still age thirteen, she joined an even more serious drug-using crowd that hung out at a discotheque. There she became the girlfriend of a sixteen-year-male who was both a heroin addict and a homosexual prostitute. At the beginning of their relationship, she initially gave him only what money she had to help him buy his heroin. Then she began "scrounging" (e.g., panhandling, bumming) for money to help him buy his heroin.[28]

In April of 1976, a month before her fourteenth birthday, Christiane first began using heroin by inhaling (i.e., "snorting") it. Shortly thereafter she began injecting heroin intravenously. At the age of fourteen she lost her virginity to her boyfriend, and during the winter of 1976 she began working as a prostitute in order to obtain money to support her own heroin habit. Initially, she defined sex with customers as a form of "scrounging" for money, rather than as prostitution. This allowed her to reject the identity of a prostitute and rationalize her behavior. Subsequently, her boyfriend began asking her to have sex with his bisexual customers. Up until this point in time, she had not thought of herself as a prostitute. However, with her boyfriend's bisexual customers becoming her customers, she began to see her prostitution as a business and herself as a prostitute with customers of her own.

While still fourteen, she was arrested by the police for possession of heroin and was questioned about prostitution. She was registered as a drug addict by the police, who then released her to her mother. This was the first time she had been publicly labeled as a heroin addict, or "junkie."[29]

Christiane immediately went back to abusing heroin and engaging in prostitution. In early 1977 she was arrested again on substance-abuse charges but was subsequently released. By this time almost all of the plainclothes police officers in the area where Christiane met her prostitution customers knew her as a "junkie." On at least one occasion, a plainclothes police officer confronted her about her prostitution activities but did not arrest her. Presumably she was treated leniently because of her age despite her known status as a **street walker** (a prostitute who stands on the sidewalk or roadway to solicit men who pass by).[30]

Christiane F. was finally indicted on an illegal-substance-abuse charge in Berlin, Germany, in July 1977. She was found guilty of continuous purchase of narcotic drugs in coincidence with continuous tax evasion. Her sentence was suspended and she was placed on probation. In November 1977 her mother forced her to go to live with relatives in a rural community. After moving there, she broke away from her Berlin drug-using friends and, as of the spring of 1980 (the last date for which information is available), was completely free of drugs.[31]

By isolating her from audiences that had labeled her as a prostitute-junkie, Christiane's mother helped her reestablish a "normal" identity. By sending her

Level of Importance	Fact	Type of Fact
Primary	Christiane F.'s family environment	Predisposing
Secondary	Christiane F.'s substance-abusing peer groups	Attracting
Tertiary	Christiane F.'s boyfriend	Precipitating

Exhibit 8.4

Summary of facts and their role in the explanation of the Christiane F. case

to a rural area, she simultaneously removed her from the influence of differential reinforcement and association by her drug-abusing peers. This allowed Christiane to retreat from her status of a secondary, or labeled, criminal and from the ostracism that accompanies such a label. Christiane was fortunate to have this opportunity early enough in the process of labeling and learning. She was thus able to avoid the cycle of labeling, ostracism by conventional society, and reinforcement by the criminal subculture that produces hardened criminal self-images and behavior patterns. Exhibit 8.4 summarizes the facts of her case.

Christiane F.

The case of Christiane F. is especially appropriate for a labeling-consequences explanation because of her age and the relatively minor nature of her crimes. Christiane's experiences reflect Lemert's concepts of primary and secondary deviance. In Lemert's terminology, her initial crimes of substance abuse and prostitution were acts of primary deviance. That is, when she initially committed these acts, she did not perceive herself to be either a drug addict or a prostitute. However, after her boyfriend's bisexual customers became her customers, her informal treatment as a prostitute by the police, and the court's application of the official label of substance abuser, she began to perceive herself as both a substance abuser and a prostitute. The activity with the bisexual customers was significant enough to break through her rationalization of normality, while the experience of being arrested carried formal labels with it.

As mentioned earlier, Lemert and the other labeling theorists are not concerned with the original causes of criminal behavior, nor do they attempt to explain them. In Christiane F.'s case, the original causes of her criminal behavior may best be explained by psychological or social-learning explanations. Labeling theorists would not disagree with this. What is important to remember is that Lemert's theory provides an explanation for the continuation and intensification of the criminal behavior over time. Christiane F. saw her master status as that of a schoolgirl prior to her involvement with her boyfriend's bisexual customers, the courts, and the police. Her feelings of rejection at school weakened this identity and encouraged her to associate with others who did poorly at school. This led her into a situation of differential association-reinforcement which was deepened by the subsequent labeling of her acts as criminal. She saw her master status as that of a heroin addict/prostitute and continued in that role until her mother forced her out of it.

Interactionist Approach

Schur suggests that there are three types of social audiences whose reactions are critical to the labeling process: the significant other, the social control agency, and the society-at-large (see Exhibit 8.5).[32] All three levels contribute to both social control and personal identity. **Significant-Other audiences** are made up of people who live in direct daily contact with one another (i.e., family members, relatives, friends, neighbors, co-workers, etc.). A significant other is anyone whose opinion matters to the other person. **Social control agency audiences** are made up primarily of people who, because of their employment, serve as official representatives of public agencies (e.g., police officers, probation officers, judges, the staff of mental institutions, etc.). They have formal labeling powers. **Society-at-large audiences** are made up principally of people who belong to social groups within society who would ordinarily not come into direct contact with criminals except for their involvement in some group with political interests (e.g., national, state, and local legislative bodies and political parties, right-to-life and pro-choice activist groups, parent-teacher associations, etc.).

Different subgroups exist within each of these audiences, and each subgroup reacts differently to various sorts of acts because each has different values and concerns. For example, one significant-other social audience's reaction might be to define spouse battering as noncriminal, whereas another's might be to want the batterer executed. The following hypothetical scenario about two men stabbed by their wives highlights the practical consequences of differing significant-other societal reactions.

> Two men are stabbed by their respective wives. Both stabbings occur during arguments over the husbands' infidelity. When the police arrive at the scene of the first stabbing, the husband is angry and tells the police that his wife has just attempted to kill him. This man's wife is arrested and taken to jail. However, when the police arrive at the scene of the other stabbing, the husband feels guilty about having had an affair and informs the police that his wife slipped on the floor and accidentally stabbed him. This wife is not charged with any crime and not taken into custody. As you can see, the reaction of the husbands as significant-other audiences resulted in two completely different consequences for the identical acts committed by their wives.

Exhibit 8.5

Interactionist approach

Restrictive Assumptions

1. Social audiences determine whether an act is criminal or not.
2. Definitions of behavior as criminal or noncriminal are dependent on social audiences' responses to the behavior.
3. There are three levels of societal reactions to behavior:
   a. significant other,
   b. social control agency, and
   c. society-at-large.

Source: E.M. Schur, *Labeling Deviant Behavior: Its Sociological Implications* (New York: Harper & Row, 1971), pp. 12–14.

Many crimes are never reported to police because the victims or witnesses do not feel that a "real" crime has occurred. Furthermore, the way in which an act is initially explained to police has much to do with their subsequent actions in regard to prosecuting the case.

In addition to the importance of significant-other definitions in the reporting of criminal acts to agents of social control, there is another important aspect to these definitions—the perpetuation of criminal behavior. This aspect of significant-other definitions is readily apparent in cases of unreported spouse abuse. In many of these situations the abused spouse calls the police while being battered in an attempt to stop the violence rather than to report a crime. This has the effect of temporarily interrupting spousal violence, but not deterring it or labeling the abuser as a criminal. In these types of situations, the significant others' noncriminal definition of the act (despite the criminal label that control agents would give it) allows for the perpetuation of the criminal behavior.

The formal definition of what constitutes a criminal act is typically found in state penal, family, and criminal procedure codes. These are the definitions used by the official agents of social control. For example, the act of unlawfully taking property with the intent to deprive the owner of it is defined by the social control agents within the criminal justice system as a criminal act of theft.[33] As with significant-other audiences, social control agents have much discretionary power over their reactions to acts. That is, they must decide whether each act reported to them is criminal, and if so, what type of violation it constitutes. This is true in spite of the fact that legislative bodies have already provided formal definitions of crime that are further refined by court decisions.

A hypothetical example of differences in control-agent audience reactions can be seen in the following scenario:

> Two young men take radios from a store without purchasing them. One is apprehended with the unpurchased radio outside the store by a policeman. The policeman takes this person back into the store. The man returns the radio and the policeman releases him. A second man is apprehended under the same circumstances. This time the policeman arrests the man and charges him with theft by shoplifting.

As can readily be seen in this hypothetical scenario, the different reactions of social control agents lead to some of the same acts being treated as criminal while others are not. Such judgments must be made on a daily basis by control agents and often result in controversial charges of favoritism and bias.

This also illustrates the importance of the relationships between the reactions of the three types of audiences. Social-audience interrelatedness was vividly pointed out by Mechanic, a mental health researcher who found that, due to the time limits imposed on them by institutions, physicians in large mental hospitals assume the patients brought before them to be ill and accordingly apply labels to alleged, if not recognizable, mental illness symptoms.[34] Therefore, most of the actions of stigmatized people are interpreted as symptoms of their supposed pathological condition regardless of their actual source.

Goffman used the term **looping** to describe this sort of phenomenon wherein a person's attempts to prove a stigma false are used by agency personnel (or any other audience) to demonstrate the continued presence of that trait and to increase the severity of the label.[35] Looping indicates that the label is unquestioned and that all of the stigmatized person's actions are perceived as evidence of that label's validity. Looping may occur with any type of audience but is most common among "people-processing" agencies.[36]

An example of looping would be a parole officer who witnesses a parolee under his supervision assisting an elderly woman across the street and assumes the parolee is attempting to steal the woman's purse. The parole officer "loops" the parolee's act of altruism (i.e., helping the elderly woman) into a criminal act (i.e., stealing a purse). No matter what the parolee does to attempt to prove to the officer that she or he is attempting to live a decent life, the officer will interpret all acts as symptomatic of the label "parolee," which implies criminality. The label thus serves as a sort of lens that colors the officer's interpretation of all the parolee's actions.

Similarly, the basic decision regarding the criminality of many acts occurs prior to the person being taken into custody for a criminal act and is made by professional members of the community such as the police or probation officer. Like the mental health professionals, these control agents usually assume that their need to be involved with the person is sufficient evidence that the person is a criminal. The significant-other conceptual definition of "crime" or "a criminal act" is therefore important because this definition often determines whether or not an act is reported to control agents. This informal level of labeling also influences the manner in which the act will be reported. These factors, in turn, strongly affect the sort of labels that official control agents will apply when and if they become involved in the situation.

Scheff's Interactionist-Labeling Theory

Although Scheff's theory was originally designed to address serious mental illness, it is also a general theory of labeling that can easily be applied to other forms of deviant behavior such as crime (see Exhibit 8.6). In this text we have taken the liberty of modifying the language of Scheff's theory to specifically address criminal behavior.

In the last of the assumptions listed in Exhibit 8.6, Scheff identifies six variables as predicting the likelihood of an official societal reaction to law-breaking, as well as the severity of that reaction. Three of the variables identified were the visibility, degree, and amount of law-breaking.[37] The more obvious the rule violation is to others (i.e., the more visible), especially formal control agents, the greater the likelihood of societal reaction. Visibility is closely related to accessibility. The more observable a person is to control agents, the greater the likelihood that she or he will be apprehended for a rule violation. Since wealth and power allow people to restrict access to themselves, these variables are inversely related, with the poor being the easiest to observe and label.

Typically, societal reactions are more severe when the behavior involves laws governing serious felony crimes than they are for misdemeanor-type offenses. For example, social audiences (e.g., significant-other or agents of social control) that observe actions violating drug laws may easily ignore them, while audiences that observe acts of homicide cannot. However, the chance of a societal reaction to illegal drug sales increases proportionately with the number of illegal drug sales in which a person is involved (frequency) and the size of the transactions (severity).

Exhibit 8.6
. . . .
Scheff's interactionist-labeling
theory

Specific Assumptions

1. Criminal behavior originates from a variety of diverse sources and much of it is of so little consequence that it is never reported.

2. Criminal stereotypes are learned in early childhood and are constantly reaffirmed in everyday social interaction.

3. Persons assigned criminal labels may be rewarded for adhering to the stereotypical role of the criminal.

4. Persons labeled as criminals may be penalized for attempts to return to conventional, noncriminal roles.

5. In the crisis of being publicly labeled, people are highly vulnerable and may surrender to the role of the criminal as the only available alternative.

6. Criminal labels are the most important cause of criminal careers.

7. The likelihood and severity of societal reaction to violations of the law are predicted by
   a. the visibility of the act,
   b. the severity and amount of the behavior(s),
   c. the power of the rule violator,
   d. the amount of social distance between the rule violator and the control agents,
   e. the rule violator's similarity to the stereotype of a criminal, and
   f. the community's tolerance for that sort of crime.

Source: T.J. Scheff, *Being Mentally Ill* (Chicago: Aldine Publishing, 1966).

Among the other variables identified by Scheff as having an effect upon societal reactions to law-breaking is the *social power* of the person breaking the law relative to that of the audience. Social power is a result of wealth and prestige. It also aids in reducing the visibility of one's actions. Audiences that observe acts of law-breaking by socially powerful people are less likely to react with coercive sanctions than if these same acts were committed by individuals with little or no social power. When audiences are in a dominant position of power, they are much more likely to react in a negative manner. Simultaneously, non-powerful rule-breakers have less ability to defend themselves from accusations of criminality and from the consequences of such a label.

Closely related to social power, and of equal importance in Scheff's theory, is the *social distance* between the law-breaker and the audience. Social distance is a function of (sub)cultural membership. Virtually all control agents are firmly entrenched in the mainstream culture. Thus, when they encounter values, norms, and perceptions that are not typical of their group, they are likely to respond in a negative fashion. Whereas social power is a result of the stratification system (i.e., socioeconomic), social distance is a product of group or culture membership. People from the same or similar groups understand each other's behavior much better than do persons from very different backgrounds. When a great deal of social distance exists between two people, they will inevitably have difficulty communicating with one another and will be likely to misinterpret the meaning of each other's actions.[38]

Scheff points out that there is a fairly wide range of tolerance for various rule violations across various communities. Acts that are tolerated by some communities are completely unacceptable in others. For example, there is a much higher level of tolerance toward prostitution in large metropolitan areas than there is in most small towns. Different geographical regions of the United States also vary in their cultural outlook and thus in their tolerance for certain types of rule violations. Homosexuality is more readily accepted in highly cosmopolitan cities like San Francisco and New York than it is more provincial cities like St. Louis or Dallas.

The availability of noncriminal roles in one's group or culture is also related to the likelihood of labeling and consequent societal reaction.[39] High tolerance levels for illegal substance abuse are generally recognized to exist in impoverished urban neighborhoods, as well as in extremely wealthy jet-set and entertainment communities. The same behaviors are not tolerated at all among government employees and professionals.

The societal-reaction perspective is the foundation upon which Scheff's theory emerged as a competing theory with the biological and psychiatric perspectives. Indeed, this perspective was developed as a response to the bio-determinism of traditional psychiatric views of mental illness. Like Lemert, Scheff proposes that the causes of initial criminal behavior are numerous and fundamentally diverse. They include factors such as organic or psychological illnesses, external stress, social learning within subcultures, and voluntary acts of innovation or defiance. This theory concentrates attention on the continuation and intensification of criminal behavior (careers of crime) that often follow initial apprehension. Scheff's theory suggests that the official, public stigmatization that occurs through the societal reaction process is the single most important factor in the perpetuation of criminal behavior.[40] The effects of labels are well illustrated in the case of the Martin brothers, which follows. Here virtually all the background factors are the same for both brothers. However, the assignment of stigma to the older brother resulted in a life of crime while the absence of stigma in the younger brother's life allowed him to become a police officer.

· · · · · · · · · **APPLICATION** · · · · **The Case of Jackie and Mike Martin**

Jackie Martin's mother turned him and his brother and sister over to a children's home in Dallas, Texas, to be raised. She told officials at the home that she was not prepared to raise three children (she was young and her husband was not around much); however, she kept in touch with the children, and when they grew older, she did provide a home for them.[41]

Jackie Martin was five years old when he was placed in the children's home. This event was very upsetting to him and caused him to feel insecure. The placement was not as upsetting to his year-and-a-half-old brother, Mike, whose first memories in life are of the children's home.[42]

The Martin children lived there for several years. They were once placed in foster care with a police officer and his family for a little over one year.

However, the placement did not work out satisfactorily and they were returned to the children's home.[43]

At age fifteen, Jackie Martin ran away from the children's home and returned to his mother. Such an action defined him as a delinquent in terms of the formal control agencies that had supported his placement in the home. His mother was struggling to make a living and did not have much free time to spend with him. He began skipping school and made friends on the street, where he began abusing drugs. He was caught robbing a couple of stores and sentenced to two and one-half years in a state reform school. This strengthened his identification of himself as a criminal. He was released from the state reform school in 1969 at the age of nineteen. He returned to abusing drugs almost immediately after his release. For approximately the next fifteen years of his life he bounced between prisons and halfway houses as a result of his continual burglaries and sales of heroin. He was last arrested in 1982 for robbing a drugstore and confined by the Texas Department of Corrections. He was scheduled to be paroled in 1988 or 1989.[44]

Jackie's brother, Mike Martin, also returned to live with his mother at the age of fifteen. Unlike Jackie, however, he did so legally, without running away from the children's home. Thus, he had little to fear from the authorities and was able to perceive himself as a fairly normal youngster.

While living with his mother, he quit school as had his older brother but found employment at a tree-cutting company and began moving around the country. This legitimate form of employment reinforced his "normal" self-image and showed him that he could indeed find adventure and excitement without violating the law. He eventually returned to the children's home but was no longer content there. He began causing trouble and was discharged. After being released, he joined the United States Marine Corps. He took several college correspondence courses during his four years in the Marine Corps, then attended a university and earned a bachelor's degree. All of these activities strengthened his view of himself as a respectable citizen and encouraged others to define him as such. In 1984 he became a police officer.[45]

Both of the Martin brothers were exposed to institutional conditions early in their lives and each had significant exposure to a somewhat dysfunctional mother. However, the course of their lives was completely different—one became a control agent while the other became a criminal. This difference seems to be largely due to the differences in the development of their self-images that occurred as a result of labeling. Exhibit 8.7 summarizes the facts of the Jackie Martin case.

Level of Importance	Fact	Type of Fact
Primary	Jackie Martin labeled criminal	Attracting
Secondary	Jackie Martin's substance abuse	Precipitating
Tertiary	Jackie Martin's peer group	Predisposing

Exhibit 8.7

Summary of facts and their role in the explanation of the Jackie Martin case

Types of Labels

The interactionist approach to the labeling perspective is concerned with the nature and validity of the labels that are assigned to people. The same behavior may be defined in different ways by different people. For example, some perceive addicts as people suffering from a disease-like condition for which they need to be treated. Others see them merely as criminals deserving punishment. Still others believe that they are enemies of the established social order who are trying to undermine society by seducing others into their lifestyle.

Joseph Gusfield identified four ideal types of labels that may be applied to known deviants. Each has different implications for the preservation of the existing social order. The type of label assigned to a particular deviant has much to do with how that person is treated and thus with the nature of the changes that will occur in their identity as a result of labeling.

Sick deviants are those whose rule-violations are thought to result from internal pathologies that are beyond their control. These people are felt to be more in need of treatment than punishment. They pose no threat to the social order because their acts are so deviant that only a disease could account for their abnormality. The sick deviant thus actually helps to support the social order because his or her acts are such that they are interpreted as being so different from society's norms that only a "sick" person would perform them.[46]

Repentant deviants are rule-violators that have seen the error of their ways and now express great sorrow over their crimes. These deviants also support the moral order by advertising the liabilities of rule violation and demonstrating remorse over their crimes.[47] People in organizations like Alcoholics Anonymous are typical of repentant deviants. So also are ex-convicts who devote the rest of their lives to working with youths in an effort to keep them out of trouble.

Cynical deviants are a more problematic category. These criminals are quite aware that their acts are illegal but have no regrets for them or their consequences.[48] The cynical deviant openly admits that the moral order of society is correct and acknowledges that his/her behavior is inappropriate. Professional killers and thieves are excellent examples of cynical deviants. Such offenders are dangerous enough to require much attention from the criminal justice system, for practical reasons. Because of their open cynicism, however, they do not pose a symbolic threat to the moral order.

The last type of rule-violator identified by Gusfield is the **enemy deviant** who does pose a threat to the moral order. The enemy deviant is one who believes that certain rules supported by the society are wrong and that her or his violations are appropriate behavior. These offenders directly confront the moral order of society and seek converts to their belief system.[49]

The way in which society defines a particular offender is crucial in understanding the sanctions it imposes. Repentant deviants are treated most leniently since they provide testimony to the wisdom of the moral order. Sick deviants may gain sympathy and most people would argue that they need treatment more than punishment. Cynical deviants are usually thought to require incapacitation and punishment for their acts and attitudes. Enemy deviants, however, generally receive the harshest treatment since their crimes are interpreted as acts explicitly directed against the moral order as well as the victim.

Depending on the audience, an offender may be defined as belonging to any of these categories. Drug users are an especially good example of how the definition of a single criminal act can result in any of these four labels. Some see addiction as a disease and argue that the "sick" addict requires treatment, not punishment. Users who become repentant and proclaim the evils of drugs often become involved in rehabilitative agencies and thus contribute to strengthening the moral order. Others perceive the drug user as one who has cynically chosen to make money from drug sales regardless of the costs to others. Still others believe that addicts seek out nonusers and urge them to use drugs so as to legitimate their subcultural belief system.

Who feels threatened by the act and the status of the offender has much to do with the type of label that is applied. Groups with much investment in a particular law are the most likely to attempt to control the labeling and sanctioning processes. When a powerful group is threatened, the sanctions desired tend to be severe. The more powerful the offender, the more likely that a label of "sick" will be attached.

For example, most people can understand why an impoverished slum dweller would want to "escape" the reality that surrounds him or her through drugs. But most cannot comprehend why the children of our wealthiest and most powerful families would have the same desire (i.e, only a "sick" person would commit this crime in such circumstances). In addition, the children of the wealthy are not likely to victimize members of powerful groups, while the poor are more likely to engage in predatory crimes. Thus, when a slum dweller is arrested for drugs, he or she is seen as a threat to society and is likely to be labeled as a cynical or enemy deviant. When the same act is performed by someone from a wealthy family, the label of "sick" is likely to be applied and treatment or some other lenient sanction applied.

Gusfield's typology of labels presumes that rule violation(s) and labeling have occurred. Becker points out that labels are not always attached to acts of crime and that, in other cases, labels may be falsely applied to people who have not committed the violation for which they are labeled. Much of the complexity associated with the labeling phenomenon stems from the existence of three different labeling circumstances for criminal behavior:[50]

1. Criminal behavior has occurred and is labeled as such—the *pure criminal*.
2. Criminal behavior has not occurred, but the person is nonetheless labeled as having violated the law—the *falsely accused criminal*.
3. Criminal behavior has occurred but has not been recognized or labeled as such—the *secret criminal*.

The typologies developed by Gusfield and Becker share the important trait of emphasizing the linkage of the interactionist-labeling approach with that of the consequences approach. Both typologies therefore have serious implications for the criminal justice system as well as the effects of labels on individuals. In order to fully illustrate the application and dynamics of the labeling perspective, these ideas will be applied to a second case to illustrate the role of the secret criminal who was killed by his son, who was then handled as a sick deviant.

The Case of Richard Jahnke, Sr.

Indecency with a Child
The act of engaging in sexual contact with a child under the age of seventeen.[51]

Injury to a Child
The act of intentionally, knowingly, recklessly, or with criminal negligence causing serious bodily injury or serious physical or mental deficiency to a child.[52]

In his book, *The Poison Tree*, Alan Prendergast provides an account of the murder of Richard Jahnke, Sr., a *secret criminal* in labeling terminology. He was shot and killed by his fifteen-year-old son, Richard Jahnke, Jr., in Cheyenne, Wyoming, on November 16, 1982.[53] Seven months previously, he had fought with his son over the beating of Mrs. Jahnke. Although the elder Jahnke had beaten his wife and children on numerous occasions over the years, these beatings had never been reported to the police. However, after this particular fight with his father, Jahnke, Jr., reported his father's battering of his mother to authorities. He also reported the past battering of his mother, his sister, and himself.[54] This was the son's attempt to have his father labeled and punished as a *true* (or *pure*) *criminal*.

Although of secondary importance, this incident was the *precipitating factor* in this case. When Jahnke, Jr., was unable to get help from the formal agents of social control (the police) he decided to solve his family's problem by killing his father. His lack of social power, which was due to his age, along with the invisibility of the battering episodes in this rural area, allowed his father to remain a so-called secret criminal. He was unable to get his (significant-other) definition of his father as a true criminal accepted by the authorities. They told him that all they could do was put him, Jahnke, Jr., in jail for his own protection. The police called in the Department of Public Assistance and Social Service Agency, which sent Jahnke, Jr., back to his parents, and a child-protection caseworker was assigned. The caseworker defined the son's complaint as an isolated incident and recommended counseling for the family. This was the caseworker's only contact with the Jahnke family before the case was placed on inactive status.[55]

The elder Jahnke's battering of his wife and children illustrates a very common situation of secret criminality. In addition, the fact that Jahnke's violence toward his family was not reported for so long supports Scheff's suggestion that the rate of reported crime is relatively low in comparison to the rate of unreported crime. Most criminologists agree that the majority of domestic violence cases, for example, are never reported to the police. The same is true of many other types of crimes.

Other social audiences (e.g., Jahnke, Jr.'s teachers and neighbors) also contributed to keeping Jahnke, Sr., a secret criminal. Although these social audiences did not directly witness the battering, they were very aware of the symptoms displayed by his children that resulted from his battering. Yet they failed to act. School personnel, for example, noticed Jahnke, Jr., did well on intelligence tests, but they failed to seek an adequate explanation for his erratic academic performance, poor grades, and isolation from other students. The Jahnke neighbors, too, had noticed Jahnke, Jr.'s strange behavior but never reacted to it. This lack of action allowed Jahnke, Sr., to remain a secret criminal.[56]

Of tertiary importance were the *attracting factors*. Jahnke, Jr. was attracted to a violent solution to his problem by several facts. He had the ability to use firearms; there were an unusually large number of firearms present in the home (situational availability); and his long-term exposure to his father's violent behavior had taught him that problems were to be resolved with the use of force.[57]

Richard Jahnke Jr. arrives at court in Cheyenne, Wyoming to be tried for the murder of his father.

The *predisposing factor,* which is also of primary importance in this case, was Jahnke, Sr.'s physical and psychological abuse of his seventeen-year-old daughter. Jahnke, Jr., essentially killed his father because he could no longer stand to watch his father beat his sister any more. Throughout Deborah Jahnke's entire life she had been abused by her father. Jahnke, Sr. would assault her in response to the most trivial of incidents. He also sexually molested her when she was thirteen and fourteen years old. She constantly complained to her brother about their father's abuse and they had numerous conversations in which killing their father was the central topic.[58]

One of Deborah Jahnke's teachers was convinced that Deborah was a "screwed-up kid". She talked to another teacher about her, and both faculty members agreed that Deborah Jahnke needed psychological treatment. The teacher's primary concern was with her potential for suicide. However, psychological counseling was hard to obtain without parental permission, which Jahnke, Sr., refused to give.[59] This exercise of parental power helped him to keep his criminality secret from the authorities. No further action was ever taken on the observations of the neighbors and teachers, or on the son's formal complaint, allowing Jahnke, Sr., to remain a secret criminal until his death. His criminal behavior was exposed to the public only when his son stood trial for his murder. The severity of his secret criminality helps to explain the leniency of the sentence that Jahnke, Jr. ultimately received. Convicted of voluntary manslaughter, he was sentenced to the Wyoming State Penitentiary

Exhibit 8.8
. . . .

Summary of facts and their role
in the explanation of the
Jahnke, Sr., case

Level of Importance	Fact	Type of Fact
Primary	Jahnke, Jr.'s need to protect his sister	Predisposing
Secondary	Agents of social control's failure to help	Precipitating
Tertiary	Jahnke, Jr.'s ability to use firearms	Attracting
Tertiary	Firearms in home	Attracting
Tertiary	Family violence	Attracting

for a period of five to fifteen years. However, the governor of Wyoming commuted this sentence to two to four months in a Denver, Colorado, psychiatric hospital, followed by placement in the Wyoming Industrial Institute for Juveniles until he reached the age of twenty-one. Jahnke, Jr.'s total sentence thus amounted to only three years and thirteen days.[60]

The original sentence of five to fifteen years indicates that Jahnke, Jr. was initially labeled as a *cynical deviant*. This was probably due to the fact that parricide (killing one's parent) is seen as an especially horrendous crime. The governor's commutation of the sentence appears to be based on the idea that Jahnke, Jr., was relabeled as a *sick deviant* by public opinion when the facts of his father's abuse came to light. Exhibit 8.8 summarizes the facts of the Jahnke case.

The reluctance of police to arrest Jahnke's father can best be explained by the power of the parental role, the invisible nature of domestic violence, and possibly by the community's tolerance of family "disciplinary" methods. Having exhausted the available legal means, Jahnke, Jr., chose to become a true criminal himself. He was willing to be labeled a murderer by killing his father in order to rid his family of the abuse.

The reader needs to keep in mind that this case and its interpretation was provided primarily for the purpose of illustrating the importance of the presence and type of label. It is very important to remember that labeling theories are also attempting to expand explanations of criminal behavior to include unreported acts of crime as well. Although other theories may provide better explanations for the actions of both Jahnke, Jr., and his father, Scheff's labeling theory at least posits the need to account for unreported crimes, it also helps to explain the reactions (or lack thereof) on the part of criminal justice authorities.

Conclusions
. . . .

The societal-reaction perspective has made some unique contributions to criminology. Some conservatives argue that stigmatization, or the threat thereof, serves as a cheap and effective method of deterring and punishing crime. Labeling theory draws attention to the negative aspects of such deterrence policies. These insights into the effects of societal reactions are especially relevant to members of disenfranchised groups who have little initial investment in acceptable roles and/or societal approval.

Labeling theories lead to policies that divert minor offenders from the criminal justice system whenever possible so as to help them retain their "normal" identities. **Diversion** programs attempt to place juveniles and/or first offenders in situations where they can be integrated back into conventional society before they have been formally labeled. This usually means that the first offender is referred to the mental health or welfare system by the criminal justice system. Some have charged that entrance into the mental health system is just as stigmatizing as labels signifying criminality.

Societal-reaction theories also redirect our attention from the criminal to the interactions of the criminal with others. In particular, this perspective demands that criminology examine the behaviors of control agents as well as those of the offender. Predominantly focused at the micro level, the perspective has certain ramifications for the meso and macro levels of analysis as well. Agency priorities are often critical in determining which types of offenders are likely to remain secret criminals and which are to be labeled as pure, or true, criminals. Agency priorities may result from either national issues (e.g., the war on drugs) or more local concerns (e.g., prostitution sweeps). The same is true of the beliefs of individual control agents. This idea is best explained by reference to the vicious cycle of self-fulfilling prophecy that results from beliefs about group levels of criminality.

As the diagram in Exhibit 8.9 shows, agency expectations are confirmed as a result of implicit or explicit bias on the part of individual control agents. As with any vicious circle, this cycle is self-perpetuating unless some outside force intervenes. The labeling perspective is designed, in part, to have such an effect by making people aware of the consequences of agency biases. Thus, societal-reaction theories direct criminological attention to the study of agency and practitioner behavior. Other theories tend to presume that agency behavior is constant over time, or at least that it is consistently focused on meeting current social needs. In contrast, the labeling perspective posits that control agencies respond to political and internal pressures that may or may not be related to the distribution of crime in society, and that the personal biases of individual control agents have much the same effect, though on a smaller scale.

This is especially relevant to the interpretation of crime statistics at the meso and macro levels. Law enforcement agencies are very responsive to political pressure. As a result, different types of crime get varying amounts of attention at different times. In this sense there is a close relationship between the pluralist-conflict perspective (see Chapter 14) and the societal-reaction perspective. The difference between them is the level at which they tend to

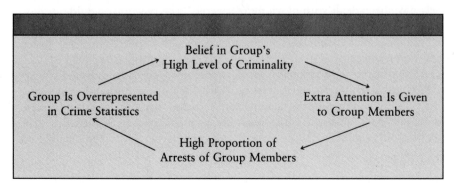

Exhibit 8.9

Cycle of the self-fulfilling prophecy

focus. Labeling focuses on the micro level, but has macro implications, while conflict theories are principally concerned with the macro level, though they have implications for the micro level.

For example, federal statistics indicate that arrests for drugs and drunk driving increased dramatically between 1978 and 1987.[61] One could interpret this fact as indicating that the actual frequency of these behaviors in society increased during this period. Most criminologists, however, would offer a different explanation based on the insights of the consequences approach to the labeling perspective. In 1978 many people favored the legalization of at least some drugs (e.g., marijuana) and there was no real sense of urgency to enforce these laws. By 1987, however, the nation had declared "war" on drugs and the police felt pressure to maximize all types of arrests for drugs. Similarly, groups like Mothers Against Drunk Driving (MADD) began mobilizing in the late 1970s and forced the authorities to increase their enforcement of drunk-driving laws. These factors are related to the rate at which people are labeled for certain types of offenses and the type of labels used. Official statistics therefore do not necessarily correspond to the rate at which these behaviors actually occur in society.

Self-report and victimization data are used to offset these sorts of biases in official statistics. **Self-report data** is produced by surveys that ask large samples of people if they have committed certain crimes and if they were apprehended for them. **Victimization studies** ask people if they have been the victims of various sorts of crimes and if they reported the crime to police. Comparison of official records, self-report data, and victimization surveys allow us to estimate a more accurate figure for various offenses and speculate on the reasons for changes in the frequency of arrests for certain crimes.

The incidence of a behavior in society and its prominence in official records can be very different over time and in different places. This is also true of the nature of the labels used to classify specific types of rule violations. Again, drug use is an excellent example. During the 1970s the drug user was often defined as a person in need of psychological and/or medical help and was treated accordingly (i.e., sick deviant). Today, the user is more likely to be seen and treated as a criminal (i.e., cynical or enemy deviant). While these changes in our perception of drug use are partly due to the introduction of "crack cocaine" in the early 1980s, they also reflect changes in the national political climate. Likewise, many rural jurisdictions are more severe in their treatment of drug users than are urban ones.

The same is true of the severity of the societal response to law violations. Had Richard Jahnke, Jr., killed his father a decade or so earlier, he would likely have been dealt with much more severely. The governor would not have been as sensitive to public sympathy for the victims of domestic violence and Richard, Jr., might well have been labeled a cold-blooded murderer rather than a quasi-victim.

The political implications of labeling theories lead us to question the activities of the criminal justice system. Thus, they allow criminology to contribute to the maintenance of democracy, because such a form of government cannot survive unless official agencies are kept under constant scrutiny. The role of group values in the process of law creation and enforcement is dealt with more directly and in more detail in Chapters 13 and 14.

Glossary ·····························

Control Agents People with the legal power to attach official labels to others that will affect their social and material well-being.

Cynical Deviants People who are quite aware that their acts are illegal but have no regrets for them or their consequences. While often dangerous to themselves, society and/or others, they pose no threat to the moral order because of their obvious cynicism.

Diversion Refers to programs that place first offenders in situations where they can be integrated back into conventional society before they have been formally labeled.

Dramatization of Evil Refers to the idea that rule violations, even isolated ones, are often given a disproportionate amount of attention by some audiences, especially control agents. This attention results in the characterization of the person in terms of acts that often are not typical of the person's usual behavior. By focusing on such acts, attention comes to rest on the rule violation rather than on the entire person and labeling occurs.

Enemy Deviants People who believe that certain rules supported by the society are wrong and that their violations are appropriate behavior. These offenders pose a serious threat to the moral order of society because they directly challenge it and seek converts to their belief system.

Looping Occurs when a person's attempts to prove a stigma false are used by agency personnel to demonstrate instead the presence of that stigma. This practice results from the fact that officially assigned labels often go unquestioned by social control agencies. Looping results in an attitude that encourages all of the stigmatized person's actions to be judged on the basis of his or her label.

Master Status The major social status a person uses to define him or herself. This status is the central feature of the person's self-image and serves to define and modify the content of all the other roles that individual occupies.

Primary Criminal Behavior (or Primary Deviance) Refers to the initial and unlabeled rule violations committed by a person that have few, if any, consequences for the individual's self-image or social and material well-being.

Repentant Deviants Rule-violators that have seen the error of their ways and now express great sorrow over their crimes. These deviants act to support the moral order by advertising the liabilities of rule-violation and demonstrating remorse over their crimes.

Secondary Criminal Behavior (or Secondary Deviance) Results from official and/or well-known criminal labels that have negative consequences for a person's social and material welfare and lead the individual to adopt a criminal master status. This criminal behavior is habitual and is the mainstay of the person's identity.

Self-Report Data Data produced by surveys that ask large samples of people if they have committed certain crimes and if they were apprehended for them.

Sick Deviants People whose rule violations are felt to result from internal pathologies beyond individual control. They pose no threat to the social order because their acts are so deviant that only a "sickness" could account for them.

Significant-Other Audience   Made up of people who live in direct daily contact with one another. Their opinions are valued by the stigmatized person.

Social Control Agency Audience   Made up primarily of people who are employed as official representatives of public agencies and have the legal power to formally stigmatize others.

Society-At-Large Audience   Made up of people who belong to social groups within society that would ordinarily not come into direct contact with individual people involved with crime except for their membership in the group.

Stigma   Refers to a negative label, usually assigned by social control agency audiences, that has negative social and/or material consequences for its holder.

Victimization Surveys   Surveys that ask people if they have been the victims of various sorts of crimes and if they reported the crime to police.

■ Notes

1. F. Tannenbaum, *Crime and the Community* (Boston: Ginn and Co., 1938); E. M. Lemert, *Social Pathology* (New York: McGraw-Hill, 1951); J. I. Kitsuse, "Societal Reaction to Deviant Behavior: Problems of Theory and Method," *Social Problems* 9 (1962): pp. 247–256; Howard S. Becker, *Outsiders: Studies in the Sociology of Deviance* (Glencoe, IL: Free Press, 1963); Howard S. Becker, "Labeling Theory Reconsidered" in P. Rock and M. McIntosh (eds.), *Deviance and Social Control* (London: Tavistock Publication, 1974).
2. Ibid., pp. 42–45.
3. Ibid., p. 47.
4. Ibid., pp. 42–45.
5. T.F. Cullen and J. B. Cullen, *Toward a Paradigm of Labeling Theory* (Lincoln, NE: The University of Nebraska, 1978), p. 5.
6. Howard S. Becker, *Outsiders: Studies in the Sociology of Deviance*, p. 9.
7. K. T. Erikson, "Notes on the Sociology of Deviance," *Social Problems* 9 (Spring 1962): p. 311.
8. J. P. Gibbs, "Concepts of Deviant Behavior: The Old and the New," *Pacific Sociological Review* 9 (Spring 1966).
9. Erikson, "Notes on the Sociology of Deviance."
10. Donald J. Shoemaker, *Theories of Delinquency,* 2d ed. (New York: Oxford University Press, 1990): p. 214.
11. Tannenbaum, *Crime and the Community;* Lemert, *Social Pathology;* Becker, *Outsiders: Studies in the Sociology of Deviance;* E. Goffman, *Asylums* (Garden City, NY: Doubleday, 1961); T. J. Scheff, *Being Mentally Ill* (Chicago: Aldine Publishing, 1966); R. Quinney, *The Social Reality of Crime* (Boston: Little, Brown and Company, 1970).
12. Lemert, *Social Pathology.*
13. C. E. Frazier, *Theoretical Approaches to Deviance: An Evaluation* (Columbus, OH: Charles E. Merrill Publishing, 1976), p. 25.
14. Ibid., pp. 33–34.
15. H. Garfinkel, "Conditions of Successful Degradation Ceremonies," *American Journal of Sociology* 61 (1956): pp. 420–424.
16. Erikson, "Notes on the Sociology of Deviance," p. 311.

17. Edwin Lemert, "Primary and Secondary Deviation," in Joseph E. Jacoby (ed.), *Classics of Criminology* (Prospect Heights, IL: Waveland Press, 1979): pp. 193–195.
18. Ibid.
19. Ibid.
20. Ibid.
21. E. M. Lemert, "Paranoia and the Dynamics of Exclusion," *Sociometry* (1962): pp. 2–20.
22. George E. Rush, *The Dictionary of Criminal Justice,* 2d ed. (Guilford, CT: Dushkin Publishing Group), p. 198.
23. Jean L. McKechnie, *Webster's Deluxe Unabridged Dictionary*-2d ed (New York: Simon & Schuster, 1979), pp. 1800–1801.
24. Christiane Vera F. with Kai Hermann and Horst Rieck, *Christiane F.,* trans. Susanne Flatauer (New York: Arlington Books, 1980).
25. Ibid.
26. Ibid.
27. Ibid.
28. Ibid.
29. Ibid.
30. Ibid.
31. Ibid.
32. E. M. Schur, *Labeling Deviant Behavior: Its Sociological Implications* (New York: Harper & Row, 1971): pp. 12–14.
33. Texas Penal Code, 8th ed. (St. Paul, MN: West Publishing, 1990): p. 50.
34. D. Mechanic, "Some Factors in Identifying and Defining Mental Illness," *Mental Hygiene* 46 (1962): pp. 66–74.
35. Erving Goffman, *Asylums* (Garden City, NY: Anchor Books, 1961), pp. 35–37.
36. Ibid.
37. Frazier, *Theoretical Approaches to Deviance: An Evaluation,* p. 39.
38. Ibid.
39. Ibid.
40. Scheff, *Being Mentally Ill,* p. 40.
41. Clara Tuma, "Brothers: One's a Cop, the Others' a Convict," *Fort Worth Star-Telegram,* October 12, 1985.
42. Ibid.
43. Ibid.
44. Ibid.
45. Ibid.
46. Joseph R. Gusfield, *The Culture of Public Problems: Drinking, Driving and the Symbolic Order* (Chicago: University of Chicago Press, 1981).
47. Ibid.
48. Ibid.
49. Ibid.
50. Becker, *Outsiders: Studies in the Sociology of Deviance;* Shoemaker, *Theories of Delinquency,* p. 212–214.
51. Texas Penal Code, 8th ed., pp. 30–31.
52. Ibid., pp. 36–37.
53. Alan Prendergast, *The Poison Tree* (New York: G.P. Putnam's Sons, 1986).

54. Ibid.

55. Ibid.

56. Ibid.

57. Ibid.

58. Ibid.

59. Ibid.

60. Ibid.

61. Katherine Jamieson and Timothy Flanagan (eds.), U.S. Dept. of Justice, Bureau of Justice Statistics, *Sourcebook of Criminal Justice Statistics, 1988* (Washington D.C.: U.S. Government Printing Office, 1988): p. 489.

■ Suggested Readings

Howard S. Becker, *Outsiders: Studies in the Sociology of Deviance* (Glencoe, IL: Free Press, 1963).

K. T. Erikson, "Notes on the Sociology of Deviance," *Social Problems* 9 (Spring 1962): pp. 307–314.

J. P. Gibbs, "Concepts of Deviant Behavior: The Old and the New," *Pacific Sociological Review* 9 (Spring 1966).

E. Goffman, *Asylums* (Garden City, NY: Doubleday, 1961).

J. I. Kitsuse, "Societal Reaction to Deviant Behavior: Problems of Theory and Method, " *Social Problems* 9 (1962): pp. 247–256.

E. M. Lemert, "Paranoia and the Dynamics of Exclusion," *Sociometry 25* (March 1962): pp. 2–20.

Edward Sagarin, *Odd Man In: Societies of Deviants in America* (Chicago: Quadrangle Books, 1969).

T. J. Scheff, *Being Mentally Ill* (Chicago: Aldine Publishing, 1966), pp. 40–93.

■ Suggested Readings for Additional Application

Jack Henry Abbott, *In The Belly of the Beast* (New York: Vintage Books, 1982).

Malcolm Braly, *False Starts: A Memoir of San Quentin and Other Prisons* (New York: Penguin, 1977).

Jeanne Cordelier, *The Life: Memoirs of a French Hooker,* trans. Harry Matthew (New York: Viking Press, 1978)

Billy G. McCune, *The Autobiography of Billy McCune* (San Francisco: Straight Arrow Books, 1973).

Albert Race Sample, *Racehoss: Big Emma's Boy* (New York: Ballantine Books, 1984).

CHAPTER

Social-Disorganization Perspective

Overview of Social-Disorganization Perspective

The social-disorganization perspective is among the oldest of the sociological perspectives on crime. This perspective was developed to explain why some social phenomena tend to occur in epidemics, or "waves," within societies or their subgroups. Although first applied to the distribution of suicides in Europe, the social-disorganization perspective is commonly used to explain the concentration of crime and other social problems in particular regions, time periods, and/or groups. To a limited degree, its assumptions (see Exhibit 9.1) overlap with those of the strain and control perspectives.

The social-disorganization perspective is unique in its macro-structural concern with institutions. In its effort to explain differences in group rates of criminal behavior over time and space, it focuses on the relationship between crime rates and social institutions. This perspective implies that ecological forces and/or group memberships determine individual behavior. It does not directly address individuals because of its macro orientation. It also assumes that social institutions, and the structures they form, have evolved into the most efficient type of organization possible. Efficiency and stability are the

Exhibit 9.1

Social-disorganization perspective

Common Assumptions

1. Societies are most efficient when in a state of equilibrium or stability.

2. Institutions evolve into the most stable and efficient structure possible for the society.

3. Institutions serve to regulate behavior and integrate people into the group.

4. Rapid changes in technology and organization affect the social structure.

5. Changes in social structures alter human environments and expectations.

6. Changes in human environments and expectations decrease the effectiveness of informal mechanisms of social control and integration.

7. Ineffective social control and integration make life unpredictable and stressful.

8. Stress can cause psychological disorganization, which can lead to crime.

Source: Emile Durkheim, *Suicide*, trans. J.A. Spaulding and G. Simpson (New York: Free Press, 1951 [1897]); Emile Durkheim, The Division of Labor in Society, trans. G. Simpson (London: Free Press of Glencoe, 1933 [1893]); Jack P. Gibbs and Walter T. Martin, "On Assessing the Theory of Status Integration and Suicide," *American Sociological Review* 31 (1966): pp. 533–541; Jack P. Gibbs, "Status Integration and Suicide Rates," *American Sociological Review* 47 (1982): pp. 227–237; Donald J. Shoemaker, *Theories of Delinquency* (New York: Oxford University Press, 1984), pp. 72–73; Melvin L. DeFleur, *Social Problems in American Society* (Boston: Houghton-Mifflin, 1983), pp. 16–17.

criteria by which social structures are evaluated under this and related perspectives. Widespread consensus on social rules is also presumed by this view.

Institutions are established patterns formed to accomplish goals that are important to the maintenance and stability of society.[1] They are of direct relevance to criminology because they perform many functions that affect human behavior and perception. According to this perspective, crime is the result of social disorganization at the macro level. In particular, this perspective is concerned with the intraorganizational and interorganizational disruptions and dysfunctions that lead to *anomie,* or normlessness. **Anomie** results from the inadequate regulation of behavior by social organizations and the inadequate integration of citizens into society. It is a property of large groups, not of individuals.[2] Therefore it is appropriate to speculate that a group or community is experiencing anomie, but the effect on the individual members of the group would be referred to as *strain, stress,* or *anomia.*

In essence, this perspective is designed to deal with crime as an "act of passion" rather than as an "act of want." Thus, it is much better suited to the explanation of expressive crimes than of instrumental ones. However, instrumental acts can often be dealt with by this perspective by restating the instrumental act as an expressive drive related to the individual's status or self-image.

Generally, this perspective infers that crime results from disorganized **social structure**—defined as the pattern of interaction between institutions.[3] Social structure both provides and limits the range of methods available to solve a given problem. Simultaneously, it facilitates the integration of the individual into various groups and into the society. Control and integration are seen here as two sides of the same coin.

This perspective is very concerned with **social control,** which refers to the means used by institutions and groups within societies to encourage their members to abide by the norms, assume appropriate roles, and assist in achieving institutional and group goals. Criminologists are primarily interested in the use of **sanctions** to ensure that the norms are obeyed. Although the term refers to all types of incentives to behave in a particular way (i.e., rewards and punishments), in criminology it is generally used to denote punishments.[4]

Social control can be administered by either formal or informal organizations. **Formal organizations** are bureaucratically organized groups united by a very limited number of highly specific goals. The agencies of the criminal justice system, as well as those of universities, businesses, and charities are formal organizations. **Informal organizations** have little or no official structure, are non-bureaucratic in operation, and have a wide variety of functions. The family, the community, and the peer group are examples of informal organizations. Social control by formal organizations is referred to as **formal** or **secondary social control,** whereas control provided by informal organizations is called **informal** or **primary social control.**[5]

Primary social control is considered to be far more effective than secondary social control for four reasons. First, people are likely to be exposed to informal groups on a more regular basis than they are to formal ones. Second, people belong to more informal groups, and are likely to take the opinions of these groups more seriously than they are formal ones. Third, society must depend mainly on the informal groups to socialize and control its members. Thus, from a social-learning perspective, interaction in informal groups has greater frequency, duration, intensity, and priority than that which occurs in formal ones. Therefore, more learning occurs in these groups than in formal ones. Finally, and perhaps most importantly, the control functions of social institutions overlap with their integrating functions. By integrating individuals into meaningful social groups (e.g., the family, community, and society), incentives to invest and believe in the social order are provided. Such investment and belief are the most effective form of social control known.

To the degree that primary forms of social control are effective, the role of the criminal justice system is to deal with conflicts between groups (culture conflicts) and with aberrant personalities. When social integration is inadequate, undue pressure is placed on secondary control mechanisms (e.g., the criminal justice system) and crime increases rapidly. The declining role of the family in American society over the last 100 years is exemplary of this kind of institutional dysfunction.

Social control functions overlap with integrative functions, especially among informal groups. Approaches stressing the breakdown of social control without equal focus on the integration of the individual into the group are dealt with under the control perspective because additional assumptions about human nature are needed to properly elaborate that micro-meso perspective. The focus of this chapter is on the social-organizational causes of anomie (discussed earlier), a macro-level form of disorganization in which individuals are uncertain as to how they should behave and thus lose their sense of belonging to the society. Many theorists see anomie as a result of rapid changes in society that undermine the regulatory and integrative functions of institutions.

Change is perceived as a major threat to the stability, or equilibrium, of a society by this perspective. Through their institutions, societies attempt to perpetuate their norms and thus assure continued stability. When change in the environment or the organization of society occurs, it disrupts the operation of the institutions and organizations upon which people depend for both sustenance and guidance. As these institutions become disorganized, people are no longer able to maintain their previous lifestyles and often feel threatened by the stress of a new, unfamiliar, and unpredictable situation. In essence, as institutions become disorganized due to change, lifestyles crumble and life becomes extremely stressful.

In explaining crime, the social-disorganization perspective is best suited for use at the macro or meso levels of explanation. That is, it can best explain crime as a product of social disorganization in a large social setting (e.g., at the national, state, or city level) or in an institutional setting. For example, institutional disorganization resulting from extreme economic conditions, such as occur during national depressions or economic boom times, can be seen as causal forces, resulting in crimes of want, greed, etc. Under such conditions, the old rules and norms are no longer trustworthy because they were developed for a situation that no longer exists.

In essence, informal institutions like the church and the family are seen as the principal means of social integration and control at the meso and micro levels. Unfortunately, technology and social organization change more quickly than do the norms and values that guide behavior. Because institutions are unable to keep pace with the changes that surround them, they become less effective in guiding behavior. This inability of norms to keep pace with technological and/or organizational changes is known as **culture lag.**[6] At any point in time, some institutions, or the structures they compose, are more stable than others. Therefore, crime and other forms of deviance tend to impact one or several groups most heavily at a given point in time, while leaving the rest of society in a fairly stable (and thus unsympathetic) situation.

Major business areas exert a strong influence on individual patterns of behavior that often overcomes that of the institutional control systems. This is because such businesses represent the new technologies, and the structures that accompany them, in the most favorable way possible. Heavily commercialized areas also provide an opportunity for many groups to come together and share their views of right and wrong, thus broadening the individual's repertoire of motives and justifications for action. Finally, such areas provide increased levels of temptation and opportunity for those most adversely affected by social changes.[7]

Application of the social-disorganization perspective to an individual crime requires linking its macro- and meso-level concepts to the micro or individual level of analysis at which behavior occurs. The *strain perspective* was designed to perform just this function. Case-specific applications of macro-level perspectives tend to violate the original intent of the theorists, who were concerned with explaining group rates. However, the concept of **personal disorganization** allows us to make this link in a tentative way as follows: When the social structure and/or institutions are disorganized, they are no longer able to exert adequate control over individuals. These individuals then become personally disorganized, resulting in a greater likelihood of criminal behavior.

This perspective has been used primarily to explain the correlation of crime with urbanization. In an urban setting, informal social control mechanisms

Vietnam veteran in a subway station, New York City.

are undermined by contact with other cultural groups, as well as by the anonymity, crowding, and mobility of urban life that simultaneously weaken formal controls. Thus, the perspective's principal use in criminology has been to explain the criminogenic influence of the city on behavior.[8]

Concentric-Zone Theory

As a result of its macro-level focus, the social-disorganization perspective has led to much interest in the role of **social ecology** in explaining or predicting crime rates. Social ecology is the study of how people and institutions use space and resources. The social-disorganization perspective has most often been used to explain the disproportionately high crime rates of certain areas of a city. Social-disorganization theories appeared in the United States when urbanization and immigration were the dominant social trends. Early in this century it was noted that some urban communities had consistently high crime rates, even though they were occupied by different groups of immigrants at different points in time. Most of the educated people of this era had been socialized in rural or small-town settings, and perceived the city as a source of degeneracy and chaos. Their scientific ideas were thus tinged with their own values and prejudices. These biases led to a view of the city as a disorganized setting that promoted deviance.[9]

The social-disorganization perspective was very useful in explaining the changes in the moral structure of society during the early part of this century. Immigrants arriving in American cities were no longer part of their original culture but had yet to be integrated into the fabric of American society. This transitional status was felt to be *anomic* by social scientists.

It was observed that newly arrived immigrants initially settled in the most deteriorated areas of the city. Within a generation or so they integrated into American culture and moved away from the inner city into progressively better neighborhoods. Other groups of new immigrants replaced them in the deteriorated inner city. It was noted that crime rates were linked to the neighborhood, rather than the ethnic group, during this period of immigration. This led theorists to speculate that it was the disorganized neighborhood, not the nature of the groups that came to occupy it, that was the criminogenic element. That is, the people that had most recently arrived from their homeland lived with serious disorganization until they became integrated into the society. This integration was reflected in both their rate of crime and the status of their neighborhood.[10]

It was demonstrated that banking and governmental concerns dominated the **central business district (CBD)** at the center of the city. So long as the economy is reasonably healthy, this area must expand in order to continue to accommodate the growing needs of the area. The CBD is the integrative and regulatory center for economic activity in the city. Because capitalism requires growth to function properly, it is inevitable that the CBD will expand into surrounding areas and displace activities based there to areas more distant from the city's center.

Just beyond the CBD is a very deteriorated area of aging homes and apartments. This is an unpleasant place to live because housing is in bad repair and residents are exposed to the dirt and crowding of the city's industry. However, it is the only place that the poorest (i.e., most recently arrived) can afford to live. Land in this area is worth a great deal of money because it is expected that future CBD expansion will require its use. However, the buildings on this land are old and not appropriate for CBD use. The land is purchased for its future value to the CBD, not as a residential area. Since this area is in transition from residential to commercial use, it is economically wise for landlords to invest in this area, but put no money into improving the housing conditions. Labeled the **zone in transition,** this area has significantly higher rates of crime, delinquency, suicide, and other social problems than any other part of the city. Any group living there is thought to be affected by the disorganization that results from economic growth.

This view of the city's organization and growth came to be known as **concentric-zone theory** (see Exhibit 9.2) because it posited the existence of zones organized into rough circles. The CBD was at the center, with the zone in transition surrounding it. Then came progressively better residential areas that eventually graded off into suburbs. The process of growth by which these zones expanded was called **succession** because one use of the land replaced, or succeeded, another as the city grew. As immigrants integrated into American society, they also moved into successively better neighborhoods farther from the CBD.[11]

As mentioned earlier, the social-disorganization perspective is among the oldest, and until fairly recently its place in modern criminological thought was generally viewed as marginal.[12] But in the mid 1980s an interest in this per-

Children manage to play among the trash in one of North Philadelphia's zones in transition.

Exhibit 9.2
· · · · · · · · · · · · · · · ·

Concentric-zone theory

Specific Assumptions

1. The most important economic functions will be based at the city's center.

2. So long as the economy is healthy, this zone will expand to keep pace with demands for economic regulation and integration.

3. The area surrounding the city's center will always be in a state of change—housing will soon be replaced by economic centers.

4. Because of constant change, this transitional zone will be the most disorganized and have the highest rate of crime.

Source: Clifford R. Shaw and Henry D. McKay, *Juvenile Delinquency and Urban Areas* (Chicago: University of Chicago Press, 1942): Robert E. Park, "Human Ecology," American Journal of Sociology, vol. 42 (1936), pp. 1–15; Ernest W. Burgess, "The Growth of the City: An Introduction to a Research Project," in Robert E. Park, Ernest W. Burgess, and Roderick D. McKenzie (eds.), *The City* (Chicago: University of Chicago Press, 1967).

spective was renewed,[13] largely because of increases in the number of gangs and the amount of gang violence occurring in large metropolitan areas throughout the United States.[14]

Research conducted since the mid 1980s has demonstrated the importance of change in urban ecological systems for crime in general. Other recent studies have also indicated that gang crime, in particular, is more closely associated with social disorganization than is poverty; and that gang homicide conforms to the explanations generated by the social-disorganization perspective. Curry and Spergel's study of gang homicides in Chicago found the gang problem to be concentrated in low-income, public-housing projects and poor black and Hispanic sections of the city. They concluded that because gangs are residual subsystems (groups/organizations) concerned with territoriality, status, and the control of human behavior, social disorganization and poverty may better explain the growth of gangs throughout the United States than suggestions of secret and massive criminal organizations and conspiracies do.[15]

The reader should note that some cities do not conform to the concentric-zone pattern. In fairly recent times, urban renewal and changes in transportation methods have resulted in the relocation of some urban poor. Some cities have multiple CBD's and conform to a pattern of organization called **multiple nuclei** in which each small CBD is surrounded by a set of concentric zones that overlap one another.[16] Other cities are organized in a star-like pattern, with businesses clustering along traffic arteries that radiate from the area's center. These star-like patterns usually follow the routes of old streetcar lines which once provided the main form of transportation for area residents. Other exceptions to the concentric-zone model occur as a result of geographical features like rivers and flood plains as well as man-made barriers like highways and railroad tracks. The government and finance centers take the most attractive pieces of land. The homes of the wealthy occupy the most pleasant and least at-risk areas while other sectors are relegated to less powerful groups.[17]

In the 1970s the deteriorated areas of aging homes and apartments in many large metropolitan areas began experiencing **gentrification,** the reclaiming of deteriorated residential areas by the more affluent, more highly educated managerial-professional class.[18] The goals of gentrification are urban renewal and the preservation of the area's residential nature. Tax incentives are used to attract new residents who will improve the quality of the buildings in decaying areas of the city. Complaints about gentrification include the fact that apartment buildings that once housed many families are often converted to single-family homes, and thus fewer people can be housed in the area. Additionally, the mixing of middle-to-upper-class families with the urban poor creates a heightened sense of inequality and frustration among the latter group as well as providing increased opportunities for the criminal poor. Taylor and Covington concluded from their study of neighborhood changes involving gentrification that rapid changes in neighborhoods are problematic in that disorder is increased relative to other neighborhoods.[19]

The social-disorganization perspective is not restricted to urban settings. Indeed, some of the most dramatic changes in American social structure in recent years have impacted rural areas the hardest. Since the crowding, contacts between cultures with different norms, and anonymity of the city make it a complex setting, we have chosen to use a more simplistic rural case to illustrate this perspective. The case of James Jenkins and his son occurred in a rural Minnesota farming community where they were not affected by the direct transition of adjusting to city life, but instead were victims of urban economic norms becoming dominant in rural communities. This change in financial practices disorganized their farming life and caused Jenkins to become personally disorganized. The personal disorganization led him to strike back at two men who, for Jenkins, represented an alien and oppressive social structure. His was not a rational act, but it is a very understandable one if the assumptions of the social-disorganization perspective are used.

Social-disorganization theorists do not explicitly specify the mechanism by which disorganization at the macro level (social) causes disorganization at the micro level (personal). However, it can be readily inferred that as social institutions lose their ability to provide for and control people, individuals become stressed and therefore susceptible to psychological problems such as were discussed in Chapters 4, 5, and 6. When life becomes far less predictable and loses institutional guidance, frustration certainly can be the result. In addition, as institutions become unpredictable, people feel less invested in the status quo, including the moral codes under which they had previously operated. This also could lead to crime.

Because they are perceived as beyond individual or even group control, many institutional systems come to be seen as villainous by the individuals they impact. Since the institution or structure itself appears "untouchable" to the individual, other persons are likely to become symbols of those institutions and therefore the target of personal feelings of anger. Such is the case when we complain to a police officer about a poorly positioned traffic control sign— we are frustrated by the inevitable fine that accompanies the ticket, and cannot "tell off" the entire city engineering department, the mayor that hired them, and the schools that trained them. Therefore, we vent our rage at the police officer, even though it was not his decision to hang the sign in an easily obstructed area. A similar dynamic appears to have affected James Lee Jenkins' relationship with a major financial institution.

The Case of James Lee "Jim" Jenkins

In his book, *Final Harvest,* Andrew H. Malcolm provides an account of an *expressive crime* committed by James Lee "Jim" Jenkins that can be explained by the social-disorganization perspective. Malcolm's account of James Lee Jenkins traces the origin of his personal disorganization to the disruption of rural social structures that began to occur in American farming communities around 1950 and became acute in the early 1980s. The disorganization of rural farming and banking structures was a part of the larger financial disruption occurring within the United States during this period of time.[20] Malcolm's account of Jim Jenkin's personal disorganization can be used as the link between this macro-structural dysfunction and Jenkin's failed attempts to purchase the farm he had been earlier dispossessed of. This structural disorganization set the stage for Jenkins to commit two homicides before taking his own life.

On September 29, 1983, James Lee Jenkins telephoned Rudy Blythe and pretended to be a potential buyer for his old farm. He arranged a meeting with Blythe at the farm. Then James Lee and his eighteen-year-old son, Steve, went to the farm with a rifle and hid, awaiting Rudy Blythe's arrival. When Rudy Blythe and a loan officer of the Buffalo Ridge State Bank named Deems A. "Toby" Thulin, arrived at the farm, James Lee and Steven Jenkins shot and killed both of them. On October 2, 1983, three days after the murders, James Lee Jenkins used a shotgun to commit suicide in Paducah, Texas.[21]

Steve Jenkins was tried and convicted on one count of second-degree murder for the death of Deems A. "Toby" Thulin, and one count of first-degree murder for the death of Rudy Blythe. First-degree murder in Minnesota

Steven Todd Anderson, formerly Steve Jenkins, flanked by his unidentified girlfriend and a sheriff's deputy after being sentenced to life in prison. The 18-year-old's name was legally changed when his defense attorney adopted him.

carries a mandatory life sentence, which means Jenkins will have to serve a minimum of seventeen and one-half years before he can be considered for parole. He was also given a ten-year sentence for the death of Thulin, but it was to run concurrently with his life sentence, essentially not adding any additional sentencing time.[22]

To understand this crime according to the social-disorganization perspective, we need to consider the fact that the rural social structure of the United States changed significantly between 1950 and 1980. During these thirty years, approximately 18.4 million Americans left their farms. Rural towns like Ruthon, Minnesota, where James Lee Jenkins lived, were increasingly seen as no longer necessary or important in the United States. This was the reward rural communities received for increased production and efficiency.[23] The family farm could no longer compete with corporation-sponsored agribusinesses because of the expense involved in the new farming technologies.

These changes resulted in farmers no longer being able to work as farmers. Their traditional lifestyle was destroyed and the norms and strict morality by which they had lived their lives undermined. In short, life became very unpredictable and stressful.[24]

Also in the early 1980s, financial stress in the U.S. economy began disorganizing the structural links between farmers and rural bankers. Farmers began to think that the bankers were deceiving them with advice to borrow more money in order to buy more expensive equipment so as to have bigger farms. The bankers began believing the farmers were being deceitful about their inability to pay back the money they borrowed. The trust that once existed between these two groups (and the institutions they represented) was gone.[25] This trust had been pivotal to the earlier farm financing structure and thus to the survival of farming communities like Ruthon.

James Lee Jenkins was born in 1936. Among the *predisposing factors* in Jenkin's life was the fact that he had quit school to work on a farm. Thus, he lacked the ability to change occupations later in life. He also lacked the behavioral norms needed to guide a transition to a new lifestyle. He had worked his entire life as a farmer, supplementing this income by working as a farm-equipment repairman. Despite his hard work, however, he and his family had barely eked out a living. His wife divorced him because she could not endure the lifestyle he was able to provide as a farmer. To illustrate the financial problems confronting James Lee Jenkins, we can refer to the fact that in 1974 a bushel of soybeans was bringing $10, but by 1986 it was bringing only $6 — 40% less than in 1974. In 1974 a new tractor cost $14,360, and in 1986 one cost $55,000 — almost four times more than in 1974.[26]

The predominant *attracting factor* for James Lee Jenkins was the fact that in 1977 he had borrowed $30,000 from the Buffalo Ridge State Bank in Ruthon to buy a small farm. In 1980, when he could not make enough money off the farm to pay back his loan, the Buffalo Ridge State Bank foreclosed the loan, repossessed his farm, and evicted him. The bank had to foreclose on James Lee Jenkins and others like him because the rural banks had to borrow money from urban centers in order to make loans to farmers. Urban bankers were far less trusting and much more bureaucratic than their rural counterparts. Therefore, the rural financing structure, which had been based on personal trust, collapsed as urban banking norms became dominant.

Exhibit 9.3
. . . .

Summary of facts and their role
in the explanation of the
Jenkins case

Level of Importance	Fact	Type of Fact
Primary	Bank foreclosure on farm and eviction of the Jenkins family	Precipitating
Secondary	Jenkins's inability to buy a new farm because of bad credit rating from bank	Attracting
Tertiary	Disrupted relations between rural bankers and farmers	Predisposing
Tertiary	Jenkin's inability to work at nonfarming jobs	Predisposing

After the foreclosure, the Buffalo Ridge State Bank was unable to sell James Lee Jenkins' repossessed farm without taking a loss in the process. In essence, between 1977, when Jenkins bought his farm, and 1980, when Buffalo Ridge State Bank repossessed it, the value of farmland had decreased and banking interest rates had increased. As more farms surrounding Ruthon, Minnesota were repossessed, the value of farmland continued to drop. As a result, the Buffalo Ridge State Bank, and the local people it served, became increasingly disorganized.[27]

The origin of James Lee Jenkin's personal disorganization can be traced to the repossession of his farm and his eviction from it. This personal disorganization can be named as the primary *predisposing factor* in the case. Just why Jenkins was attracted to such a violent resolution to his problems is unclear. However, the major *precipitating factor* occurred in 1983 when he wanted to buy another farm. At that time Jenkins found that he was unable to secure a loan to buy another farm because of his credit history with the Buffalo Ridge State Bank. The bureaucratic impersonality of urban financial institutions had become dominant over the more informal and qualitative standards preferred by rural Americans. James Lee Jenkins became angry and ultimately blamed Rudy Blythe, owner of the Buffalo Ridge State Bank, for his predicament. These causal factors are summarized in Exhibit 9.3.

Conclusion
. . . .

The social-disorganization perspective is very useful in explaining the impact of macro-level situations on the perceptions of individuals and groups. It is these perceptions that, in turn, guide behavior and result in crime. Social-disorganization theories assert that at any given point in time certain subgroups of society are more affected by change than others. These effects must then be translated into behavior before a crime (or other act) occurs. And such a translation has been provided by the authors of this text.

This perspective is best suited for dealing with predisposing and attracting factors, but fails almost entirely to confront precipitating factors. It should be noted, however, that some current social-disorganization theorists are attempting to integrate the dynamics of individual behavior with the group-level forces described by this perspective. If they succeed, the perspective will also be able to explain precipitating factors as well.[28]

The social-disorganization perspective is one of the oldest explanatory frameworks for deviant behavior in the social sciences. A major weakness of this theory is its tendency to promote, or at least excuse, **ethnocentricity** on the part of observers who belong to the dominant cultural group in a society.[29] Ethnocentricity is the human tendency to see one's group's method of doing things as the "right" way and to use this method to evaluate the actions and beliefs of members of other groups.[30] It is all too easy to attribute disorganization to situations with which we are not familiar. Situations that appear disorganized to us may be very coherent from the standpoint of those involved. As outsiders, we are likely to fail to perceive this organization because the participants in the situation under scrutiny are using the logic of their own culture, which is different from our own. It was this weakness of disorganization theory that Sutherland and Cressey initially addressed with their idea of differential social organization (see Chapter 7).

It appears to be true that urban settings contribute to crime by creating an atmosphere of anonymity in the context of mobility, cognitive and sensory overload, and normative heterogeneity.[31] These factors set the stage for social controls to disintegrate and various social learning processes to develop. The stresses that result from disorganization may also play a "triggering" role in bringing biological predispositions into play. This strain may force subconscious conflicts between desires and norms to surface as behavior. However, this is in no way indicative of the goal of the social-disorganization perspective. Social disorganization is a structural phenomenon, which, by definition, occurs at the institutional (i.e., macro) level and is then passed on to ever smaller groupings through incidents such as, in the Jenkins case, the repossession of his farm. Culture-conflict theory is similarly focused, but emphasizes the lack of consensus across groups as to what constitutes proper behavior. Social disorganization is concerned with loss of consensus and certainty *within* groups. Such a loss of consensus is seen as a predisposing factor that sets the stage for criminal behavior.

Glossary ·······························

Anomie   A situation of normlessness brought about by inadequate integration and regulation that affects societies or groups within them.

Central Business District (CBD)   Area located at the center of the city. It is the integrative and regulatory center for economic activity in the city. So long as the economy is reasonably healthy, this area must expand in order to continue to accommodate the growing needs of the area.

Concentric-Zone Theory   describes the organization and growth patterns of American cities early in this century. It posits the existence of zones organized into rough circles, with the CBD (central business district) at the center and the zone in transition surrounding it. Progressively better residential areas eventually grade off into suburbs.

Culture Lag   Refers to inability of norms to keep pace with technological, organizational, and similar social changes.

Ethnocentricity   The human tendency to see one's group's method of doing things as the "right" way and to use this view of proper behavior as a standard for evaluating the actions and beliefs of members of other groups.

Formal Organizations   Bureaucratically organized groups united by a very limited number of highly specific goals.

Gentrification   The reclaiming of deteriorated residential areas within large cities by the more affluent, higher educated managerial-professional class.

Informal Organizations   Organizations with little or no official structure, non-bureaucratic in operation, and having a wide variety of functions.

Institutions   Established patterns formed to accomplish goals important to the maintenance and stability of society.

Personal Disorganization   Refers to situations in which the individual's relations with basic institutions like the family and community are abnormal, and even the reverse of what would normally be expected. This situation results from uncertainty and stress and can predispose some people to crime.

Primary Social Control   The use of sanctions by informal organizations to guide individual behavior.

Sanctions   Refer to all types of incentives to behave in a particular way (i.e., rewards and punishments), but generally denote punishments in criminology.

Secondary Social Control   The use of sanctions by formal organizations to guide human behavior.

Social Control   Refers to the use of rewards and punishments by a group to encourage its members to abide by the norms, assume appropriate roles, and assist in achieving group goals.

Social Ecology   The study of how people and institutions use space and resources.

Structure   The interaction of institutions.

Succession   The process of growth by which the concentric zones of the city expand into one another. As immigrants integrated into American society, they also moved into successively better neighborhoods farther from the CBD (central business district).

Zone in Transition   Area surrounding the CBD (central business district) where the land is valuable but the buildings are not. Therefore, this is a slum area where owners invest in land but allow buildings to deteriorate so that the land can be sold at a profit when CBD expansion reaches it. This is the poorest and least well-organized area of a city, characterized by high rates of crime and other social pathologies.

■ Notes

1. Melvin L. DeFleur, William D'Antonio, and Lois DeFleur, *Sociology: Human Society* (Scott, Foresman and Co., 1977).
2. Emile Durkheim, *Suicide: A Study in Sociology,* trans. J.A. Spaulding and G. Simpson (New York: Free Press, ([1897](1951)).
3. DeFleur, D'Antonio, and DeFleur, *Sociology: Human Society,* p. 92.

4. Ibid., pp 41-45.

5. Ibid., pp. 41, 56-57.

6. William Ogburn, *Social Change with Respect to Cultural and Original Nature* (New York: Viking Press, 1950).

7. Robert Park, Ernest Burgess, and Roderick McKenzie, *The City* (Chicago: University of Chicago Press, 1967).

8. Park, Burgess, and McKenzie, *The City;* Clifford R. Shaw and Henry D. McKay, *Juvenile Delinquency and Urban Areas,* rev. ed. (Chicago: University of Chicago Press, 1972 [1942]); Louis Wirth, "Urbanism as a Way of Life," *American Journal of Sociology* 44 (1938); James F. Short, "Gang Delinquency and Anomie" in Marshall Clinard, *Anomie and Deviant Behavior* (New York: Free Press, 1964); Harold J. Vetter and Ira J. Silverman, *Criminology and Crime: An Introduction* (New York: Harper & Row, 1986).

9. C. Wright Mills, "The Professional Ideology of Social Pathologists," *American Journal of Sociology* 49 (1942): pp. 165–180.

10. Shaw and McKay, *Juvenile Delinquency and Urban Areas.*

11. Ernest W. Burgess, "The Growth of the City" in R. E. Park, E. W. Burgess, R. D. McKenzie and L. Wirth, *The City* (Chicago: University of Chicago Press, 1925); Robert Park, "Succession: An Ecological Concept," *American Sociological Review* 1 (1936): pp. 171–179.

12. Robert J. Bursik, Jr., "Social Disorganization and Theories of Crime and Delinquency: Problems and Prospects," *Criminology* 26 (1988): pp. 519–551.

13. Ibid.

14. G. David Curry and Irving A. Spergel, "Gang Homicide, Delinquency, and Community," *Criminology* 26 no. 3 (1988): pp. 381–405; Cheryl L. Maxson, M. A. Gordon, and Malcolm W. Klein, "Differences between Gang and Nongang Homicides," *Criminology* 23 (1985): pp. 209–222; Irving A. Spergel, "The Violent Gang Problem in Chicago: Local Community Approach," *Social Service Review* 60 (1986): pp. 94–131; Paul E. Tracy, "Subcultural Delinquency: A Comparison of the Incidence of Gang and Nongang Member Offences" in Marvin E. Wolfgang, Terrence P. Thornberry, and Robert M. Figlio (eds.), *From Boy to Man, from Delinquency to Crime* (Chicago: University of Chicago Press, 1988).

15. Curry and Spergel, "Gang Homicide, Delinquency, and Community," pp. 381–405.

16. C. D. Harris and E. L. Ullman, "The Nature of Cities," *The Annals of the American Academy of Political Science* 242 (1945): pp. 7–17; W. A. Schwab, *Urban Sociology* (Reading, MA: Addison-Wesley, 1982), pp. 257–283.

17. H. Hoyt, *The Structure and Growth of Residential Neighborhoods in American Cities* (Washington, D.C.: Federal Housing Administration, 1939); Schwab, *Urban Sociology,* pp. 257–283.

18. Ralph B. Taylor and Jeanette Covington, "Neighborhood Changes in Ecology and Violence," *Criminology* 26, no. 4 (1988): pp. 553–589.

19. Ibid.

20. Andrew H. Malcolm, *Final Harvest* (New York: Signet, 1987).

21. Ibid.

22. Ibid.

23. Ibid.
24. Ibid.
25. Ibid.
26. Ibid.
27. Ibid.
28. Bursik, Jr., "Social Disorganization and Theories of Crime and Delinquency," pp. 519–551.
29. Mills, "The Professional Ideology of Social Pathologists," pp. 165–180.
30. DeFleur, D'Antonio, and DeFleur, *Sociology: Human Society,* pp. 103, 617.
31. Louis Wirth, "Urbanism as a Way of Life," *American Journal of Sociology* 44 (1938).

■ Suggested Readings

Joseph Barry and John Dereviany (eds.), *Yuppies Invade My House at Dinnertime: A Tale of Brunch, Bombs, and Gentrification in an American City* (Hoboken, NJ: Big River (1988).

Robert J. Bursik, Jr., "Social Disorganization and Theories of Crime and Delinquency: Problems and Prospects," *Criminology* 26 (1988): pp. 519–551.

James M. Byrne and Robert J. Sampson (eds.), *The Social Ecology of Crime* (New York: Springer-Verlag, 1986).

G. David Curry and Irving A. Spergel, "Gang Homicide, Delinquency, and Community," *Criminology* 26, no. 3 (1988): pp. 381–405.

Emile Durkheim, *Suicide: A Study in Sociology,* trans. J.A. Spaulding and G. Simpson (New York: Free Press, 1951 ([1897]).

Janet L. Heitgerd and Robert J. Bursik, Jr., "Extra-Community Dynamics and the Ecology of Delinquency," *American Journal of Sciology* 92 (1987): pp. 775–787.

C. Wright Mills, "The Professional Ideology of Social Pathologists," *American Journal of Sociology* 49 (1942): pp. 165–180.

Ora Simcha-Fagan and Joseph E. Schwartz, "Neighborhood and Delinquency: An Assessment of Contextural Effects," *Criminology* 24 (1986): pp. 667–703.

Rodney Stark, "Deviant Places: A Theory of the Ecology of Crime." *Criminology* 25 (1987): pp. 893–909.

Ralph B. Taylor and Jeanette Covington, "Neighborhood Changes in Ecology and Violence," *Criminology* 26, no. 4 (1988): pp. 553–589.

Jackson Toby, "The Differential Impact of Family Disorganizations," *American Sociological Review* 22 (1957): pp. 505–512.

■ Suggested Books for Additional Application

J. Wambaugh, *The Onion Field* (New York: Dell Publishing Company, 1974).
J. E. Wideman, *Brothers and Keepers* (New York: Penguin Books, 1984).

CHAPTER **10**

Culture Conflict Perspective

Overview of Culture Conflict Perspective

The culture-conflict perspective focuses on conflicts between the normative prescriptions of different groups to which individuals belong. It is concerned with behavior promoted by one group as being admirable that may be labeled as criminal by another group. Crime is therefore a deviation from consensus on the guidelines that define behavior as appropriate or criminal within groups. The perspective is especially concerned with conflicts between subgroup norms and those of the dominant society. Because of the emphasis on group membership, these explanations are mainly at the macro to meso levels. Exhibit 10.1 gives the common assumptions.

Examination of crime rates for various social groupings often reveals that one group is much more heavily involved in crime than others. This observation, especially with regard to homicide rates, has led some theorists to assert the existence of **subcultures of violence** that have norms defining certain types of crime as appropriate under some circumstances.[1] A **subculture** is a group with distinctive patterns of norms, beliefs, attitudes, values, and concerns that has evolved within the dominant society and shares many of its traditions. Subcultures often emphasize themes found in the dominant culture but to a greater, or more exclusive degree, than the dominant culture.[2] Several subcultures of violence have been identified in the United States. Wolfgang defined poor urban blacks as such a group in 1958, his research showed that people possessing structural traits of being poor, urban, and black were disproportionately involved in acts of homicide.[3] Other research has posited the existence of a similar subculture among white southerners.[4] This definition of a subculture of violence emphasizes the common traditions of the group, and may be termed a cultural, or tradition-based definition. Other research has used the term to refer to people having a particular interest in common, such as involvement with illegal drugs.[5] The difference between these definitions lies in the way in which the group is defined, not in the manner by which affiliation with the group leads to crime. In each case, the (sub)cultural group provides the means for transmitting norms, beliefs, and values across time and space through the processes of socialization.

Exhibit 10.1

Culture-conflict perspective

Common Assumptions

1. The difference between appropriate behavior and crime is defined by the norms of the dominant cultural group of a society.

2. Cultural groups often do not agree as to what should be considered criminal behavior.

3. Acts that are normative for some groups may be defined as criminal by the dominant cultural group.

4. Thus, to obey the rules of one's native culture, one may have to break the laws of the dominant culture.

Source: Thorsten Sellin, *Culture Conflict and Crime* (New York: Social Science Research Council, 1938).

Primary and Secondary Culture Conflict Approach

Thorstein Sellin lived and wrote during the period of American history in which the nation was urbanizing with the aid of many different groups of immigrants. Most of these immigrants were from southern and eastern Europe and had been born into cultures that were very different from those of the original settlers of the country. He theorized that much crime was the result of conflicts between the norms of the different cultural groups.

Inherent in Sellin's primary and secondary culture conflict approach is the belief that the norms of individual cultures and subcultures dictate individual desires, as well as the preferred methods of achieving them. This approach views crime as primarily *instrumental*, in the sense that establishing and acting upon the unique (sub)cultural norms held by the individual is considered to be the cause of the criminal act. This is true of the entire structural perspective on crime (see our discussions of the strain, social-disorganization, and control perspectives). However, the culture-conflict approach is also well-suited for dealing with *expressive* acts by conceptualizing self-esteem and a sense of belongingness as commodities that can and do enter into rational decision-making processes.

Sellin developed this approach to explain the high rates of crime and delinquency among immigrants to this country early in the 1900s. *Culture conflict* results from differences in the norms governing the behavior of individuals who belong to various different groups within a society. Each culture prescribes certain goals and the methods by which they should be achieved. **Primary culture conflict** occurs when the norms of the native culture are unacceptable (i.e., criminal) in the new, dominant culture of the society in which a person lives. This sort of culture conflict occurs primarily as a result of migrations or conquests that bring divergent cultural groups into close, permanent contact. These groups have distinct histories and traditions that contain contradictory prescriptions as to what is appropriate behavior. The

Exhibit 10.2

Primary and secondary culture-conflict approach

Restrictive Assumptions

1. Behavior is governed and evaluated by conduct norms specified by one's cultural group.

2. Consensus as to the value of conduct norms exists only in simple, homogeneous societies.

3. Consensus as to the conduct norms is never complete in complex, diverse societies.

4. Interaction between members of divergent cultures leads to "primary culture conflict."

5. Interaction between members of subcultures and the dominant culture leads to "secondary culture conflict."

Source: Thorstein Sellin, "Culture Conflict and Crime," Social Science Research Council, *Bulletin* 41, New York, 1938); George B. Vold and Thomas J. Bernard, *Theoretical Criminology*, 3d ed. (New York: Oxford University Press, 1986), p. 270.

conflict is, in part, a result of the unequal power of the two groups that reside together.

For example, laws against drugs in the United States arose as part of a culture conflict early in this century between the dominant white-Anglo society and black, Asian, and Hispanic minorities.[6] While these cultures do not necessarily condone drug use, their view of it was very different from that of Anglo-Americans. This fact still places many of the foreign drug dealers in a dual conflict with American law. First, they are trafficking in a forbidden substance and have no recourse to formal means of resolving disputes. Second, many of the cultures involved in the drug trade (e.g., Colombian) assert that it is appropriate to traffic in these substances and to enforce their "rights" in whatever manner is feasible.

The history of Colombia is one of lawlessness and violence. As a result of this history, Colombian males have learned to enforce their own contracts rather than to address their grievances in the courts. Many members of this culture would see use of government authority to protect one's interests as unmanly.[7] They are thus caught in a double-bind situation sociologically, because no matter which norm they obey, they must violate the norms of one cultural group and face its rejection. This is the sort of situation that Sellin labeled as a primary culture conflict.

Secondary culture conflict occurs when the norms of one social grouping are defined as criminal by another social grouping within the same culture. That is, different segments within a single cultural group have contradictory norms governing a particular aspect of social behavior.[8] Whereas primary

Culture conflict, economic disparity, and unequal access to centers of political power have spawned a bitter rivalry between the Black and Hasidic communities of Crown Heights, New York. This tension between cultures erupted into riots during August, 1991 after a Hasidic Jew's car struck and killed Gavin Cato, 7.

culture conflict is concerned with differences in traditions and laws across historically distinct groups, secondary culture conflict focuses attention on segments within a society that share a common history but have developed distinctive traditions and norms as a result of social position and/or environmental factors. The subgroups in secondary culture conflict are generally defined in terms of structural variables (e.g., socioeconomic class) and are formed by the process of **segmentation**, meaning that as a society increases the size of its population by natural, internal means, roles become more specialized. With increased specialization, especially in the workplace, different groups develop on the basis of divergent interests.

The cultural group that can get its norms enacted into law and enforced by government institutions has both practical and symbolic advantages over the group whose behavior has been deemed illegal. These advantages often spill over from legal questions into more general definitions of group morality. The use of moral-legal questions to take and/or hold symbolic and political power over another group is known as **status politics**.[9] Virtually all moral issues on the social agenda have some degree of status politics inherent in them.

Like other conflict-based theories discussed in this book, culture conflict theorists see society as a mosaic of groups competing for scarce resources (e.g., good jobs, nice homes). The morality and efficiency of various norms often become key issues in the formal (e.g., legal) manifestations of this conflict. That is, they form the basis of the arguments used to protect the dominant group from losing power over resources and social organization.

This approach presumes that all culture groups generate *conduct norms* to govern the behavior of their members. These norms are the product of the group's unique environment and history. That is, groups determine what is to be considered criminal and noncriminal behavior within their respective cultures. Criminal behavior occurs when an individual commits an act defined as appropriate by the norms of his or her own group in the presence of another group that defines the same act as criminal.[10] In such situations offenders believe that they are following the "right" course of action and that the prohibitions against their actions by the other group are wrong. If the other group is dominant—for example, middle socioeconomic class versus lower class in the case of secondary culture conflict—the individual can avoid criminal behavior only by abandoning the norms of his or her own group and attempting to live by the norms of the dominant group. In doing so, of course, people risk being rejected by their own group while still being refused acceptance by the dominant group, of which they are not true members.

For example, in primary culture conflict, this approach can be correctly interpreted as predicting that the *machismo* norm of Latin American societies will produce behavior that will conflict with U.S. norms and laws. In these cultures, an affront to one's masculine pride would demand a direct and physical response rather than resorting to the legal authorities. Thus, Latin American males must often fail to do what they feel to be correct in order to abide by U.S. laws and norms.

Many actions taken by a person caught in a culture-conflict situation will result in some sort of norm violation. A choice must be made between the norms they were socialized to follow and those of the society that surrounds them at the moment of decision. Since the norms of one's original group are usually the most familiar, these are the ones that are generally followed.

As modern technologies shrink travel time, contacts between divergent cultures increase. Similarly, with the growth of technology, specialization and segmentation increase. Therefore, this theory correctly predicts that crime will increase as differing norm systems come into close contact with one another.

APPLICATION

The Case of Ali Bayan

Kidnapping
The act of intentionally or knowingly abducting another person against her or his will.[11]

Interference with Child Custody
The act of taking or retaining custody of a minor in violation of a court order awarding custody of that child to another person.[12]

In October of 1987 Ali Bayan kidnapped his own seven-year-old daughter, Barbara Lauren Bayan, and took her to Jordan, his native country. Bayan had been divorced from Barbara's mother, Ms. Cathy Mahone, for approximately six years. Legally this sort of kidnapping by a noncustodial parent is known as *interference with child custody*. Ali Bayan showed little interest in his daughter immediately after his divorce from Cathy. Gradually, however, he began to develop an interest in her. He began visiting her, taking her on outings, and to visit with his other two children from a second marriage.[13]

The *precipitating factor* in this case appears to be Bayan's loss of his restaurant. His restaurant business began doing poorly and he sold it. The evidence suggests that after the sale of the restaurant, Bayan began planning to return to his native Jordan. Just prior to his fleeing the United States with his kidnapped daughter, he made a down payment on a $23,000 automobile and had it sent to Jordan. In addition, he made purchases on his credit cards up to their limits. His credit rating had been excellent up until the time he defaulted on these debts.[14]

There do not appear to be any clearly definable *attracting factors* in this case. The fact that he had to pay $175 a month in child support to Barbara's mother may have played such a role, however. On at least one occasion, she had to sue Bayan for failing to make his child-support payment.[15]

The primary *predisposing factor* in explaining Bayan's crime is culture conflict. Cathy Mahone met Bayan while she was going to college and working as a waitress at a Dallas, Texas, restaurant. Although Bayan was from a wealthy Jordanian (Sunni) Moslem family, he was working at the same restaurant as Cathy to earn his college tuition. After a brief courtship, they were married in 1976.[16]

In 1980, when Cathy informed Bayan that she was pregnant, he told her that the child must be raised in the Islamic faith. This was unacceptable to Cathy, who was a practicing Christian. In Jordanian culture, women play a very subservient role and Bayan became very angry at Cathy's refusal to accede to his demands. Six weeks after Barbara's birth in September of 1980, Cathy filed for divorce from Bayan. A Texas court awarded her custody of Barbara, and Bayan was granted visitation rights.[17]

As with most Moslem countries, Jordanian courts (unlike American courts) almost always award custody to the father in divorce cases, and they have certainly never been known to award custody to an American mother. Thus, Bayan was denied by a court in the United States what he normally would have received in his native Moslem culture—custody of his daughter. This was a matter of contradictory traditions in the two nations. Thus, Bayan was caught up in a cultural conflict between the norms of his native Jordanian

Exhibit 10.3
. . . .
Summary of facts and their role
in the explanation of the Ali
Bayan case

Level of Importance	Fact	Type of Fact
Primary	Culture conflict	Predisposing
Secondary	Child-support payments	Attracting
Secondary	Loss of restaurant	Precipitating
Tertiary	Divorce	Predisposing

culture and those of the United States.[18] The motivating facts of this case are summarized in Exhibit 10.3.

There are more than 600 cases similar to this one currently on file with the U.S. State Department. Another 25,000 such cases are known to the State Department on an informal basis. But the U.S. government can provide no assistance to the parents of kidnapped children in these cases. When a person enters another country, that nation's laws become applicable.[19] Although a Dallas grand jury indicted Ali Bayan on charges of interference with a child-custody agreement, and a warrant was issued for his arrest, the court was powerless to assist Cathy Mahone because there is no extradition treaty between the United States and Jordan. The Jordanian government, of course, believed its child-custody norms to be correct and refused to cooperate with Mahone.[20]

In December 1987 Cathy Mahone hired Don Feeney and Dave Chatellier to rescue her daughter from Bayan in Jordan. Feeney was a fifteen-year veteran of the army with service in the First Ranger Battalion of the Seventy-fifth Airborne and Special Forces. Chatellier was a former military-intelligence specialist. Together they operated a company called Corporate Training Unlimited, which provided anti-terrorist training to employees of private companies and government agencies. Feeney and Chatellier solicited Jim Hatfield, a thirty-one-year-old former intelligence analyst with the Special Forces, and J. D. Robert, a Vietnam veteran, to assist them in abducting Barbara from Bayan. In January 1988 Cathy Mahone and these four men, along with a Jordanian by the name of Adil Abbadi, abducted Barbara on her way to school and crossed the border into Israel so as to return with her to the United States.[21]

Cathy Mahone has gone into hiding with her daughter. The State Department expressed regret to the Jordanian government over the incident. Feeney, Chatellier, Hatfield, and Robert have returned to their normal, routine work. Abbadi was arrested in Jordan for his part in the abduction and remains in a Jordanian jail.[22]

Subcultural Approach
. . . .

The primary and secondary culture conflict approach, just discussed, is best equipped to explain crimes that appear to result from membership in large, impersonal groups (e.g., neighborhoods, social classes, etc.), while the subcultural approach (see Exhibit 10.4) focuses attention on the role played by membership in small and relatively intimate groups (e.g., gangs, clubs, etc.) in

Exhibit 10.4
. . . .
Subcultural approach

Restrictive Assumptions
1. Subcultural membership assists in obtaining goods, services, status and belongingness.
2. Subcultural membership provides guidelines and justifications for group and individual behavior.
3. Subcultural norms may be considered criminal by the dominant society but are defined as normal and proper by members of the subculture.
4. Subcultural membership can lead to conflicts with the dominant culture.
5. Subcultural membership enhances criminal techniques.

Source: Melvin L. DeFleur, William D'Antonio and Lois DeFleur, *Sociology: Human Society,* 2d ed. (New York: Scott, Foresman and Co., 1977), pp. 118–20; J.H. Vetter and I.J. Silverman, *Criminology and Crime: An Introduction* (New York: Harper & Row, 1986), p. 309.

the creation of criminal behavior. The subcultural approach implies the operation of social-learning theories in a much more direct fashion than did Sellin's original statement of the culture-conflict perspective.

The distinction between the two approaches is consistent with Mannheim's position that subculture is based on differences between the social classes, and the conflicts that exist between them.[23] Thus, in terms of application, Sellin's concept of secondary culture conflict better explains the motives for criminal acts that are closely linked to membership in large, impersonal social groupings while crimes committed by members of small groups, communities, or gangs are better explained by the subcultural position.

The subcultural approach can explain criminal behavior in any class (e.g., white-collar crime in the upper classes, street crime in the lower class). However, it is most often used to explain crimes that are committed by members of the lower class or other groups outside the dominant culture (e.g., white southerners).[24]

Countercultures, for criminological purposes, may be considered a type of subculture in which certain mainstream social norms are deliberately inverted. Countercultures are almost constantly in conflict with the mainstream, while subcultures come into direct conflict in only one or a very few areas of behavior.[25]

While some theorists include Cohen's middle-class measuring-rod theory and Cloward and Ohlin's theory of differential opportunity structures under the subcultural position, others classify them as part of the strain perspective. We have chosen to include them under the latter. However, we see the two perspectives as complementing one another in terms of their explanation of the development of actual behaviors. Though both these theories are discussed in greater detail under the strain perspective (see Chapter 11), a brief discussion here of their contribution to the subcultural orientation towards delinquent gang behavior is in order.

Cohen maintains that delinquent subcultures purposefully develop deviant norms for behavior that are in direct opposition to the larger adult culture. That is, these subcultures develop norms that are "negativistic" toward those that exist in the larger culture. According to Cohen, this accounts for why youth gangs in many cases steal, vandalize, and terrorize others simply for the fun of it. Cohen also proposes that a conflict exists between the norms of school systems functioning on the basis of middle-class values and those of the lower-class youth attending them. This value conflict results in lower-class youth doing poorly in school, which in turn results in them turning primarily to gangs that provide them with a sense of success and autonomy.[26]

Many poor urban teens seek out a social setting in which their failure to achieve according to middle-class norms will not be held against them. Street gangs provide such a setting and assure youths who are "failures" by middle-class academic standards a set of norms under which they can define themselves as "successes." Thus Cohen's view of the delinquent gang characterizes it as a countercultural group whose members believe they are not able to achieve success through legitimate opportunities.

Cloward and Ohlin suggest that there is not only a different degree of access to legitimate opportunities within lower-class delinquent subcultures, but that there is also a differential amount of access to illegitimate opportunities. They posit that crime results from the high availability of criminal role models for the young urban poor. Such access to these criminal roles is not equally available to everyone. That is, access to both criminal and noncriminal roles is limited by both social and psychological factors.[27]

Cloward and Ohlin further propose that these socially structured differences in access to illegitimate opportunities are important predictors of the type of delinquent subcultures that arise in various situations. According to these theorists, the degree and type of criminality that exists in lower-class neighborhoods determines whether or not youth gangs will arise, and if they do, what type of behaviors they will most often engage in.[28]

Essentially, they suggest that lower-class youth are integrated into criminal activity through their interactions with adult criminals in their neighborhoods.[29] They propose that if no successful criminal activity exists in a neighborhood, illegitimate opportunities for youth are very limited, and legitimate methods of achieving success are likely to be sought out. On the other hand, if organized criminal activities by adults are the most available models of success for local youths, then community teens will be most aware of the illegitimate opportunities available to them. If neither type of opportunity is present in the community, youths will drift toward expressive forms of crime like gang violence.[30] This type of neighborhood offers virtually no opportunities for material success, legal or illegal, but violence promises youth gang members increased status within their group.

Then there are some youths who are unable to succeed in either the gang subculture of their neighborhood or in the legitimate pursuits of conventional society. These youths, according to Cloward and Ohlin, are prone to form loosely knit *retreatist* gangs whose activities center on substance abuse of some kind. They are "double failures," according to these theorists, because they were forced to drop out of both conventional society and the local gang subculture.[31] In sum, Cloward and Ohlin propose that youth gangs model their goals and behaviors after those of the most successful adults in their neighborhoods. They are therefore integrated into one or another type of criminal activity depending on the type of criminal activity in which the adults in the neighborhood are involved.

The "double failure" view of substance-abusing groups has lost much of its popularity in recent years. This is partly due to the fact that an addict must be fairly successful as a criminal in order to continually finance the costs of supplying a drug habit.[32] However, with the increasing presence of drugs in lower-class urban neighborhoods, the use of drug dealers as role models is inevitably a factor leading many youths to define drug involvement as a means of achieving financial success. Furthermore, as drugs become more important within the criminal world, they attact the attention of organized groups of adult criminals and the delinquent gangs that imitate and work for them. Simultaneously, the huge amounts of money involved in the drug trade create a need for gang members that can perform exceedingly violent actions upon command. Thus, the modern gang has elements of the violent, organized delinquent, and of the retreatist gang combined in its structure. It appears to be developing into a multifaceted organization that supplies its members with physical, social and emotional necessities wherever they may find themselves.[33]

Gangs constitute a distinctive type of subculture. They vary in organization from the loosely knit *near-group* described by Yablonsky —a collection of individuals who remain in a state of partial organization over a fairly long period of time—to the well-organized networks constructed by biker groups like the Hell's Angels.[34] Near-groups are better organized than a mob of rioters but lack the kind of predictable internal structure that typifies most organized social or criminal groups. Yablonsky described the street gangs of the early 1960s as near-groups led by sociopaths. The more severe the individual's sociopathy, the higher a position of leadership he was likely to hold. (Virtually all gang members studied were males.) Special roles were constructed by each individual to suit his own emotional needs. Group behavior was expressive with roles and leadership positions shifting to meet the demands of the situation as well as the needs of individual members. Membership in these groups was never constant, and there was no consistently used set of rules for defining just who was a member. These groups thus had an inner core of permanent members and an outer core of occasional members. Others were sometimes "drafted" into membership if needed, but estimates of group size were generally exaggerated to a fantastic degree.[35] The groups described by Yablonsky created a culture that was neither well-organized nor constant over time. Such a set of shifting norms served the emotional needs of the core members, who were felt to suffer from personality problems of a severe nature.

At the other end of the continuum of subculture organization are the "one-percent" biker clubs that jointly subscribe to a set of norms that has changed very little since the late 1960s. These gangs emerged just after the second world war. Returning servicemen with weak family ties grouped together, especially on the west coast, where they united around a love of motorcycling and wild living. Most had found comfort of some sort in the combat situations the war forced them into but had little patience with military discipline. They formed "clubs" like the Hell's Angels, Gypsy Jokers, and Diablos, using norms that were often just the opposite of those in the mainstream culture. Initially these were near-groups that fought among themselves almost as frequently as they

Sons of Silence

fought with one another. Over time they became increasingly well-organized, especially as a result of their involvement in illegal enterprises like drug manufacturing and sales.[36] In essence, these near-groups of counterculturalists gradually evolved into a subculture of criminal syndicates. Much the same seems to be occurring with some street gangs today as the lucrative drug trade creates the need for increasingly effective organization and at least a semblance of social acceptability.[37]

Lower-Class Culture Conflict Theory

Walter Miller developed a theory of lower-class culture conflict (see Exhibit 10.5) based on the general assumptions that compose the subcultural approach. This theory also contains elements of the learning perspective discussed earlier, since it asserts that the norms that make criminal acts acceptable are passed on from one generation to the next, as are more conventional norms.

Miller suggests that a "lower-class" subculture exists in the United States, distinguished by six focal concerns that often contribute to gang formation and delinquency:[38]

1. *Trouble*—which for males means negative interactions with officials from the police, school, etc., and for females means unwanted pregnancy and/or conflicts within romantic relationships.

2. *Toughness*—which for males means "macho," or manly, often in a rough or violent way.

3. *Smartness*—which means the ability to cheat, hustle, or "con" others.

4. *Excitement*—which refers to thrills/danger.

Exhibit 10.5
. . . .
Lower-class culture-conflict
theory

Specific Assumptions

1. Specific lower-class focal concerns exist independently of other values held by members of other classes within a society.

2. These focal concerns modify the meaning of commonly held moral values for lower-class persons.

3. The resulting worldview is unique to the lower class and can be used in a number of ways to guide behavior.

4. Lower-class households tend to be matriarchal.

5. This form of family organization is different from that prescribed by the dominant culture and can cause lower-class adolescent males to join delinquent groups dominated by males.

Source: Walter B. Miller, "Lower-Class Culture as a Generating Milieu of Gang Delinquency," *Journal of Social Issues* 14 (1958): pp. 5–19.

5. *Fate*—which refers to the individual's lack of control over what happens to him or her.

6. *Autonomy*—which means achieving or seeking independence.

Miller suggests that these focal concerns are endemic in, and unique to, the lower class of this country. He theorizes that their influence is more important in explaining juvenile delinquency than the formation of "delinquent subcultures" as Cohen suggested or the impact of "differential opportunity" described by Cloward and Ohlin. He proposes that it is the lower-class cultural system that exerts the most direct pressure on behavior.[39]

This sort of pressure is seen as a motivating factor in the creation of gangs.[40] As has been demonstrated by theoreticians, both street and motorcycle gangs have values based heavily on norms that originated in this lower class,[41] and members' adherence to these values, as well as their avoidance of the mainstream culture and its norms, is akin to that of a deviant religious sect.[42] Many gang members report that they first joined these groups in search of protection from other gangs, to gain status, meet girls, and find friends.[43] Their nearly religious view of the gang as a source of hope and belongingness, as well as the physical and social resources necessary for survival, leads to intense loyalty to the group. Such loyalty, along with the value placed on toughness, often leads to violence between groups as well as disdain for conventional society and its values.[44]

Another important component of Miller's theory is that lower-class families tend to be matriarchal, or female-based. This, along with status as a racial minority, is typical of street gang membership.[45] According to Miller, in a relatively large number of lower-class families the male parent is either totally absent from the household, only occasionally present in the household, or, if present, only very minimally or sporadically engaged in supporting or parenting the children. Matriarchal households of this type are thought to lead to the emergence of age-graded *single-sex peer groups* for males over the age of puberty. These groups are highly prevalent in lower-class communities. Miller believed that they provide a stable reference group of same-sex role models for youths raised in female-dominated households—especially important for the adolescent male, who, in the absence of a father to model himself after, seeks a peer-group setting in which to learn the male sex role.[46]

Miller's thesis suggests that these one-sex peer groups/gangs commit criminal behavior because of the way in which they interpret the focal concerns of the lower class. Thus, for example, assaultive behavior (e.g., gang fights and assaults on individuals) could be attributed to the focal concern of "toughness," auto theft to the focal concern of "excitement," and so on.[47] Miller's theory thus predicts the emergence of gangs among the poor whenever matriarchal family structure becomes so dominant that young males lack same-sex role models.

It must be stressed that Miller's theory presumes human behavior to be controlled by free will. Individuals *choose* how to interpret and employ these concerns. These focal concerns are not values, but interests that help define the meaning of values in the context of lower-class urban life. These concerns are produced by the problems unique to the lower-class. It must be emphasized that Miller does not believe that there is a single lower-class morality. Rather, each member of the lower class must deal with these concerns to a much greater degree than would members of other classes. The manner in which these concerns are defined and linked to one another, as well as to conventional values, is what determines the individual's perception and behavior. For example, a lower-class youth may join a gang to prove his toughness or may avoid gangs out of fear of trouble. Miller's central point, however, is that the importance of these concerns among the lower class distinguishes them as a unique subculture. The focal concerns also tend to stress factors that can easily lead to criminality under some circumstances.

The Case of Perry Smith · · · · · · · · · · · · · · · · · APPLICATION · · · · · · · ·

Truman Capote's *In Cold Blood* provides an account of Perry Edward Smith, who, along with Richard Eugene Hickock, murdered and robbed a family in Holcomb, Kansas, on November 16, 1959. Smith and Hickock were executed for the murders of Mr. and Mrs. Herbert W. Clutter and their two children, Bonnie and Kenyon, on April 14, 1965.[48]

Capote's account suggests that Smith committed these crimes primarily as a result of what Miller identified as lower-class focal concerns. Smith was a single, white, thirty-one-year-old, lower-class male when he and Hickock murdered the Clutter family. The main *predisposing factor* affecting Smith was his unhappy childhood. His alcoholic mother left his father and took Smith and his siblings with her when she went to San Francisco to lead a wild life. Smith was six years old at this time, and his brother and sister were pre-teenagers. His mother would have sex with anyone who would buy her a drink. While he and his brother and sister lived with their mother, they had to constantly clean up her vomit and usually went without decent clothes or sufficient food. Smith's sister, Fern, and his brother, Jimmy, both committed suicide as adults.[49]

Committed to an orphanage at the age of seven, Smith was later returned to his mother for a short time. After several confinements in institutions and children's detention centers, he was sent to live with his father. His formal education had ended at the third grade, further predisposing him to crime. He

Perry Edward Smith

and his father drifted around the country in a house trailer until Smith was sixteen and joined the merchant marines. After discharge in 1952, he went to help his father build a lodge in Alaska. In 1955, after the lodge was built, Smith had an argument with his father, who then threw him out.[50]

The central *attracting factor* for Smith was his early involvement in crime and prison life. After separating from his father, he had no money and nowhere to go. As a result of this, he committed a burglary in 1955 and was subsequently convicted of breaking and entering. He received a five-to-ten-year sentence in the Kansas State Penitentiary and was paroled on July 6, 1959.[51]

While in prison, one of Smith's acts demonstrated the lower-class concern with toughness and smartness. During his confinement, he bragged of having killed a man several years earlier in Las Vegas, Nevada (i.e., toughness). He claimed to have done this "just for the hell of it" and maintained that he had "gotten away with it." He actually made up this story (i.e. smartness or "conning") to impress the other inmates. He later rationalized that his reason for telling the story was that if he and Hickock were ever arrested for the Clutter murders, he would know (i.e., smartness in handling "trouble") that Hickock had confessed to the police about the murders if the police also knew about his story of killing a man in Las Vegas.[52]

Chief Detective Dewey, who was in charge of the investigation of the Clutter murders for the Kansas Bureau of Investigation, tried to understand "how two individuals could reach the same degree of rage, the kind of psychopathic rage it took to commit such a crime," but the detective could not

Richard Eugene Hickock,
after admitting to taking
part in the slaying of the
Herbert Clutter family.

come up with an answer.[53] The explanation offered here is that Smith was looking for *excitement*, that he believed it was *fate* that brought him to the Clutter home, and that he was seeking *autonomy*, which he believed could result from the money obtained from the robbery aspect of this crime. These beliefs helped Smith to (1) define his actions as acceptable and (2) feel no personal responsibility for these actions.

The *precipitating factor* for Smith was the desire to expose Hickock to excitement (i.e., danger) by showing Hickock that he (Smith) could commit cold-blooded murder. Once he cut Mr. Clutter's throat, there was no turning back. Smith did the actual killing of all four members of the Clutter family. He later maintained that he did not initially intend to kill them—that when he put the knife to Mr. Clutter's throat, he thought that Hickock would stop him. In effect, he was trying to bluff Hickock into "chickening out" first so as to demonstrate his own *toughness*. Another example of concern with excitement (i.e., danger) occurred when Smith and Hickock pulled into the Clutter driveway. Smith said he did not want to go through with the crime at that point. Hickock, however, told Smith he would prove who had the most guts and do it all by himself.[54]

Smith defined his participation in this crime as being a result of *fate* (i.e., he believed it to be beyond his control). For example, it was fate that had prevented him from meeting up with an old cellmate friend (as he had planned) after being released from prison. Had this occurred, he would not have become involved with Hickock, and the Clutter murders would not have occurred.

Exhibit 10.6
. . . .
Summary of facts and their role
in the explanation of the case of
Perry Smith

Level of Importance	Fact	Type of Fact
Primary	Pathological childhood	Predisposing
Primary	Desire to demonstrate toughness and achieve autonomy	Precipitating
Secondary	Early experience with crime and prison	Attracting
Secondary	Fatalistic view of life	Attracting
Tertiary	Limited opportunities due to lack of education	Predisposing

He also took a fatalistic view of their being apprehended for the Clutter murders—that is, he felt they would be caught, whereas Hickock thought they would not. As mentioned, another aspect of this crime was Smith's desire for autonomy. By committing the robbery of the Clutter home, he hoped to achieve the independence to do what he always dreamed of, which was to hunt for sunken treasure off the coast of Mexico.[55] Exhibit 10.6 summarizes the facts of this case.

Conclusion
. . . .

The culture-conflict perspective emphasizes the lack of consensus as to what constitutes proper behavior across the groups that compose a society. This perspective thus serves as a necessary counterbalance to the ethnocentric tendencies of theories stressing social disorganization. Like that of Sutherland, the perspective stresses the idea of differential social organization. It asserts that the causes of crime lie in the contradictions between group norms within a society.

The central point made by the cultural-conflict perspective is that obeying the conduct norms of certain groups is likely to result in the individual being defined as criminal by the dominant society. Yet, obeying the conduct norms of the dominant society makes the individual a traitor to his or her own group. Such conflicts can occur between the norms of distinct cultures or between the norms of segments of a single society, such as between lower- and middle-class citizens.

This was the situation with Ali Bayan. His Islamic norms maintained that fathers should have custody of children in divorce cases—exactly the opposite of the U.S. norm. His response to this problem was just what Sellin's primary culture-conflict approach would predict—he enforced the norms of his culture and thus violated the U.S. legal code. Cathy Mahone and the men she hired to return her daughter to her were also caught in a culture-conflict situation in Jordan. Their acts were clearly classified as criminal by Jordanian law and Islamic norms.

The culture conflict perspective is best suited for dealing with predisposing and attracting factors, but is completely unable to predict precipitating ones.

This perspective predicts that the presence of certain norms (e.g., machismo) among participants in an illegal enterprise will result in heightened rates of violence. However, this perspective tends to neglect the individual, and thus can be misinterpreted as being deterministic. The culture-conflict perspective cannot resolve the questions that deal with why particular victims were killed by particular assailants in a particular situation (i.e., precipating factors).

This is to say that (1) culture conflict occurs primarily at the macro or meso level but results in difficult choices at the micro level; (2) it does not predict specific crimes or criminals but rather explains trends in the rate at which certain crimes occur; and (3) it has political implications, because it is concerned with the creation and enforcement of laws that support one normative system at the expense of another.

The subculture approach helps to offset some of these limitations by focusing on micro- to meso-level forces that create relatively small groups with very similar norm systems. Gangs are typical of such groups. This perspective, along with that based on the idea of strain, is critical to explaining gang behavior. Cloward and Ohlin's theory uses the range of opportunities for achieving success that are present in a community to predict the nature of the gangs that arise. Cohen explains how the educational system's use of middle-class norms creates frustration in many lower-class youths and thus attracts them to gangs. Gangs enable such youths to determine their own criteria for success rather than forcing them to conform to conventional standards. Miller argues that the matriarchal family structure typifying the urban poor of this country forces youths into gangs as a result of their need for a same-sex peer group that will help them define the masculine role. The interpretations of the lower-class focal concerns that originate in such single-sex peer groups are also seen as criminogenic, especially in regard to gang activities.

The subculture approach is not entirely restricted to use with crimes committed by groups, however. As we have illustrated with the Smith-Hickock case, the norms that facilitate gang formation in the inner city are also used by individuals to evaluate themselves and their acts. A distorted sense of masculinity is common both in gang members and others from the lower classes because of the lack of conventional male role models.

The subculture approach is also useful in explaining much of the crime that is currently labeled as "drug-related." Use of illegal drugs forces individuals to participate in a deviant social system. As members of such a system they have little chance of success in using the formal system of courts and police to deal with their conflicts. They also learn that having a reputation as "tough" helps them to avoid problems with others. Aggression is rewarded at all levels of the illegal drug trade and vicarious learning processes (see chapter 7) transmit this norm from dealers and traffickers to users. The reasons for such violence include territorial disputes between traffickers/dealers, rule enforcement within distribution organizations, disputes over drug quality, elimination of police informants, disputes over use of paraphernalia and drugs, and robberies of dealers who are unprotected by agents of formal social control. This **systemic model** of drug related violence explains many of the crimes related to illegal drugs by referring to the norms of the underworld as a source of guidance for its members. It is thus a complement to the psychopharmacological and economic-compulsive models that were presented in chapter 4.[56] Like the other two models, however, the systemic model of drug-related crime fails to address the question of how many of these crimes would have occurred had drugs not been involved. That is, because most drug users were involved in crime and illicit subcultures prior to their drug use,[57] it is very likely that they would have become involved in an illegal subculture and followed its norms even if they had not become drug–involved.

The culture conflict perspective presumes the presence of social learning to a great extent. That is, the interpersonal dynamics described by social-learning theories are presumed to occur in gang and other small group settings. Subcultural theorists may also subscribe to some aspects of the social-disorganization perspective. This is especially true of the ecological approach in the disorganization perspective. The association between gang leadership roles and sociopathy that Yablonsky proposed means that gang norms may often be set by persons afflicted with antisocial-personality disorder. Drug use and the stresses unique to lower-class urban life add to the criminal potential of such subcultures.

The pivotal issue in all the theories contained in this perspective is that the offender(s) are obeying the norms of the group(s) to which they belong. They see their behavior as appropriate for the situation. In the language of control theorists, we could say that they are well-bonded but to the wrong group. Because they perceive the (criminal) action as proper, policies based on deterrence are unlikely to affect the sorts of crimes produced by culture conflict.[58] Like other forms of conflict theory, the ideas in this perspective focus on the import of group membership in the development and evaluation of behavior as well as the role of group power in the process of creating and enforcing law.

Glossary ·

Countercultures For criminological purposes, may be considered a type of subculture in which certain mainstream social norms are deliberately inverted. Countercultures are almost constantly in conflict with the mainstream, whereas subcultures come into direct conflict in only one or a very few areas of behavior.

Primary Culture Conflict Occurs when the norms of a person's native culture are unacceptable (defined as criminal) in his or her new culture.

Secondary Culture Conflict Occurs when the norms of a person's social grouping within society are defined as criminal by other social groupings within that society.

Segmentation A process that occurs as a society increases the size of its population by natural, internal means, causing roles to become more specialized. With increased specialization, especially in the workplace, different groups develop on the basis of divergent interests. These groups are referred to as *segments* and are distinguished by their differing normative systems.

Status Politics Refers to the use of moral-legal questions to take and/or hold symbolic and political power over another group.

Subcultures Groups with distinctive patterns of norms, beliefs, attitudes, values, and concerns that have evolved from the dominant society and share much of its traditions. They often exaggerate minor themes of the dominant culture to the exclusion of the major ones.

Subcultures of violence   Groups within a society that have both disproportionately high rates of violence and traditions or norms that encourage violent behavior deemed criminal by the dominant culture. These subcultures can be defined in terms of structural, traditional, or behavioral commonalities.

Systemic model of drug related violence   Uses the subculture approach to explain much of the crime that is currently labeled as "drug-related" by referring to the fact that involvement with illegal drugs forces individuals to participate in a deviant social system. As members of such a system they have little chance of success in using the formal system of social control to deal with their conflicts. Aggression is rewarded at all levels of the illegal drug trade and social learning processes transmit this norm among users, dealers and traffickers. It is a complement to the psychopharmacological and economic-compulsive models that were presented in chapter 4.

■ Notes

1. Marvin Wolfgang and Franco Ferracuti, *The Subculture of Violence* (New York: Tavistock, 1967).
2. Melvin L. DeFleur, William D'Antonio and Lois DeFleur, *Sociology: Human Society*, 2 ed. (New York: Scott, Foresman and Co., 1977), pp. 112–118, 624; J. Milton Yinger, *Countercultures* (New York: Free Press, 1982), pp. 41–43.
3. Marvin Wolfgang, *Patterns of Criminal Homicide* (Philadelphia: University of Pennsylvania Press, 1958).
4. M. D. Smith and R. N. Parker, "Type of Homicide and Variation in Regional Rates," *Social Forces* 59 (1957): pp. 136–147; J. Reed, *One South*, (Baton Rouge, LA: Louisiana State University Press, 1982); R. Gastil, "Homicide and a Regional Culture of Violence," *American Sociological Review* 36 (1969): pp. 412–427; W. Bankston, R. St. Pierre, and D. Allen, "Southern Culture and Patterns of Victim-Offender Relationships in Homicide," *Sociological Spectrum* 5 (1985): pp. 197–211.
5. M. Zahn and G. Snodgrass, "Drug Use and the Structure of Homicide in Two U.S. Cities" in Flynn and Conrad (eds.), *The New Criminology and the Old Criminology* (New York: Praeger, 1978).
6. James Inciardi, *The War on Drugs* (Mountain View, CA: Mayfield, 1966).
7. Marshall Clinard and Daniel Abbott, *Comparative Criminology* (New York: Free Press, 1975); Peter Lupsha, "Drug-Trafficking: Colombia and Mexico in Comparative Perspective," *Journal of International Affairs* 35, no. 1 (1981): pp. 95–115; Wolfgang and Ferracuti, *The Subculture of Violence*; Thomas Schorr, "The Structure and Stuff of Violence in a North Andean Valley" in Miles Richardson (ed.), *The Human Mirror* (Baton Rouge, LA: Louisiana State University Press, 1974), pp. 269–297.
8. Sellin, "Culture, Conflict and Crime."
9. Joseph Gusfield, *Symbolic Crusade* (Urbana, IL: University of Illinois Press, 1963).
10. Sellin, "Culture, Conflict and Crime"; Harold J. Vetter and Ira J. Silverman, *Criminology and Crime: An Introduction* (New York: Harper & Row, 1986).
11. *Texas Penal Code*, 8th ed. (St. Paul, MN: West Publishing, 1990), p. 29.

12. *Texas Criminal Laws 1989–90*, Austin, TX: Texas Department of Public Safety, Austin, Texas, 1989, pp. 44.

13. Neil C. Livingstone and David Halevy, "Operation Lauren," *The Washingtonian*, September 1988, pp. 143–256.

14. Ibid.

15. Ibid.

16. Ibid.

17. Ibid.

18. Livingstone and Halevy, "Operation Lauren," pp. 143–256; Allison L. Jernow, "A Part of Me Is Missing," *The Washingtonian*, September 1988.

19. Ibid.

20. Ibid.

21. Ibid.

22. Ibid.

23. Hermann Mannheim, *Comparative Criminology* (Boston: Houghton-Mifflin, 1965).

24. Reed, *One South*.

25. Yinger, *Countercultures*.

26. Albert K. Cohen, *Delinquent Boys* (New York: Free Press, 1960).

27. Richard A. Cloward and Lloyd E. Ohlin, *Delinquency and Opportunity* (New York: Free Press, 1960).

28. Ibid.

29. Cloward and Ohlin, *Delinquency and Opportunity*.

30. Ibid; See also Donald J. Shoemaker, *Theories of Delinquency*, 2 ed. (New York: Oxford University Press, 1990), pp. 124–135.

31. Ibid.

32. Inciardi, *The War on Drugs*, pp. 25–26.

33. Jeffrey Fagan, "The Social Organization of Drug Use and Drug Dealing among Urban Gangs," *Criminology* 27, no. 4 (1989): pp. 633–670.

34. Lewis Yablonsky, *The Violent Gang* (New York: Macmillan, 1962); Howard Abadinsky, *Organized Crime*, 2 ed. (Chicago: Nelson-Hall, Inc., 1989), pp. 24–40; Fagan, "Social Organization of Drug Use and Drug Dealing among Urban Gangs."

35. Yablonsky, *The Violent Gang*, pp. 272–273.

36. Abadinsky, *Organized Crime*, pp. 24–40; Hunter S. Thompson, *Hell's Angels* (New York: Ballantine Books, 1967); James F. Quinn, "Sex Roles and Hedonism among Members of 'Outlaw' Motorcycle Clubs," *Deviant Behavior* 8, no. 1 (1987): pp. 47–63.

37. Fagan, "Social Organization of Drug Use and Drug Dealing among Urban Gangs."

38. Walter B. Miller, "Lower Class Culture as a Generating Milieu of Gang Delinquency," *Journal of Social Issues* 14 (1958): pp. 5–19.

39. Ibid.

40. Fagan, "Social Organization of Drug Use and Drug Dealing among Urban Gangs"; J. Mark Watson, "Outlaw Motorcyclists as an Outgrowth of Lower Class Values," *Deviant Behavior* 4, (1980): pp. 31–48.

41. Watson, "Outlaw Motorcyclists as an Outgrowth of Lower Class Values."

42. Robert K. Jackson and Wesley D. McBride, *Understanding Street Gangs* (Sacramento, CA: Custom Publishing Co., 1985), pp. 36–38; J. Mark

Watson, "Righteousness on Two Wheels: Bikers as a Secular Sect," *Sociological Spectrum* 2 (1982): pp. 333–349.

43. Jackson and McBride, *Understanding Street Gangs*, pp. 5–9; Fagan, "Social Organization of Drug Use and Drug Dealing among Urban Gangs."

44. Quinn, "Sex Roles and Hedonism among Members of 'Outlaw' Motorcycle Clubs," pp. 47–63.

45. Jackson and McBride, *Understanding Street Gangs*, p. 11.

46. Walter B. Miller, "Lower Class Culture as a Generating Milieu of Gang Delinquency," *Journal of Social Issues* 14 (1958): pp. 5–19.

47. Ibid.

48. Truman Capote, *In Cold Blood* (New York: Random House, 1965).

49. Ibid.

50. Ibid.

51. Ibid.

52. Ibid.

53. Ibid.

54. Ibid.

55. Ibid.

56. P. J. Goldstein, "The Drugs-Violence Nexus: A Tripartite Conceptual Framework," *Journal of Drug Issues* Fall (1985): pp. 493–506.

57. J. A. Inciardi, *The War on Drugs*, (Palo Alto, CA, 1984): pp. 124–6.

58. P. Reuter, "Social Control in Illegal Markets" in Donald Black (ed), *Towards a General Theory of Social Control: Selected Problems*, vol. 2 (Orlando, FL: Academic Press, 1984).

■ Suggested Readings

Anne Campbell, *The Girls in the Gang* (New York: Basil Blackwell, 1984).

M. Clinard and D. Abbott, *Comparative Criminology* (New York: Free Press, 1975).

S. N. Eisenstadt and Luis Roniger, *Patrons, Clients, and Friends: Interpersonal Relationships and the Structure of Trust in Society* (Cambridge, England: Cambridge University Press, 1984).

Joseph Gusfield, *Symbolic Crusade* (Urbana, IL: University of Illinois Press, 1963).

P. Lupsha, "Drug-Trafficking: Colombia and Mexico in Comparative Perspective," *Journal of International Affairs* 35, no. 1 (1981): pp. 95–115.

W. Miller, "Lower Class Culture as a Generating Milieu of Gang Delinquency," *Journal of Social Issues* 14 (1958): pp. 5–19.

C. Wright Mills, "The Professional Ideology of Social Pathologists," *American Journal of Sociology* 49 (1942): pp. 165–180.

Randall Montgomery, "The Outlaw Motorcycle Subculture," *Canadian Journal of Criminology* (October 1976): pp. 332–342.

Randall Montgomery, "The Outlaw Motorcycle Subculture II," *Canadian Journal of Criminology* (October 1977): pp. 356–361.

James F. Quinn, "Sex Roles and Hedonism Among Members of 'Outlaw' Motorcycle Clubs," *Deviant Behavior* 8, no. 1 (1987): pp. 47–63.

Thorstein Sellin, "Culture, Conflict and Crime," Social Science Research Council, *Bulletin* 41, New York, 1938.

Thomas Schorr, "The Structure and Stuff of Violence in a North Andean Valley" In M. Richardson (ed.), *The Human Mirror* (Baton Rouge, LA: Louisiana State University Press, 1974), pp. 269–297.

Jackson Toby, "The Differential Impact of Family Disorganization," *American Sociological Review* 22 (1957): pp. 505–512.

J. Mark Watson, "Outlaw Motorcyclists as an Outgrowth of Lower Class Values," *Deviant Behavior* 4 (1980): pp. 31–48.

J. Mark Watson, "Righteousness on Two Wheels: Bikers as a Secular Sect," *Sociological Spectrum* 2 (1982): pp. 333–349.

Louis Wirth, "Culture Conflict and Misconduct," *Social Forces* 9 (1931): pp. 484–492.

Louis Wirth, "Urbanism as a Way of Life," *American Journal of Sociology* 44 (1938): pp. 1–24.

Marvin Wolfgang, *Patterns of Criminal Homicide* (Philadelphia: University of Pennsylvania Press, 1958).

M. Wolfgang and F. Ferracuti, *The Subculture of Violence* (New York: Tavistock, 1967).

J. Milton Yinger, *Countercultures* (New York: Free Press, 1982).

■ Suggested Books for Additional Application

John Dillman, *Unholy Matrimony* (New York: MacMillan, 1986).

Donald Goddard, *Joey* (New York: Dell Publishing Co., 1974).

Yves Lavigne, *Hell's Angels: Three Can Keep a Secret If Two Are Dead* (New York: Carol Publishing Group, 1987).

P. Meyer, *The Yale Murder* (New York: Empire Books, 1982).

Frank Reynolds and Michael McClure, *Freewheelin' Frank: Secretary of the Angels* (New York: Grove Press, 1967).

Hunter S. Thompson, *Hell's Angels* (New York: Ballantine Books, 1967).

J. Wambaugh, *The Onion Field* (New York: Dell Publishing Company, 1974).

J. E. Wideman, *Brothers and Keepers* (New York: Penguin Books, 1984).

CHAPTER **11**

Strain Perspective

Overview of Strain Perspective

. . . .

The strain perspective originated in sociology, and versions of it are common throughout the sociological community. It has been extremely popular in criminology since the late 1950s. Strain theories developed as attempts to link the macro-level issues identified by the disorganization perspective with the micro level at which behavior actually occurs. Exhibit 11.1 gives the general assumptions of the strain perspective. Both the strain and disorganization perspectives presume that, like animals in Darwin's theory of evolution, human societies evolve into the most efficient structural form possible for their situation. These theorists believe that what exists is present because it is the most effective form at the time. By "effective" they mean that the organizational form (e.g., capitalism, democracy) allows the society to successfully compete with other societies while maintaining its stability, or equilibrium.

The strain perspective assumes that society is built on a consensus as to what is right and wrong (goals). It follows, then, that similarly strong consensus exists as to the best ways of achieving what is "right" (methods). Crime is a challenge to this consensus and thus threatens society's stability. However, as long as the crime rate is fairly low, rule violations have three important **latent functions**—unintended and often unrecognized results—that actually contribute to social stability. First, crime provides the mainstream society with a source of *solidarity* in that it gives law-abiding citizens something to unite against in moral outrage. Second, by punishing criminals, society makes a statement as to which of its rules are the most important. This is known as **boundary setting**. For example, in western civilizations, human life is given

Exhibit 11.1
. . . .

Strain perspective

General Assumptions

1. Societies evolve into the most efficient form of organization possible.

2. Not all groups within the society benefit equally from this form of organization.

3. A widespread consensus as to the goals that individuals should strive for results from this efficiency.

4. All societies attempt to control the methods by which their citizens attain these goals.

5. Human behavior is based on free will and tends to be self-serving (egocentric).

6. Individual choices are, in large part, a result of group membership.

7. Deviance and crime result from individuals choosing to violate these regulations.

8. Rule violations pose a serious threat to the social order of the culture.

Source: Melvin L. DeFleur, *Social Problems in American Society,* (Boston: Houghton Mifflin, 1983) pp. 13–17; Emile Durkheim, *Suicide: A Study in Sociology,* trans. J.A. Spaulding and G. Simpson (New York: Free Press, [1897] 1951).

high value. Therefore, the punishment for murder is more severe than for most other crimes. By setting the penalities in this way, society announces that this is a very important boundary that citizens should not cross. Finally, the public punishment and humiliation of criminals provides people with a motive to obey the law. We may say that the punishment of crime thus acts to *affirm the value of conformity*. To the degree that crime serves these functions, therefore, it contributes to social stability and is seen as a necessary evil by strain theorists.

Like the classical frame of reference, this perspective attributes behavior to individual free will and presumes it to have self-serving motives. However, group memberships are seen as predisposing individuals to certain types of choices. Membership in some groups can result in crime being chosen as an appropriate form of behavior more than is normal in the society as a whole. This happens because all of the groups within a society do not benefit equally from its form of organization. The strain perspective is specifically concerned with the ways in which members of groups that benefit the least from their society's form of organization adapt to their disadvantaged situation.

Problems in the structure of a society could lie in (1) the sorts of goals the culture has defined as most desirable, (2) the sorts of methods commonly used to achieve these goals, or (3) the discrepancy between the cultural goals and the socially approved means of attaining them. The assumption of the perspective that the society's form of organization is the best possible prevents questioning of the appropriateness of the goals and methods of attaining them that the society prescribes. Therefore, its focus is on the last type of problem — the discrepancy between universally desired goals and differentially available means of achieving them.

Strain theorists see the illegitimate acquisition of goods and status as a result of the fact that our society instills in its members a felt need for certain standards of comfort and success but does not provide equal opportunities for members of all groups to attain them. The tension experienced by certain segments of the population as a result of this discrepancy between universal goals and unequally distributed means is referred to as **strain.** At the aggregate level of analysis, strain predisposes certain groups to high rates of criminality. However, because human behavior is governed by the free will of individuals, other events in the person's life must be examined to predict *which* members of the group are likely to become criminal.

Some people maintain that the American media has exacerbated strain in our society by, for example, making "get rich quick" schemes socially acceptable, even though our capitalist system demands long-term investment and frugal use of resources. To give another example, sexual satisfaction is a commonly advertised goal, and many movies, books, and TV shows link it to the use of violence. Learning theories have addressed these issues at some length.[1]

In its concern for the relationship between the macro-level organization of society into groups (e.g., rich and poor, black and white, urban and rural) and the effect of the group's position in the society's hierarchical structure on the behavior of the group's members, the strain perspective is a decidedly meso-level one. In essence, it links the macro-structural organization of society to the micro-social choices of its individual members. The ability of people in various positions in the society to meet their goals is the critical factor in strain-based analyses of crime. But these theorists are not concerned with personality traits or individual abilities. They look for explanations primarily in the dynamics of group memberships and the hierarchical relations between groups.

Anomie Approach

The general assertion underlying Merton's approach to societal strain (see Exhibit 11.2) is that tension (strain) exists between the desire to meet goals and the distribution of methods for doing so in the society. For example, virtually all Americans seek a comfortable lifestyle in which they can feel that they are successful. However, not all citizens are able to obtain the training required to get a well-paid and secure job. Group memberships are the best overall predictor of how likely a person will be to achieve these goals. Merton's approach focuses primarily on economic groups. The higher the status of those groups is, the more likely the achievement of the goals without resorting to crime.

Each group is unique in this regard because it occupies a different position in the structural hierarchy of society. These positions change in a slow but constant manner so that different groups experience strain at different points in time. Each individual also has a unique set of group memberships that jointly define his or her position in the society and determine the level of strain he or she will experience — that is, the amount of tension between goals and available means to reach them. When the strain is great, the result is both a lack of normative guidelines for individual behavior and inadequate integration into mainstream society — what the sociologist Emile Durkheim defined as **anomie**.[2]

Exhibit 11.2

Anomie approach

Restrictive Assumptions

1. Society defines goals and the socially approved methods of achieving them.

2. All members of a society have similar goals but are not equally equipped to obtain them.

3. Strain results from the discrepancy between desired goals and the available means of achieving them.

4. Strain is a specific form of anomie that leads to stress.

5. A person's group memberships are the best predictors of how much strain she or he will experience.

6. The individual must choose approved or illicit goals, and methods of achieving them, in order to adapt to this strain.

7. There are five basic and common reactions to strain.

8. These reactions are defined on the basis of their use of socially approved or disapproved goals and means.

Source: Robert K. Merton, "Social Structure and Anomie," *American Sociological Review* vol. 3 (1938): pp. 672–682.

Anomie was presumed to generate stress and a propensity for criminal behavior.[3] However, Durkheim never specifically described the means by which this macro-social phenomena came to impact individual choices of behavior. He merely inferred that the values and beliefs of the group, as well as its position in the social structure, were pivotal in this regard.[4]

The student should be aware that the strain perspective was designed to link such macro-level factors to the micro level where criminal behavior is actually committed; it is a meso-level approach.[5] (Anomie at the macro level of analysis has also been linked to crime, as discussed in Chapter 9.) In this meso-level approach, Merton attempts to explain the fact that low socioeconomic status has long been disproportionately associated with criminal behavior. The original focus of the approach was on differences in group rates of criminality.[6] Our use of this approach to explain micro-level actions is thus an embellishment of the original approach.

Merton's approach defines all crimes as fundamentally *instrumental* acts that result from individuals attempting to obtain goals related to their material well-being and/or their social status. Under this approach, expressive crimes are, in effect, redefined as instrumental ones so as to allow for the conceptualization of emotional goals as instrumental ones. Thus, emotional goals become a sort of commodity, and the distinction between expressive and instrumental motivation becomes meaningless. So long as the emotional goal is recognized by the dominant group's norm system, the approach is able to deal with it in this fashion.

Merton refined Emile Durkheim's concept of anomie to create the basic statement of the anomie approach:[7] To the degree that normative methods of achieving goals are perceived as unavailable by members of a social group, strain is experienced by the group. This strain is uncomfortable to the individual, who is likely to define it as a form of stress. The individual must then choose a method of adapting to that stress, and a way—whether approved or illegal — of implementing this adaptive method. It is this personal choice of adaptation that determines which individuals will act in a criminal manner. However, Merton's anomie approach neglects the micro-level variables that influence choices of adaptation in various situations.[8]

Culturally defined goals are interests that are held to be legitimate objectives for members of all groups within the society (e.g., comfort and success). These goals, or symbols of them, are ranked by the individual according to their perceived value. Group norms play a large role in determining such rankings, however, since self-esteem and belongingness needs are rooted in the relationship between the individual and the group.[9]

Although some of these goals are directly related to human biological drives, they are not determined by them. Acceptable means of attaining the goals are determined by *regulatory norms,* those based on the moral beliefs of most members of the society or of those best able to promote their sentiments through the use of power.[10] The most important of these regulatory norms are enacted as laws in modern societies.

A stable relationship between culturally defined goals and the regulatory norms for achieving those goals is maintained as long as individuals who conform to both sets of guidelines experience satisfaction. In this way, the value of conformity is constantly reaffirmed, and society remains stable. In the event that this stability is disrupted or challenged, criminal behavior is likely to ensue. Criminal behavior may thus be regarded as a symptom of a poor fit between culturally prescribed goals (aspirations) and socially structured methods for achieving those goals (means).[11]

Social structure produces a strain on group members and a state of anomie within the group. Our capitalist social order, for example, creates pressure for each individual to outperform every other individual in the quest for success. Merton does not regard this competition as harmful provided the norms regulating the relationship between the prescribed goals and the accepted means are stable. This equilibrium is disturbed whenever a greater emphasis is placed upon the outcome (goal) than upon the methods by which it is attained (means). The result of such a disturbance of social equilibrium is a breakdown of the institutional norms, the creation of anomie at the group (macro to meso) level, and increased stress at the individual (micro) level.[12] Thus, when "success at any price" becomes a dominant norm in society, or a subgroup thereof, the regulatory norms lose their effectiveness, and the resulting state of anomie encourages some people to choose criminal methods of attaining their "success" goals.

Merton focuses on societies in which there is an exceptionally strong emphasis upon specific goals without a corresponding emphasis on the acceptable procedures for achieving those goals. In such a society, the most effective means, whether culturally legitimate or not, become preferable to alternative forms of conduct. As the institutional norms lose their effectiveness in assuring success for members of a specific group, the society becomes unstable, and an environment of normlessness, or *anomie,* develops within the group.[13]

Merton believed that American culture places great emphasis upon certain goals without providing an equivalent emphasis upon the acceptable means for achieving those goals.[14] For example, retaining the goal of monetary success in the face of repeated frustration is entrenched in American culture. A normative system that emphasizes the accumulation of wealth will create ever-increasing disparities between the goals and the means for achieving them among its less privileged members. Regardless of whether wealth is acquired illegally or legitimately, the money can be used to purchase the same goods and services. Therefore, the universally desired goals have been achieved and reinforced, but the norms controlling the methods of achievement have been undermined by the same process.

Merton's anomie approach, also known as *means-end theory,* includes a typology of adaptations to the strain imposed on their group by the social structure.[15] The classification of behavior within these **modes of adaptation** is based on individuals' acceptance or rejection of the goals and the means that society provides for them when they are confronted with anomie. Because people often shift from one adaptation to another as they engage in different kinds of social activities at various points in their lives, Merton confines the adaptations to economic activity (the production, exchange, distribution, and consumption of goods and services). However, to the degree that social statuses and emotional needs are related to an individual's economic position in the social hierarchy, Merton's strain approach is also capable of dealing with the crimes that result from status-seeking and related *expressive* needs. This is done by treating the status or need as a commodity or goal, regardless of how it is perceived by the individual. Merton identified five ways people choose to adapt to strain (see Exhibit 11.3).[16]

First are those individuals who accept both the goals and means of society—the **conformists.** When conformity to both cultural goals and institutionalized means is the most common and widely available adaptation, the society is stable, and crime occurs mainly as a result of culture conflicts such as those discussed in Chapter 10. Because Merton's interest centered on the causes of significant and lasting differences in group rates of deviant behavior, he concluded that little more needed to be said regarding this type of adaptation.[17] Slum dwellers who become police officers or clergymen are exemplary of this mode of adaptation.

Those who reject the socially approved goals but not the means of achieving them are **ritualists.** Ritualism involves the abandoning or scaling down of lofty cultural goals such as financial success and upward social mobility to the point where the individual's aspirations are fully satisfied in the present. Having reduced the scope of their horizon, ritualists will continue to abide by institutional norms. They are merely "going through the motions" of conforming so as to avoid potential threats to their welfare. This adaptation to strain is permitted, but not culturally preferred, in American society. Although it may or may not be described as deviant, it is a departure from the cultural model in which individuals are obliged to constantly strive for upward mobility in the socioeconomic hierarchy.

Merton observes that this type of adaptation should be common in a society (such as that of western capitalism) where an individual's social status is dependent upon her or his personal achievements. The acute status-anxiety that this produces in many people can be reduced by lowering their aspirations.

Merton's approach predicts that ritualism will be heavily represented among the lower middle class, where parents typically exert a great deal of pressure upon children to succeed according to the accepted norms of society, even though such success is likely to be difficult to attain.[18]

Those who accept the goals but reject or significantly alter the means of achieving them are **innovators.** Most crimes, as well as technological and organizational inventions, result from this mode of adaptation to strain. Society encourages innovation by allowing the emphasis on attaining cultural goals to become more important than the socially approved means by which they are to be attained. It is expected that many lower-class individuals will exhibit

Exhibit 11.3

Modes of adaptation to strain

Mode	Means	Goal
Conformity	Accept	Accept
Ritualism	Accept	Reject
Innovation	Reject	Accept
Retreatist	Reject	Reject
Rebellion	Replace	Replace

Source: Robert K. Merton, "Social Structure and Anomie," *American Sociological Review* vol. 3 (1938): pp. 672–682.

innovative behavior in response to the emphasis on goal attainment and the lack of legitimate opportunities for achieving the goals.

The distinction between business-like striving within the boundaries of institutionalized norms and the "sharp" practices that are beyond institutionalized norms is frequently erased by the pressure toward innovation as a means to an end. This emphasis on goal achievement at the expense of attention to the propriety of the methods used tends to blur the distinction between criminality and creativity in many cases. The history of many great American fortunes is threaded with the use of ethically, if not legally, questionable innovations. Drug dealers, white-collar criminals, and organized-crime figures are also excellent examples of innovative adaptations to strain.

Merton points out that whatever the rates of deviant behavior in the various levels of the social hierarchy may be, the greatest pressure is almost always exerted upon the lower levels. Deviant behavior, he argues, is thus a "normal" response to a situation where the cultural emphasis upon wealth has been absorbed but where there is little access to conventional and legitimate means for becoming wealthy.[19]

Those who abandon both the goals and the means of the dominant society are termed **retreatists** in Merton's scheme. This mode of adaptation is most likely to occur when the institutionally approved practices are perceived as unlikely to produce success and conventional goals are rejected as unobtainable. Retreatism becomes an escape vehicle for those who are unable or unwilling to go through the motions of conforming to the approved methods. Strain is reduced by abandoning both the cultural goals and the accepted means

Those who reject the goals of mainstream society and culture often see the institutional system as corrupt, and rebellion as the only acceptable response.

of achieving them. In contrast to the conformist, who keeps the wheels of society turning, the retreatist sees no value in the success-goals so highly prized by the culture. In contrast to the ritualist, who at least conforms to the institutional norms, the retreatist is an asocial individual.[20] This mode of adaptation is commonly associated with substance abusers and certain subgroups of the mentally ill.

Those who reject both the goals and means and replace them with new goals and means are **rebels.**[21] In American society, organized rebellion movements usually aim to introduce a form of social organization in which the cultural standards of success would be sharply modified and provision would be made for a closer correspondence between reward and merit, effort, or need. When the institutional system is regarded as the main barrier to the satisfaction of legitimized goals, rebellion becomes an adaptive response to strain. Merton defined rebellion in terms of organized political action, but it can also take the form of highly antisocial gang activity.[22] Rebellious groups that lack a unifying ideology are likely to drift rapidly into innovation, however (see J. Milton Yinger's discussion of the transition from "countercultural" rebellion to "subcultural" innovation in *Countercultures*).[23] The history of street and motorcycle gangs illustrates how inverted mainstream norms (e.g., drug use) can lead to profitable innovation (drug sales). In the absence of a deeply held ideology, the group will likely adopt at least some conventional goals.[24]

Merton's anomie approach is best equipped to explain *instrumental* crimes such as murder for remuneration (contract murder), kidnapping for ransom, insurance fraud, robbery, burglary, theft, fraud, bribery, prostitution, gambling, organized crime, and the manufacture or sale of drugs. However, innovative methods for obtaining status or physical gratification can be dealt with to a limited degree by this approach also. To apply Merton's anomie approach at the micro level, rather than merely explaining rates of behavior, one must take some liberty in how goals are interpreted. In particular, the goal of the crime must be very specific. For example, Sutherland proposes that if the goal is simply wealth, then the goal is no different for the person who steals or works for it, and Merton's strain approach should not be used as the sole explanation of the crime. However, one can easily recognize the difference between a person who steals for "generalized goals" (e.g., the professional criminal for whom crime is a livelihood) or "random goals" (e.g., the youth who steals a car for a joyride) and those who steal for a "specific goal" (e.g., cash for a date). Typical street crimes and juvenile offenses are better explained by theories other than those that are critically dependent on general goal orientations such as Merton's approach. His approach provides a better explanation for crimes of emotion in the lower class, and instrumental crimes committed by members of the middle and upper classes, than it does for instrumental crimes committed by members of the lower class.

Compared with the number of instrumental crimes committed by "occasional property offenders" of the lower class, offenders from the middle or upper classes usually commit relatively few crimes. Those from the lower classes are under greater pressures than are those from the middle and upper classes. These pressures are both instrumental (e.g., lack of money) and expressive (e.g., low self-esteem). For the lower classes, general goals like autonomy are closely related to more specific ones like money. Simultaneously, the concern with trouble and fate may make law-abiding behavior less attractive to some lower-class persons (see Chapter 10's discussion of lower-class focal conerns).

······· **APPLICATION** ···· # The Case of Muneer Deeb

Carlton Stowers, in his book *Careless Whispers: The Lake Waco Murders,* provides an account of a "murder-for-hire" that occurred in Waco, Texas, in 1982. Muneer "Lucky" Deeb, David "Chili" Spence, Gilbert Melendez, and Tony Melendez were all convicted for the murders of Jill Montgomery, Raylene Rice, and Kenneth Franks. Deeb, a Jordanian national, came to the United States in 1979 on an education visa. He became co-owner of a small convenience store named "The Rainbow," located across the street from the Methodist Home (a residential treatment facility for troubled youth with family problems) in Waco, Texas.[26]

The *predisposing factors* in Deeb's life that can be gleaned from the information provided by Stower's account of the case were that (1) he lacked the capability to successfully operate a business, (2) he was financially dependent on his family to maintain his business, (3) he was impotent but allowed young adolescent females to take financial advantage of him (i.e., they played him for a "sucker").[27]

The primary *precipitating factor* for Muneer Deeb to become what Merton describes as an innovator was that his family eventually refused to continue providing the financial assistance required to sustain his business. A tertiary *attracting factor* was that Deeb's numerous attempts to marry adolescent American females for the purpose of becoming a United States citizen failed: all the women refused him.[28]

In 1982 Deeb was in a near-destitute financial state. He had purchased a $20,000 accident insurance policy on Gayle Kelley, a young girl living at the Methodist Home, when she was employed in his store. He named Kelley as his common-law wife on the policy and himself as the beneficiary.[29] Under the particular accident insurance policy that Deeb purchased, murder was considered a form of accidental death. The existence of this policy predated Deeb's idea of hiring Spence to kill Gayle Kelley and thus constitutes a *attracting factor* in this crime. Rather than choosing to be a ritualist (noncriminal) when confronted with the structural discrepancy between retaining his goal of being co-owner of a convenience store and the legitimate means available to him to do so, Deeb choose to become an innovator by retaining his goals but seeking illegal means to attain them.

Deeb told David Spence he would give him $5,000 of the insurance money he would collect from the policy on Kelley if Spence would kill Kelley for him. This was not the first time Deeb had attempted insurance fraud. On a previous occasion, he had asked Spence to wreck his (Deeb's) car so he (Deeb) could collect the insurance on it. Spence wrecked Deeb's car for him, but Deeb did not know that when a car is financed, the insurance claim paid for damage repair goes to the finance company and not the owner of the car.[30]

Gayle Kelley, the intended victim, and Jill Montgomery, one of the actual victims, looked strikingly similar. Even their close friends had trouble telling them apart. Montgomery was also a former resident of the Methodist Home.

She had returned to Waco with a friend, Raylene Rice, to get a paycheck owed her from a part-time job she had held while living at the Methodist Home. Montgomery had been close friends with Kenneth Franks, also a former resident of the home who still resided in Waco with his father. Montgomery and Rice picked up Franks at his home, and the three of them went to Koehne Park. David Spence, Gilbert Melendez, and Tony Melendez also went to Koehne Park on Lake Waco that night. While at the park, Spence saw Jill Montgomery and mistook her for Gayle Kelley.

An autopsy indicated that Montgomery's throat had been cut and that she had been stabbed nine times in the chest, as well as having been sexually assaulted. Raylene Rice's autopsy indicated that her throat had also been cut and that she had been stabbed numerous times in the chest. She also had suffered genital injuries. Kenneth Frank's autopsy indicated that he had been stabbed ten times in the heart, six times in the chest, and twice in the liver.[31] Exhibit 11.4 summarizes the facts of this case.

In January of 1985 a jury found Deeb guilty of the first-degree murder of Montgomery in less than two hours and subsequently sentenced him to death by lethal injection. Spence was also found guilty in the death of Montgomery and given the death penalty. The Melendez brothers struck a plea bargain in exchange for their testimony against Deeb, and each received consecutive life sentences for two murder convictions for their roles in the crime.[32] It is unlikely that Deeb could have been convicted without their testimony, because successful prosection of a murder for remuneration (murder-for-hire) case is extremely difficult to prove without the cooperation of a co-conspirator.

Merton's anomie approach can usually be applied as an explanation for crimes of an instrumental nature. That is, criminals motivated by instrumental concerns (they commit a crime in order to obtain a socially approved goal) can almost automatically be classified as innovators. If they abandon their goal, they become ritualists instead. Noncriminals, who use legitimate means to secure their goals, are conformists. Of course, in crimes involving multiple offenders, the application of a theoretical explanation for one of the offenders involved may not be equally appropriate in explaining the involvement of the other offenders. This we believe to be the case in the Lake Waco murders.

David Spence, Gilbert Melendez, and Tony Melendez were all innovators under a strict interpretation of Merton's anomie approach. They were attempting to secure a socially legitimate goal (money) by the use of socially disapproved means (murder). However, other criminological theories are nec-

Level of Importance	Fact	Type of Fact
Primary	Family's refusal to continue financial assistance	Precipitating
Primary	Insurance policy on Gayle Kelley	Attracting
Secondary	Inability to run a profitable business	Predisposing
Tertiary	History of unsuccessful relationships with girls from Methodist Home	Attracting

Exhibit 11.4

. . . .

Summary of facts and their role in the explanation of Muneer Deeb's role in the Lake Waco murders case

essary to fully explain their involvement in this crime. Lower-class deprivations and frustrations seem at least as much to blame as an innovative adaptation to strain. This is in contrast to Muneer Deeb, who was simply attempting to obtain a middle-class goal through illegal means. We will extend our analysis to the Melendez brothers, two of Deeb's co-conspirators, after introducing Cohen's delinquency and frustration theory.

Delinquency and Frustration Theory

Cohen's delinquency and frustration theory (see Exhibit 11.5) is a direct extension of Merton's work, and therefore is contained within Merton's anomie approach. Unlike Merton, however, Cohen emphasizes the effects of the dysfunctional relationship between the socioeconomic classes on the thoughts, perceptions, and behavior of individuals.[33] In this way, his theory links Merton's meso-level presumptions and concepts to social-psychological variables at the micro level.

Cohen's theory assumes that delinquency usually occurs in groups and is primarily a lower-class male phenomenon. He associates middle-class values with approval for such qualities as punctuality, neatness, cleanliness, nonviolent behavior, etc.,[34] which are often in opposition to the behavior rooted in lower-class focal concerns (see Chapter 10). For this reason, his thesis is often referred to as the *middle-class measuring-rod* theory.

Crucial to this theory are the concepts of status frustration, reaction formation, and middle-class values. According to Cohen, the American education system has a middle-class bias, and lower-class youths feel that they are inferior when they are unable to "measure up" to the middle-class standards.[35] Because all humans have the need to attain status, Cohen refers to this dynamic as **status frustration**.[36] As individuals (i.e., lower-class youths) attempt to meet their needs, they find that they are categorically denied their status goal (success

Exhibit 11.5

Delinquency and frustration theory

Specific Assumptions

1. School officials generally use middle-class norms to evaluate students.

2. Lower-class males tend to perform poorly in school.

3. Poor school grades predict delinquency.

4. Poor school grades are mainly the result of the conflict that exists between the norms of lower-class students and the middle-class values of the school.

5. Lower-class expressive crime is primarily committed in a group, or gang, context.

6. Lower-class expressive crimes are often a means of nurturing positive self-concepts through the use of antisocial values.

Source: Albert Cohen, *Delinquent Boys* (New York: Free Press, 1955); Donald J. Shoemaker, *Theories of Delinquency* (Oxford University Press, 1984).

and/or approval) because of their ascribed position in the social structure. This frustration occurs as a result of the unique relationship between the individual, the group, and the dominant society.

Reaction formation, a sort of "sour grapes" reaction, is the internal mechanism by which status frustration is often resolved. Thus, lower-class youths who are judged lacking by middle-class standards tend to reject the means and goals of the dominant (i.e., middle class) society. New means and goals which seem more attainable are substituted. Freud used the term *reaction formation* to describe the phenomenon of wanting something but rejecting it because you cannot obtain it. An example of this would be a young man who would have liked to have gone to college and become an attorney, but since he could not afford to go to college, he now voices the attitude that being part of a street gang is preferable to attending school.

Cohen hypothesized that many lower-class youths are placed in this sort of situation — where they experience status frustration and attempt to resolve it by reaction formation — by the structure of our society (i.e., the interaction of the economic stratification system and the education system). He maintains that this problem is the basis for the formation of lower-class subcultures and gangs.[37] Indeed, his original intention was to explain the process of gang formation in the urban lower class (See chapter 10 for a discussion of gang-formation theories). Cohen proposed that the delinquent subculture was **nonutilitarian, malicious,** and **negativistic.** By **nonutilitarian** he meant that most youth gang and criminal behavior had no rational purpose. That is, he proposed that gang youths steal mostly for the fun of it or for status within the gang, not for the purpose of keeping or selling what they steal. By **malicious,** he meant that youth gangs gain enjoyment and pleasure by creating discomfort for others. They gain satisfaction from frightening youths who are "good kids" and nongang members. They enjoy ridiculing, challenging, and defying others. Cohen termed the norms developed by delinquent gangs **negativistic,** meaning they are in direct opposition to those of the larger adult culture.[38]

Gangs and similar groups help to relieve status frustration by providing a social setting in which the disenfranchised youths can "write their own rules" and thereby assure themselves of "success" under an alternative, often criminal value system. Whenever large numbers of disadvantaged people live in close physical proximity to one another, they are likely to be affected by this social-psychological dynamic. The substitution of alternative goals and means of achievement suggested by Cohen would be considered a form of **rebellion** in Merton's scheme.

The Case of Gilbert and Tony Melendez · · · · · · · | APPLICATION | · · · · · · · ·

Along with Muneer Deeb and David Spence, the Melendez brothers were convicted of committing the "Lake Waco Murders".[39] The crime itself has already been discussed in a preceding section of this chapter. Unlike Muneer Deeb, Gilbert and Tony Melendez were from the lower class, and their participation in the Lake Waco murders seems best explained by Cohen's theory. This explanation could be expanded by referring to the lower-class focal concerns discussed in Chapter 10 and the social-learning theories covered in Chapter 7.

Exemplary of the secondary *predisposing factors* for Gilbert Melendez, the older of the two brothers, was that he ran away from home when he was sixteen years old. This suggests that his early home life was unhappy and that he perceived violation of the expectations of the dominant society as an appropriate method for resolving problems. Another factor was that the Melendez brothers were Hispanic in ancestry and appearance, but they both spoke like Anglos. In essence, they did not fit in with the Hispanic youth of Waco because they spoke like Anglos, and they did not fit in with the Anglo youth because they were obviously Hispanic in name and appearance. This left them without a social group to satisfy their need for belongingness. Gilbert Melendez also had a serious alcohol-abuse problem. Around the age of twenty-four, he was very attracted to a young woman and they began living together. However, she soon left him because she could not tolerate his drinking problem.[40]

The *attracting factors* for Gilbert Melendez began in April of 1974, when, at the age of eighteen, he shot and wounded a man in a Waco parking lot during an argument. He was sentenced to the Texas Department of Corrections for four years for assault with intent to murder but was paroled after serving sixteen months. This conviction further limited his range of opportunities for achieving success and also introduced him to the norms of the prison subculture.

It should also be noted that, shortly before the Lake Waco murders, Gilbert Melendez and David Spence sexually assaulted an eighteen-year-old male. This indicates their acceptance of prison norms. This sort of behavior further linked violent action to the attainment of physical gratification for both men. By 1982, the year in which the Lake Waco murders were committed, Gilbert Melendez was, essentially, a twenty-eight-year-old man going nowhere. The *precipitating factor* occurred in the first week of July 1982, when David Spence asked Gilbert Melendez if he wanted to become involved in Muneer Deeb's murder-for-hire offer.[41]

Gilbert Melendez made a plea bargain arrangement in exchange for testifying against Deeb, in which he pled guilty to two counts of murder and was given two life sentences. He would have to serve a minimum of forty years for these life sentences. He also pled guilty to the aggravated sexual-abuse charge in the sexual assault of the teenage male and was given a seven-year sentence for this crime.[42]

Much the same *predisposing factors* that existed for Gilbert Melendez also existed for his brother, Tony Melendez. The *attracting factors* for Tony Melendez lay in the fact that he was wanted by the Corpus Christi, Texas, police on a three-year-old warrant for robbery and rape at the time of the Lake Waco murders. Like his older brother, Tony Melendez was a young man "going nowhere" at the time of the Lake Waco murders. The *precipitating factor* in his case, as in his brother's, was Muneer Deeb's murder-for-hire offer to David Spence.[43]

In June 1983 Tony Melendez was allowed to plea bargain in exchange for his testimony against Deeb and Spence. In exchange for two concurrent life sentences, he admitted that he had participated in the murders and pled guilty to the murders of Jill Montgomery and Kenneth Franks. According to his testimony, he raped Montgomery and stabbed her twice. He also testified that he and his brother Gilbert used the latter's pickup truck to transport the victims' bodies from Koehne Park to Speegleville Park, where they were dis-

Exhibit 11.6

- - - - - - - - - - - -

Summary of facts and their role in the explanation of the Melendez Brothers' role in the Lake Waco murders case

Level of Importance	Fact	Type of Fact
Primary	Deeb's "murder for-hire" offer	Precipitating
Primary	Experience in prison (Gilbert)	Attracting
Primary	Failure to fit in either anglo or Hispanic subgroup	Predisposing
Secondary	Past history of violence	Attracting
Secondary	Unhappy home life as child/teen	Predisposing
Tertiary	Fugitive status (Tony)	Attracting
Tertiary	Alcoholism (Gilbert)	Predisposing

covered. All of Tony Melendez's statements about the Lake Waco murders were confirmed by the pathologist's report.[44] Exhibit 11.6 summarizes the facts of the Melendez brothers' case.

It should be noted that the excessive viciousness with which these murders were performed would have been predicted by Cohen's theory. Cohen maintains that lower-class youths often feel that they cannot achieve "success" according to the "middle-class measuring rod" by which school officials and society judge them. Consequently, they often adopt an inverted version of middle-class norms resulting in negativistic and malicious illegal expressive behavior.[45] The Melendez brothers and David Spence could have fulfilled their murderous contract with Muneer Deeb with far less violence to the victims' bodies. However, Cohen's theory would suggest that this "overkill" aspect of the murders was a trait of the lower class offender's reaction formation against basic middle-class norms of decency and nonviolence. The homosexual rape of the Anglo teenager was "appropriate" behavior only by the standards of the prison subculture. Such an act is appalling to most middle-class Americans, as well as to most lower-class males, who are almost homophobic in their sexual attitudes.[46]

Theory of Differential Opportunity Structures
- -

Opportunity structure, the central concept in Cloward and Ohlin's theory, is best defined as the set of methods perceived by the individual to be available and useful in obtaining desired goals. This theory of differential opportunity structures (see Exhibit 11.7) extends Merton's approach with the additional assumption that members of each social class and type of neighborhood are aware of a limited set of opportunities for goal attainment. It is postulated that various types of both legal and illegal opportunities (i.e., means) for gaining economic success are unevenly distributed across each of the social classes as well as across different types of neighborhoods. This means, as mentioned in Chapter 10, that access to criminal as well as noncriminal role models is limited by both social and psychological factors.[47]

Specific Assumptions

1. When individuals perceive that their economic aspirations cannot be attained, the result is often frustration and a loss of self-esteem.

2. Frustrations resulting from blocked economic aspirations often lead to participation in criminal subcultures.

3. Discontent with lower-class status is not a result of frustration among the lower class in obtaining middle-class goals, but rather the frustration of not obtaining lower-class goals.

4. The type of criminal subculture people join is dependent on the opportunities they perceive as available to them through their observations of "successes" with whom they can identify.

Source: Richard A. Cloward and Lloyd E. Ohlin, *Delinquency and Opportunity* (New York: Free Press, 1960); Donald J. Shoemaker, *Theories of Delinquency* (New York: Oxford University Press, 1990), p. 109; J.H. Vetter and T.J. Silverman, *Criminology and Crime: An Introduction* (New York: Harper & Row, 1986), pp. 322–323.

This theory presumes that the more "successful" residents of communities provide role models for youths seeking the most efficient means of achieving success. As the number and type of role models vary, so also do the opportunity structures of those around them.[48] While personal characteristics (e.g., intelligence) and decisions (e.g., dropping out of school) undeniably affect one's opportunity structure, this theory emphasizes the influence of available role models and the groups in which the person participates. In essence, it proposes that lower-class youth are integrated into criminal activity through their interactions with or observations of adult criminals in their neighborhoods.[49] Thus, the theory bridges the gap between the micro and meso levels of analysis but does not explicitly deal with the micro level.

The frustrations and deprivations experienced by members of the lower classes are believed to result in the development of three different ideal types of deviant subcultures within various types of (urban) neighborhoods: **Criminal subcultures** are primarily involved in instrumental crimes such as theft and gambling and are associated with working-class areas. This type of gang is heavily influenced by the presence of organized-crime figures like drug dealers and bookmakers. These criminals are of the type Merton described as innovators. **Conflict subcultures** are primarily involved in expressive crimes of violence, usually over gang "territories." They are usually found in the most deteriorated of the lower-class neighborhoods, where there is a complete lack of "successful" residents. Their mode of adaptation to strain is best described as rebellious. **Retreatist subcultures** are primarily involved in expressive crimes involving drug and alcohol use. Their members are thought to be "dropouts," or failures from criminal and conflict gangs. Cohen's view of these substance-abusers therefore labels them as a *double failures* because they have failed to attain success in both the legitimate (i.e., middle-class) world and the world of the lower-class gang.[50]

In short, Cloward and Ohlin propose that youth gangs model their behavior and attitudes after the "successful" adults in their neighborhoods.

Therefore, they are integrated into various types of criminal activity depending on the type of successful adults to which their neighborhood and/or group memberships expose them.

The Case of David Spence · · · · · · · · · · · · · · · · [APPLICATION] · · · · · · · ·

David "Chili" Wayne Spence, along with the Melendez brothers and Muneer Deeb, was convicted for his involvement in the Lake Waco murders.[51] Spence was twenty-five years old at the time he helped commit the murders. *Predisposing factors* for Spence included the facts that (1) he was a junior high school dropout, having quit school in the ninth grade, thus greatly limiting his opportunity structure; (2) his father drank heavily, was rarely at home, and, when he was at home, often beat David for no reason; and (3) early in his childhood he regularly watched his father beat his mother.[52]

At age sixteen, Spence married a fifteen-year-old girl who was living at the Methodist Home in Waco, Texas. They had two sons before she left him because of his excessive drinking and constant abuse. In 1978 he checked into an Austin, Texas, drug treatment center for two months. He had also joined the Army, but was given a medical discharge after only four months.[53]

Spence was diagnosed as an antisocial personality. Like other sociopaths, he expected and sought out immediate gratification in all his endeavors, was extremely self-centered and irresponsible, was incapable of loyalty or other deep and abiding emotions, was unable to empathize with others, and felt justified in lying or distorting the truth whenever it was convenient and served his purposes (see Chapters 5 and 6 for more details on sociopathy). He was also a full-fledged alcoholic and drug abuser.[59]

In 1982 Spence was regularly beating his live-in girlfriend, who finally realized he could reach a sexual climax only after physically abusing her. During sex he would bite her savagely, drawing blood from her neck, shoulders, and breasts. Sometimes he would even force her to spend the night naked in the front yard tied to a tree with a dog collar around her neck.[55] Such an aberrant view of sexual gratification (i.e., sadism) cannot be dealt with by Merton's approach. However, the linkage of violence to sex by an uneducated and abused youth from the lower-class "street" culture is quite comprehensible under Cloward and Ohlin's theory if we presume that the processes defined in the social-learning perspective were operating as well. That is, the media's linkage of violence with sexual success was reinforced by the lower-class focal concern with "toughness" which Spence came to comprehend first through observing his father and later through his prison experiences.

The *attracting factors* for David Spence in the Lake Waco murders began with his prison experience. Having served fifteen months (April 1980 to July 1981) of a four-year sentence in the Texas Department of Corrections for the aggravated robbery of a convenience store in Fort Worth, Texas, he was released from prison with no support from family or friends. Those who knew Spence before his incarceration noticed a significant change in his demeanor after his release. He now dressed like a biker, drank more, and displayed tattoos. He talked almost nostalgically about penitentiary life. He told everyone that he had been a respected leader among the prison inmates, when in reality he had been treated as an outcast by the other prison immates and

Exhibit 11.8
. . . .

Summary of facts and their role in the explanation of David Spence's role in the Lake Waco murders case

Level of Importance	Fact	Type of Fact
Primary	Early life in pathological lower-class home	Predisposing
Primary	Deeb's "murder for-hire" offer	Precipitating
Primary	Experience in prison	Attracting
Secondary	Sexual sadism	Attracting
Secondary	Antisocial personality	Predisposing
Tertiary	Broken marriage/wife beating	Attracting
Tertiary	School dropout	Predisposing

served his time quietly.[56] He had fit in no better in prison than he had in free society—even the role of the "good convict" or "right guy" had eluded Spence.[57] This constituted a major failure to achieve the kind of lower-class status that he so urgently desired.

In September 1982, after the Lake Waco murders, Spence was arrested for the aggravated sexual abuse of an eighteen-year-old Anglo male. Gilbert Melendez was a co-perpetrator in this crime. During the assault, Spence stabbed the victim in the leg, leaving the teenager with a four-inch gash. In addition to this crime, and prior to the Lake Waco murders, David Spence had also raped two teenage girls in Waco, Texas.[58]

The *precipitating factor* for Spence was Muneer Deeb's $5,000 murder-for-hire offer. On March 23, 1983, Spence was convicted of aggravated sexual abuse for his attack on the male teenager and was given a ninety-year sentence. In June 1984 he was found guilty of raping Jill Montgomery and stabbing her to death. In October 1985 he was found guilty of murdering Kenneth Franks and was sentenced to death by lethal injection by the state of Texas.[59] Exhibit 11.8 summarizes the facts of the David Spence case.

Conclusion
. . . .

Each of the components of the strain perspective has unique strengths and weaknesses. The areas of greatest strength for these three conceptualizations of criminality are summarized in Exhibit 11.9. Like many forms of social theory, they tend to address the gaps between levels, rather than being isolated at one level of analysis. In most cases, the strengths and weaknesses of a theory are a direct result of the use for which the theory was originally designed. However, the intent of the original theorist and the ultimate use of the theory are independent of one another in the final analysis.

Several limitations of the strain perspective have been addressed by Merton himself. He noted that this approach tends to neglect the influence of social-psychological processes in the choice of specific modes of adaptation. Cohen and Cloward and Ohlin only partially address this shortcoming. The need to limit the scope of Merton's anomie approach to certain types of crime has

Exhibit 11.9
. . . .
Relative strengths of theories
within the strain perspective

Theory/Approach	Level of Analysis	Type of Factor Addressed
Mertonian anomie	Meso	Precipitating
Delinquency and frustration	Meso-micro	Predisposing and attracting
Differential opportunity structures	Meso-micro	Predisposing, attracting and precipitating

already been mentioned in this chapter, but it bears repeating.[60] The approach was developed to explain why rates of crime in the lower class are disproportionately high. Some writers question the perspective's assumption that a set of generally accepted cultural goals exists in the lower class.[61]

When anomie theory is limited in its application to a case like Muneer Deeb's, its major explanatory strength is at the precipitating-factor level. That is, when anomie theory is applied to crimes specifically motivated by monetary goals and viewed as a "money-is-the-root-of-all-evil" explanation of the crime, the precipitating factor (the need for money) becomes self-explanatory.[62] This factor is classified as being at the meso level of analysis because it is so closely tied to the offender's group memberships and relationships with social institutions.

It may be tempting to use the strain perspective as an explanation of predisposing influences, because the perspective is oriented to instrumental crimes of the lower class. However, to use the perspective in this way has little explanatory value since such a use inevitably leads to the question of why many lower-class persons resist the temptation to innovate, or otherwise violate social rules, in their pursuit of success. Thus, the perspective can be said to have arisen *ex post facto*, or on the basis of prior empirical observations, but has little predictive power at the micro level.

Regardless of how it is used, the strain perspective and its theories are weakest at the attracting-factor level of analysis. In the case of Muneer Deeb, it is extremely difficult, if not impossible, to determine why he was attracted to an innovator mode of adaptation versus one of the other modes of adaptation available. Similarly, the perspective is unable to explain why a criminal form of innovation, as opposed to an acceptable one, was chosen. Clinard suggests that it is not the pressure arising from failure to achieve goals, as the strain perspective suggests, but rather the interaction with other criminals that results in the commission of criminal acts. Even with the assistance of Clinard's suggestion, it remains difficult to determine why Deeb was attracted to such a highly criminal solution to his problems. In Stower's account of Deeb's life, there is no indication that his family would have condoned his committing any criminal act. More importantly, there is no explanation for why he was not attracted to one of the other modes of adaptation based on his association with his noncriminal business partner (the co-owner of the convenience store), rather than his association with David Spence. We can, however, speculate that his history of unsuccessful relationships with girls from the Methodist Home may have attracted him to such a violent form of retribution. Conflicts between cultural definitons of masculinity may also have played a tertiary role.

The *diasthenia-stress model* could be invoked to deal with this issue. Inadequate opportunities to achieve one's goals create strain for groups and stress for individuals. This stress may then act as a trigger mechanism to unleash dormant pathologies within the individual. It may also be that living with chronic stress retards the development and use of appropriate problem-solving skills that are required to help individuals avoid crime.

The perspective is also weak in addressing predisposing factors. That is, using the mode of adaptation chosen as an explanation for being predisposed to that mode of adaptation is a circular and repetitious argument. For example, to suggest that a person is predisposed to criminality or alcoholism after a person is a criminal or alcoholic is not a convincing argument for the existence of a predisposition towards criminal or alcoholic behavior. The predisposition that dictates the choice made between these types of behavior needs to be identified before the behavior occurs if the perspective is to have any explanatory value.

Although Cohen's delinquency and frustration theory is derived from Merton's anomie approach, the reverse seems to hold true in terms of its strengths at various levels of analysis. This is due, in part, to the fact that Cohen was more explicitly concerned with the micro level of analysis than was Merton. Environmental conditions and conditioning processes can be used to explain how the predisposing and attracting factors contribute to the decision to commit criminal acts. However, this theory addresses precipitating factors in a way that is so ad-hoc, or random, that it would appear to be completely unpredictable. This is true in the Lake Waco murder case where the analogy of the Melendez brothers being like bombs just waiting to explode seems appropriate at first glance; but what, when, and who lit the fuse remains unexplained.

Cloward and Ohlin's theory of differential opportunity structures appears to be relatively strong at all three levels of analysis when applied to cases such as that of David Spence. That is, the predisposing factors are consistent with the attracting factors, and the attracting factors are consistent with the precipitating factors in the case of Spence. Spence's life history, in short, can easily be seen as the predisposing factor that was pivotal in creating his opportunity structure. This set of perceived opportunities for "success," in turn, led him ever further into crime.

Glossary

Anomie   A condition affecting a society or group in which a high degree of confusion and/or contradiction between norms exists due to inadequate regulation and integration.

Boundary Setting   The erection and maintenance of rules, in terms of their priority in the society, that allows citizens to be constantly aware of the limits society has placed on their behavior.

Conflict Subcultures   Primarily involved in expressive crimes of violence. They occur most often in the most deteriorated neighborhoods, which lack residents who could be considered "successful" role models.

Conformists   Those individuals who accept both the goals and means of society.

Criminal Subcultures   Primarily involved in instrumental crimes. They are associated with communities in which the "successful" residents are involved in (organized) criminal activities.

Innovators   Those individuals who accept the goals of society, but reject or significantly alter the acceptable means of achieving these goals.

Latent Functions   The unintended and often unrecognized results of a pattern of social activity.

Malicious   Describes delinquent or criminal behavior that is committed for enjoyment or pleasure gained by discomforting others.

Modes of Adaptation   Five methods that Merton predicts individuals will use to deal with strain: conformity, ritualism, innovation, retreatism, and rebellion. Each is defined by the manner in which the individual reacts to culturally prescribed goals and the means of achieving them.

Negativistic   Describes delinquent or criminal behavior that is directed against the norms that exist in the larger culture.

Nonutilitarian   Describes delinquent or criminal behavior that is committed for no rational purpose; e.g., stealing for the fun of it or for status.

Opportunity Structure   Set of methods perceived by an individual to be both available and useful in obtaining desired goals. It is heavily influenced by role models upon which individuals pattern their behavior.

Rebels   Those individuals who not only reject the goals and means of society, but also replace them with new goals and means with which they feel assured of success.

Reaction Formation   Phenomenon of wanting something but rejecting it because you cannot obtain it.

Retreatists   Those individuals who reject both the goals and the means of the dominant society.

Retreatist Subcultures   Primarily involved in expressive crimes involving drug and alcohol use.

Ritualists   Those individuals who reject the socially approved goals of society but retain the means of achieving them.

Status Frustration   A condition in which an individual is unable to achieve a desired social status or other reward because of the society's normative structure.

Strain   The tension produced by the discrepancy between universally desired goals and differentially distributed means of attaining them in a society. It is a specific form, or subtype, of anomie.

■ NOTES

1. Albert Bandura, *Social Learning Theory* (Englewood Cliffs, NJ: Prentice-Hall, 1977).
2. Durkheim, *Suicide: A Study in Sociology.*
3. Jack E. Bynum and William E. Thompson, *Juvenile Delinquency: A Sociological Approach* (Needham, MA: Allyn and Bacon, 1989).
4. Durkheim, *Suicide: A Study Sociology,* trans. J.A. Spaulding and G. Simpson (New York: Free Press, [1897] 1951).
5. Robert K. Merton, *Social Theory and Social Structure,* rev. ed. (London: The Free Press of Glencoe, 1957).
6. Ibid.
7. Merton, *Social Theory and Social Structure;* Durkheim, *Suicide: A Study in Sociology.*
8. Merton, "Social Structure and Anomie," pp. 672–682.
9. Abraham Maslow, *Toward a Psychology of Being,* 2 ed. (New York: Van Nostrand Reinhold, 1968).
10. Merton, "Social Structure and Anomie," pp. 672–682.
11. Ibid.
12. Ibid.
13. Ibid.
14. Ibid.
15. Merton, *Social Theory and Social Structure.*
16. Merton, "Social Structure and Anomie," pp. 672–682.
17. Merton, *Social Theory and Social Structure.*
18. Merton, "Social Structure and Anomie," pp. 672–682.
19. Ibid.
20. Ibid.
21. Ibid.
22. Ibid.
23. J. Milton Yinger, *Countercultures* (New York: Free Press, 1982).
24. James F. Quinn, "Sex Roles and Hedonism among Members of 'Outlaw' Motorcycle Clubs," *Deviant Behavior* 8 (1987): pp. 47–63.
25. *Texas Penal Code,* 8th ed. (St. Paul, MN: West Publishing, 1990), p. 27.
26. Carlton Stowers, *Careless Whispers: The Lake Waco Murders,* (Pocket Books: New York: 1987).
27. Ibid.
28. Ibid.
29. Ibid.
30. Ibid.
31. Ibid.
32. Ibid.
33. Albert Cohen, *Delinquent Boys* (New York: Free Press, 1955).
34. Ibid.
35. Ibid.
36. Ibid.
37. Ibid.
38. Ibid.
39. Stowers, *Careless Whispers: The Lake Waco Murders.*
40. Ibid.
41. Ibid.

42. Ibid.

43. Ibid.

44. Ibid.

45. Cohen, *Delinquent Boys.*

46. John H. Gagnon and William Simon, "The Social Meaning of Prison Homosexuality," *Federal Probation* 32 (1968): pp. 23–29.

47. Richard A. Cloward and Lloyd E. Ohlin, *Delinquency and Opportunity* (New York: Free Press, 1960).

48. Ibid.

49. Ibid.

50. Ibid.

51. Stowers, *Careless Whispers: The Lake Waco Murders.*

52. Ibid.

53. Ibid.

54. Ibid.

55. Ibid.

56. Ibid.

57. John Irwin, *Prisons in Turmoil* (Boston: Little, Brown and Co., 1977) pp. 31–33).

58. Stowers, *Careless Whispers: The Lake Waco Murders.*

59. Ibid.

60. Merton, *Social Theory and Social Structure.*

61. M. B. Clinard and R. F. Meier, *The Sociology of Deviant Behavior* (New York: Holt, Rinehart and Winston, 1985); Marshall B. Clinard, *Anomie and Deviant Behavior* (New York: Free Press, 1964), pp. 213–242; E. M. Lemert, *Human Deviance, Social Problems, and Social Control* (Englewood Cliffs, NJ: Prentice-Hall, 1967): A. Thio, *Deviant Behavior* (Boston: Houghton Mifflin, 1983).

62. E. Sagarin, *Deviants and Deviance: An Introduction to the Study of Disvalued People and Behavior* (New York: Praeger, 1975).

∎ Suggested Readings

Robert S. Agnew, "Social Class and Success Goals: An Examination of Relative and Absolute Aspirations," *The Sociological Quarterly* 24 (1983): pp. 435–452.

Daniel Bell, "Crime as an American Way of Life," *The Antioch Review,* 13 (1953): pp. 131–154.

Richard A. Cloward, "Illegitimate Means, Anomie, and Deviant Behavior," *American Sociological Review* 24 (1959): pp. 164–176.

Albert K. Cohen, "The Sociology of the Deviant Act: Anomie Theory and Beyond," *American Sociological Review* 30 (1965): pp. 5–14.

Albert K. Cohen, "Reference Group Identification and Deviant Behavior" in Robert K. Merton, Leonard Broom, Leonard S. Cottrell, Jr. (eds.), *Sociology Today* (New York: Basic Books, 1959).

Emile Durkheim, "The Normal and the Pathological" in Emile Durkheim, *The Rules of the Sociological Method,* trans. George E. G. Cathn, edited by Sarah A. Solovay and John H. Mueller (New York: The Free Press, 1965), pp. 65–73.

Robert A. Dentler and Kai T. Erickson, "The Functions of Deviance in Groups," *Social Problems* 7 no. 2 (1959): pp. 98–102.

Kai T. Erickson, *Wayward Puritans: A Study in the Sociology of Deviance* (New York: John Wiley and Sons, 1966).

James F. Short, Ramon Riviera, and Ray A. Tennyson, "Perceived Opportunities, Gang Membership, and Delinquency," *American Sociological Review* 30 (1965): pp. 56–67.

J. Milton Yinger, *Countercultures* (New York: Free Press, 1982).

▪ Suggested Books for Additional Application

Jonathan Coleman, *At Mother's Request* (New York: Simon & Schuster, 1985).

Richard Hammer, *The CBS Murders* (New York: New American Library, 1988).

Clifford Irving, *Daddy's Girl: The Campbell Murder Case* (New York: Kensington Publishing, 1988).

B. Taubman, *The Preppy Murder Trial* (New York: St. Martins Press, 1988).

CHAPTER **12**

Social-Control Perspective

Overview of Social-Control Perspective

Unlike most criminological perspectives, which try to explain why some people engage in criminal behavior, the social-control perspective tries to explain why all people do not engage in criminal behavior on a regular basis.[1] Exhibit 12.1 gives the common assumptions of this perspective. Like Freud, the social-control perspective assumes that humans are by nature "bad" or self-serving, rather than "good" or altruistic. Therefore, criminal behavior is to be expected of people, and conformity to noncriminal norms is the fact that must be explained.[2] This is a very different starting point than that of most theories, which propose that people are basically conforming and those who become criminals have been driven to commit crimes by physical and/or environmental forces.

The central idea in social-control theories is that society binds individuals to the moral order so as to control them. Society does this by both external controls (social institutions such as the family, church, schools, and community) and internal controls (individuals' learned inhibitions against committing criminal acts). Internally generated controls are preferred because they are less costly to society and provide greater assurance that people will follow the rules even when unsupervised. Such internal controls are established through the process of socialization in which the individual makes emotional, ethical, and practical investments in the moral order of society as a result of the influence of the various social institutions just mentioned. Criminal behavior is seen as the result of a weakening or breaking of these social ties.[3]

Consistent with this perspective's view of human behavior is the assumption that all societies have defined some forms of behavior as criminal.[4] And since according to this perspective, criminal behavior is to be expected unless social-control mechanisms are working properly, the subject of interest is not criminal motivation, but rather the methods by which society restrains people

Exhibit 12.1

Social-control perspective

Common Assumptions

1. Criminal behavior is natural and to be expected.

2. Human beings must be controlled if society is to be orderly and safe.

3. There is a consensus within society as to the most appropriate beliefs and norms.

4. Control mechanisms are required to force people to adhere to these norms and beliefs in their daily behavior.

5. There are two basic types of control mechanisms:
   a. personal or internal, and
   b. social or external.

6. Criminal behavior is a result of a deficiency or absence of such control mechanisms.

Source: Donald J. Shoemaker, *Theories of Delinquency* (New York: Oxford University Press, 1984), pp. 153-154.

from committing criminal acts.[5] The assumption that unites social-control theories is the idea that people commit criminal acts because some controlling factor in their life is ineffective or missing. These controls, then, are the logical focus of all these theories, which presume that all people must be controlled in order to prevent the criminal acts that they would otherwise be tempted to commit.[6]

Containment Approach

Reckless' idea of containment is defined as an approach in this text (see Exhibit 12.2) because several other theories have been developed on the basis of its assumptions. According to the containment approach, both internal forces and external forces operate on individuals as they make decisions to commit or avoid crime in diverse situations.[7] The approach proposes that both criminal and noncriminal behavior result from the interactions of these inner and outer forces.[8]

Reckless subdivides these motivating and restraining forces into four subtypes: (1) "inner pushes and pulls" toward committing criminal behavior; (2) "inner containments" (constraints), or the internal personal controls that inhibit criminal behavior; (3) "outer pressures and pulls" toward committing criminal behavior; and (4) "outer containments" (constraints), or the environmental controls beyond the individual that inhibit criminal behavior. In Reckless' view, "inner pushes and pulls" and "outer pressures and pulls" are those internal and external forces that influence the individual to make the decision to commit a criminal act. "Inner containments" and "outer containments" are those internal and external forces that would incline the individual to avoid the impulse to commit a criminal act.[9]

Outer pressures and pulls toward committing criminal behavior are environmental in nature and include such things as living conditions, (un)employment, and deviant (or nondeviant) associates. The pressures are seen as social forces driving the individual away from conventional, law-abiding behavior (e.g., the ostracism that accompanies labeling). Pulls are usually

---

Exhibit 12.2
. . . .

Containment approach

Specific Assumptions

1. To conceive of one's self in a positive way, one must have the acceptance of the dominant moral order.

2. Negative self-concepts encourage criminal behavior.

3. Positive self-images insulate against criminal behavior.

4. Individuals have several layers of psychological and social forces simultaneously pushing and pulling them in criminal and noncriminal directions.

5. The type of self-image one has is a major predictor of which of these forces will dominate one's behavior.

Source: Walter C. Reckless, "A New Theory of Delinquency and Crime," *Federal Probation* 25 (1961): pp. 42–46.

defined as the rewards of criminality, which include sensory gratification, sub-cultural status and financial gain with a minimum of effort.

Outer containments inhibiting criminal behavior are the external factors by which society keeps the individual's behavior within the norms and rules. These are forces that provide discipline and supervision. Policies aimed at "deterring" crime consist of constructing and implementing outer containments. The **inner containments** that inhibit criminal behavior consist of the individual's own tendencies to follow the conventional norms and rules. Inner containments are, in many respects, similar to Freud's idea of the superego. They are the rules of behavior that the individual has internalized and uses to judge her or his own actions. **Inner pushes and pulls** toward committing criminal behavior are the id-like desires that define a person's needs and wants.[10]

Reckless asserts that a conception of one's self as a socially acceptable person serves to discourage the individual from criminal involvement, since to maintain this self-image requires the maintenance of institutional approval, and that comes only as a result of following the rules. In other words, the power of inner constraints is dependent on the nature of the individual's self-image.[11] To the degree that people can define themselves as "good" in conventional terms, they have an investment in the moral order. Such an investment motivates them to internalize the rules of society and act in accordance with them so as to protect both their self-image and their investment in the moral

Reckless argues that the unique pressures of lower-class life and the stigma attached to it can damage individuals' self-concept and their commitment to the moral order.

order on which it is based. Reckless proposes that this principle applies especially to members of the middle and upper classes. Although this same concept of self as "good" can also insulate those in the lower class from committing criminal acts, the unique pressures of lower-class life, and the stigma that accompanies membership in this group, mitigate against the strength of these pro-social constraints.[12]

Problem-Behavior Theory

Jessor and Jessor's problem-behavior theory (see Exhibit 12.3) focuses on how distinctions in information received from the environment are made, and how these distinctions impact behavior. This theory is similar to Reckless' in that it concentrates on the relationship between the individual and variables in the environment, or what Reckless termed external pushes, pulls, and containments. Jessor and Jessor's theory proposes that differences in the individual's perceptions of various environmental forces determine the extent to which they influence the individual's behavior. The theory is especially relevant to the role of group memberships in prioritizing the norms by which an individual lives. That is, group memberships are considered to be the most important of the environmental factors that influence behavior.

According to this theory, the individual perceives each variable in the environment as either distal or proximal. **Distal perceptions** contain variables that are perceived as not directly relevant (i.e., distant) and somewhat innocuous to the individual. Distal perceptions, then, have only a little influence over the individual's behavior. An example of a distal perception would be an individual's perception of norm consensus between different reference groups. (It is believed that a perception of norm consensus, would only indirectly influence behavior.)

Proximal perceptions, on the other hand, are those ideas that are defined by the individual as highly relevant and therefore have much direct effect on behavioral choices.[13] An example of a proximal variable would be the individual's perception of a specific reference group's norms. For example, an individual's perception of the substance-abuse norm of a particular peer group would be proximal, whereas his or her perception of the consensus between that peer group's norm and his or her family's would be distal.

Exhibit 12.3
. . . .

Problem-behavior theory

Specific Assumptions

1. As part of one's social environment, groups are perceived through distal and proximal structures.

2. Variables contained in the distal structure provide indirect links between the juvenile and delinquent acts.

3. Variables contained in the proximal structure provide direct links between the juvenile and delinquent acts.

Source: Richard Jessor and Shirley L. Jessor, *Problem Behavior and Psychosocial Development: A Longitudinal Study of Youth* (New York: Academic Press, 1977).

Although Jessor and Jessor's theory is applicable to all social variables in the external environment, the theory's main emphasis is on what Haskell termed *normative* and *deviant personal reference groups*.[14] (We will discuss Haskell's ideas later in this chapter under the heading of "Expansions and Extensions of Social-Bonding Approach.") The concept of **personal reference group** was developed by Jennings to refer to groups in which individuals receive support, recognition, approval, and are appreciated for just being themselves (e.g., family and friends.)[15] The Jessors identified the perceived norms and behaviors of these personal reference groups as the major variables in predicting criminal activity.[16]

This theory essentially proposes that variables perceived as proximal provide a direct link between the individual and criminal acts, whereas those perceived as distal provide only an indirect link. Thus, an explanation is provided for why some environmental variables have a great impact on the individual while others do not. This conception of the process by which the decision to commit crimes is made in some ways resembles Sutherland's notion that individuals assign differing priorities to assorted sources of definitions of acts as "good" or "bad." The ultimate distinction between which factors are defined as distal and which as proximal is made by the individual. That decision, is, however, influenced by the availability of opportunities for group memberships, as implied by the subcultural strain theories of Cohen and of Cloward and Ohlin.

· · · · · · · · · | **APPLICATION** | · · · · ## The Case of Marlene Olive

> **Delinquent Conduct**
> An act committed by a juvenile (a person under the age of seventeen in most states) that violates a state penal law and which is punishable by imprisonment or confinement in jail.[17]
>
> **Status Offense**
> An act that is declared by statute to be an offense, but only when committed by a juvenile (e.g., running away from home, liquor possession, truancy).[18]

In June 1975, in Terra Linda, California, Marlene Olive and her boyfriend, Chuck Riley, conspired to murder her parents, Jim and Naomi Olive. On the day of the murders, Marlene Olive called Chuck Riley and told him her mother was asleep in their house, and that she and her father were going out to the store. Riley went to the Olive house and hit Naomi Olive several times in the head with a hammer, killing her. Marlene and Riley had originally planned to murder only Marlene's mother. However, Marlene and her father returned from the store earlier than expected and entered the house while Riley was still there. Riley shot Mr. Olive four times. Marlene and Riley then took her parents' bodies to an old fire pit and burned them. After her parents' disappearance was discovered, Marlene Olive confessed to the crime and implicated Riley.[19]

This crime came to represent the ultimate nightmare of middle-class suburban parents throughout the United States. Jim and Naomi Olive had at one time held great hopes for success and "upward mobility". However, they eventually lost faith in the middle-class values of the 1950s that had formed the basis of their belief system, primarily because of economic frustrations. Like many other middle-class Americans, the Olives believed that they were failing to attain success and were instead experiencing "downward mobility," or a loss of socioeconomic status. In essence, economic survival began to take precedence over serving as an outer containment for their daughter.[20]

Several months prior to the murders, Marlene Olive began speaking to her friends, their parents, and others about her hatred of her mother and her desire to kill her. Almost all of the older women who befriended her became a substitute mother figure for her. Marlene would tell them about her mother's bizarre and abusive behavior and her hatred for her. In January 1975 Marlene began making extensive plans for running away from home. This was an alternative *attracting factor* (i.e., alternative solution) that Marlene acted upon, but in a very feeble way. Her plan consisted of making a big drug deal and running away on the profits. She did in fact run away, but with the intention of not going very far. She ran away to a friend's house, and after a few days her father found her and took her back home. Although she did not want to live at home, she was even more afraid of the alternative.[21]

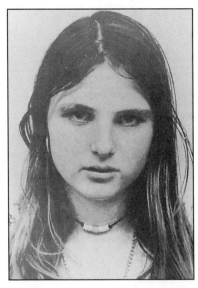

Marlene Olive

In May 1975 Marlene began to look for someone who would kill her parents for $25,000. She started by asking her boyfriend, Riley, to solicit one of his friends to kill them. Riley found a friend who initially considered killing them but backed out. On two other occasions, Marlene even attempted to poison her mother.[22]

After Marlene's failed attempts at homicide and running away, she began to fight more with her father. This was the immediate and primary *precipitating factor* of the actual crime—her increased fighting with her father over the combination of her deteriorating schoolwork, long-distance telephone calls, "fast" friends, shoplifting, and illegal drug use. Up until this time her relationship with her father had been a fairly good one.[23] That is, his beliefs and opinions were proximal to her. Conflicts with her father served to greatly reduce his influence and control over her. He thus became a distal influence, and, in Reckless' terms, ceased to be an effective outer containment on her behavior.

Marlene had been adopted at birth by the Olives. She had not been able to get along with her mother for a number of years. Naomi Olive's behavior had provided outer pushes on Marlene to commit deviant acts of defiance ever since early childhood. About six months before the murders, Marlene's relationship with her mother began to grow even worse. Her parents discovered her habitual truancy from school and her shoplifting escapades, which had begun a few months earlier. Truancy, like running away, is a status offense. Marlene and her mother now no longer talked, they just screamed at each other. Naomi Olive would also tell Marlene that Marlene's biological mother was a prostitute and that Marlene was also likely to become one. These behaviors of Naomi's served as powerful outer pushes towards crime for Marlene. They also had a negative effect on Marlene's self-concept, which further worsened the situation in the Olive home. For example, she began to fantasize about becoming a prostitute and having a "pimp."[24] These proximal perceptions of her mother's behavior served to increase the severity of Marlene's criminal behavior.

The *attracting factor* was Marlene's peer group. You might say she fell in with the "wrong crowd" in junior high school. She had been a model pre-adolescent child, except perhaps for being overprotected by her mother. In junior high school, however, she became involved with a group of adolescents and young adults who used illegal drugs. This group provided additional outer pulls on Marlene to commit illegal acts. As with most adolescents, Marlene's peer group had a very proximal impact on her. Her schoolwork began to suffer and her grades declined after she became involved with this group.

Twenty-one-year-old Chuck Riley, a small-time illegal drug dealer, was part of this group. The largest drug deal he had ever made was for $5,000.

Charles Riley, 19, and James Olive, 58.

He dealt in illegal drugs because it was a way for him to make friends, become needed, and feel important. He lived at home with his parents and had no permanent job. In many ways he was a person going nowhere—except for his relationship with Marlene. She was Riley's first girlfriend even though he was twenty-one years old. He had always been extremely overweight and became so infatuated with Marlene that he would do anything to keep her. An example of the level of his infatuation is that on one occasion when Marlene threatened to leave him, he attempted suicide by taking a drug overdose. She could easily control him simply by threatening to stop seeing him.[25]

Although Riley thought of Marlene as his girlfriend, she did not define their relationship in these terms. She used Riley to drive her and her friends to numerous places and supply them with free drugs. She became sexually promiscuous and had sex with Riley as well as with many of his friends. She began engaging in what might be described as bizarre or weird sex. For example, she wanted to have more group sex and have Riley watch her having sex with his friends. She also began reading about the occult and wanting others in the group to think that she was a witch. This occult involvement was very superficial, or distal, however.[26] All of these behaviors—the sexual promiscuity, the desire to have others witness her having sex, and the desire to have others believe she was a witch—are further evidence of the impact of her declining self-image on her behavior, according to the containment approach.

A tertiary *attracting factor* was that the juvenile probation authorities under whom she was placed as a result of her shoplifting provided Marlene with no relief from her mother's verbal attacks. Marlene proposed that she be placed in a foster home in order to escape her mother and resolve her behavior problems. The probation authorities told her that it was unlikely that she could be placed in a foster home because it required a court order and the court was unlikely to grant the request because her parents wanted to retain custody of her.[27]

Even when, shortly before the murders, the investigating officer reported that Olive's mother probably should be hospitalized because of her disturbed mental condition, the juvenile authorities did not remove Marlene from her home. This officer reported to her superiors that Marlene's anger toward her parents was legitimate in that she was being forced to live with a disturbed mother and an ineffective father. The officer believed that Marlene was "acting out." She described the situation as explosive.[28] This lack of action on the part of the juvenile authorities provided another outer push toward more serious criminal behavior.

Although somewhat tertiary, an additional *attracting factor* was the fact that Jim Olive chastised Marlene for telling the school guidance counselor about her mother's alcohol problems and their poor relationship, and then transferred her to a private school. At the private school Marlene continued her truancy.[29] Her father's chastisement reduced his ability to serve as an outer containment over her behavior.

The primary *predisposing factor* in this case was Marlene's family environment. The Olive family might best be described as the typical, dysfunctional schizoid family (i.e., where one parent supports the psychotic behavior of the other parent). Naomi Olive suffered from alcoholism and a psychotic disorder. Jim Olive supported and defended his wife's psychotic behaviors against his daughter's protests.

Naomi's alcoholism and psychosis had become serious when Marlene was about five years old. The family had moved to South America, where Naomi simply could not adjust to the change in lifestyle. She began drinking more, and her psychosis worsened as a result. She refused to give up her role of parent—indeed, she was overprotective—even though she was not capable of acting suitably in that capacity. She also refused to seek treatment for her alcoholism and mental illness. She blamed all of Marlene's subsequent school and delinquency problems on Marlene's use of drugs and the influence of Riley.[30] However, the evidence strongly suggests that the original source of the problem in the Olive household lay in Naomi's problems.

Jim Olive denied the reality of his wife's mental condition. For example, Naomi Olive would hold conversations with four or five nonexistent persons simultaneously (e.g., ghosts from her past such as her brother and father, and her husband's mother and father). Marlene would call her mother "crazy lady" to her face and in front of her friends. Jim Olive did nothing about his wife's behavior. He was a "bound for glory" salesman who never quite succeeded. In many ways he was a victim of society's values. He suffered under the illusion that if he was successful in his work, he could buy his family everything they needed. While trying to earn enough to give his family the best money could buy, he ignored his wife's psychosis, her alcohol problem, and the way she interacted with their daughter. He somehow expected that his wife's alcoholism and psychotic behavior would not affect Marlene. He tried to compensate Marlene for Naomi's behavior by spoiling her with material goods (e.g., buying her toys and dolls). Like his wife, he refused to release Marlene to the custody of a foster family, yet he would do nothing to change the dysfunctional family situation. He fully supported Naomi's belief that Riley was the cause of their daughter's problems.[31] Exhibit 12.4 summarizes the facts of this case.

Marlene and Riley were both found to be legally sane and guilty of murder in the first degree. Fortunately for Marlene, she was sixteen years old at the

Exhibit 12.4
. . . .

Summary of facts and their role in the explanation of Marlene Olive's role in the murder of her parents

Level of Importance	Fact	Type of Fact
Primary	Dysfunctional mother	Predisposing
Secondary	Deviant peer group	Attracting
	Juvenile authorities refuse to assist	Attracting
Tertiary	Disintegrating relationship with father	Precipitating

time of the crime. Therefore, she was not tried as an adult and was sentenced to the Ventura School, a coeducational institution for offenders, until she reached the age of twenty-one. The judge indicated that he would have liked to have sent her to a state prison.[32]

Riley received the death sentence. However, the supreme court of California struck down the state's death penalty in 1977, so his sentence was commuted to life in prison. He was initially incarcerated in San Quentin, and then transferred to the California Men's Colony in 1978. After six years in prison, he was denied parole in 1981. Lifers without an expiration date in California can theoretically be released after serving seven years in prison. However, Riley expects to spend at least twenty more years in prison.[33]

In essence, the behavior patterns of Marlene's parents caused her internal containments against criminality to collapse. Her mother's behavior pushed her towards substance abuse and delinquency, while her father's behavior resulted in his loss of influence and control over her. As she became more and more enmeshed in substance abuse, sexual promiscuity, and delinquency, her self-concept gradually worsened to the point where it would no longer insulate her against murdering her own parents.

Social-Bonding Approach
. . . .

Like Reckless' containment theory, Hirschi's social-bonding theory is defined as an approach in this text, because several theories have been developed on the basis of its principal assumptions (see Exhibit 12.5). Hirschi proposed that the social bond was critical to understanding the causes of delinquency.[34] Like Reckless's containment approach, Hirschi's concept of the social bond is social-psychological in nature. It focuses on the relation between social factors and individual activities.[35] The central idea is that individuals become free to commit crimes when their ties to society are broken or diminished. Thus, people who are not bonded to society are freer to commit criminal acts than those with strong bonds.

The social bond is the tie between the individual and society. It is the force that keeps mainstream society proximal to the individual despite the temptation to commit crime. Like other social-control theories, Hirschi's approach proposes that links to conventional institutions are all that prevent most people from acting on criminal motives most of the time.[36]

The social bond between the individual and the society is composed of four major, interrelated elements: attachment, commitment, involvement, and belief.[37] A breakdown in one element will cause a failure of the entire bond.[38]

Exhibit 12.5

. . . .

Social-bonding approach

> **Specific Assumptions**
>
> **1.** The social bond is the link between the individual and society consisting of four parts:
>
>   **a.** attachment,
>
>   **b.** commitment,
>
>   **c.** involvement, and
>
>   **d.** belief.
>
> **2.** A strong bond to conventional society is required to prevent criminality.

Source: Travis Hirschi, *Causes of Delinquency* (Berkeley and Los Angeles: University of California Press, 1969); Shoemaker, *Theories of Delinquency,* pp. 161–162.

Attachment to others consists of the emotional and psychological ties a person has with other individuals and groups.[39] This is the emotional dimension of the social bond, which is hypothesized to discourage a person from committing criminal acts through personal affection and loyalty.[40] Some examples of attachment are the sentiments that caring parents have towards their children or even that dedicated employees have to their employer. Marlene Olive's relationship with her father just prior to the murders is an excellent example of a weakened or broken attachment to others.

Commitment is concerned with the individual's practical investment in the socio-moral order. It involves the weighing of potential losses in these investments in conformity against the possible profits of criminal behavior.[41] Commitment is, essentially, the cost factor involved in engaging in criminal acts. People who have invested in conventional goals and activities will be reluctant to risk losing their investments by committing criminal acts.[42] For such people, legitimate institutions and groups are proximal influences that provide internal containment of impulses to commit crime.

The principle of commitment suggests that the more conforming assets (e.g., job, home, automobile) people have, the less likely they will be to commit crimes. Thus, one who owns his or her own home and has a well-paid job is unlikely to rob a gas station for a few hundred dollars. An unemployed person with no job skills or material assets is much more likely to commit such a crime.

Many factors affect the degree of containment and bonding experienced by individuals. In the discussion of the social-disorganization perspective in Chapter 9, it was noted that internal controls are always more effective than external ones. However, internal controls are not easily manipulated by policymakers, whereas external controls are a normal part of government power. The salience of deterrent forces like the police and stiff prison sentences act as outer containments, as does the fear of stigmatization.

Many people argue that the fear of being stigmatized with a negative label as a result of apprehension for criminal conduct is a very effective containment device that bridges the gap between inner and outer control mechanisms. This **deterrence** argument leads to an emphasis on swift, certain, and reasonably severe punishment as one method of keeping law a proximal influence over people's behavior. However, those with inadequate commitments to society are little affected by deterrence policies, especially if their attachments are to nonconventional others. The higher one's socioeconomic level, the greater one's commitment to the moral order is likely to be and thus the more influenced by deterrence-based crime control policies. It is for this reason that such policies have much popular appeal among members of the middle and upper classes but prove largely ineffective in controlling the behavior of the typical street criminal, who is of lower-class origin. Nevertheless, the great majority of people who vote in elections are of middle- to upper-class status so such policies do help politicians get elected.

Involvement relates to the individual's participation in conforming activities.[43] Such involvements include legitimate employment, church, sports, recreational clubs, etc. It is assumed that these kinds of activities occupy enough of the individual's time to assure that there will be no spare time for indulging any temptations to commit crimes.[44] This aspect of the bond implies that certain acts, such as dropping out of school without having a full-time job, make time available for individuals to become interested in criminal behavior.

Belief refers to the level of the individual's acceptance of conforming values. This is the moral component of the social bond.[45] The assumption is that people's faith in the conventional values, norms, and laws of the society will restrain them from committing crime; those without such beliefs are free to commit crimes.[46] Thus, criminal behavior is thought to occur when conventional norms and rules are not internalized by the individual, since social controls are less effective in securing law-abiding behavior

Persons of upper socioeconomic class who have benefited from society's status quo are likely to approve of the moral order and of deterrence-based crime policies. Deterrence is largely ineffective, however, in controlling the behavior of lower-class criminals.

from those who have not internalized the norms and rules as part of their self-concept.[47]

Lofland suggests that there are five basic dimensions involved in facilitating affective social bonding: exposure, practical aid, actual or potential peership, understanding, and warmth. He further proposes that the more these dimensions are associated with representatives of conventional society (i.e., individuals, groups, organizations, institutions), the greater the likelihood of positive affective bonding.[48] This insight has been largely ignored by our correctional system but has been used in some crime prevention programs (e.g. DARE—Drug Abuse Resistance Education).

It is assumed by the social-bonding approach that individuals will bond with the conventional society. Bonding is, however, equally possible with deviant subcultures. When this is the case, a culture-conflict situation is likely to arise and lead to criminal conduct.[49]

Expansions and Extensions of Social-Bonding Approach

Reference-Group Theory of Delinquency

As mentioned in the discussion of Jessor and Jessor's problem-behavior theory, the concept of the personal reference group is used to refer to groups in which individuals receive support, recognition, approval, and are appreciated by the others just for being themselves (e.g., the family).[50] Haskell's reference-group theory of delinquency (see Exhibit 12.6) extends this idea by developing the

Exhibit 12.6

Reference-group theory of delinquency

Specific Assumptions

1. The first personal reference group for children is the family.

2. Families are normative reference groups.

3. Street groups become the personal reference groups of juveniles prior to their engaging in delinquent acts.

4. Lower-class street groups are part of a delinquent subculture.

5. In decisions preceding delinquent acts, juveniles having street groups as their personal reference groups are more likely to decide in favor of the commission of delinquent acts than those with conventional reference groups.

6. Individuals are inclined to bring their socio group life attitudes and behavioral ways into personal reference groups.

7. Satisfying relationships in normative socio groups exert a decisive influence against entering into delinquent acts where the juvenile is both a member of a normative and delinquent personal reference groups.

Source: Martin R. Haskell, "Toward a Reference Group Theory of Juvenile Delinquency," *Social Problems* 8, Winter 1961: pp. 221–224.

Johnson argued that juveniles are "pushed" and "pulled" into delinquency when success and self-esteem cannot be achieved in family or school contexts.

concept of **socio reference groups** to identify groups in which the objectives of the group are not solely those of the individual, and the concerns and obligations of the group are held in common (e.g., work group) among its members.[51] Haskell's **normative personal reference group** is a collection of individuals who associate with one another for nonspecific reasons and transmit norms that define group membership. These are the same norms that are usually internalized as part of the self-image and act as internal containments.

Although Haskell did not fully address how his theoretical formulation was related to other theories of crime, his work does suggest much reliance on control and strain theories.[52] Parts of Haskell's theory are also very compatible with Cohen's middle-class measuring-rod theory, which bridges the gap between the culture-conflict and strain perspectives.[53] The presumption that social learning is critical to the definition of rewards and the development of behaviors also seems to be implied in Haskell's formulation.

Haskell's theory focuses on the causal relationship between reference groups and juvenile delinquency. At the core of his theory is the idea that conflict arises between lower-class juveniles and their families as a result of the juveniles' use of attitudes and behaviors from normative socio group norms, primarily from school, in the context of their family (a personal reference group).[54] In effect, Haskell argues that the same juveniles reject or break the bonds with their families because the latter are not living up to the socio groups' middle-class standards.

Haskell suggests that even deviant families often supply a normative personal reference group for juveniles because they attempt to instill the norms of the larger society in their offspring rather than their own deviant norms. Haskell also argues that our schools (as socio group settings) turn some juveniles against not only our families, but also against the school itself. He suggests that part of the answer is for our educational system to provide counseling to help juveniles choose realistic occupational goals and part- or full-time employment that is suited to their immediate needs.[55] This suggestion is consistent with other studies that have identified basic differences in ability among students.[56]

Attachment Theory of Delinquency

Johnson's attachment theory (see Exhibit 12.7) uses several divergent orientations, and could have been included under the containment approach.[57] However, it also requires knowledge of social bonding if it is to be properly understood and used. His theory also seems to acknowledge the operation of the social-learning process. Johnson developed what he called an *attachment* brand of control theory.[58] Like Reckless, Johnson sees the juvenile's self-esteem as the critical variable in the formation of controls within the individual. His focus on the attachment of juveniles to their parents, peers, and schools is consistent with Hirschi's social-bonding theory. Indeed, after examining the empirical evidence, Hirschi came to emphasize the attachment component over the other three in his own work.[59] Johnson concluded that attachments to parents and school are the most important factors in determining the probability of a juvenile committing delinquent behavior and should receive emphasis in theories of the origin of criminal behavior patterns.[60]

As Merton's strain approach pointed out, American society is very achievement-oriented. Youths who are unable to achieve "success" at school or within the family are thus forced to find it in peer groups. The peer groups that are most supportive for youths who have failed to achieve conventional success

Exhibit 12.7

. . . .

Attachment theory of delinquency

Specific Assumptions

1. Adolescent self-esteem affects susceptibility to peer influence.

2. Adolescents whose self-esteem is not based on school-related successes or family-related experiences are more vulnerable to peer influences.

3. Acquiring prestige in adolescent peer groups frequently requires committing delinquent acts.

Source: Richard E. Johnson, *Juvenile Delinquency and Its Origins* (New York: Cambridge University Press, 1979), p. 70.

are likely to be similar to those described by Cohen and Cloward and by Ohlin in their strain theories of delinquent subcultures. The commission of illegal acts is often a virtual requirement for acceptance and "success" in these groups. Thus, when self-esteem cannot be developed through the family or other legitimate opportunities (i.e., school), the juvenile is likely to be "pushed" and "pulled" into delinquency and adopt a self-image that encourages criminality.

· · · · · · · · ┃ **APPLICATION** ┃ · · · · # The Case of Candace Montgomery

Adultery
The act of a married person voluntarily engaging in sexual intercourse with a partner other than his or her spouse. Although criminal laws prohibiting adultery still exist in many states, they are rarely enforced.[61]

Betty Gore, a thirty-year-old suburban housewife with three children, was killed on June 13, 1980, in Wylie, Texas. On the day of the murder, Candace "Candy" Montgomery went over to Betty Gore's house to pick up a swimsuit for Betty Gore's daughter, who was going to spend the night with Candace Montgomery's daughter at the Montgomery's house. The two women had become friends as a result of attending the same church.[62]

As Candace Montgomery was about to leave Betty Gore's home, Betty asked Candace if she were having an affair with Betty's husband, Allan Gore. Candace said they had had an affair but that it had ended eight months ago and was over for good. At this point Betty Gore went into her garage and returned with a three-foot ax. She cornered Candace Montgomery in a utility room and swung the ax at her, saying that she was going to kill her. This action was the *precipitating factor* in this case. The two women struggled, and Montgomery got the ax away from Gore and killed her with it. According to Candace, Betty Gore would not stay down, even after being hit numerous times with the ax, until she was dead. Candace proceeded to take a bath at Betty's house to clean the blood off and then left.[63]

Candace Montgomery became a police suspect because she was the last person known to have seen Betty Gore alive. The police had also learned of her affair with Allan Gore. Several days after the crime, Candace confessed to her attorney. She was subsequently arrested and charged with the murder.[64]

The *attracting factor* in this case is attributed to Betty Gore's motives for her behavior, even though she ultimately became the victim. Betty Gore initiated the violence with her attack on Candace Montgomery because she saw this as a way of keeping her husband. She already had one small child and was pregnant with another. She was determined not to have her marriage break up and lose her family to Candace Montgomery. Because Betty Gore initiated the dispute that led to her death, this was a case of victim-precipitated homicide.

The *predisposing factor* in this case was Candace Montgomery's extramarital affair with Allan Gore. Candace, a thirty-year-old housewife with two children, had been married to her husband for approximately ten years. Pat Montgomery was a research scientist who earned over $70,000 a year.[65] Her extramarital affair with Allan Gore had lasted about three months.

Candace Montgomery had started the extramarital affair because she felt a need for more excitement in her life. Although she had talked to her minister and a close friend about the affair, neither of them could talk her out of it. Her beliefs had changed, and she no longer believed that committing adultery was wrong. Allan Gore's willingness to engage in adultery provided further support for her new belief concerning adultery.

The extramarital affair was not nearly as exciting as Candace had hoped it would be, and she and Gore ended their romantic relations without hard feelings. Both had wanted extramarital sex without emotional involvement, and both also wanted to remain married to their respective spouses.[66]

Very soon after her affair with Allan Gore ended, Candace had a second extramarital affair with another man. This second affair lasted about three weeks. Her husband had learned of her affair with Allan Gore by finding a love letter Allan had given to Candace. Pat and Candace Montgomery talked about her affair, and Pat forgave her for it. He felt that her affair with Gore was his fault because he had neglected her. He did not learn of the second affair until the trial.[67]

Montgomery pled not guilty to the murder charge. At her trial, her attorney argued that she had killed Betty Gore in self-defense. The jury believed this argument and found her not guilty. Her claim of self-defense against Betty Gore was recounted under hypnosis by a psychiatrist and again under polygraph examination. Both the hypnosis and polygraph examinations fully supported her account of what happened at the Gore residence on June 13, 1980.[68]

Candace Montgomery's changed beliefs about adultery allowed for the weakening and finally the breaking of her social bond. In particular, it weakened her attachment to her husband and encouraged her to become involved with other men. It also weakened her commitment to her children. Because of these changed beliefs, she became willing to risk losing her family, as well as her standing in the community (i.e., loss of status in neighborhood and church). Although she claimed to have no intention of leaving her family, church, and community, few people are naive enough to assume that adulterous behavior is not going to have adverse effects on these types of relationships.

Her new beliefs found social support first in Allan Gore and then in the second man with whom she had a liaison. Her discussions of adultery with her minister and friend indicated her need for social support for her new, unconventional beliefs (though she failed to obtain it from those two people). Such a need appears to be fairly strong among humans and illustrates the importance of normative reference groups, no matter what the group's size. Exhibit 12.8 summarizes the facts of this case.

Conclusion

As you have undoubtedly noticed by now, new theories are often developed on the basis of assumptions and propositions contained in older theories. Thus,

Level of Importance	Fact	Type of Fact
Primary	Candace Montgomery's extramarital affair with Allan Gore	Predisposing
Secondary	Betty Gore's attack on Candace Montgomery	Precipitating
Tertiary	Betty Gore's fear of losing husband and family	Attracting

Exhibit 12.8

Summary of facts and their role in the explanation of Candace Montgomery's role in the death of Betty Gore

most of the newer theories are variations or expansions of older ones. One of the reasons that more micro-oriented theories are developed out of macro or meso ones is that the more macro-oriented ones are generally very difficult to link to the particular acts of individuals. Some are also very difficult to test in an empirical fashion. In some respects, many of the micro theories within particular perspectives are designed to serve as empirically testable subtheories. This is in keeping with Schrag's contention that in order for a belief to be a theory, it must be possible to reduce it to a set of interconnected propositions from which testable hypotheses can be derived.[69]

Many of these newer theories complement older ideas about the origins of crime by either (1) linking them together or (2) expanding upon one or more of their assumptions or propositions regarding criminal behavior. This is especially true of the theories that are contained within the social-control perspective. For example, both the containment and social-bonding approaches view human nature as essentially egocentric and both refer to a specific set of methods by which society tries to keep individuals under its control. They differ primarily in their focus rather than their presumptions.

The containment and social-bond approaches also lend themselves to linkage with other theories, or what is commonly referred to as the *synthesizing* of theories. The use of Hirschi's notion of bonding to explain how inner containments, as well as pushes and pulls, operate within an individual illustrates how these two theories easily lend themselves to combination. Reckless' containment approach, the older of the two, is an attempt to link individual behavior to the relative strength of social institutions. This is an example of the general goal of linking micro-level behaviors to meso- and even macro-level structures. This goal was also a major factor in the development of the strain perspective. Similarly, although Hirschi's bonding theory is set at a more micro level with its focus on family and peer relations, macro-level variables like socioeconomic factors clearly affect the bonding process as well.

In addition, both control approaches tend to complement the strain perspective and both implicitly assume that social learning is an important mechanism in the acquisition of attitudes and behaviors. Strain theory, especially in regard to the innovator role, could also be used to help explain why people with significant investments in conformity are disinclined to commit crimes. The use of such combinations of theories to explain facts, especially at the level of individual actions, is encouraged by the authors of this text because it provides more comprehensive explanations than could any single theory.

Glossary •

Attachment   The part of the social bond that refers to the emotional and psychological ties a person has toward other persons' or groups' opinions and feelings.

Belief   The part of the social bond that refers to the level of the individual's acceptance of conforming values.

Commitment   The part of the social bond that refers to an individual's investments in conformity.

Deterrence   Refers to attempts to prevent or discourage crime by use of actual or threatened punishments. It is the theoretical basis of policies claiming to "get tough" on crime.

Distal Perceptions   Perceptions of variables that are defined by the individual as having only indirect relevance to his or her thoughts and acts and/or are somewhat innocuous in their behavioral impact.

Inner Containments   The individual's own internal inhibitions against criminal behavior.

Inner Pushes and Pulls   The individual's organic or psychological drives and/or defects that encourage criminal behavior.

Involvement   The part of the social bond that relates to the degree and amount of participation individuals have in conforming, legal activities.

Normative Personal Reference Groups   Collections of individuals who associate with one another for nonspecific reasons and transmit norms that define group membership.

Outer Containments   Environmental forces outside the individual that inhibit criminal behavior.

Outer Pressures and Pulls   Environmental forces outside the individual that encourage criminal behavior.

Personal Reference Groups   Groups where people receive support, recognition, approval, and are appreciated for just being themselves.

Proximal Perceptions   Perceptions of variables that are defined by the individual as having much direct effect on behavioral choices.

Socio Reference Groups   Groups that have communal objectives; the concerns and obligations of the group are held in common.

▪ Notes

1. R. L. Matseuda, "Testing Control Theory and Differential Association: A Causal Modeling Approach," *American Sociological Review* 47, pt. 2 (1982): pp. 489–504.
2. M. Mathur and R. A. Dodder, "Delinquency and the Attachment Bond in Hirschi's Control Theory," *Free Inquiry in Creative Sociology* 13, no. 1 (1985): pp. 99–103.
3. Terence P. Thornberry, "Toward an Interactional Theory of Delinquency," *Criminology* 25, no. 4 (1987): pp. 863—891; R. D. Conger, "Social Control and Social Learning Models of Delinquent Behavior: A Synthesis," *Criminology* 14, no. 1 (1976): pp. 17–40.
4. D. Dressler, *Readings in Criminology and Penology* (New York: Columbia University Press, 1964).
5. A. E. Liska and M. D. Reed, "Ties to Conventional Institutions and Delinquency: Estimating Reciprocal Effects," *American Sociological Review* 50, no. 4 (1985): pp. 547–560.
6. Donald J. Shoemaker, *Theories of Delinquency*, (New York: Oxford University Press, 1984): pp. 153–154.

7. Walter C. Reckless, "A New Theory of Delinquency and Crime," *Federal Probation* 25 (1961): pp. 42–46.

8. J. H. Rankin, "Investigating the Interrelations among Social Control Variables and Conformity," *The Journal of Criminal Law and Criminology* 67, no. 4 (1977): pp. 470–480.

9. Reckless, "A New Theory of Delinquency and Crime"; W. Reckless and S. Dinitz, "Pioneering with Self-Concept as a Vulnerability Factor in Delinquency," *Journal of Criminal Law, Criminology, and Police Science* 58 (1967): pp. 515–523.

10. Rankin, "Investigating the Interrelations among Social Control Variables and Conformity."

11. Ibid.

12. Walter C. Reckless, Simon Dinitz and Ellen Murray, "Self-Concept as an Insulator against Delinquency," *American Sociological Review* 21 (1956): pp. 744–746.

13. Richard Jessor and Shirley L. Jessor, *Problem Behavior and Psychosocial Development: A Longitudinal Study of Youth* (New York: Academic Press, 1977).

14. Ibid.

15. Helen H. Jennings, "Sociometric Structure in Personality and Group Formation" in Muzafer Sherif and M. O. Wilson (eds.), *Group Relations at the Crossroads* (New York: Harper, 1952).

16. Jessor and Jessor, *Problem Behavior and Psychosocial Development: A Longitudinal Study of Youth.*

17. George E. Rush, *The Dictionary of Criminal Justice*, 2 ed. (Guilford, CT: Dushkin, 1986), p. 73; *Texas Family Code* (St. Paul, MN: West Publishing, 1990): pp. 150–151.

18. Ibid., p. 229.

19. Richard M. Levine, *Bad Blood: A Family Murder in Marin County* (New York: Random House, 1982).

20. Ibid.

21. Ibid.

22. Ibid.

23. Ibid.

24. Ibid.

25. Ibid.

26. Ibid.

27. Ibid.

28. Ibid.

29. Ibid.

30. Ibid.

31. Ibid.

32. Ibid.

33. Ibid.

34. Travis Hirschi, *Causes of Delinquency* (Berkeley and Los Angeles: University of California Press, 1969); Shoemaker, *Theories of Delinquency*, pp. 161–162.

35. Conger, "Social Control and Social Learning Models of Delinquent Behavior: A Synthesis."

36. A. E. Liska and M. D. Reed, "Ties to Conventional Institutions and Delinquency: Estimating Reciprocal Effects," *American Sociological Review* 50, no. 4 (1985).

37. M. D. Wiatrowski, D. B. Griswold, and M. K. Roberts, "Social Control Theory and Delinquency," *American Sociological Review* 46, no. 5 (1981): pp. 525–541.

38. R. R. Lyerly, J. K. Skipper, Jr., "Different Rates of Rural-Urban Delinquency: A Social Control Approach," *Criminology* 19, no. 3 (1981): pp. 385–399.

39. Shoemaker, *Theories of Delinquency*, pp. 161–162.

40. R. L. Matsueda, "Testing Control Theory and Differential Association: A Causal Modeling Approach," *American Sociological Review* vol. 47, pt. 2, (1982): pp. 489–504.

41. Shoemaker, *Theories of Delinquency*, p. 162.

42. M. D. Krohn and J. I. Massey, "Social Control and Delinquent Behavior: An Examination of the Elements of the Social Bond," *Sociological Review* 21, no. 4 (1980): pp. 529–543.

43. Shoemaker, *Theories of Delinquency*, p. 162.

44. Krohn and Massey, "Social Control and Delinquent Behavior: An Examination of the Elements of the Social Bond"; Matsueda, "Testing Control Theory and Differential Association: A Causal Modeling Approach."

45. Shoemaker, *Theories of Delinquency*, p. 162.

46. Krohn and Massey, "Social Control and Delinquent Behavior: An Examination of the Elements of the Social Bond."

47. A. J. Reiss, Jr., "Delinquency as the Failure of Personal and Social Controls," *American Sociological Review* 16, no. 1, (1951): pp. 196–207.

48. John Lofland, *Deviance and Identity* (Englewood Cliffs, NJ: Prentice-Hall, 1969).

49. S. A. Cernkovich, "Evaluating Two Models of Delinquency Causation: Structural Theory and Control Theory," *Criminology* 16, no. 3 (1978): pp. 335–352.

50. Helen H. Jennings, "Sociometric Structure in Personality and Group Formation," in Muzafer Sherif and M. O. Wilson (eds.), Group Relations at the Crossroads (New York: Harper, 1952).

51. Martin R. Haskell, "Toward a Reference Group Theory of Juvenile Delinquency," Social Problems 8 (Winter 1961): pp. 220–230.

52. Ibid., pp. 220–230.

53. Ibid.

54. Ibid.

55. Ibid.

56. Hirschi, *Causes of Delinquency*.

57. Richard E. Johnson, *Juvenile Delinquency and Its Origins* (New York: Cambridge University Press, 1979), p. 70.

58. Ibid.

59. Hirschi, *Causes of Delinquency*.

60. Johnson, *Juvenile Delinquency and Its Origins*.

61. Rush, *The Dictionary of Criminal Justice*, p. 4.

62. John Bloom and Jim Atkinson, *Evidence of Love* (New York: Bantam Books, 1985).

63. Ibid.
64. Ibid.
65. Ibid
66. Ibid.
67. Ibid.
68. Ibid.
69. C. Schrag, *Crime and Justice: American Style* (Washington, DC: United States Government Printing Office, 1971).

■ Suggested Readings

S. A. Cernkovich, "Evaluating Two Models of Delinquency Causation: Structural Theory and Control Theory," *Criminology* 16, no. 3 (1978): pp. 335–352.

R. D. Conger, "Social Control and Social Learning Models of Delinquent Behavior: A Synthesis, *Criminology* 14, no. 1 (1976): pp. 17–40.

M. D. Krohn and J. I. Massey, "Social Control and Delinquent Behavior: An Examination of the Elements of the Social Bond," *Sociological Review* 21, no. 4 (1980): pp. 529–543.

A. E. Liska and M. D. Reed, "Ties to Conventional Institutions and Delinquency: Estimating Reciprocal Effects," *American Sociological Review* 50, no. 4 (1985): pp. 547–560.

J. H. Rankin, "Investigating the Interrelations among Social Control Variables and Conformity," *The Journal of Criminal Law and Criminology* 67, no. 4 (1977): pp. 470–480.

Walter C. Reckless, "A New Theory of Delinquency and Crime," *Federal Probation* 25 (1961): pp. 42–46.

Walter C. Reckless, Simon Dinitz and Ellen Murray, "Self-Concept as an Insulator against Delinquency," *American Sociological Review* 21 (1956): pp. 744–746.

A. J. Reiss, Jr., "Delinquency as the Failure of Personal and Social Controls," *American Sociological Review* 16, no. 1 (1951): pp. 196–207.

■ Suggested Books for Additional Application

Joe Sharkey, *Death Sentence: The Inside Story of the John List Murders* (New York: Penguin Books, 1990).

Linda Wolfe, *The Professor and the Prostitute* (New York: Ballantine Books, 1986).

CHAPTER **13**

The Marxist Perspective

Overview of Marxist Perspective

. . . .

Marx was not directly concerned with crime and criminality. His major concern was with the relationships between economics, history, and social organization. Marx's work was heavily influenced by the misery that he saw throughout Europe as industrialization took firm hold over the economy and capitalist power replaced that of the monarchies. Although he wrote very little on the subject of crime, some of his successors developed a Marxist perspective on crime based on his view of socioeconomic organization. It was thus designed to deal with macro-level phenomena like socioeconomic classes and societal institutions. Exhibit 13.1 gives the common assumptions of this perspective.

Because Marxists are primarily concerned with the use of, and interactions between, economic and political power, much of their work has been devoted to the study of law and its development over time. However, Marxism does address criminality as a social phenomena and those are the insights that will be stressed here.

Marx saw crime as an inevitable result of certain types of social organization at the macro level. He believed that the predominant **mode of production** in a society—meaning the manner in which the production of goods and

Exhibit 13.1

. . . .

Marxist perspective

Common Assumptions

1. The method by which a society organizes the development, production, and distribution of goods and services is the basis on which all other aspects of that society's organization and structure develop.

2. All societies are plagued, to some degree, by contradictions in their mode of production.

3. Capitalist societies are essentially composed of two groups—the bourgeoisie, who control the mode of production, and those without such control, or the proletariat.

4. The difference in the power available to these two groups, in combination with the capitalist stress on profits, results in bourgeois exploitation of the proletariat.

5. As a result of their exploited status, alienation is endemic among the proletariat.

6. Alienation, a sense of meaninglessness and powerlessness, results in attitudes and beliefs that lead to crime.

7. The alternative to alienation among the capitalist proletariat is class consciousness, which will lead to revolution by the masses.

8. Such violent revolutionary changes in the organization of society are the source of progressive improvement for mankind.

Source: C. Wright Mills, *The Marxists* (New York: Dell Publishing, 1962), pp. 47–58; Karl Marx, *Capital*, edited by Friedreich Engels (New York: International Publishers, 1967); Karl Marx, *Critique of Political Economy* (New York: International Library, [1904] 1859).

services is organized (e.g., capitalism, feudalism)—created the social conditions that typified that society. Crime was merely one of the many social conditions that resulted from the socioeconomic organization of society. As the mode of production changed, so also did the nature of crime and other conditions of life. This view of society and human behavior is known as **economic determinism**. It can be defined as the belief that a person's view of the world and their social behavior is a result of their position in the economic system. One's position in the economic hierarchy is, in turn, largely a product of the method by which the society's economy is organized. For modern America, this means capitalism.[1]

According to Marx, capitalist societies are composed of two basic groups— the **bourgeoisie**, or elite, who control (i.e., own) the mode of production, and the **proletariat**, the masses of workers who actually produce the goods and services available in the society. The vast majority of citizens in any capitalist society are proletarians. Marx believed that this mode of societal organization was doomed because of the internal contradictions in its structure. Marxists point out that capitalism's emphasis on profits diverts attention from meeting many basic human needs—even though economic organization is created for the purpose of meeting human needs efficiently.[2] From this perspective the fact that each American family is encouraged to possess several televisions while many citizens are homeless, unemployed, and malnourished is irrational and contradictory.

In the Marxist view, capitalism has an inherent need to continue to grow. Economic growth can be accomplished in either of two ways. New markets can be located, as when we sell cigarettes and televisions to developing nations in the Pacific. Alternatively, new needs can be created, as when we convince people that they should smell, dress, and transport themselves in particular and fashionable ways. Since most of the potential markets on the planet are already being tapped by capitalism, we cannot expect that avenue of growth to continue for long. However, by creating desires for new luxuries while some people are still in desperate need of the basic necessities, capitalism exposes its greedy indifference to human welfare and undermines itself.[3]

The Marxist View of Social Organization

Marx was interested in the history of civilization. He identified three stages in the development of western societies and predicted the emergence of a fourth stage. He conceived of man in an original natural state in which the production and use of various items was an individual matter and people found inner fulfillment in the course of meeting their daily needs. This idyllic lifestyle, he theorized, was subverted by wars and greed into a system dominated by slavery, as in ancient Greece and Rome.

With slavery as the dominant mode of production, rebellion was the predominant form of crime, and any act that might contribute to rebellion was feared and outlawed. Thus, for example, it was once a felony in most southern states to teach a slave to read, because reading could expose a slave to the idea that slavery was unnatural, immoral, and unchristian.

Because it was ultimately unprofitable, the slavery of the ancient world gave way to feudalism in the Middle Ages. This was a system in which serfs were dominated by royalty but not actually possessed by it. Under the feudal mode of organization there was great concern with loyalty to the monarchs as well as to the church that legitimated their power and status. Crime took on moral, as opposed to practical, implications. A "good" person was one who did not question the beliefs and actions of the church and state. Any act that brought religious authority into question was defined as criminal, because any doubt about religious principles could bring the supremacy of the monarchy into question as well. Thus, public discussion of the scientific findings of men like Galileo and Copernicus was considered to be a criminal act during this period of history.

As society grew increasingly complex and technological, feudalism ceased to be a viable mode of production, and capitalism emerged. For Marx, capitalism's most essential feature was its emphasis on private control of the mode of production, which under slavery and feudalism, had been controlled by the same groups that controlled the government. Capitalism essentially put government in the service of the bourgeoisie.[4]

It was the private ownership of factories and farmlands, not of homes and toothbrushes, that Marx objected to in capitalism. In a capitalist society, the law is structured to protect the interests of the bourgeoisie—to defend their factories and keep the labor force that operates them well disciplined. For this reason most Marxist analyses of crime focus on acts by businesses or the government that serve to repress the proletariat. These activities, according to the Marxists, are in contradiction to the needs of the majority of citizens. Capitalist factory owners strive to minimize the expense of producing their goods while maximizing the cost of the product so as to assure the highest profits possible. So long as maximization of profits, rather than meeting the needs of the majority of citizens, is the goal of the predominant mode of production, the masses remain needy and exploited.[5]

Since the mode of production determines the nature and content of the society's institutions, the nuclear family comes to predominate over the extended family in a capitalist society because the former provides greater mobility for the labor force. This has criminological implications in that as the family unit shrinks in size, informal social-control mechanisms are weakened. Although formal control mechanisms are expected to take over, they can never be as effective as informal controls.

The institutional format of society in turn molds the **superstructure** of the society. That is, institutions interact with one another in the context of the mode of production to form the society that is actually perceived by individuals on a daily basis. Again, this insight has powerful implications for criminology. The capitalist form of economic organization is responsible for the relationships between vital concerns like law, religion, reproduction, and leisure activity. According to Marx, changes in the mode of production inevitably result in alterations of the social superstructure. However, little can be done to change the superstructure without first altering the mode of production. Policies aimed at superstructural changes without questioning the mode of production are seen as methods of diverting the proletariat's attention to issues that will divide rather than unite them. Thus, Marxists generally conclude that it is not possible to significantly reduce the amount of crime in society, or change its nature, without abandoning capitalism.

Marxist Approach to Crime

Unlike many other criminological perspectives, the Marxist one (see Exhibit 13.2) does not accept the assumption that there is widespread consensus in society as to the basic values and goals of individual citizens. Socioeconomic factors are seen as the fundamental organizational force in human society by this perspective. Marxists distinguish between a moralistic conception of crime as acts that harm others, and the legal conception of crime as violations of government decrees.[6] They maintain that the bourgeois exploitation of the proletariat is extremely criminal, though it is rarely recognized as such by the justice system. In a capitalist society, criminal law is a means of controlling the proletariat and promoting **false consciousness** among its members. This term refers to belief in an ideology or belief system that runs counter to one's actual material interests.[7]

Two separate pathways to crime can be discerned in the Marxist approach. The most obvious pathway is centered around the potential for revolution by the proletariat. This is the central concern of orthodox Marxism. As members of the proletariat come to realize that they are being exploited, Marx predicted that they would unite and rebel against the elite bourgeoisie. Such actions would be defined as criminal by the state, which consistently acts to protect the interests of the elite.

The realization among proletarian workers that they have a common problem and suffer under the same oppressors is referred to as **class consciousness**. Class consciousness has two components: (1) the recognition that the prole-

Exhibit 13.2

Marxist approach

Restrictive Assumptions

1. The proletariat will eventually develop an awareness of their exploitation and oppression by the bourgeoisie.

2. Such an awareness will result in the unification of the workers against the elite.

3. The natural outcome of such unity among the masses is the overthrow of the oppressive bourgeoisie.

4. Such revolutionary activities will be labeled as criminal by the capitalist government.

5. The bourgeoisie will attempt to undermine the unification of the workers by encouraging divisions among them based on criteria other than social class.

6. Such divisions will result in the separation of workers from themselves, their products, and their society.

7. This estrangement is a symptom of the perversion of human nature by capitalism.

8. As human nature is perverted and class unity is undermined, the workers will behave in a criminal fashion toward one another, as well as toward the bourgeoisie.

tariat constitutes a single class; and (2) loyalty to, and identification with, that class despite other divisions within this large group. This sort of consciousness is a prerequisite to the revolutionary sentiment that Marx predicted would lead to the overthrow of capitalism and the development of a socialist mode of production.[8] From this approach, crimes committed by proletarians against the bourgeoisie establishment or its representatives can be described as "the struggle of the single individual against the dominant conditions."[9]

The other pathway to crime described by the Marxist approach focuses on the proletariat's failure to achieve class consciousness. False consciousness is a result of the failure of the proletariat to achieve class consciousness. Any subjective view of one's situation that is in contradiction with the objective facts is a source of false consciousness. The fact that the leaders of society permit, and at times even encourage, racism, sexism, and unionization would be taken as methods of promoting false consciousness among the working class by a Marxist. These beliefs lead to false consciousness by emphasizing divisions within the proletariat that are secondary to the fact that they have common problems rooted in their exploitation by the bourgeoisie. Similarly, religion was portrayed as having a drug-like effect because of its tendency to

A union meeting of coal miners in Gilbert Creek, West Virginia. Marx argued that the desire to perform constructive labor is a basic human drive, but that capitalism perverts this by exploiting the working class and denying them the right to develop their many talents and to control the products of their labor.

define the life of an oppressed person as something holy and worthy of redemption in the afterlife. Thus, religion helped the bourgeoisie keep the proletariat divided and unaware of their class unity, allowing it to rule them in an exploitative fashion.[10]

The result of this situation is **alienation** among the workers—a sociological term for a condition typified by sentiments of powerlessness and meaninglessness that lead to self-estrangement. According to Marx, alienation is rooted in the organization of the workplace. Marx believed that humans were distinct from all other creatures in their drive to perform constructive labor.[11] The capitalist mode of production, he reasoned, denies most people the opportunity to explore and develop their many talents while it simultaneously destroys their right to control the products of their labor. Because the desire to accumulate profits and property is so intense in capitalism, basic human traits are suppressed and human nature is adversely affected. Crime is often a result of this perversion of man's basic nature.[12] Because this text is primarily concerned with explaining individual acts of crime, this second pathway to law violation is the most critical concern here. This pathway is best described by the work of Willem Bonger.

Orthodox Marxist Theory of Crime Causation

In 1916 Willem Bonger, a prominent European socialist, applied Marx's ideas directly to the issue of criminality in his book *Criminality and Economic Conditions*.[13] His was the orthodox Marxist view of the issue. His theory (see Exhibit 13.3) is relevant to modern criminology because it explicitly links the motives of the individual to group memberships and the values of the dominant system.

Like the labeling and social-learning theorists, Bonger saw crime as a set of behaviors that were within the normal range of human activities. These behaviors were distinguished only by the fact that they were labeled as illicit by authorities with the power to punish. Thus, the content of a society's criminal law was unique—there was no act that was inherently criminal.

Political authorities, said Bonger, assign criminal meaning to acts that they feel are harmful to society. Because the political authorities represent the bourgeoisie class, the content and enforcement of law is designed to serve them at the expense of the proletariat.[14] In particular, acts that are threatening to those who hold power are defined and treated as criminal. Also, the excessive competition that typifies modern capitalism means that such societies must be held together by force rather than consensus.

Like Bentham and the classical frame of reference, Bonger felt that human behavior was based on the search for pleasure. In a capitalist society, access to pleasure is not equally distributed. Rather, the more power possessed by an individual, the greater her or his ability to pursue and obtain pleasure. Money, of course, can easily be equated with the ability to obtain pleasure in capitalist societies, and its distribution summarizes the distinction between the classes.[15] These ideas directly parallel those of the strain perspective but substitute the idea of pleasure for success as the basic goal.

Bonger insisted that capitalism encourages egocentricity and pleasure seeking. Such tendencies are perversions of man's basically altruistic nature, according to Marx and his followers. Capitalism is seen as encouraging the

Exhibit 13.3

. . . .

Orthodox marxist theory of crime causation

Specific Assumptions

1. All societies are politically divided into ruling and subservient classes.

2. All people seek pleasure, but members of the ruling elite are more able to actually obtain it than are members of the subservient class.

3. No act is inherently criminal—crime is defined by social and political forces.

4. Poverty encourages crime by creating intense need while simultaneously weakening the individual's sentimental bonds to the culture's moral order.

5. The desire for success motivates some members of the elite to commit crime.

6. Personal pathologies are intensified by the values of the capitalist mode of production, and this can lead to increased criminality among the masses.

7. Crime will persist as a social problem until society provides for the needs of all of its citizens.

8. A socialist mode of production will reduce crime to the point where only a few deranged individuals are drawn to it.

Source: Willem Bonger, *Criminality and Economic Conditions,* abridged ed. (Bloomington, IN: Indiana University Press, 1969); Larry J. Siegel, *Criminology,* 2d ed. (St Paul, MN: West Publishing, 1986), pp. 272–273; J.M. van Bemmelen, "Willem Adrian Bonger" in Hermann Mannheim, *Pioneers in Criminology,* 2d ed. (Montclair, NJ: Patterson Smith, 1973), pp. 443–457.

development of criminal values in members of both classes. Thus, it is the moral environment of capitalism itself that encourages crime. While both classes are equally exposed to this moral environment, it is the proletariat that is most likely to be identified as criminal, since the bourgeoisie control the content and enforcement of the law. The self-serving activities of the bourgeoisie are protected by law while those of the proletariat are restricted or forbidden by the same authorities.[16]

Members of the bourgeoisie may commit crime to gain further power and pleasure. They may also be motivated to criminality by a lack of moral insight brought about by capitalism's emphasis on competition and self-centeredness. Proletarians may be motivated to crime either by outright need (e.g., stealing bread because one is hungry) or by a lack of sentimental attachment to others and to the general moral order (i.e., lack of social bonds). The idea that most crime is a result of proletarian poverty and alienation is thematic in Bonger's work.[17] The linkage of society's economic and political organization to the content of individuals' values is a classic example of Marxist materialism.

Bonger was especially influential in turning the attention of criminology from absolute to relative poverty in the explanation of crime. **Absolute poverty** refers to a condition in which a person lacks the resources required to maintain life—adequate amounts of food, clothing or shelter. **Relative poverty,** on the other hand, refers to the condition of having less than those around you. According to Bonger (as well as many non-Marxists) it is relative poverty, not absolute need, that is at the root of most criminal acts.[18] For example, crime is relatively rare in many rural areas of this country despite the fact that they are populated by sharecroppers and others with very meager resources. It is in the cities, where rich and poor live in close proximity to one another, that crime is most rampant. This is despite the fact that welfare and similar services are more readily available in urban areas. Bonger's emphasis on the unequal distribution of wealth and pleasure in a society is well-suited to explain these empirical anomalies.

Bonger also used aspects of positivism in his theory of criminality. He maintained that proletarians with psychological problems are especially prone to become criminal due to their disadvantaged situation. He inferred that the relative poverty these individuals endure can make minor psychological problems more extreme and thus cause criminal behavior in many persons. This is to say that the economic inequality that is the hallmark of a capitalist society makes preexisting personal problems worse and thereby contributes to both the crime rate and the level of human misery in the society.[19] Many psychiatrists believe that stress, which is at constantly high levels in the lower classes, acts as a trigger for many mental disorders.[20]

Bonger believed that a socialist mode of production would, in large part, solve the crime problem. In a socialist society wealth would be distributed on the basis of individual needs. That is, those with the greatest need would receive the most resources. He believed that such a system would eliminate relative poverty and equalize the power of the various groups that composed the society. It would also replace the legal approach to law creation and enforcement with the moral one that would not provide any particular subgroup with an advantage over the others. Under such a system, Bonger predicted, crime would only occur as a result of extreme psychological problems and would be relatively rare.[21]

Social Reality of Crime Theory

Richard Quinney is probably the most prominent of American Marxist criminologists. His theory of criminality (see Exhibit 13.4) combines the basic assumptions of orthodox Marxism with more conventional criminological theories, such as differential association, labeling, and strain. The fundamental assumption underlying his analysis is that crime exists in the judgments of others, not in the acts themselves. Like the more orthodox Marxists, Quinney presumes that definitions of what is criminal are created and used by the ruling class to control the masses. Other prominent neo-Marxists like William Chambliss and Gilbert Meier echo this belief.

In essence, these writers maintain that society is dominated by a small elite group. The interests of this elite form the basis of the legal code. The police powers of the state are thus consistently employed to maintain the status quo and protect the interests of the elite. Therefore, criminal sanctions are disproportionately applied to the poorer subgroups in society. Crime results from conflict between the two basic classes; its nature and form is a product of the dominant capitalist mode of production. Like Bonger, the neo-Marxists are hopeful that the socialist overthrow of capitalism will bring about a new form

Exhibit 13.4
· · · · · · · · · · · · · · · ·

Social reality of crime theory

Specific Assumptions

1. Crime is a definition of behavior that is assigned to certain acts by those with political power.

2. Acts that conflict with the interests of those powerful enough to create and enforce law are defined as criminal.

3. Which laws are enforced and under what conditions they are enforced is a result of the power of various societal segments to shape public policy.

4. Individual behavior is produced by the normative systems of various groups—therefore, one's position in the class structure predicts the likelihood of one's behavior being defined as criminal.

5. The idea of what constitutes crime is created and transmitted through normal forms of human communication.

6. The social reality of crime results from the formulation of legal definitions of behavior, their enforcement, the development of behavior patterns specific to social subgroups, and the creation of concepts as to what is criminal.

Source: Richard Quinney, "The Social Reality of Crime" in Jack D. Douglas, *Crime and Justice in American Society* (Indianapolis, IN: Bobbs-Merrill, 1971), pp. 119–146.

of economic organization in which crime will become a relatively rare event. Unlike Bonger, these theorists also take advantage of the insights of modern criminological theories and explicitly incorporate these views into a Marxist framework. This effort is most complete in Quinney's work, and we shall therefore concentrate attention there.

Quinney's theory of the social reality of crime borrows heavily from other sources that have already been outlined in this text. The first assumption in his theory is a definition of what constitutes crime—it is virtually the same as that used by labeling theorists such as Howard Becker.[22] This view of crime stresses the social and political symbolism of criminal law as a mechanism of group conflict in a society. The important point here is that all cultures divide behavior into approved and disapproved categories but there is often a lack of consensus across groups as to the category to which a particular behavior should be assigned.

The second proposition describes how such decisions are made in politically organized societies. It is also virtually identical to that found in the labeling perspective. The key concept here is power. Quinney maintains that the groups with the sociopolitical ability to shape public policy are in control of which acts are defined as criminal. Although he stresses the political aspect of group power in this context, it is inferred that political power is a result of economic power. Thus, Quinney's theory is united by a distinctly Marxist theme. It can also be inferred that the content and interpretation of criminal law changes as the power structure of society is altered.

Quinney's third proposition addresses the enforcement power of the same segments of society that create law. Groups within society that can enact laws that protect their status usually have the power to assure that these laws will be enforced. Without effective enforcement, law has no practical value and very little symbolic utility. Thus, laws from past eras may remain "on the books," but without enforcement they have no power to guide behavior. Laws against fornication and adultery are excellent examples of this situation.

The fourth proposition in this theory asserts that group membership predicts which individuals are most likely to be involved in behaviors that will be officially defined as criminal. Here the joint influence of the strain and social-learning perspectives can be discerned. Strain theory was developed to explain why the lower socioeconomic classes have disproportionately high crime rates. It does so without examining the political nature of the law creation and enforcement processes, however. Quinney links these two observations together in his theory. He posits that behavior is a result of the individual's group membership, which in turn is largely a product of socioeconomic status. Such group memberships also predict the degree to which the norms that the society supports through its legal system will correspond with those of the individual's reference group.

Quinney's fifth proposition is concerned with human perception and the individual's interpretation of the world. It is clearly drawn from the social-learning perspective. Quinney distinguishes between a physical reality that is independent of human activity and a **social reality** that is entirely the product of human efforts. He contends that law, crime, and related concepts are entirely within the social reality of human invention rather than a "natural" or physical fact that transcends human endeavors. This is important because people tend to take social reality for granted and often presume that it is beyond human control. Quinney is pointing out that anything created by humans can be changed by them as well. Therefore, since law and crime are social realities, we are free to change our definition of these ideas in ways that we believe will benefit our group and/or society.

The theory's final assumption is a summary statement of Quinney's view of the law creation and enforcement process. It ties the process of law creation and enforcement to the distribution of political and economic power across the various segments of society. It then links these factors to the notion that behavior is guided by subgroup norms.

Social reality is the world created, experienced, and believed in by a group; it is the sum total of their knowledge, experience, and ideas as they interpret and apply their insights to the world around them. Law, and therefore crime, is a human creation. As such it easily becomes the tool of those with the ability (i.e., power) to enforce it. As the law is consistently enforced, it seems to take on a life of its own that appears to be independent of the forces that created it.

When human creations come to be perceived as causal forces in their own right, it is said that **reification** has occurred. Reification refers to the belief that the human creation is actually a phenomenon independent of human actions and biases. This leads to false consciousness by creating the illusion that the law is always right and its violators are always wrong. Anyone who doubts the illusory quality of human creations such as the criminal law should examine what was defined as legal and proper behavior in the era of American slavery or under Hitler's nazi regime in 1930s and 1940s.

Based on the above theoretical formulation, Quinney suggests that there are two general types of crimes: crimes of domination and repression and crimes of accommodation and resistance. **Crimes of domination and repression** are generally considered to be those committed by the ruling class (i.e., capitalists, bourgeoisie) in order to remain in power and maintain their position of supremacy over the working class (i.e., proletariat). Included in this category are (1) crimes committed by the government and its agents of social control to maintain the status quo, (2) white-collar crime, (3) organized crime, and (4) crimes committed by businesses and industries, such as environmental pollution. These are the sorts of moral crimes with which Marxism has traditionally been concerned.

If the moral definition of crime is employed from a Marxist viewpoint, then the Vietnam War is an excellent example of a crime of domination and repression on several levels. First, this war consisted of the most powerful nation in the world attempting to control the organization of an impoverished culture. Therefore, at the macro level, the United States played the role of a bourgeoisie nation oppressing a proletarian one by attempting to impose a capitalist mode of production and values upon it. Second, it was commonly pointed out that those drafted to serve in the war were disproportionately from the lower class, while most middle- to upper-class youths were able to obtain draft deferments. Thus, the proletariat was victimized by the sacrifice of its sons while the elite profited from war industries. In addition, the war sparked much protest in this country and had the effect of diverting the proletariat's interest from class consciousness to debates about the "righteousness" of the war. That is, the war produced false consciousness in the proletariat.

Crimes of accommodation and resistance are usually considered those crimes committed by the working class in order to survive under capitalism. In this category are so-called street crimes (e.g., burglary, robbery), personal crimes (e.g., assault, rape, murder), and clandestine crimes against the ruling class (e.g., business and industry sabotage, civil disobedience, rioting).[23] Most street crimes identified under modern American penal codes are in this category.

········ **APPLICATION** ···· # The Case of Joe Gamsky and the Billionaire Boys Club

The Billionaire Boys Club (henceforth referred to as the BBC) was composed of a group of young men from Beverly Hills, California. All of them were from wealthy or influential families with the exception of Joe Gamsky, the group's founder and leader. And even Gamsky, although he had middle-class origins, had attended an exclusive preparatory school on a scholarship. The goal of the BBC was to acquire more wealth and power for its members. Within a few years, however, the BBC faced virtual bankruptcy. This financial pressure led Gamsky and other members to increasingly resort to overtly criminal acts. The BBC committed a string of crimes during the early 1980s that ranged from extortion to various forms of fraud and culminated in two murders that eventually exposed the rest of their activities. Our focus, however, is upon the activities of the BBC as a group of young members of the social and financial elite.

The *attracting factor* was that Joe Gamsky, also known as Joe Hunt, thought he had talked Ron Levin into investing $5 million with the BBC, which would have solved its financial problems. Ron Levin was an experienced con man who had formed dozens of companies to cheat investors out of their money. By the late 1970s, he had defrauded various people of enough money to move to Beverly Hills, California. Although not a violent criminal, he had served a short jail term as a result of one of his con games. He openly told people about his criminal record, and when asked what he did for a living, he told people he was a thief. In Beverly Hills, where the eccentric are more eagerly accepted than elsewhere, he was well known and popular.[24]

Levin, however, did not actually invest any money with Gamsky's BBC. He had pulled one of his con games on Gamsky. Without Gamsky's knowledge, Levin had talked a brokerage firm into establishing a dummy account with no money in it in Gamsky's name. Levin told the brokerage firm that it was part of a documentary he was doing on commodity trading. The brokerage firm was also told that Gamsky was not to know it was a dummy account. If he did not think the trading was real, he might not take it seriously enough. The brokerage firm went along with Levin's scheme and let Gamsky believe that he was using real money. Levin had agreed to give Gamsky half of the profits from his $5 million investment with the BBC. When Levin closed the dummy account, Gamsky's share of the profits from Levin's dummy account was more than $4 million. Gamsky vowed to get revenge when he found out that Levin's commodity account was a fake. Beginning in February of 1983, he discussed killing Levin with other BBC members.[25]

On June 6, 1984, Gamsky and Jim Pittman went to Levin's home and shot and killed him. Jim Pittman, also known as Jim Graham, had been hired to serve as the BBC's security director. Pittman was a twenty-eight-year-old small-time hoodlum who had fled to California from Virginia to avoid prosecution on a felony theft warrant. He worked as a security guard in California before he was hired by the BBC. With Pittman's help, Gamsky forced Levin to sign a check for $1½ million before they killed him. The Swiss bank on which the check was written refused to cash it for Gamsky, however.[26]

The attraction to solve the BBC's financial problems by criminal methods did not end with the death of Ron Levin. Gamsky and Pittman, now joined by three other BBC members—Dean Karny, Ben Dosti, and Reza Eslaminia—kidnapped and killed Reza Eslaminia's father, Hedayat Eslaminia. Karny and Dosti had met Gamsky while attending the same exclusive preparatory school with him. Karny was the son of a prominent Los Angeles real-estate developer and Dosti was the son of an influential Los Angeles food writer and critic.[27]

Reza Eslaminia was twenty-four years old at this time. His father was an opium abuser who battered both his wife and his children. Reza Eslaminia abused many drugs, including marijuana, cocaine, and LSD. He was arrested three times in 1980—once for possession of a dangerous weapon, once for drugs, and once for burglary. He had frequent and violent fights with his father. He had seen a psychologist who, under California legal requirements, wrote his father that he was in danger of loss of life and property at the hands of his son.[28]

On July 30, 1984, Gamsky, Pittman, Karny, Dosti, and Reza Eslaminia kidnapped Hedayat Eslaminia for the purpose of extorting money from him. Their plan was to abduct him, force him to sign his assets over to his son, and then kill him. Although he died during the kidnapping, they hid his body to keep his death a secret and forged his signature to have his assets turned over to his son. This forgery attempt also failed.[29]

Reza Eslaminia facing
murder chargers for the
slaying of his father.

The *precipitating factor* in these crimes was the fact that the BBC was on
the verge of bankruptcy. Joe Gamsky was its president and founder. Gamsky
had established the BBC in the winter of 1982 as a combination business
venture and social club. He developed what he called "Paradox Philosophy"
for the club, the idea that any means were justified in obtaining ones' goals.[30]
BBC members were quick to adopt this philosophy as their own. This philosophy reflects precisely those aspects of capitalism that Bonger felt created the
moral climate in which crime flourished. The intense desire for extreme wealth
and power that united the BBC was acquired through social learning that
reflects the values of capitalism. Quinney's linkage of group membership to
social learning is thus critical in explaining the predisposition to these crimes
that existed among the BBC's membership. As the paradox philosophy became
a social reality for BBC members, it became increasingly easy for them to
commit crimes.

The BBC members were young men who wanted to excel in life and make
a lot of money without starting at the bottom of the corporate ladder and
working their way up as is usually required. Gamsky's BBC business plan
presented these young men with a way to achieve their goals. They would
solicit investors for BBC business ventures and then they would run the businesses. Gamsky gave them corporate job titles and proclaimed them to be
business executives, which was exactly what they wanted. By 1983 the BBC
had over thirty members and the organization had raised several hundred
thousand dollars in capital.[31]

Gamsky was able to keep the BBC viable by pulling a confidence game on its investors whereby he took new investment money and used it to return large profits to initially small BBC investors so as to secure more capital from them. Gamsky was returning profits of this nature when in fact the BBC was losing large sums of money.[32] This is a fairly common method of defrauding business investors.

The primary and *predisposing factor* in this case was Gamsky's intense desire for extreme wealth. The BBC was spending up to $70,000 dollars a month on excessively expensive living with extravagant cars, dinners, and parties. Although Gamsky was born into a middle-class Chicago family in 1959, he was identified as a gifted child and received a scholarship to attend an elite preparatory academy for boys from extremely wealthy families. He began attending the preparatory academy in the seventh grade. While at the academy he became an excellent debater, but was caught cheating and was banished from the debate team.[34]

In his senior year at the academy, Gamsky took accounting courses at the University of California at Los Angeles. He claimed that he passed the California CPA exam at the age of nineteen, and that he was the youngest person ever to have passed it. After high school he attended the University of Southern California. While there, he became president of a social fraternity. Due to his obsession with his power as president of the fraternity, he was later asked to resign. After he resigned, he dropped out of the university.[35]

In 1981 Gamsky raised enough money to buy a seat on the Chicago Mercantile Exchange. He was suspended in 1982 for trading with other than his own money, which was illegal. He then returned to California, looked up his old friends from the academy, and founded the BBC. One of the BBC's early business ventures was a company called Westcars, which imported expensive foreign cars. However, Westcars could not sell the cars because they could not pass the California emission test. Gamsky sent Jim Pittman out to the emission testing facility to shoot up the place in the hope that this would scare the emission inspector into passing their cars. Their scare attempt failed.[36] This increased the financial pressure on Gamsky and the BBC that led to the murders of Levin and Eslaminia. Exhibit 13.5 summarizes the facts of this case.

Gamsky's BBC investment con game serves as a good example of Quinney's white-collar crimes of domination and repression. The BBC was able to commit this type of white-collar crime because of its bourgeoisie position. In many cases, the investors who were defrauded had trusted the BBC because of the

> **Deceptive Business Practice**
> The act of making false or misleading statements (misrepresentation) of fact involving the commodities exchanged (e.g., money, stocks, property) in business transactions.[33]

Level of Importance	Fact	Type of Fact
Primary	BBC on the verge of bankruptcy	Precipitating
Secondary	Levin's con game on Gamsky	Attracting
	Hedayat Eslaminia's wealth and bad relations with son	Attracting
Tertiary	Gamsky's intense desire for extreme wealth	Predisposing

Exhibit 13.5

Summary of facts and their role in the explanation of the Joe Gamsky case.

reputations of its members' families. According to the social reality of the investors, young men from such fine families could not possibly be involved in criminal activity.

Gamsky's personal pursuit of extreme wealth illustrates Bonger's concept of relative deprivation in the explanation of crime. Since seventh grade, Gamsky had seen himself as his having less than those around him, and thus felt relatively deprived. In addition, Gamsky, Karny, and Dosti's criminal behavior epitomizes Bonger's insistence that capitalism encourages egocentricity and pleasure seeking while perverting man's altruistic nature. These men committed crimes to gain power and pleasure. They were motivated to criminality by a lack of moral insight that was brought about by the emphasis on competition and self-centeredness that is characteristic of capitalist elites. Gamsky, Karny, and Dosti all developed criminal values and used the "paradox philosophy" to justify them in the context of their BBC membership. Because this philosophy dominated the BBC, it quickly became their social reality. Their moral values were, in large part, perverted as a result of their attempts to have the BBC succeed in a competitive economic environment.

Marxian Paradigm of Crime and Criminal Law

Chambliss' model of crime and criminal law (see Exhibit 13.6) was created to explain the fact that the nature and rate of crime varies in different countries. Chambliss asserts that these variations are due to the differences in their modes of economic production. He proposes that the various modes of production are all variations of two basic types—privately owned (capitalist) ones and publicly owned (socialist) ones. He sees the development of social classes as inevitable in societies where the modes of production are privately owned. He then states that the ruling classes in these societies create the notion of crime as a result of the contradictions that are inherent in the social structure that evolves from them,[37] and he gives the United States as an example. Societies with publicly owned modes of production should anticipate much less crime than capitalistic ones, according to this theory. Crime in these societies will at first result from the residual influences of capitalist values, and later from internal pathologies such as brain tumors as socialist values come to predominate.

According to Chambliss there are two contradictions in the structure of capitalism that create a need for crime. The first contradiction is that a capitalist system needs a large working class market to consume its products. At the same time, however, the society needs to keep a portion of its work force in poverty so that the proletariat will be motivated to work by the threat of falling into poverty if they don't. People thus accept jobs and/or wages that they would ordinarily refuse. Such poverty, however, reduces the spending power of the market on which capitalism is dependent for profits. Second, he points out that a capitalist system divides a society into a ruling class and a working class in such a way that conflict between these two classes is inevitable even though it disrupts the flow of goods and services.[38] In short, the first contradiction is that capitalism creates the desire to consume but fails to provide adequate legitimate means for this consumption on the part of most people. The second contradiction is that the social classes created by capitalism are doomed to be in conflict with each other even though such strife undermines

Exhibit 13.6

• • • • • • • • • • • • • • • • •

Marxian paradigm of crime and criminal law

Specific Assumptions

1. The ruling class defines certain acts as criminal because it is in their best interests to do so.

2. The proletariat is often punished for violating laws, but the ruling class is only rarely punished for similar acts.

3. In capitalist societies, criminal law continually expands its coverage so as to pressure the proletariat into submission.

4. Crime creates employment in the criminal justice system, and in the ancillary systems supporting it, which helps to reduce society's surplus labor pool.

5. Crime distracts members of the proletariat from their exploitation and focuses their attention on divisions among themselves rather than on their oppression by the ruling class.

6. The notion of crime exists as a reality only because it serves the interests of those who created it.

7. Criminal and noncriminal behavior represent rational acts consistent with social class. Crime is thus a response to social-class life circumstances.

8. The nature of crime varies among societies according to their political and economic structures.

9. Socialist societies should have less crime because they have less severe class struggles.

Source: William J. Chambliss, "Toward a Political Economy of Crime," *Theory and Society* 2, no. 2 (Summer 1975): pp. 152–153.

the efficiency of economic production. The more conflict between the classes, the greater the number of acts that will be defined as criminal in the society.[39]

Creating the idea of crime is thus a method of maintaining false consciousness among the proletariat in order to prevent the development of class consciousness, which could result in the overthrow of the elite. Furthermore, by creating and maintaining poverty, the bourgeoisie assures itself a large pool of easily obtained and relatively cheap labor. Attempts to escape this poverty by proletarians are often defined as criminal so that the bourgeoisie can remain as a powerful, but small and exclusive, elite. The same values that motivate the capitalist to maximize profits are thought to encourage criminality in the proletariat.

The Case of Mary "Lee" Orsini • • • • • • • • • • • • •   APPLICATION • • • • • • • •

Mary "Lee" Orsini arranged for Eugene James "Yankee" Hall and Larry Darnell McClendon to shoot Alice McArthur, age forty-one, to death in McArthur's own home in Little Rock, Arkansas, on July 2, 1982. Eugene Hall was a heavy substance abuser who sold illegal drugs for a living. Hall saw himself as a lady's man, and Orsini was his latest girlfriend. McClendon, age twenty-seven, was a long-time friend of Hall's and they had been in jail together several times. Hall did not tell McClendon about Orsini's role in the murder. He simply told McClendon that McClendon's share for the murder-for-hire killing would be $6,000.[40]

Orsini convinced Hall to help her kill McArthur by lying to him. She told Hall that by killing McArthur they could make easy money with which they could go into the cocaine business. She told him that McArthur's husband, William Charles McArthur, would pay $30,000 to have his wife killed, which simply was not true. Orsini told him that William McArthur wanted his wife murdered because she was threatening to leave him and destroy his law practice.[41]

Several weeks prior to Hall and McClendon killing Alice McArthur, Orsini and Hall had made an attempt on her life. They planted a bomb in her car, but she escaped the explosion with only a very minor injury to one leg. The police thought this attempt on her life was related to a nightclub her husband owned. Like the police, both McArthur and her husband also thought that he was the intended victim of this bombing.[43]

The *precipitating factor* in this case was Orsini's delinquent $30,000 bank note. In 1981 the bank foreclosed on Orsini's mother's home because Orsini had used it as collateral to finance the purchase of her own home. This factor was of secondary importance, however. The *predisposing* and primary factor in this case was Orsini's intense desire for upper-middle-class status. She longed to be accepted in the part of society that is made up of professionals and their families. She wanted to shop in the finest stores, be seen in the best places, and live in a home in the most privileged of local neighborhoods. Using the name "Lee" instead of Mary was her first move toward attaining this lifestyle.[44]

Orsini's maiden name was Mary Myrtle Hatcher. She was born August 17, 1947, in Searcy, Arkansas to an alcoholic cattleman from Houston, Texas, and his wife. When under the influence of alcohol, her father would threaten her, as well as her mother and sister, with a shotgun, causing the three of them to run out of their home and not return until they were positive he was sound asleep. Henry Hatcher died of cancer at the age of fifty-two, when Mary was three years old.[45]

Although the Hatcher family lived in a large house and owned land, they were poor. Mary's mother worked as a schoolbus driver and in the school cafeteria. Although Mrs. Hatcher did not verbalize her feelings toward her husband in front of the children, they could sense her hostility toward him. They were also under the impression from their mother that he had killed a man in Texas.[46]

Mary dropped out of school at the age of sixteen. In 1963 she married Douglas Sudbury, a twenty-year-old airman stationed at the Little Rock Air Force Base. They were soon divorced, but remarried in 1966. A year later, she divorced Sudbury for the second time. In 1971 she married David Raymond but left him after six months.[47]

In 1976, at the age of twenty-nine, she married Ronald Gary Orsini, age thirty-four. Ronald Orsini worked hard in a heating and air conditioning business in which he held a 25 percent interest. Five years later, in 1981, he was found shot to death in his bed. With her husband dead, the *attracting factor* in Mary "Lee" Orsini's subsequent crime was her attraction to her

---

Possession and/or Transport of a Destructive Device
An illegal act under sections 921–922 of the United States penal code unless the person is duly licensed by the Department of the Treasury. The term *destructive devices* refers to bombs, grenades, rockets with more than four ounces of propellant charge, a mine, or any similar device.[42]

Mary "Lee" Orsini, after being convicted of murdering her husband.

Exhibit 13.7
. . . .

Summary of facts and their role
in the explanation of the Mary
"Lee" Orsini case

Level of Importance	Fact	Type of Fact
Primary	Orsini's pursuit of an upper-middle-class lifestyle	Predisposing
Secondary	Orsini's delinquent bank note	Precipitating
Tertiary	Orsini's attraction to William McArthur	Attracting

attorney, William McArthur. She had hired him to assist her in dealing with the police investigation of her husband's death in which she was a suspect.

William McArthur, a fairly well-to-do attorney, appeared to be the type of man who could provide the lifestyle that "Lee" had always wanted. She believed that Alice McArthur stood in her way, so she arranged to have her murdered.[48] Exhibit 13.7 summarizes the facts in this case.

Orsini was found guilty of capital murder for her involvement in the death of Alice McArthur and was sentenced to life in prison without possibility of parole. She was also convicted of the slaying of her husband, Ronald Orsini, and received a second sentence to life in prison without parole. This gave her two life sentences in the Arkansas Department of Corrections.[49]

In return for a plea bargain agreement, Eugene "Yankee" Hall implicated Orsini in McArthur's murder and received a life sentence without the possibility of parole. Larry McClendon received a twenty-year prison sentence for his role in the slaying of McArthur. Since he was on parole at the time of the McArthur murder, this sentence was added to his existing one, which gave him a total sentence of over fifty-one years.[50]

Orsini's desire to live in the style of the bourgeoisie elite is an excellent example of the internal contradictions of capitalist values pointed out by Chambliss' theory. For most people, the desire to consume far outstrips the available means for consumption. The societal value system had clearly created the desire in Orsini to consume, but failed to provide her with adequate means to do so.

The second contradiction pointed out by Chambliss, that the social classes created by capitalism are doomed to conflict with each other, is illustrated by the bank's foreclosure on Orsini's home. As a member of the working class, Orsini was in conflict with members of the ruling class, her bankers. There was no other realistic source of loan money for her that would have allowed her to avoid indebtedness to the bourgeoisie. Further, banks are aware that notes of such a size frequently cannot be repaid. This allows them to repossess and resell the property involved. Thus, the bourgeoisie bankers can accumulate further profits even though the stated purpose of such loans is to assist home buyers.

Finally, and perhaps most importantly, Orsini's criminal behavior appears to have been a response to the circumstances in which she found herself. Because life circumstances are heavily influenced by one's social class, her acts can be interpreted as rational and consistent with her social class, given the capitalist valuation of material wealth. From a Marxist perspective, Orsini's natural drives to altruism and constructive labor were distorted by the dominant social values of capitalist society. Chambliss's theory would say that capitalist values distracted her from consciousness of her oppression by the economic system in general and the bankers in particular. This distraction led her into crime rather than into rebellion against the system—the result of false consciousness, according to the Marxist perspective.

Conclusion

Marxist theories are fundamentally concerned with **political economy**, or the manner in which the economic system of production is related to the political system that controls decision-making structures at the societal level. Crime is not often a major concern to these thinkers because they see it as a merely a symptom of capitalism's inequalities. Their perspective, however, is most useful in understanding (1) the law creation and enforcement processes, (2) the role of social inequalities in producing crime, and (3) the role of capitalism's value system in producing crime.

Marx was primarily concerned with the development of societies and the internal structure of their institutions. For this reason, he focused on the nature and content of history. His reasoning was based on a form of logic distinct from that of most non-Marxist social scientists, who use either inductive or deductive reasoning to develop theories and apply them to criminological facts.

Inductive reasoning begins with an examination of the available, pertinent facts, seeks common themes among them, and then produces a series of propositions that accurately summarize and explain them. This form of logic is the type advocated by the positivist school of criminological thought. **Deductive reasoning** is the opposite. It begins with a set of propositions that make sense intuitively and are logically congruent with one another. Once a set of logical propositions is assembled, the deductive thinker then tests their applicability to the real world. This is the form of logic that dominated the work of the classical school. It is also used in creating and interpreting law.

Marx used **dialectical reasoning** (involving theses, antitheses, and syntheses) to argue that history was a progression of social forms in which there was no repetition even though elements of the past were constantly found in the present and appeared to influence the future. A Marxian-informed theory of crime is important to criminology because it stresses the fact that actions (i.e., **theses**) encounter responses (i.e., **antitheses**) and some form of compromise (i.e., **syntheses**) is eventually reached. This compromise, or synthesis, is a new social form that includes elements of the original one (thesis) as well as ideas from its opponents (antithesis).

Law is one aspect of social organization, and dialectical reasoning is very applicable to its development. For this reason most dialectical analyses in criminology focus on relationships between law, the state, and the social classes or interest groups that represent them. For example, sexual battery statutes were necessary because older versions of the law defined rape as a property crime (thesis). As social attitudes toward women's rights to control their bodies and destinies became predominant through the activities of the women's movement (antithesis), the older view of rape came to be offensive to many citizens. The new laws improved on the old by offering greater protection to potential victims of sexual assault. It recognized the new respect for the individual in general and women in particular, while simultaneously keeping the older view of rape as distinct from other forms of violent crime (synthesis).

A Marxian-informed theory of crime is also important to criminology because it forces us to examine our own social ideology and how that ideology was formed. Marx proposed that because our ideologies are grounded in our material existence and the method by which we produce it, everyone is vulnerable to false consciousness. This is as true for macro-level institutions like the criminal justice system as it is for individuals. An example of false consciousness is *sentencing disparity*—that is, the wide range of sentences that offenders, who are similar in all other ways, often receive from the courts. For example, one offender may get five years while another gets ten even though they committed very similar offenses and have very similar social backgrounds and criminal histories. Such disparity in sentences cannot be rationally justified. It is problematic for correctional facilities because it often creates unrest in our prisons due to the fact that some offenders feel victimized. It also creates problems for the parole boards that must even out such disparities. Even though the practice causes problems throughout the system, it has been tolerated for many years. This illustrates the practical consequences of false consciousness in terms of macro-level institutions. At the individual level, false consciousness is present, for example, among inmates who form racially biased gangs rather than uniting with all other inmates to protest their common plight.

Multiple forms of Marxist thought are in use today. We have concentrated our attention on what is known as **structural Marxism** because it is the oldest version of the perspective and the easiest to explain. This form of Marxism is based primarily on Marx's allusions to economic determinism. **Critical Marxism** is a much newer variety of Marxist thought that is primarily based on the dialectic. There are many subvarieties of these forms of Marxism as well as other, less well known forms.

Critical Marxism does not accept the idea of determinism as such and is suspicious of all the social phenomena that have evolved under capitalism. A social science like criminology is but one such social phenomenon. This form of Marxism focuses on the use (and abuse) of power in society. It stresses the mental health needs of the individual and the ways in which society forces people into artificial categories for the sake of bureaucratic convenience. Crime is one such set of categories.

Critical Marxism is useful to criminology because it points out the validity problems of scientific classification schemes and typologies as it questions the way in which much aggregate research is performed. It is especially concerned with the tendency of social scientists to reify the dominant form of social organization in their society. In other words, many critical Marxists do not trust standard scientific procedures because they were developed largely within social superstructures based on capitalist values. Critical Marxists stress the unique needs of the individual and the way in which macro-level structures often work to frustrate these needs. Such analyses inform criminology of its own logical and methodological weakness. Critical analyses also provide valuable suggestions on how we can help reduce crime by changing macro- and meso-level structures to better serve human needs.

More generally, the Marxist perspective is valuable because it highlights the **latent functions**, or unintended but significant results, of capitalist social organization. There is widespread agreement among social scientists that many beneficial and well-intended policies and plans have unanticipated results that create problems. Capitalism is an example. While most Americans would argue that capitalism has brought our nation many advantages and has been beneficial to many individuals, this does not mean that it is perfect or cannot create problems at the same time. Thus, at the very least, the areas of agreement between the strain and Marxist perspectives are extremely noteworthy to criminology. Both perspectives stress the inability of certain segments of society to meet the goals that they have defined as worthy. Such definitions originate in the values promoted by social institutions. Marxism is especially effective in linking macro forms of organization to the individual situations that lead to criminality.

Glossary ·

Absolute Poverty   Condition of lacking the resources required to maintain life—that is, adequate amounts of food, clothing, or shelter.

Alienation   Sociological term for a condition typified by sentiments of powerlessness and meaninglessness that lead to self-estrangement.

Antithesis   Marx's term for a new ideology or version of social organization that arises in opposition to an older, more established one.

Bourgeoisie   The ruling class of people who control the mode of production in their society. In particular, the term refers to the capitalist class of persons who own the property that is used in the production and/or distribution of goods and services. Marx felt that this elite class exploited the masses for its own benefit.

Class Consciousness   Entails both the recognition that the proletariat constitutes a single class and the growth of loyalty to, and identification with, that class, despite other divisions within this large group.

Crimes of Domination and Repression   Acts committed by the ruling class (i.e., capitalists, bourgeoisie) in order to remain in power and maintain a position of supremacy over the working class (i.e., proletariat). Examples are crimes committed by the government and its agents of social control to maintain the status quo, white-collar crime, organized crime, and crimes committed by businesses and industries, such as environmental pollution.

Crimes of Accommodation and Resistance   Acts committed by the working class in order to survive under capitalism. Examples are street crimes (e.g., burglary, robbery), personal crimes (e.g., assault, rape, murder), and clandestine crimes against the ruling class (e.g., business and industry sabotage, civil disobedience, rioting).

Critical Marxism   A subtype of the Marxist perspective that stresses the dialectical nature of human and social development. It focuses attention on the unique nature and needs of individuals and points out the shortcomings of social structures in meeting those basic human needs.

Deductive Reasoning   Opposite of inductive reasoning. Begins with a set of propositions that make sense intuitively and are logically compatible with one another. These are tested for applicability to the real world. This is the form of logic that dominated the work of the classical school. It is also used in creating and interpreting law.

Dialectical Reasoning   A form of logic used by Marxists. It maintains that as a *thesis* encounters its opposite, or *antithesis*, the result is a *synthesis* of the two, which is composed of elements of both the thesis and the antithesis but is in itself a new social form. Thus, new social forms contain elements of earlier ones but evolve as unique entities.

Economic Determinism   The belief that people's view of the world and their social behavior are a result of their position in the economic system.

False Consciousness   The acceptance of an ideology or belief that runs counter to one's actual interests. Any subjective view of one's situation that is in contradiction with the objective facts is a source of false consciousness.

Inductive Reasoning   Begins with an examination of the available, pertinent facts, seeks common themes among them, and then produces a series of propositions that accurately summarize and explain them. This form of logic is the type advocated by the positivist school of criminological thought.

Latent Functions   The unintended but nonetheless significant results of a social policy or mode of organization.

Mode of Production   The manner in which the production of goods and services is organized (e.g., capitalism, feudalism).

Political Economy   The manner in which the economic system of production is related to the political system that controls decision-making structures at the societal level.

Proletariat   The masses of relatively impoverished workers who are under the control of the ruling class in a capitalist society. They produce goods and services but are prevented from controlling the fruits of their labor.

Reification   Occurs when human creations come to be perceived as causal forces in their own right; the belief that a human creation is actually a phenomenon independent of human actions and biases.

Relative Poverty   Condition of having less than those around you and being uncomfortably aware of this fact.

Social Reality   The world created, experienced, and believed in by a group; it is a human creation that is often perceived as beyond human control.

Structural Marxism   Subtype of the Marxist perspective that focuses attention on the deterministic influences of political-economic organization on group welfare and activities.

Superstructure   Marxist term for the patterned way in which institutions interact with one another. It is ultimately determined by the mode of production. This is the form of society that is actually perceived by individuals on a daily basis.

Synthesis Marx's term for the combination of a thesis and antithesis. While it contains elements of both, it is actually an entirely new form of organization.

Thesis Marx's term for the ideological and organizational logic used to bring order to a society. It is associated with the older, more established, and powerful elements of the society.

■ Notes

1. C. Wright Mills, *The Marxists* (New York: Dell Publishing, 1962), pp. 41–43.
2. Karl Marx, "Class Conflict and Law" in Joseph E. Jacoby (ed.) *Classics of Criminology* (Prospect Heights, IL: Waveland Press, 1979), p. 69; William Chambliss and Robert B. Seidman, Law, Order and Power—2nd Ed. (Reading, MA: Addison-Wesley, 1982), pp. 202–203.
3. Mills, *The Marxists*, pp. 32–33, 49–58.
4. James M. Inverarity, Pat Lauderdale, and Barry C. Feld, *Law and Society* (Boston: Little, Brown and Co., 1983), pp. 68–88.
5. Mills, *The Marxists*, pp. 32–33, 39.
6. Richard Quinney, *Criminal Justice in America* (Boston: Little, Brown and Co., 1974), pp. 16–17.
7. Thomas Bernard, "The Distinction between Conflict and Radical Criminology," *Journal of Criminal Law and Criminology* 72, no. 1 (1981): pp. 366–370.
8. Karl Marx and Friedreich Engels, *The Communist Manifesto*, edited by Samuel Beer (New York: Appleton-Century-Crofts, 1955); Marx, *Capital*. See also Melvin L. DeFleur, William D'Antonio, and Lois DeFleur-Nelson, *Sociology: Human Society* (Glenview, IL: Scott, Foresman & Co., 1977), pp. 210–215.
9. Karl Marx, "Class Conflict and Law" in Joseph E. Jacoby *Classics of Criminology* (Prospect Heights, IL: Waveland Press, 1979), p. 73.
10. DeFleur, D'Antonio, and DeFleur-Nelson, *Sociology: Human Society*, pp. 7–8; Ian Robertson, *Social Problems*, 2d ed. (New York: Random House, 1980) p. 193.
11. Mills, *The Marxists*, pp. 25–26.
12. Marx, "Class Conflict and Law," pp. 73–74.
13. Willem Bonger, *Criminology and Economic Conditions* (Boston: Little, Brown & Co., 1916).
14. Ibid.
15. Ibid.
16. Ibid.
17. Ibid.
18. Ibid.
19. Ibid.
20. Robert C. Carson, James N. Butcher, and James C. Coleman, *Abnormal Psychology and Modern Life* (Glenview, IL: Scott Foresman and Co., 1988), pp. 504–505; "Schizophrenia and the Brain," *Harvard Medical School Mental Health Letter* 4, no. 12 (June 1988): pp. 1–3.

21. Bonger, *Criminality and Economic Conditions*; Larry J. Siegel, *Criminology*, pp. 272–273; Van Bemmelen, "Willem Adrian Bonger," pp. 443–457.
22. Howard Becker, *Outsiders: Studies in the Sociology of Deviance* (The Free Press of Glencoe, 1963), pp. 7–9.
23. Richard Quinney, *Class, State, and Crime* (New York: McKay, 1977).
24. Sue Horton, *The Billionaire Boys Club* (New York; St. Martin's Press, 1989).
25. Ibid.
26. Ibid.
27. Ibid.
28. Ibid.
29. Ibid.
30. Ibid.
31. Ibid.
32. Horton, *The Billionaire Boys Club*.
33. *Texas Penal Code*, 8th ed. (St. Paul, MN: West Publishing, 1990), pp. 61–62; Rush, *The Dictionary of Criminal Justice*, p. 154.
34. Ibid.
35. Ibid.
36. Ibid.
37. Ibid, pp. 149–150.
38. Ibid, pp. 150–151.
39. Ibid.
40. Jan Meins, *Murder in Little Rock* (New York: St. Martin's Press, 1987).
41. Ibid.
42. *Federal Criminal Code and Rules* (St. Paul, MN: West Publishing, 1989), sections 921–923, pp. 493–507.
43. Meins, *Murder in Little Rock*.
44. Ibid
45. Ibid
46. Ibid
47. Ibid
48. Ibid
49. Ibid
50. Ibid

■ Suggested Readings

Howard Becker, *Outsiders: Studies in the Sociology of Deviance* (The Free Press of Glencoe, 1963), pp. 7–9.

Thomas Bernard, "The Distinction between Conflict and Radical Criminology," *Journal of Criminal Law and Criminology* 72, no. 1 (1981).

James M. Inverarity, Pat Lauderdale, and Barry C. Feld, *Law and Society* (Boston: Little, Brown and Co., 1983).

Richard Quinney, *Criminal Justice in America* (Boston: Little, Brown and Co., 1974).

Richard Quinney, "The Social Reality of Crime" in Jack D. Douglas, *Crime and Justice in American Society* (Indianapolis, IN: Bobbs-Merrill, 1971).

Jeffrey H. Reiman, *The Rich Get Richer and the Poor Get Prison*, 2d ed. (New York: John Wiley & Sons, 1984).

■ Suggested Books for Additional Application

Joe Barboza with Hank Messick, *Barboza* (New York: Dell Publishing, 1975).

Carl Bernstein and Bob Woodward, *All the President's Men* (New York: Simon & Schuster, 1974).

Fenton Bresler, *Who Killed John Lennon* (New York: St. Martin Press, 1989).

Martin A. Gosch and Richard Hammer, *The Last Testament of Lucky Luciano* (New York: Dell Publishing, 1974).

Robert Lindsey, *The Falcon and the Snowman* (New York: Pocket Books, 1980).

Peter Maas, *The Valachi Papers* (New York: Bantam Books, 1968).

Nicholas Pileggi, *Wise Guy: Life in a Mafia Family* (New York: Pocket Books, 1985).

Barry Sussman, *The Great Coverup: Nixon and the Scandal of Watergate* (New York: Crowell Publishers, 1974).

Peter Tompkins, *The Murder of Admiral Darlan* (New York: Simon & Schuster, 1965).

CHAPTER **14**

Conflict Perspective

Overview of Conflict Perspective

The idea that the essence of society is conflict and change is very old. It is found in the works of ancient Chinese, Greek, and Arabic philosophers as well as in Machiavelli's writings, which had great influence on European thought. Ibn Khaldun, an Arab from what is now Tunisia, is often credited with being the first conflict theorist.[1] Thomas Hobbes was probably the first to articulate these ideas to the English-speaking world. Hobbes' view of human nature was not flattering and is quite the opposite of that taken by Marx. It is however, similar to the view of Freud, Bentham, and the control theorists.

Hobbes believed that humans have an instinctive desire for power that results in a state of perpetual warfare until brought under control by governments. He saw humans as basically rational but amoral. Because of their rationality, they construct social systems that will reduce violence and conflict to a minimum. Thus, the concepts of morality and justice are used by governments as devices to help control the natural human inclination to fight for status and resources. The idea of proper behavior, therefore, is entirely dependent on the dictates of those who hold power, and the uniformities in the law that are found across most cultures exist because of their roots in rationality. Hobbes declared that as long as a government is able to protect its citizens from one another and from outsiders, it is owed respect and obedience, but if it becomes unable to provide such protection, it is deemed of no value and is owed nothing.[2]

Bear in mind that the conflict perspective (see Exhibit 14.1) is not identical in all respects with Hobbes' views; however, it does contain his concept of a **relative morality** that assumes crime is a matter of definition. This perspective therefore assumes that only some rule–violators are caught and labeled, and that criminology must focus on the processes of law creation and enforcement as much as it does upon the traits associated with criminality.[3] In this sense it is closely related to the labeling perspective. It stands in diametric opposition to the strain and social-disorganization perspectives, which presume that there is widespread consensus within society as to the nature of crime and claim that such a consensus is necessary for the stabilizing effect it has on society.

Exhibit 14.1

Conflict perspective

Common Assumptions

1. Society is composed of multiple, overlapping groups with differing interests, values and norms.

2. These groups are, to some extent, in competition with one another for scarce resources.

3. This competition often results in conflicts between groups.

4. Intergroup conflict is normal and widespread.

5. Social change and progress are often the result of resolving conflicts between groups.

Source: Melvin L. DeFleur, "Introduction" in Melvin L. DeFleur (ed.) *Social Problems in American Society* (Boston: Houghton-Mifflin, 1983), p. 18.

Modern conflict theorists believe that instead of consensus, there is continuing conflict among the various groups of society and that social change brought about by the resolution of such conflicts is what benefits society and keeps it healthy. In this way the conflict theorists are much more optimistic than Hobbes.

The strain and disorganization perspectives emphasize the similarity of the groups that make up a society while the conflict perspective stresses their differences. Criminologically, however, this is less of a contradiction than it may at first appear. Most social scientists see these two major views of the nature of society (i.e., consensus versus conflict) as opposite sides of the same coin. That is, both consensus and conflict are present in society; both stability and change have many potential benefits; and both views add to our comprehension of crime and its causes.

Perspectives stressing consensus within society tend to focus their attention on acts that are fairly universally defined as crime (e.g., murder, robbery, rape). These sorts of acts are referred to as **mala en se**, or bad in themselves. They are obviously injurious to society or its members. Most predatory street crimes are in this category. On the other hand, the conflict perspective emphasizes acts that only some groups define as illicit (e.g., white-collar crime, drugs, prostitution, gambling). These sorts of acts are referred to as **mala prohibita**, or bad because they are defined as such.[4]

The conflict perspective shares this emphasis with the Marxists. In addition, both conflict and Marxist theorists take a macro-level view of crime. Rather than being concerned with the behaviors and motives of individuals, their attention is primarily focused on the relationships between the groups that compose society. For this reason, both the conflict and Marxist perspectives focus on the distribution and use of power in society and, consequently, are primarily interested in the processes of law creation, interpretation, and enforcement.

However, as mentioned before, the conflict theorists have a different view of human nature than the Marxists; they see humans as basically amoral. Furthermore, the conflict perspective's view of society, law, and crime differs from that of the Marxists in two major ways. First, whereas Marxists assume that society is made up of two basic groups based on the ownership of the mode of production, the conflict perspective recognizes a multitude of groups to which individuals simultaneously belong.[5] For example, some conflict theories have focused on religious affiliation while others have concerned themselves with three or more socioeconomic classes.

The conflict perspective also differs from that of the Marxists in its view of the relationship between morality and crime. While Marxists believe in the existence of a single, absolute moral code that stresses equality and the fulfillment of human needs, the conflict perspective views morality as a relative phenomenon that results from the situation of the group in society. That is, Marxists presume that there are certain norms that define right and wrong under virtually all circumstances (i.e., the "moral" view of crime discussed in Chapter 13).[6] They are thus able to contrast "moral crimes" with crimes recognized by the society's legal code. Conflict theorists, on the other hand, define the notion of crime simply as a creation of government power. It is an inherently political phenomenon to them that is always subject to redefinition by those in power.

Marxism can thus be said to employ an **absolute morality**. All absolute moralities presume that certain acts are always undesirable and harmful.[7] Conservative ones further presume that rule-violators are inherently different from the law-abiding and that criminology should restrict itself to discovering the nature of the pathology within the rule-violator. Marxists and liberals prefer to focus on the inadequacies and biases of the structure of the social organization from which law emanates.

The conflict perspective, on the other hand, views morality as a result of the unique set of overlapping group memberships that define each individual's position in society. Each group has its own interests and problems. Therefore morality is relative to one's group memberships. These groups form along a wide variety of dimensions. Ethnic, religious, and occupational groupings are easily recognized but many issues have the effect of uniting people along ideological lines that cross such boundaries as well. At any given time, certain of these memberships will be of greater importance to the individual than will others. The more threatening an issue is to group members, the more likely they are to be aware of their membership in the group.[8]

There are some things (good jobs and housing, for example) that are not easily available to all members of a society. This problem was the primary theme of the strain perspective. When many people desire something that only a few can actually have, the result is intense competition and, very often, conflict. Society establishes the formal rules for this competition through its government authorities. However, not all of the involved groups are likely to agree that these formal rules are fair and appropriate. Members of some groups are likely to compete in the manner they find to be most advantageous to them and in doing so may violate the prescriptions of the legal authorities.

Strikers burn their contracts. The conflict perspective sees the ongoing conflict between groups with opposing desires as basic and essential to modern society.

Unlike the strain and disorganization perspectives, which encourage the maintenance of social stability, the conflict perspective is not troubled by the presence of dissent and social change.[9] While the Marxists believe that conflict is a means to an end—a utopian social order—the conflict perspective perceives the ongoing battle of groups as the very fabric of a modern, democratic society. This perspective presumes that the process of dissension and conflict resolution encourages a society to change and progress. Thus, despite the fact that some individuals may suffer as a result of intergroup strife, the society ultimately benefits from its continuance. Please recall that this perspective's focus is on the society, not the individual.

Law Approach

Ralf Dahrendorf attempted to modernize Marx's view of social organization by recognizing that certain divisions within the working class were natural and inevitable. While some writers classify him as a Marxist, we have placed him within the conflict perspective because his division of the proletariat into subgroups is independent of the society's mode of production. He also uses a relative view of morality that is more typical of the conflict perspective than of the Marxists.

Dahrendorf's law approach to crime (see Exhibit 14.2) is typical of those referred to as **radical** because of its fundamental and intensive scrutiny of the most basic aspects of social organization. These are precisely the aspects of society that most people take for granted in their daily lives. Any theoretical

Exhibit 14.2

Law approach

Restrictive Assumptions

1. Levels of skill in the workplace translate into levels of socioeconomic power in society.

2. These levels of skill and power represent meaningful divisions within the proletariat that will not be altered by any sort of change in mode of production.

3. Coercive power is based on the group's status and ability to control resources and is found in all societies. It is especially important in the processes of law creation and enforcement.

4. Dissent, conflict, and change are natural processes for all societies at all points in time.

5. All of the subgroups of a society are involved in its conflicts and changes—law reflects the relative power of various groups at a particular point in time and space.

6. Society is held together by the legal coercion of some citizens and groups by others.

7. Progress towards greater efficiency and equality is often the final outcome of conflicts within a society.

Source: Ralf Dahrendorf, *Class and Class Conflict in Industrial Society* (Stanford, CT: Stanford University Press, 1959).

view that emphasizes the political nature of crime and the law while focusing on the repressive aspects of law creation and enforcement is termed radical by modern criminologists.[10] Most Marxists, and many modern conflict theorists, are considered to be radical criminologists.

Rather than asking how and why the criminal is different from the law-abiding citizen, radicals focus on the role of power in creating and enforcing the law. In the tradition of relative morality, they often make no presumptions as to the ultimate meaning of ideas like right, wrong, and justice. Instead they focus attention on the actual predictors of the routine operation of the criminal justice system. In the opinion of the authors of this text, thoughtful consideration of the contradictions between these observations and one's own ideas of what law and justice should entail can lead to significant improvements in the existing system of social control.

According to Dahrendorf, the crucial divisions in the proletariat are those resulting from differences in occupational skill and status. These differences are direct predictors of group power. Law is created by the more powerful groups in society and reflects their interests. The more skilled, and thus more powerful, segments of the proletariat are allowed just enough input into the law creation process to assure their loyalty to the status quo. Orthodox Marxism would, of course, consider such loyalty to be a symptom of false consciousness. Dahrendorf, however, sees the outcome of the process as beneficial to the entire society since it assures progressive change while simultaneously maintaining social stability. This balance between change and stability is referred to as a **fluid equilibrium** and is a major theme in Dahrendorf's work.[11]

The coercive use of power is a natural and inevitable part of the process by which law is created and enforced. This is unavoidable because it is impossible to give equal representation to competing groups with contradictory goals. The more powerful a group is at the time a law is created, the greater the impact of that group's interests on the content of the law. Similarly, the enforcement process is symbolic of the power of the various groups at the time. The more powerful groups will be better protected by enforcement actions than will the less influential ones.[12]

Turk's Theory of Criminalization

Although Austin Turk's theory of criminalization (Exhibit 14.3) relies heavily upon Marxist concepts, it uses a relativist view of morality. It defines crime as acts which violate official proclamations such as state and federal statutes. Turk's theory explicitly addresses issues that are only briefly mentioned in other works. While other conflict theories have devoted much attention to the law-creation process, Turk simultaneously focuses on the law-creation and law-enforcement processes. Indeed, he really does not fully distinguish between the two in much of his work. This is because he assumes that police activity is heavily influenced by political concerns at all jurisdictional levels.

Turk asserts that individuals with similar traits and problems will form groups through which they attempt to protect and extend their interests. He is primarily concerned with the group traits that predict how much attention a particular segment of the criminal population will receive from the legal

Exhibit 14.3

· · · · · · · · · · · · · · ·

Turk's theory of criminalization

Specific Assumptions

1. Society is composed of many groups whose members are distinct from one another by their traits and/or norms.

2. The likelihood of conflict between any of these groups and the legal authorities is best predicted by examination of the group's behavioral and organizational traits.

3. Groups whose values and behaviors simultaneously violate the law are more likely to attract enforcement attention than are others.

4. All other things being equal, groups with a high level of organization are most likely to attract the attention of law enforcers.

5. All other things being equal, groups that are not sophisticated in the processes of law creation and enforcement are most likely to attract official attention.

Source: Austin Turk, *Criminality and Legal Order* (Chicago: Rand McNally 1969), pp. 55–60.

authorities. Such an orientation is typical of most radical theorists. Turk is unconcerned with the individual motivations to crime. His goal is to explain why the authorities direct their attention towards the behavior of some groups while ignoring others.

Turk proposes that a group that advocates a behavior that has been defined as illegal but does not actually practice that behavior will attract little official reaction. At least in the United States this is true, because American legal codes do not recognize "thought crimes" as illegal acts. The First Amendment to the U.S. Constitution expressly forbids legal encroachment on citizens' rights to free speech. Thus, for example, a group favoring the legalization of marijuana will not be the target of official sanctions so long as its members do not actually possess, distribute, or use the substance.

Likewise, groups that are not well organized are unlikely to attract official attention, because they do not pose a significant threat to the status quo. The better organized the group, the more it is able to assert its power over the law-creation and law-enforcement processes and thus come into direct conflict with them.

Finally, groups with sophisticated knowledge of the political and police systems are better able to successfully defend themselves from official sanctions and therefore attract less attention from them. Such groups are not easily prosecuted even when they have repeatedly violated the law. They are also likely to pose substantial challenges to the status quo if targeted for sanctions by lawmakers. Thus, it is generally in the best interests of the authorities to leave them alone unless very extreme or obvious forms of criminality are noticed. This is often the case in attempts to bring criminal charges against major businesses. The lobbyists and lawyers employed by such entities make them extremely difficult to defeat in either the legislative or judicial arenas.

Chambliss and Seidman's Theory of Law Enforcement

Chambliss and Seidman's theory of law enforcement (Exhibit 14.4) focuses on the discretionary power of law-enforcement agencies. **Discretion** is a term for the use of individual judgment in choosing between courses of action in various situations. For example, the police must constantly exercise discretion in deciding which law violators to arrest and which to ignore. Without the use of discretion, the system would quickly be overloaded with minor cases and rendered unable to deal with serious crimes.[13]

This theory proposes that law-enforcement agencies discriminate in enforcing laws on the basis of their own self-interest. Like all organizations, law-enforcement agencies need certain resources to function effectively. In essence, without resources there can be no organization. Law-enforcement agencies are completely dependent on public funds, which are controlled by elected officials. Thus, people with socio-political power can adversely affect the supply of resources for police agencies. Therefore, these agencies must cooperate with the desires of elected officials and those who support them. The theory further assumes that elected officials can be influenced by others who possess power greater than their own, such as campaign contributors.

This theory is similar to labeling theories in that it focuses on the problems inherent in the use of discretionary power by agents of the criminal justice

North Philadelphia police officers and a 15 year old. Chambliss and Seidman argue that law enforcement agencies discriminate when deciding which laws to enforce and who to arrest, based on their own self-interest.

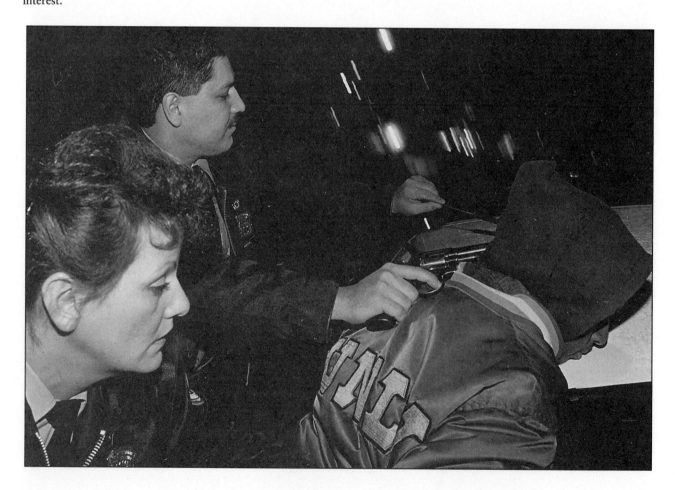

Exhibit 14.4
. . . .
Chambliss and Seidman's theory
of law enforcement

Specific Assumptions

1. Law-enforcement agencies are bureaucratic organizations whose activities and resources are controlled by political authorities.

2. The official goals and norms of law-enforcement organizations are of less import in determining agency activities than the informal ones which increase rewards and decrease pressure on the organization.

3. The replacement of official organization goals and norms is possible in law enforcement because
   a. there is a lack of resistance to such changes within these organizations,
   b. the legal code allows these organizations much situational freedom, and
   c. there is a lack of effective sanctions for rule violations by these organizations.

4. Law-enforcement agencies can increase their rewards and decrease pressures on the organization by processing the powerless but not the powerful.

5. A disproportionately high number of individuals from powerless groups will be processed by law-enforcement agencies, while many crimes committed by the powerful will be ignored.

Source: William J. Chambliss and Robert B. Seidman, *Law, Order, and Power* (Reading, MA: Addison-Wesley Publishing Company, 1971), p. 269.

system. It differs from labeling theories, however, in that it is more concerned with the interaction of groups and agencies than with individuals. It sees the use of discretionary power as a means of controlling conflicts between the social classes and other interest groups.

The Case of Mark Hofmann · · · · · · · · · · · · · · · · · **APPLICATION** · · · · · · · ·

On October 15, 1985, Mark Hofmann placed a bomb concealed in a package outside Kathy Sheets' home in Salt Lake City, Utah. When Kathy Sheets, age fifty, picked up the package, the bomb exploded and killed her. That same day Hofmann placed a similar bomb outside the office of twenty-eight-year-old Steve Christensen. When Christensen picked up the package it, too, exploded and killed him. Later that day, while Mark Hofmann was attempting to deliver a third bomb, it exploded in his parked car. This third bomb was intended for a high ranking official of the Church of Jesus Christ of the Latter Day Saints (LDS Church), also known as the Mormons. Unlike Sheets and Christensen, Hofmann survived the explosion.[14]

The bombings were actually an attempt to cover up a string of frauds that Hofmann had committed against the LDS Church. The LDS Church is a very powerful institution in Utah. It is also a rather controversial denomination with many critics and internal divisions. Therefore the church is quite sensitive

Mark Hofmann arriving at the courthouse with his wife, Doraleen, during his trial for first-degree murder in the bombing deaths of two people.

to how the stories of its origin and early days are portrayed to the public. For this reason, the fact that it had been victimized by a forger like Hofmann was especially problematic for church leaders. While the case's notoriety sprang from the bombings, focus should really be on Hofmann's forgeries and the LDS Church's attempts to avoid embarrassment if the dynamics of the situation are to be properly understood.

The *precipitating factor* in this case was Mark Hofmann's financial indebtedness. By the time of the bombings, Hofmann owed more than $1.3 million to business associates, bankers, and realtors, and they all wanted their money immediately. Hofmann had developed much credit on the basis of his earlier successful forgeries and had to continue with these schemes to maintain his lifestyle. His creditors believed that he was in possession of historical documents related to the history of the LDS Church—one known as "The Oath" the other as "The McLellin Collection." Hofmann was in the process of attempting to sell the Oath, which was actually a forgery that he had prepared, to the New York Public Library for $1.5 million. He was also in the process of negotiating the sale of the McLellin Collection, which he did not actually possess, to either the LDS Church or another party.[15]

Hofmann was not able to forge the McLellin Collection rapidly enough to pay his debts in a timely fashion. He decided to kill Christensen to delay the McLellin transaction and buy himself more time with his creditors. Christensen was serving as the LDS Church's representative in the sale of the McLellin Collection. Hofmann placed the bomb at the Sheets' home to divert attention for the murder of Christensen away from himself. He reasoned that since Christensen had worked for Kathy Sheets's husband, and because the Sheets' business was in financial trouble, everyone would think that both bombings were somehow related to their business problems rather than to him.[18]

The *predisposing factor* in the forgeries was Hofmann's obsession with acquiring money by selling forged historical items. This obsession had begun early in his adolescence. At age twelve he altered the mint marks on some coins to make them appear to be rare and valuable collector's pieces. He also began collecting Mormon memorabilia at about this time.[19]

In 1980 Hofmann traded a forgery of "The Salamander Letter" to the LDS Church for other historical documents worth $20,000. The church traded for documents instead of purchasing them because it appeared more reverent. The Salamander Letter, supposedly written by one of the founders of the LDS Church, undermined some of the major doctrines of the LDS Church. Hofmann's forgery of this letter passed standard ultraviolet and infrared examinations for alterations, and the ink was determined to be from the appropriate time period by the church's scientific experts. After its sale, Hofmann dropped out of college and became a documents dealer. Because of the credibility he developed with church experts in the trade for the Salamander Letter, they, and others, were willing to trade or purchase documents from Hofmann without first thoroughly authenticating them.[20] This was an *attracting factor* for him to continue dealings with the church.

The LDS Church's wealth and power in the area also made it an attractive target for a scheme such as Hofmann's. The church has always had a strong desire to add to its collection of documents related to its early history in order to control its public image. It maintains important historical documents in a vault that is accessible to only a selected few of its leaders. It is widely suspected that some of these historical documents could be embarrassing to the church were their contents to become known to the public. Leading Mormon dissidents and publishers of anti-Mormon literature also wanted access to the documents for their own purposes.[21]

Another important *attracting factor* in this case lay in Hofmann's anti-Mormon sentiments. In 1890 the church banned plural marriages due to pressure from the federal government. By the early 1900s, polygamy was considered shameful behavior and a polygamist could be excommunicated from the church. In 1965 the church reversed itself, proclaiming that polygamy was not only permissible but had been divinely revealed by God; however, the disgrace associated with plural marriages—which applied to the offspring of those marriages as well—was not eliminated by this 1965 reversal. Hofmann's mother had been born into a polygamous family and this fact had tormented her for years while she kept it a secret. When she finally revealed her family secret, Hofmann became outraged at the church's hypocrisy concerning polygamy and the suffering it had caused his mother.[22]

Forgery
Consists of creating or altering a document or art object with the intention of misrepresenting its origins and/or creator.[16]

Fraud Offenses
A group of crimes in which the crucial element is deceit and the goal is to deprive the victims of property that is legally theirs.[17]

The preexisting Mormon/anti-Mormon group conflict can best be illustrated in the prosecution of Hofmann for the murders of Sheets and Christensen. All bombings are investigated by the Federal Bureau of Alcohol, Tobacco, and Firearms (ATF) because they violate federal laws. The LDS Church did not want to be involved in a scandal as a result of the bombings and Hofmann's forgeries. Prosecuting Hofmann in open court would have revealed many facts that could have embarrassed the church and its leaders.

The influence of the LDS Church on the criminal justice system became apparent when the federal prosecutor indicted Hofmann and an associate for possession of an altered Uzi submachine gun, but not for the bombings. This occurred despite the fact that ATF agents presented physical evidence for a federal case against Hofmann for possession of a destructive device—an offense punishable by a ten-year prison sentence. Fearing that a scandal might injure its power and reputation, the LDS Church used its influence to see that the entire matter was handled quietly through a plea bargain agreement. This deal allowed Hofmann to receive a relatively light sentence while minimizing the publicity surrounding the case.[23]

In his plea bargain agreement with the state of Utah, Hofmann received a sentence of five years to life for the murder of Christensen, one to fifteen years for the Sheets murder, and one to fifteen years on each count of theft by deception. The plea bargain agreement stipulated that the sentences were to run concurrently rather than consecutively. Hofmann thus received the same sentence for murdering two people and committing a multimillion-dollar series of frauds that an unarmed nineteen-year-old Utah youth received for robbing a fast-food restaurant and stealing a car.[24] Exhibit 14.5 summarizes the facts of this case.

The apparent role of the LDS Church in this case illustrates the conflict perspective's assertion that conflict is a natural process in societies. The LDS Church's influence on the prosecution of Hofmann is an example of coercive power being relative and group-based as proposed by the law approach. It is also an example of Chambliss and Seidman's contention that the official goals of law-enforcement organizations are often subverted by alternatives that decrease pressure on the organization when this is in the best interests of organization leaders or the organization itself. Certainly the lack of aggressive

Exhibit 14.5

. . . .

Summary of facts and their role in the explanation of the Mark Hofmann case

Level of Importance	Fact	Type of Fact
Primary	Hofmann's financial indebtedness	Precipitating
Primary	McLellin Collection forgery scheme	Precipitating
Secondary	Group conflict over acquisition of historical documents	Attracting
Secondary	Hofmann's anti-Mormonism due to Church's hypocrisy concerning polygamy	Attracting
Tertiary	Hofmann's forgery ability	Predisposing

prosecution by law-enforcement agencies in this case reduced the pressure being exerted on their organizations. In addition, the case illustrates Chambliss and Seidman's assumption that law-enforcement agencies can increase organizational rewards by processing the powerless (e.g., Charles Manson), whereas cases such as Hofmann's may threaten their power and supply of resources.

The attention given the Hofmann case by law enforcers also reflects Turk's assertion that groups with a high level of organization, such as the Mormon Church, are more likely to attract the attention of law enforcers. One only has to contrast the immediate law-enforcement attention focused on the Hofmann case to that focused on the first few prostitutes who were victims of the "Green River Killer"[25] to further illuminate this assertion. Of course, the church itself committed no illegal act in this case, but its leadership seems to have been seeking to conceal its own victimization in order to avoid embarrassment and divert attention from its collection of historical documents. And the law-enforcement agencies cooperated in this endeavor.

Group-Value Approach

George Vold's group-value approach (see Exhibit 14.6) assumes that law evolves into the best and most efficient form possible for a society. In this way it is similar to the strain and social-disorganization perspectives. Vold is not especially concerned with the content of the law; instead his attention is focused on its operation. Morality is relative according to this approach, and legal

Exhibit 14.6

Group value approach

Restrictive Assumptions

1. Individual lives are shaped by group memberships.

2. Social order is a product of the alliances and conflicts between the groups that compose society.

3. Social groups are produced by the presence of common needs among many individuals.

4. All social groups seek to preserve themselves and increase their power.

5. A group's struggle against other groups that seek to replace it will produce very intense loyalty in its members.

6. The processes of law-creation and law-enforcement are the product of compromises between powerful groups.

7. Crime is a behavior of non-powerful minorities.

8. Criminal groups are a source of protection and strength for their members.

Source: George B. Vold, "Group Conflict Theory as Explanation of Crime" in Stuart H. Traub and Craig B. Little (eds.), *Theories of Deviance* (Itasca, IL: F.E. Peacock, 1980), pp. 300–311; George B. Vold, "Group Conflict Theory as Explanation of Crime" in Ronald A. Farrell and Victoria L. Swiggert (eds.), (Belmont, CA: Wadsworth, 1988), pp. 76–78.

definitions of appropriate behavior result from the interests of various social groups.

Vold conceives of crime as resulting from a series of battles over group power. What is considered "right" and "just" is determined by the winners of the struggle. Due to their victory in the ongoing socio-political struggle, Vold believes them to be the most capable of creating social regulations. It is implied that just as the most "fit" animals survive and reproduce while the less fit are killed off, the most fit human groups are able to seize power while less fit groups come under their control. He is, therefore, an extreme relativist in his view of morality.

Vold's theory goes this way: Groups that are in competition for a scarce resource often take their conflict to official law-making bodies. Since each group has a different idea of how the resource should be dealt with, the government is likely to establish a compromise that more or less satisfies the desires of the most powerful (or best represented) groups. However, this inevitably results in some groups feeling left out or underrepresented. If these groups follow their own ideas on how to deal with the resource, they are likely to be labeled as criminal by the society. If they follow the government's rules, then they are at a disadvantage relative to the groups that have the most influence over how the government regulates that resource.[26]

Government regulation, including the criminal law, has both practical and symbolic power. On a practical dimension, it is clear that those who ignore social regulations will be made to suffer through stigmatization, fines, imprisonment, or other sanctions. Such suffering by group members is thought to decrease the socio-political power of the group by diverting its members' attention from the group's goals to their personal problems. In essence, the law gives government authorities considerable power over the rights and welfare of citizens. These coercive police powers are typical of the practical powers of law.

Symbolically, law has the power to give legitimacy to certain practices while defining alternatives as illicit. Therefore, the group(s) whose norms have become law are likely to be perceived as "right" and others as "wrong" simply because they have successfully enlisted the power of the state in creating social regulations.[27] This situation is a matter of *status politics* as was discussed in our earlier chapter on culture conflict.

According to Vold, the relationship between lawmakers and the more powerful segments of society is reciprocal. Each supports the other. As the structure of power in society changes, so also does the amount of influence over the law held by various segments. Thus, in Vold's view, law is a fairly accurate reflection of the distribution of social power and capability at the time it is interpreted and applied.

Vold further asserts that groups compete with one another for members as well as resources. Such intergroup competitions are of great concern to members and thus produce fierce emotional loyalty within the affected groups. Because the processes of law-creation and law-enforcement are the product of compromises between powerful groups, Vold defines crime as a behavior of non-powerful minorities. However, he also points out that group memberships are an important source of symbolic, practical, and psychological protection for their members who must deal with this minority status.

The Case of Joseph Hillstrom · · · · · · · · · · · · · · · APPLICATION · · · · · · · · · ·

Although this case involved a man called Joe Hillstrom, concern is focused primarily on the struggle between The Industrial Workers of The World (hereafter referred to as IWW), an early American labor organization, and the management of certain mining and construction companies in Utah. From 1912 until 1914 the IWW's local office in Salt Lake City organized strikes for better wages and working conditions against the Utah Copper Company and the Utah Construction Company. Other mining companies were also adversely affected by the IWW's activities in Utah.

Joseph Hillstrom was a prominent member of the IWW who was convicted and executed in 1915 for two murders, which, according to Philip S. Foner, he did not commit. Foner proposes that the real criminals in the Hillstrom case were hidden within business and government structures, identified here merely as "anti-union forces."[28] Our discussion of this case is focused on how this apparent miscarriage of justice occurred.

Joseph Hillstrom was born in Sweden in 1879 as Joel Hagglund. At the age of twenty-three, he came to the United States and changed his name to Joseph Hillstrom. He subsequently became known to millions of people throughout the world as Joe Hill, the composer of several popular songs in the *Little Red Song Book* of the IWW.[29]

The IWW, commonly known as the "wobblies," was organized in 1905 by a coalition of socialists, anarchists, trade unionists, and revolutionaries. Many members were former members of the American Federation of Labor (A.F. of L.) who had become dissatisfied with that organization, and so created a competing group. IWW members felt that the A.F. of L. was too cooperative with management and interested only in the elite of the working class. Both groups sought the loyalty of American workers and competed intensely with each other and with business management for control of industrial production. As a result, intense antagonisms existed between the IWW and both the A.F. of L. and business leaders. Essentially, the IWW solicited those workers who were treated the worst and paid the least, while the A.F. of L. came to represent skilled tradesmen.[30]

The primary *predisposing factor* in this case was the fact that the owners of companies, who wanted to maintain low wages and extremely poor working conditions, hated and feared the IWW. Worker strikes during the early 1900s often led to bloodshed and even deaths. In 1912 bitter labor struggles began to occur in Utah. In addition to writing songs for the IWW, Joseph Hillstrom traveled around the country attending IWW meetings and helping out in worker strikes. He was in Salt Lake City, Utah, when John G. Morrison and his seventeen-year-old son, Arling, were shot to death in the elder Morrison's grocery store. This was the latest in a series of unsolved homicides in Salt Lake City that were causing many citizens to complain about the inefficiency of the police.

The police arrested several suspects during their investigation of the Morrison murders, one of whom was Hillstrom. Hillstrom became a suspect in the case because he had been treated for a gunshot wound on the same night that the Morrison murders had been committed. Hillstrom claimed that he received the gunshot wound during a quarrel over a girl.[31] Thus, the Morrison murders were the *precipitating factor* in the anti-union forces' attack on Hillstrom and the IWW. However, they are only of tertiary importance in the explanation of this case.

Hillstrom was not initially arrested because of his affiliation with the IWW, but once the authorities became aware of this fact, they began a campaign to convict him.[32] Thus, Hillstrom's membership in the IWW was the primary *attracting factor* in this case. Antilabor forces wanted to halt unionism and saw an opportunity to condemn it through the conviction of Hillstrom because of his affiliation with the IWW. This constitutes an illustration of the symbolic power of the law. The anti-union forces were aided by the Salt Lake City police, who were being severely criticized for their inability to solve these killings. Public demands for an end to these killings made the idea of cooperating with the anti-union forces very attractive to the police. The power of company management to influence local politics also contributed to this attraction. Hillstrom's conviction for the Morrison murders would reduce the public's criticism of the police department. The anti-union forces were also aided by the local press, which treated Hillstrom as though his guilt was certain long before any evidence was presented in court.[33]

With the aid of the police and the press, the anti-union forces succeeded in their campaign to have Hillstrom convicted—on extremely weak evidence. After Hillstrom's conviction, the IWW conducted one of the most powerful national protest movements in the history of the United States over this miscarriage of justice. Even President Wilson appealed to the Governor of Utah for a temporary stay of execution. Nonetheless, Hillstrom was executed on November 19, 1915.[34] Exhibit 14.7 summarizes the facts in this case.

This case provides a number of illustrations of the assumptions made by Vold's group-value approach. Hillstrom's life was shaped, at least in part, by his membership in the IWW. Likewise, the Salt Lake City society in which his trial was enmeshed was painfully aware of the conflict between the IWW and the owners of companies. The area's economy was dependent on the welfare of these companies and IWW-led strikes threatened the financial well-being of many local businesses. By labeling a prominent member of the IWW a murderer, they were able to partially discredit this union.

The idea that social groups are produced by the presence of common needs among many individuals is clearly portrayed in the common need of IWW members to improve the dangerously poor conditions under which they worked. It can also be seen in the common needs of the individuals who were dissatisfied with the orientation of the A.F. of L. and consequently established

Exhibit 14.7

Summary of facts and their role in the explanation of the Joe Hill case

Level of Importance	Fact	Type of Fact
Primary	Hillstrom's affiliation with the IWW	Attracting
Primary	Desire to discredit the IWW	Predisposing
Secondary	Police department need for public support	Attracting
Tertiary	The Morrison murders	Precipitating

the IWW. Similarly, the common need to blame Hillstrom for the Morrison murders united company owners with the police and press.

The assertion that all social groups seek to preserve themselves is illustrated by the desire of the company owners to protect themselves against unionism. The IWW was a powerful union at the time and thus posed a significant threat to company management. Its struggle with the company owners produced very intense loyalty among members, evidenced in the national protest it conducted over Hillstrom's conviction. This also demonstrates how groups identified as criminal can serve as a source of protection and comfort for their members. Also, the IWW's struggle with the A.F. of L., which sought to replace it, is another example of group conflict functioning to produce group loyalty.

The anarchy and revolutionary behavior of the IWW is an example of Vold's belief that crime is a behavior of non-powerful minorities. Because this case occurred in 1915, the approach's suggestion that the processes of law-creation and law-enforcement are the product of compromises between powerful groups, is hard to address due to lack of information. However, there can be little doubt that the group conflicts described in this case ultimately resulted in the creation of laws governing unions and the conduct of labor disputes. This is the sort of social progress that conflict theorists expect to result from such group confrontations.

Bernard's Unified Conflict Theory of Crime

Bernard combined elements of Vold's approach with insights from the social-learning, strain, and Marxist perspectives to create his unified conflict theory (see Exhibit 14.8). The idea that one's position in the structure of society determines the nature of the reinforcement one can expect to receive represents the combination of Merton's strain approach with Aker's theory of differential

Exhibit 14.8
. . . .
Bernard's unified conflict theory

Specific Assumptions

1. Behavior results from conditioning processes that determine how various types of acts are defined and perceived.

2. Group memberships determine an individual's conditioning experiences.

3. Because group memberships are stable, so also are the behavior patterns of their members.

4. The more complex the society is, the wider the range of groups, behaviors and definitions of crime.

5. Criminal law is created and enforced as part of a political process in which each group attempts to promote and protect its own values.

6. Official crime rates are highest among the least powerful groups in society and lowest among the most powerful.

Source: George B. Vold and Thomas J. Bernard, *Theoretical Criminology*, 3d ed. (New York: Oxford University Press, 1986), pp. 286–287.

reinforcement. Group power results from political compromises and is directly related to the likelihood of criminality among group members. These ideas form the core of Bernard's theory.

Bernard's view of the links between social structure, behavioral learning and law creation/enforcement are very similar to those of Quinney (see Chapter 13). However, Bernard does not make any assumptions as to the ultimate nature of morality. He also recognizes the existence of multiple overlapping groups based on variables other than economic power. Bernard's theory can best be described as an updated version of Vold's approach, stressing the origins of criminal behavior as well as the processes of law creation and enforcement. It is distinct from that of Quinney in its assumption that complex societies are composed of many groups that compete for power.

This linkage of social structure, group membership, behavioral learning, crime rates, and the law-creation process is an example of a **unified,** or **integrated, theory**—one in which the insights of several different perspectives have been combined into a brief explanatory statement.[35] Such theories became popular in the 1960s while the conflict perspective was extremely popular in sociology and criminology. Unified theories can be developed within any criminological perspective, however, as will be discussed in more detail in the next chapter. Bernard's theory is introduced here because of its stress on the acquisition of criminal behaviors and the group definitions of social reality that support them.

· · · · · · · · | **APPLICATION** | · · · · **The Case of James Little**

James Richard Little began robbing banks in December of 1981. He belonged to what could loosely be defined as a gang of bank robbers. This gang began its series of crimes in 1981 and continued until apprehended in 1984. It robbed banks in Fort Collins, Colorado; Fort Polk, Louisiana; and Valley View, Texas. What was especially unusual about these bank robbers was the sophisticated equipment and military precision with which they committed their crimes. They usually disguised themselves as policemen and made an airborne assault on the banks using automatic weapons and stolen helicopters. This gang was the first to use a helicopter to commit a bank robbery in the United States.[36]

The *precipitating factor* in these bank robberies was Jim Little's need for capital to start an executive protection company. Little shared his goals and methods with Marvin Rodgers. By hiring American mercenaries they hoped to build a company that would provide extraordinarily wealthy people with various types of protection that traditional police agencies or private security services do not provide. Machine gun silencers, infrared gun scopes, bugging devices, and explosives would be needed. Little and Rodgers were convinced that traditional lending sources would not loan them the money to start such a venture. They had initially planned to steal the money from illegal drug dealers, but that plan fell through and they subsequently settled on robbing banks as a way to obtain the money.[37]

Jim Little was small-town boy from rural Texas. His father was an alcoholic who deserted the family when Little was in his early adolescence. Little rejoined his father when he was fifteen, after which his academic grades declined, and he dropped out of school in the ninth grade. In 1961, at the age of sixteen, he was arrested for stealing money from a parking meter. Under the threat of being sent to a state reform school for this theft, Little joined the army and became a helicopter pilot. He initially intended to make this his life's career, but resigned after several years of service. He then worked at numerous helicopter piloting jobs and even became a state trooper in Alaska for a while.[38]

Prior to the robberies, Marvin A. Rodgers worked as a utility lineman and part-time gun dealer licensed by Alaska. It was there that he met Little. It was rumored that Rodgers had been a soldier of fortune (i.e., a mercenary), a CIA operative, and an airline employee. He had serious financial problems and had declared bankruptcy in 1980.[39]

Other principal gang members included William Jeffrey Gross, Russel Ray Kelly, Charles Ray Holden, and Russell Earl Auzston. Gross was a forty-four-year-old ex-Marine. Prior to the robberies, he had been diagnosed as having an organic brain disorder that may have been due to his chronic alcoholism. He had been hospitalized three times for brain seizures believed to have been brought on by his drinking. Just prior to the robberies, he had been laid off as a chainman on a survey crew. Kelly, age thirty-three, had served three tours of duty in Vietnam as an Army Ranger. He had since developed a history of losing jobs, chronic problems in his romantic relationships, and barroom brawling. After his arrest for the robberies he was diagnosed as suffering from post-traumatic stress disorder brought on by his service in the military. Holden was from a lower-class economic background and had a reputation for hard drinking and chasing women, and Auzston was in constant financial difficulty.[40]

The *attracting factor* for Little was the excitement and danger of the robberies. Little had won recognition and respect as a helicopter pilot because of the risks he had taken in combat in Vietnam. As a combat pilot he had learned to accept, and even enjoy, being surrounded by violence, death, and destruction. He was proud of being cool, efficient, and impersonal in combat. He became frustrated and bored without the excitement and danger of combat. He came to view himself as perverted, referring to himself as an "adrenalin junkie," meaning a person addicted to life-and-death risk taking.[41]

The *predisposing factor* for Little was his disenchantment with society in general, and more specifically with the army and the police. Originally he had been very proud of his country, the epitome of a super-patriot. He believed everything that the government and its officials had to say. He had spent most of his adult life working to support the law in the military and police.[42] Little's disenchantment with the army resulted from the army's reductions in helicopter pilots during the later stages of the Vietnam War. Indeed, he resigned from the army because he believed that it was purging itself of its best officers and pilots while retaining those who were incompetent but held college degrees.[43]

Little was similarly disillusioned by his experience in the Alaska State Troopers. Terminated by the Alaska Department of Public Safety in 1978 due to his repeated use of unnecessary and excessive force, he was reinstated as a result of winning an appeal, but his disillusionment with government authority increased. He felt that the authorities had again betrayed him. He resigned his position as an Alaskan State Trooper in 1980 as a result of these sentiments.[44]

These experiences led Little to view society as hypocritical, corrupt and disloyal. His patriotic and pro-establishment values gave way to a belief in revolutionary goals and illegal methods. Little now saw banks as part of a system that was organized to exploit working people like himself. Bankers were giving working people very meager returns on their deposits while they made profits that he felt were obscene. In Little's mind, bankers were influential, hypocritical thieves who sent working-class kids who had no political power to die in Vietnam, but protected upper- and middle-class ones from a similar fate.[45] The system had two sets of rules, one for the rich and one for the rest. He could think of no one else who represented the upper class better than bankers. Robbing banks was not like robbing people for Little. It was simply a means of taking money from a greedy and corrupt social system.[46]

Most of the gang members were apprehended in 1984. A U.S. District Judge sentenced Little, Auzston, and Gross to the maximum of twenty-five years in prison. Holden received a twenty-year sentence, and Thomas a five-year one. Juries in two states returned sentences against Rodgers totaling fifty five years. Kelly, the three-tour veteran of Vietnam, was diagnosed by Bureau of Prison psychologists as suffering from post-traumatic stress disorder and given a ten-year sentence.[47] Exhibit 14.9 summarizes the facts of this case.

Bernard's unified conflict theory maintains that behavior results from conditioning processes that determine how various types of acts are defined. This is vividly illustrated in Little's behavior. As a result of the conditioning processes Little experienced in the army and the Alaska Department of Public Safety, he defined bank robbery as a method of obtaining justice from a greedy and corrupt system. In the terminology of control theory, his bonds to conventional society were shattered by these experiences.

Bernard's assertion that group membership determines an individual's conditioning experiences is demonstrated by Little's, Gross's, and Kelly's military experiences, and Rodgers' as a soldier of fortune. These experiences apparently conditioned them to enjoy violent and dangerous acts. This, in turn, made membership in the gang very attractive to them. The notion that when group memberships are stable, so also are individual behavior patterns is illustrated by the stability of this gang over several years and its ability to continue robbing banks.

The theory's supposition that the more complex the society is, the wider the range of groups, behaviors, and definitions is somewhat self-evident in this case (e.g., United States Army, Alaska Department of Public Safety, Little's and Rodgers' gang). Although not self-evident, it is almost a truism that criminal laws concerning the protection of the money in banks were created and enforced by groups seeking to protect and promote their own values. These values were drastically different from those held by Little and the other gang

Exhibit 14.9
. . . .
Summary of facts and their role in the explanation of the James Little case

Level of Importance	Fact	Type of Fact
Primary	Little's conflict with the Army and Alaskan State Troopers	Predisposing
Secondary	Little's and Rodgers' need for capital	Precipitating
Tertiary	Little's addiction to risk taking	Attracting

members. And this difference is largely a result of position in the social hierarchy.

This case also illustrates Bernard and Vold's assumption that official crime rates will be highest among the least powerful groups in society. One has only to contrast the criminal prosecution of Little and the other gang members with those of the people involved in the savings and loan banking scandals of the late 1980s and early 1990s in the United States to validate this idea.

Conclusion

The conflict perspective is designed primarily for use at the macro level of analysis. Its main focus is upon the various groups and institutions that influence the processes of law creation and enforcement. It also directs our attention to the manner in which group memberships and institutional structures affect the norms, values, and behaviors of the individual. This perspective is very effective in linking social problems and related issues to each other and to criminality. However, it tends to rely on other perspectives to describe the actual processes by which behavior and beliefs are acquired. In this sense it has much in common with the social-disorganization and Marxist perspectives.

The fact that it is intended to explain the attitudes and actions of groups makes it difficult to apply to the behaviors of individuals. The fact that U.S. law is written to emphasize the responsibility of individuals to control their own behavior makes this problem even more pronounced. The great majority of crimes in this country are defined in such a way that they can be perpetrated only by an individual. When groups or gangs commit illegal acts, each member's actions are judged in isolation from the others, at least in theory. This is illustrated by the variation in sentences received by members of Little's gang.

When a perspective designed for the macro level is applied to acts occurring at the micro level, there is a tendency for the application to appear weak. However, the problem lies not in the theory or the application process, but in the fit between the levels of analysis. We have chosen to keep all applications at the level of the individual in this text (keeping our view congruent with U.S. legal norms), so our case applications for macro theories may seem somewhat weaker than those for micro-oriented ones. The reader should remember that this somewhat weaker fit cannot be taken as indicating a weakness in the theories. Macro-level theories are vital to our comprehension of how both law and behavior arise from social settings. They are also crucial to our understanding of the policy construction process. These theories describe the context in which crime occurs and is defined. Without such a contextual description, the micro theories would be inadequate to explain the differences in the nature and distribution of crime over time, space, and groups. They would also be unable to link the definitions of crime to the acts of various individuals and to their group memberships.

It is by combining the insights of theories designed for different levels of analysis into explanations of concrete reality that we achieve the most comprehensive and well-rounded explanations of criminal cases possible. Ideas that are only implicit in some theories are made explicit in others. For example, Bentham, Freudian theorists, and the control perspective imply that people must be controlled by the external coercion of the state if civilization is to be preserved. However, they do not describe the process in detail because their focus is on the internal dynamics of the individual or on the relationship of the individual to society. Conflict theories make this process explicit and describe it in some detail. Conflict theories thus contribute much to the process of theory integration, as will be seen in the next chapter.

Glossary ·

Absolute Morality Presumes that certain acts are always undesirable and harmful, that rule violators are inherently different from the law abiding, and that criminology should restrict itself to discovering the nature of the pathology within the rule violator or the rule creators. It is usually associated with ideological positions that are at the leftist-liberal or rightist-conservative extreme.

Discretion The use of individual judgment in choosing between courses of action in various situations. For example, the police must constantly exercise discretion in deciding which law violators to arrest and which to ignore, otherwise, the system would quickly be overloaded with minor cases and rendered unable to deal with serious crimes. However, the use of discretion also allows bias to enter the processes of the criminal justice system.

Fluid Equilibrium Dahrendorf's term for the joint presence of stability and change that he feels characterizes modern industrial societies.

Mala in se Acts that are perceived as criminal by the vast majority of groups in a society. These acts are considered bad in themselves, not just because they are legally defined as such.

Mala Prohibita Acts that are criminal mainly because they have been defined as such by political authorities. They are often the subject of controversy in society because not all groups agree that they are wrong.

Radical Refers to any criminological theory, approach, or perspective that provides fundamental and intensive scrutiny of the basic aspects of social organization while emphasizing the political nature of crime and the law. Such theoretical statements tend to focus on the repressive aspects of law creation and enforcement. Virtually all radical theories in criminology are derived from some form of conflict-oriented assumptions and tend to stress the macro level of analysis.

Relative Morality Presumes that crime is a matter of definition, that only some rule violators are caught and labeled, and that criminology should focus on the processes of law creation and enforcement. It is usually associated with moderate to liberal ideological positions.

Unified (Integrated) Theories Theories in which the insights of several different perspectives have been combined into a comprehensive explanatory statement.

■ Notes

1. Donald Martindale, *The Nature and Types of Sociological Theory,* (Boston: Houghton-Mifflin, 1960), pp. 128–135.

2. Ibid., pp. 137–138.
3. Stuart L. Hills, *Demystifying Social Deviance* (New York: McGraw-Hill, 1980), pp. 9–10.
4. James A. Inciardi, *Criminal Justice,* 3d ed. (New York: Harcourt Brace Jovanovich, 1990), pp. 62–63.
5. Ibid., p. 17.
6. Seymour Lipset, *Political Man: The Social Bases of Politics* (Baltimore, MD: Johns Hopkins University Press, 1981), p. 26; Alex Thio, *Deviant Behavior,* 2d ed. (New York: Harper & Row, 1983), p. 80.
7. Hills, *Demystifying Social Deviance,* pp. 8–9.
8. George B. Vold, "Group Conflict Theory as Explanation of Crime" in Stuart H. Traub and Craig B. Little (eds.), *Theories of Deviance* (Itasca, IL: F.E. Peacock, 1980), pp. 300–311.
9. Melvin L. DeFleur, *Social Problems in American Society,* pp. 17–18.
10. George E. Rush, *The Dictionary of Criminal Justice,* 2d ed. (Guilford, CT: Dushkin Publishing Group), p. 204.
11. Ralf Dahrendorf, *Class and Class Conflict in Industrial Society* (Stanford, CT: Stanford University Press, 1959).
12. Ibid., pp. 47–51.
13. Rush, *The Dictionary of Criminal Justice,* p. 78; Larry J. Siegel, *Criminology,* 2d ed. (St. Paul, MN: West Publishing, 1986), pp. 502–504.
14. Steven Naifeh and Gregory White Smith, *The Mormon Murders* (New York: Weidenfeld & Nicolson, 1988).
15. Ibid.
16. Rush, *The Dictionary of Criminal Justice,* p. 103.
17. Ibid.
18. Naifeh and Smith, *The Mormon Murders.*
19. Ibid.
20. Ibid.
21. Ibid.
22. Ibid.
23. Ibid.
24. Ibid.
25. Carlton Smith and Tomas Guillen, *The Search for the Green River Killer* (New York: Penguin Books USA, 1991).
26. Vold, "Group Conflict Theory as Explanation of Crime," pp. 300–312.
27. Hills, *Demystifying Social Deviance,* pp. 37–38.
28. Philip S. Foner, *The Case of Joe Hill* (New York: International Publishers, 1965).
29. Ibid.
30. Ibid.
31. Ibid.
32. Ibid.
33. Ibid.
34. Ibid.
35. Marvin Wolfgang and Franco Ferricuti, *The Subculture of Violence* (New York: Tavistock, 1969), pp. 1–3.
36. Howard Swindle, *Once a Hero,* (Austin, TX: Texas Monthly Press, 1989).
37. Ibid.
38. Ibid.

39. Ibid.
40. Ibid.
41. Ibid.
42. Ibid.
43. Ibid.
44. Ibid.
45. Ibid.
46. Ibid.
47. Ibid.

■ Suggested Readings

William J. Chambliss and Robert B. Seidman, *Law, Order, and Power* (Reading, MA: Addison-Wesley Publishing Company, 1971).

Ralf Dahrendorf, *Class and Class Conflict in Industrial Society* (Stanford, CT: Stanford University Press, 1959).

Alex Thio, *Deviant Behavior*, 2d ed. (New York: Harper & Row, 1983).

Austin Turk, *Criminality and Legal Order* (Chicago: Rand McNally 1969).

■ Suggested Books for Additional Application

Harry J. Anslinger and Will Oursler, *The Murderers: The Story of the Narcotic Gangs* (New York: Farrar, Straus and Cudahy, 1961).

Gerald W. Clemente with Kevin Stevens, *The Cops are Robbers* (Boston: Quinlan Press, 1987).

Guy Gugliotta and Jeff Leen, *Kings of Cocaine* (New York: Harper & Row, 1990).

John Hubner and Lindsey Gruson, *Monkey on a Stick* (New York: Penguin Books USA, 1990).

Robert Lindsey, *A Gathering of Saints* (New York: Dell Publishing, 1988).

Michael McAlary, *Buddy Boys: When Good Cops Turn Bad* (New York: Charter Books, 1989).

Gary Provost, *Across the Border* (New York: Pocket Books, 1989).

Elaine Shannon, *Desperados* (New York: Penguin Books, 1989).

CHAPTER **15**

Theory Integration

Overview of Theory Integration

As noted in the introductory chapters to this text, criminological theory is derived from many disciplines, focuses on a variety of analytical levels, and makes a variety of assumptions about the nature of the individual and society. This makes it extremely difficult to employ **parsimony,** or simple, straightforward explanations, in this field, although the quality of parsimony is greatly valued in the social and physical sciences. Many theorists have tried to integrate the various perspectives on crime into a single parsimonious theory, but the contradictory assumptions involved make the task impossible without offending at least some groups of theoreticians. A more successful approach, in the authors' opinion, is to begin by acknowledging that all perspectives have some validity and that the contradictions between them simply reflect the complex nature of the individual in society. Then the process of integration can be undertaken with the understanding that it's product likewise must be complex.

Debates about underlying theoretical assumptions only lead to debates concerning the disciplines upon which criminology was founded. Therefore, the authors see theory integration as necessary to transcend these debates and help establish criminology as a distinct area of study. The dictionary defines integration as "the act or process of making whole."[1] Theory integration, then, is the combining or interweaving of separate theories into a single, though possibly complex, explanation. An **integrated theory** results from the blending of a series of empirical facts, produced by the research efforts of various scientific disciplines, into a system that assigns meaning and order to them. Theory integration is a process of treating similar questions about the causes of criminal behavior in the same way so that a cohesive and manageable explanation of crime emerges.[2] Such an explanatory scheme should have the quality of parsimony to the degree possible.

In 1967 Wolfgang and Ferracuti pointed out that criminology is an especially good field for theory integration because it is a discipline that is founded on the efforts of many other disciplines. However, they also recognized that many of the assumptions used by these various scientific communities lose their validity when jointly applied to criminological questions. They go on to say that it is unlikely that an integrated theory of crime will please all who have contributed to it. They remind us that an integrated approach to crime cannot be judged by any of the contributing disciplines but only on its own merits—the quality of the analyses it produces must be the final criteria by which it is evaluated.[3] This is possible because of the nature of criminology itself. Criminologists are not obligated to explain society, the individual, or the individual in society. They seek only to explain one aspect of the social world—the violation of law. An integrated criminological theory, therefore, is one that coordinates a range of views on why, where, and how crime occurs into a single explanation that has more explanatory value than any of its original sources.[4]

The reader should note that each attempt at integration has more material to deal with than those preceding it. This is due to the fact that new theories are constantly being proposed by criminologists and others while older theories are often modified or extended in the same way. Therefore, each attempt at theoretical integration has the advantage of having more refined and accurate material available to it. It also means that we must deal with the problem of increasing complexity as our knowledge base grows.

Wolfgang and Ferracuti's Approach to Theory Integration

Wolfgang and Ferracuti discussed the need for an integrated theory of criminal violence in 1967.[5] Their subcultures-of-violence theory was briefly reviewed in Chapter 10. They began by pointing out that many disciplines have contributed to criminological knowledge, but little has been done to integrate these nuggets of fact and theory into a cohesive whole. They used the idea of subculture as their central concept to do just this. They chose Sellin's notion of culture conflict and Sutherland's idea of differential association as their primary themes. Their integrated theory was designed to explain only violent crime, but it addresses all levels of analysis in that it explains varying crime rates by examining individual and subgroup norms regarding the use of violence. Simultaneously, it links the values of the group to the actions of the individual member. Like most integrated theories, it is based largely on the theorists' interpretation of criminological data. Exhibit 15.1 gives the specific assumptions of this integrated theory.

Wolfgang and Ferracuti assert that subcultures are groups that follow the norms of the surrounding society in many ways. That is, they are not separate and distinct from the dominant society, but rather use variations on major social themes as their dominant norms. They further point out that criminals are not constantly engaged in crime, but follow most social norms much of the time. Even the most heinous serial killers stop at red lights and eat with a

Exhibit 15.1

Wolfgang and Ferracuti's theory of subcultural violence

Specific Assumptions

1. All subcultures conform to the norms of the dominant society in some ways.
2. Members of a violent subculture will not behave violently in all situations.
3. Members of violent subcultures will use violence, or approve of its use by others, in more kinds of situations than will members of the dominant society.
4. Violent acts will be committed primarily by subculture members who are between the ages of fifteen and thirty five.
5. Differential association is the primary mechanism by which a subculture transmits its conduct norms to its members.
6. Subculture members will define their violent acts as appropriate and therefore will not experience guilt over them.

Source: M. Wolfgang, and F. Ferracuti, *The Subculture of Violence* (Beverly Hills, California: Sage Publications, 1982), p. 8.

knife and fork. Criminality is simply a part of a larger set of behaviors. We notice crimes because they are unusual in the context of the dominant society. However, such acts are often not unusual or noteworthy to the subculture members who approve of them.

The use of violence (or, more generally, crime) is more frequent among members of certain subcultures than it is among members of the dominant society. Therefore, we can identify criminal subcultures by examining statistical descriptions of crime. Particular forms of crime (for Wolfgang and Ferracuti, "violence") will be favored as methods of resolving problems by the members of a given group. However, the norms that allow and even encourage criminality will also be found in many other forms in such a subculture. For example, a violent subculture might have made major contributions to its society's military by serving bravely in combat and encouraging others to support the military. In short, military traditions would be very important to, and well respected by, this particular subculture. Such traditions are a logical correlate of its approval of violent conduct in peacetime settings.

This approach further specifies the location of the crime problem by noting that all members of the subculture will believe in similar norms, but only some will regularly act on them. Here we can most clearly see the influence of scientific research on Wolfgang and Ferracuti's theory. Age is a very significant predictor of criminality, especially at the macro level of analysis. Criminal involvement is most prevalent among young adults and older teens in all groups. This pattern is also found in criminal subcultures. Wolfgang's original research also noted that while males predominated in the homicide statistics for all subgroups, females from violent subcultures were more often involved in violence than were females from the dominant culture.[6]

Wolfgang and Ferracuti infer that differential association and related learning processes are the mechanisms by which the norms that encourage crime are transmitted to subculture members and perpetuated within the group. The processes outlined by the control perspective also seem to be implicit here. The subculture member is bonded to, or contained by, the group. Group members believe in and follow the group's norms while seeking status in ways that the group is likely to recognize. Members of criminal subcultures see nothing wrong with certain behaviors that the dominant society has defined as criminal. Indeed, their norms may even require a "criminal" response to certain situations as a condition of continued acceptance by the group.

Subculture members experience no feelings of guilt over their actions because they are convinced that their behavior is correct and the dominant society's legal code is in error. Therefore, theories that address the role of guilt in criminality cannot be applied to such people. Members of these groups do not need to "neutralize" guilt, and their behavior certainly cannot be explained by the Freudian belief that criminals seek punishment either, since they are explicitly attempting to achieve status and related rewards.

This approach is based heavily on the observation that rates of crime for different subgroups vary widely within and across societies. A *subculture of violence* is any subgroup that exhibits the traits described by the above propositions and has significantly higher rates of crime and violence than other sub-groups in the society. This integrated approach has been applied in several ways. Wolfgang himself used it to identify poor, urban blacks as a subculture of violence, based on their disproportionate involvement in homicide.[7] Wolfgang and Ferracuti also apply the term to Colombia based on their examination of national homicide rates and cultural histories.[8] Others have used the term to link white Southerners to a "code of honor" that encourages both military service and high rates of homicide.[9] Zahn and Snodgrass used the term to explain the frequency of violence among drug users and dealers in large American cities.[10] While the factors used to describe these groups vary, the norms condoning violence, the methods by which they are transmitted, and the attitudes subculture members hold regarding violence are very similar.

Some writers have compared U.S. crime rates to those of other nations and conclude that it is unfair to label any subgroup of Americans as unusually violent, since American culture as a whole is unusually violent in comparison with other nations, especially those with similar levels of industrialization.[11] This assertion seems to hold true according to Lundesgaarde, an anthropologist who performed a detailed study of homicide cases in Houston, Texas. He noted that violence was present in all social subgroups and that the legal system was often quite willing to tolerate it.[12] Observations such as these, along with our nation's long history of military involvement throughout the world, can be used to label America as a "culture of violence."

Wolfgang and Ferracuti's integrated theory was an early attempt to combine insights from sociology, anthropology, history, and psychology into a single explanation of why some relatively small groups account for a rather large proportion of violence in a society. In creating this theory they did not make any assertions that were really new to criminology. The idea instead is to combine the most applicable portions of existing theories into one comprehensive explanation. As criminological knowledge and theory grows, there is more material to be examined, accounted for, and used in explaining crime. This can only lead to a fuller understanding of crime. It is for this reason that we look with favor upon integrated theory; it takes advantage of all the knowledge available to us.

Other Attempts at Theory Integration

Several other writers have developed more sophisticated attempts at theory integration. Quinney's "Social Reality of Crime" is among these.[13] We classified it as Marxist, however, because his assumptions are clearly based on Marxist thought rather than research data (see Chapter 13). Similarly, Bernard's unified conflict theory of crime integrates most of the major theories of crime into a single explanation. It could have been placed in this chapter except that it is based more upon Vold's conflict approach than upon empirical criminological data (see Chapter 14).[14] Upon our review of these efforts, we conclude that Wolfgang and Ferracuti, Quinney, and Bernard have each done an admirable job of combining criminological insights into a single explanation without merely restating earlier explanations. However, a truly integrated theory of crime is one that is built by weaving between the criminological data at all levels of analysis and the theoretical propositions that best explain these findings in the most parsimonious manner possible. A few of the more successful attempts at such integration are briefly reviewed here.

John Mays proposed that certain combinations of personal and environmental factors were responsible for criminality. He stressed that personal variables were the primary factors in explaining adult criminality, while environmental factors were of primary importance in dealing with juvenile delinquency.[15] This assertion presumes that juveniles are much more open to the external pushes and pulls that Reckless described decades earlier.

Abrahamson improved on this formulation by concluding that it was personal tendencies, in combination with the person's living situation, that produced crime whenever the individual's ability to resist temptation was inadequate.[16] Similarities to the strain perspective, as well as Yochelson and Samenow's notion of the "criminal personality," can be detected in this view of criminality. This formulation is also similar to Reckless' idea of internal and external containments as well as Hirschi's bonding theory, though it predates the latter by almost ten years.

In a more sophisticated and thorough synthesis, Knudten approaches the phenomenon of crime from a multidimensional perspective.[17] He begins by asserting that crime is relative to the culture, subgroup, type of social organization, peer group, and individual personalities involved. His ideas of cultural and organizational relativity are derived from the conflict perspective and are also prominent in the labeling perspective. Cultural groups provide the definitions of which acts constitute crime while organizations are often crucial in determining the type of response that a crime will elicit. The importance of the peer group was stressed by the social-learning perspective and is also a factor in social-control theories. Subgroup membership is a major factor in Knudten's theory, as well as in Wolfgang and Ferracuti's work.

Knudten goes on to show that the location of an act in time and space is crucial to how that act is defined by society. Here the societal-reaction perspective plays a major role. Psychological and learning theories also informed Knudten that the way in which individuals interpret and use the norms of their society and subgroup(s) affects the likelihood of their committing a crime. Theories stressing reference groups and Jessor and Jessor's distinction between distal and proximal perceptions also have much to contribute to our understanding of this process. These same factors are also thought to affect the type(s) of crime in which people become involved.[18]

Knudten goes on to claim that an individual's socioeconomic status has as much to do with the likelihood of becoming criminal as do individual personality traits.[19] He implies that a person's position in the social hierarchy leads to particular sorts of perceptions. Role models, as well as definitions of what is rewarding, provide the basis for such perceptions. This assertion combines elements of the strain perspective with aspects of the learning, psychological and psychiatric perspectives. This, in turn, leads to relatively unique opportunity structures. Individuals use these structures to select methods of solving problems and obtaining rewards. Here Knudten combines the insights of strain, subcultural, and learning theories.

Each of these attempts at developing a single theory of crime from existing materials focuses on the joint effects of learning in a group setting and the individual's relationship with various subgroups and the dominant society. They also share the common trait of at least implicitly addressing the decision-making processes involved in individual acts of crime. Thus, they have major implications for rehabilitation policies. That is, they infer that effective rehabilitation must address the individual's need for status within a group while simultaneously altering the offender's cognitive processes. The same is true of a more recent formulation by Hirschi and Gottfredson.

Hirschi and Gottfredson's General Theory of Crime and Criminality

Travis Hirschi, originator of the social-bonding theory addressed in Chapter 12, and Michael Gottfredson have recently developed a "general" theory of crime. The intent of their theory is to organize the available knowledge on crime into a parsimonious explanation of its sources. The same assumptions about human nature that are found in control theories are used in this theory. The influence of the classical frame of reference is also very apparent in this theory. Hirschi and Gottfredson's view of crime, like that of Wolfgang and Ferracuti, among others, is based on the empirical data describing the distribution of crime and criminals.[20]

This general theory (see Exhibit 15.2) is distinct from other attempts at theoretical integration in several ways. First, Hirschi and Gottfredson explicitly reject the idea that specific types of crime (e.g., violence, white-collar crime) require unique theoretical explanations. They argue that the phenomenon of crime should be addressed as a whole by explanatory theories. Second, they point out that the great majority of crimes involve a wide range of rather petty offenses. While much of the criminological literature focuses on crimes of violence and other forms of predatory crime, our jails and prisons are full of people who have become intoxicated in public, written bad checks, or committed similarly minor offenses. Despite the fact that in this text we have, for

Exhibit 15.2

Hirschi and Gottfredson's general theory of crime and criminality

---

Specific Assumptions

1. People seek to maximize pleasure with the least effort possible.

2. Crimes are motivated by the desire to obtain pleasure or avoid pain.

3. People who commit criminal acts do so to further their immediate self-interests.

4. Criminals do not usually think in terms of the long-term impact of their actions on their well-being.

5. Crime is chosen over conventional behavior when it can more readily provide swift and certain pleasure.

6. The tendency to commit crime, if present in an individual, is relevant to all situations that present opportunities to that person.

Source: Travis Hirschi and Michael Gottfredson, "Causes of White-Collar Crime, *Criminology* 25, No. 4 (1987): pp. 949–974; Travis Hirschi and Michael Gottfredson, "The Significance of White-Collar Crime for a General Theory of Crime," *Criminology* 27, No. 2 (1989): pp. 359–372.

the most part, used rather serious crimes to illustrate theory application, we fully agree with Hirschi and Gottfredson on this point.[21] Serious crimes attract the kind of attention that leads to books and newspaper coverage because they are unusual. The typical crime is a very mundane act to which notoriety is not likely to be attached unless the offender is a famous person or the case results in a major decision by the Supreme Court.[22] The sources of both serious and minor crime are the same, however, according to Hirschi and Gottfredson's theory.

Hirschi and Gottfredson also point out that individuals vary greatly in their inclination to criminal activity and that this inclination is fairly stable over time but declines with age. Their theory has certain parallels to those of the psychological perspective, such as Yochelson and Samenow's idea of the criminal personality. This is especially true of their belief that criminals are impulsive pleasure-seekers with little foresight. They differ with the developers of most other integrated or general theories because their assumptions draw heavily upon the ideas of the classical frame of reference that were outlined in Chapter 3.[23] For example, they presume that humans tend to seek rewards in the most immediate and direct fashion possible. This idea is crucial to the classical frame of reference's support of certain policies aimed at deterring crime.

In particular, Hirschi and Gottfredson argue that acts producing swift rewards will be chosen when all other factors are equal. Crime is thought to result from the anticipation of certain rewards, just as was proposed by the classical frame of reference as well as by the social-learning perspective. Thus, crime will be chosen over conforming behavior when it produces quick and certain rewards that are equal or superior to those of legal alternatives. People also are presumed to seek out methods of self-gratification that require the least amount of effort possible. Crime is therefore often chosen because it is easier, quicker, and more certain to produce rewards than are conforming alternatives.[24]

These theorists also point out that opportunities by which the offender can gain rewards must exist if crime is to occur. Moreover, threats of punishment must be absent or very minor in importance if a particular crime is to be committed, because punishment generally outweighs and/or negates the reward value of crime. Thus, some settings and social positions are more crime prone than others. This may be due to differences in the presence of various types of control mechanisms and/or to the range of available opportunities perceived by the offender. Elements of the strain perspective's concept of opportunity structure appear here in combination with components of the learning and control perspectives.

The degree to which a person has an investment in the social order is also seen as an important predictor of who will commit crime. This was a factor in Hirschi's original bonding theory. However, people with the predisposition to commit crime are felt to carry this tendency into all aspects of their lives rather than becoming "specialists" in one type of crime.[25] Thus, Hirschi and Gottfredson differ with Wolfgang and Ferracuti in regard to the degree to which criminals specialize and on how the focus of an integrated theory should be constructed. They also deal with crime at a more micro level than do Wolfgang and Ferracuti.

Thornberry's Integrated Model of Criminological Theory

Terrence Thornberry begins his attempt at integrating criminological theory with the criticism that present models of crime are unidirectional. That is, they are concerned only with factors that cause crime and ignore the influence of crime on society and individuals. Similarly, he believes that our current models fail to adequately acknowledge the changing nature of society, crime, and criminals, nor do they fully link criminality to theories of human development. Their linkage of psychological processes to the structure of society is also very weak, according to Thornberry.[26]

On the basis of these criticisms, Thornberry uses a combination of insights from four perspectives to construct an integrated theory of crime (see Exhibit 15.3). The chief sources of this theory are (1) Hirschi's bonding theory, (2) behavioral psychology's notion of reinforcement (see Akers' differential-reinforcement theory in Chapter 7), (3) developmental psychology (see the section on moral development in Chapter 6), and (4) the strain perspective's assertion that position in the social structure affects the individual's opportunity structure. He then asserts that each of these factors affect all of the others.

He begins by pointing out that the freedom to violate the law is a result of weakened bonds to society. He further maintains that the setting in which people live and behave has much to do with what they learn and which behaviors are reinforced. It also affects the strength of their bonds to conventional behavior and norms. This is to say that his approach stresses the reciprocity of, or mutual influence between, bonding, social setting, reinforcement, psycho-moral development, and criminal behavior. In other words, the social setting affects the likelihood of bonding, but the nature of a person's bonds

---

Specific Assumptions

1. Violations of law usually result from weakened bonds to the mainstream society.

2. Social bonds are also affected by the criminality of the person and others in the same social setting.

3. The content of social learning and its reinforcement is largely a product of the social setting in which a person operates.

4. The nature and amount of crime in a particular social setting affect the content of learning and the likelihood of reinforcement for various types of behavior.

5. Criminality is affected by the nature of the social setting in which a person operates but that setting is also affected by the person's criminality.

Source: T.P. Thornberry, "Towards an Interactional Theory of Delinquency," *Criminology* 25, No. 4 (1987): pp. 863–891.

Exhibit 15.3

Thornberry's integrated model of crime.

also affects the kinds of social settings she or he seeks out. Similarly, one's level of psycho-moral development influences one's definition of what is rewarding, while the history of the rewards a person has received affects his or her level of moral development. Simply stated, Thornberry sees these four factors as the chief predictors of who becomes criminal. His theory is unique because it demonstrates that each theoretical factor simultaneously influences the other three as a person experiences society, his or her own behavior, and the full range of reactions to those behaviors.[27]

A Radical Model for Theory Integration

As we have already implied, the conflict perspective has been a productive foundation for attempts at theory integration. This seems to be the result of its stress on the importance of social definitions and group memberships on behavior and its meaning. Certainly group membership was crucial to the work of Wolfgang and Ferracuti and Thornberry, and although it is absent from Hirschi and Gottfredson's work, there is nothing in their theory that stands in direct opposition to it, either.

Taylor, Walton, and Young developed a comprehensive critique of existing criminological theories in 1973 that has the effect of combining several theories into a model of what an integrated theory should contain. Their model has

Exhibit 15.4

Taylor, Walton, and Young's requirements for an integrated theory

Specific Assumptons

1. There must be a *political economy of crime* to deal with the macro-level origins of crime and its definition.

2. There must be a *social psychology of crime* to deal with the precipitating causes of crime.

3. There must be a *processual model of the criminal act* to deal with the relationship between thought and action.

4. There must be a *social psychology of the labeling process* to deal with who reacts to crime, how specific acts are defined, and how they are punished.

5. There must be a *political economy of the societal-reaction process* at the macro level to examine the role of relationships between interest groups in the law-creation process and those between the control agencies that actually apply the labels.

6. There must be a *social-psychological explanation of response to labeling* at the micro level.

7. There must be a discussion of the nature of the entire process that links levels of analysis, as well as dealing jointly with the social-psychological and political-economy aspects of the crime phenomena.

Source: Ian Taylor, Paul Walton, and Jock Young, *The New Criminology* (London: Routledge and Kegan Paul, 1973), pp. 270–278.

seven components that range from macro- to micro-level in orientation. Group membership would play a major role in any theory developed from this model, which deals with both the causes of crime and the processes of law creation and enforcement.

In themselves, these suggestions do not constitute an integrated theory; they are merely a description of the minimum requirements of such a theory. The model is especially useful in specifying the chief areas of modern criminological interest. These writers were particularly concerned with the impact of Lemert's labeling theory on criminology. Their suggestions were intended to improve on his theory by linking it to the political economy of crime that is a dominant theme in macro-level theories originating in the conflict and Marxist perspectives.[28]

Conclusion

The integrated theories referred to in this chapter would be better described as "attempts" at theory integration, because none of these formulations takes in all of the insights of criminological theory and the empirical data associated with it. Indeed, it seems doubtful that any one theory ever will. However, these formulations have advanced our insight into the reasons for crime in our society, and future integrated theories will probably provide increasingly comprehensive explanations (separately) of (1) predatory crime, (2) habitual violations of public order, (3) the law-creation and law-enforcement processes, and (4) the relationship between stigma, sanctions, deterrence, and criminality.

Certain commonalities among the attempts at integration discussed in this text can be readily discerned: the conflict, strain, control, and social-learning perspectives figure prominently in most of these integrated theories. We believe the reason is that these theories have great intuitive appeal. That is, they make sense to both laymen, practitioners, and scholars. Of equal importance in their selection is the amount of empirical support that has been provided for them over the years. The combination of intuitive appeal and empirical support is vital for theory integration.

The conflict perspective provides theory-integration attempts with a macro-level basis due to its emphasis on group membership as a predictor of individual behavior. Like most macro-level perspectives, it is generally used to explain predisposing factors. It is also of critical importance to understanding the law-creation and law-enforcement process. Elements of this perspective are present in the societal-reaction perspective, so the use of conflict assumptions often implies the major tenets of labeling. This comes as no great surprise, because the societal-reaction perspective was created on the explicit assumption of conflicting definitions of appropriate behavior and the behavioral significance of various group memberships.

The strain perspective was designed as a meso-level link between group membership and individual choices. It serves exceptionally well as a conceptual bridge between macro and micro levels of analysis if its presumption of social consensus is ignored. The theories contained within this perspective are quite effective in explaining the factors that make the choice of criminal behavior especially attractive to members of certain groups.

The social-learning and control perspectives work well together at the micro-level and have much intuitive and empirical support. Insights from the classical frame of reference are easily combined with these perspectives, as is evident in Hirschi and Gottfredson's work. The control perspective functions to link macro- and meso-level facts into an explanation of why strain produces crime. It does this by analyzing the linkage of the individual to social groups and other individuals. Learning theories directly address the reasons why certain types of crime are chosen by particular people. The classical frame of reference provides the underlying assumptions as to the basic motives for human behavior. These perspectives thus link attracting factors to the actual precipitators of criminal acts. The classical frame of reference, like the control perspective, presumes that criminal tendencies are part of human nature when it is not adequately contained. We might also note that the evidence upon which most integrated or general theories have been built was obtained by fundamentally positivistic methods. Thus, both the positive and classical frames of references make direct contributions to the integration of criminological theory.

Following Thornberry's lead, we also must stress the reciprocal relationship between human actions, social responses to those actions, and the nature of the social settings in which they occur. Humans define behavior as they observe it, using the definitions that they have learned from the social groups to which they belong. Individuals will inevitably observe differences between their own group's definitions of what constitutes appropriate behavior and the definitions used by other groups. They not only observe these differences, but will often use them as a basis for defining themselves and others. Individuals in one group assess other groups based not only on the other group's favored behaviors, but also on that other group's responses to their own favored behaviors. Particular settings become associated with particular groups through social learning and thus take on unique meanings as well. Any change in a group's activities, its setting, or the social reaction to its actions will impact the other factors involved in this chain of associations. This view of the social world as a constantly changing entity is derived from Dahrendorf and supports the use of the conflict perspective as a basis for theory integration.

In summary, the choice of theories, both for attempts at integration and for specific explanations of actual events in the real world, is largely a matter of focus. Certain perspectives are especially prominent in the attempts at integration used in this text because we have chosen to focus specifically on the use of theory to explain criminal acts. When we focus on the criminal act, as we have in this text, one set of theories is especially designed to meet our needs. As our focus changes to other aspects of criminological interest, the prominence of the various theories is simultaneously altered.

All criminological theories are relevant to all aspects of the discipline. However, this relevance is a matter of degree that is determined by one's interest at a given point in time. Theory is a tool used by scientists to explain the world. It is constantly being improved and elaborated. Integration is one way in which logic, data, and theory can be united.

We hope that the reader has already attempted to integrate some of the theories discussed in this text in order to develop a more complete explanation of some of the cases. **Multi-theory application** (i.e., combining one or more assumptions contained in one theory, with one or more assumptions from another theory to explain a criminal act), a simpler form of theory integration, generally provides a fuller explanation than individual theories, and we encourage this practice by the reader. However, we must offer a word of caution. The assumptions combined in multi-theory explanations need to be defensible. That is, the combined assumptions need to be rational and logical in relationship to one another, or multi-theory application becomes not a more complete explanation, but rather an irrational or illogical one.

We feel most of our readers are more likely to be interested in the theories as they relate to criminal behavior rather than to criminal law. Therefore, in closing we suggest, as do Vold and Bernard, that you will find theories addressing the enactment and enforcement of criminal laws more interesting and relevant as explanations for victimless, organized, and white-collar crime than other types as you continue to apply and study theoretical criminology.[29]

Criminal behavior and criminals have fascinated people for centuries. The construction and operation of law, on the other hand, is often seen as an area reserved for specialists and scholars. As has been pointed out by many of the perspectives in this text, one cannot fully understand crime or its perpetrators without also comprehending the processes of law creation and enforcement. These areas of study are just as important to criminology as the behavior of offenders. Both ordinary citizens and criminal justice practitioners have a vital interest in overcoming the tendency to reify the law so that social policies of the future can be based on logic and fact rather than emotion and group-specific intuition. We hope that the illustrations of criminological theory and their applications to concrete cases that are contained in this book have provided some impetus in this direction.

Glossary ·

Integrated Theory   Combines the most applicable portions of existing theories into a single explanation of particular criminological facts. Most integrated theories are built by weaving between criminological data at all levels of analysis and the theoretical propositions that best explain these findings in the most parsimonious manner possible.

Multi-Theory Application   The act of combining one or more assumptions contained in one theory with one or more assumptions from another to explain a criminal act.

Parsimony   Refers to the scientific bias towards the use of the most simple, straightforward explanation of a phenomenon possible. It is often cited as a criterion for judging theories.

Political Economy   The study of social organization that examines the relationships between political organization and economic activators such as production and distribution systems. It is generally most relevant to macro-level issues.

■ Notes

1. Jean L. McKechnie, *Webster's Deluxe Unabridged Dictionary*, 2d ed. (New York: Simon & Schuster, 1979), p. 953.

2. M. Wolfgang and F. Ferracuti, *The Subculture of Violence* (Beverly Hills, California: Sage Publications, 1982), pp. 2–3.

3. Ibid., p. 3.

4. Ibid., pp. 4–5.

5. Ibid., pp. 6–7.

6. Ibid., pp. 158–161.

7. M. Wolfgang, *Patterns of Criminal Homicide* (Philadelphia: University of Pennsylvania Press, 1958).

8. Wolfgang, and Ferracuti, *The Subculture of Violence,* pp. 275–279, 325–327.

9. J. Reed, *One South* (Baton Rouge, LA: Louisiana State University Press, 1982); R. Gastil, "Homicide and a Regional Culture of Violence," *American Sociological Review* 36 (1969): pp. 412–427; W. Bankston, R. St. Pierre, and D. Allen, "Southern Culture and Patterns of Victim-Offender Relationships in Homicide," *Sociological Spectrum* 5 (1985): pp. 197–211.

10. M. Zahn and G. Snodgrass, "Drug Use and the Structure of Homicide in Two U.S. Cities" in Flynn and Conrad (eds.), *The New Criminology and the Old Criminology* (New York: Praeger, 1978).

11. Wolfgang and Ferracuti, *The Subculture of Violence,* pp. 270–275; J. E. Conklin, *Criminology,* 2d ed. (New York: Macmillan, 1986), pp. 92–93; United Nations, Demographic Yearbook, 1981 (New York: United Nations, 1983), pp. 405–411.

12. H. Lundesgaarde, *Murder in Space City* (New York: Oxford University Press, 1977).

13. Richard Quinney, "The Social Reality of Crime" in Jack D. Douglas, *Crime and Justice in American Society* (Indianapolis, IN: Bobbs-Merrill, 1971), pp. 119–146.

14. George B. Vold and Thomas J. Bernard, *Theoretical Criminology,* 3d ed. (New York: Oxford University Press, 1986), pp. 286–287.

15. Terrence Morris, *The Criminal Area* (London: Kegan Paul, 1958).

16. D. Abrahamson, *The Psychology of Crime* (New York: John Wiley & Sons, 1960).

17. R. Knudten, *Crime in a Complex Society* (Homewood, IL: Dorsey Press, 1970); R. Knudten, "A Theory of Relativity: An Integrated Middle-Range Conception of Delinquents and Criminal Behavior" in R. Knudten and S. Schaefer, *Criminological Theory* (Lexington, MA: D.C. Heath and Co., 1977), pp. 241–248.

18. Ibid.

19. Ibid.

20. Travis Hirschi and Michael Gottfredson, "Causes of White-Collar Crime," *Criminology* 25, no. 4 (1987): pp. 949–974; Travis Hirschi and Michael Gottfredson, "The Significance of White-Collar Crime for a General Theory of Crime," *Criminology* 27, no. 2 (1989): pp. 359–372.

21. Ibid.

22. Samuel Walker, *Sense and Nonsense About Crime: A Policy Guide,* 2d ed. (Pacific Grove, CA: Brooks/Cole, 1989), pp. 22–34.

23. Hirschi and Gottfredson, "Causes of White-Collar Crime," pp. 949–974; Hirschi and Gottfredson, "The Significance of White-Collar Crime for a General Theory of Crime, pp. 359–372.

24. Ibid.
25. Ibid.
26. T.P. Thornberry, "Towards an Interactional Theory of Delinquency," *Criminology* 25, no. 4 (1987): pp. 863–891.
27. Ibid.
28. Ian Taylor, Paul Walton, and Jock Young, *The New Criminology* (London: Routledge and Kegan Paul, 1973), p. 217.
29. Vold and Bernard, *Theoretical Criminology*, pp. 315–339.

■ Suggested Readings

J. W. Coleman, "Toward an Integrated Theory of White-Collar Crime," *American Journal of Sociology* 93 (1987): pp. 406–439.

J. Hagan, and A. Palloni, "Toward a Structural Criminology," *Annual Review of Sociology* 12 (1986): pp. 431–449.

T. Hirschi and M. Gottfredson, "Causes of White-Collar Crime," *Criminology* 25 (1987): pp. 949–974.

T. Hirschi and M. Gottfredson, "The Significance of White-Collar Crime for a General Theory of Crime," *Criminology* 27 (1989): pp. 359–372.

R. Knudten, *Crime in a Complex Society* (Homewood, IL.: Dorsey Press, 1970).

C. E. Reasons, "Social Thought and Social Structure," *Criminology* 13 (1975): pp. 332–365.

J. F. Sheley, "Critical Elements of Criminal Behavior Explanation," *Sociological Quarterly* 24 (1983): pp. 509–525.

M. F. Shore, "Psychological Theories of the Causes of Antisocial Behavior," *Crime and Delinquency* 17, no. 4 (1971): pp. 456–468.

NAME INDEX

N

O

P

Q

R

SUBJECT INDEX